THREE
ELIZABETHAN
FENCING MANUALS

THREE ELIZABETHAN FENCING MANUALS

Giacomo di Grassi, *His True Arte of Defence* (1594)
Vincentio Saviolo, *His Practice* (1595)
George Silver, *Paradoxes of Defence* (1599)
and
Bref Instructions Upon My Paradoxes of Defence

FACSIMILE REPRODUCTIONS
WITH AN INTRODUCTION
BY JAMES L. JACKSON

SCHOLARS' FACSIMILES & REPRINTS
DELMAR, NEW YORK
1972

Three Elizabethan Fencing Manuals

Published by Scholars' Facsimiles & Reprints, Inc.
Post Office Box 344, Delmar, New York 12054

Reproduced from copies in
and with permission of
The Folger Shakespeare Library

© 1972 Scholars' Facsimiles & Reprints, Inc.

Library of Congress Cataloging in Publication Data

Jackson, James Louis, 1916-   comp.
    Three Elizabethan fencing manuals.
    Reprint of Giamoco di Grassi, His True arte of defence, 1594,
translation of the author's Ragione di adoprar sicuramente l'arme . . .
of Vincentio Saviolo, His Practice, 1595; and Paradoxes of defence, b
George Silver, 1599.
    1. Fencing—Early works to 1800. I. Grassi, Giacomo di. Ragione d
adoprar sicuramente l'arme . . . English. 1972. II. Saviolo, Vincentio
Practice. 1972. III. Silver, George, fl. 1599. Paradoxes of defence. 1972
IV. Title.
U860.J3 1972   796.8'6   72-6321
ISBN 0-8201-1107-4

INTRODUCTION

THE ABILITY to use hand weapons well was a responsibility of Elizabethan gentlemen and yeomen, but our knowledge of Elizabethan fencing techniques, and their use in Elizabethan plays, is surprisingly meager. Our knowledge of Elizabethan fencing has been fading because of the transience of such skills and because early fencing knowledge has been hidden under three centuries of continuing fencing developments. To recover some of this fencing information, we would need an authoritative manual on the rapier and one on the sword, written in England in the 1590s. Two such manuals do survive. Perhaps spurred by the appearance in 1594 of a translation of an older rapier manual by di Grassi, Vincentio Saviolo published *His Practice* in 1595; and the advocate of the short sword, George Silver, wrote but did not publish a manual on the use of the sword about 1599.

This present volume draws together the three manuals on fencing extant in England at the height of the English Renaissance. The di Grassi volume was Englished but not significantly altered for the use of Englishmen, with the result that much of its 1570 instruction was out-of-date in the 1590s. The Saviolo volume is in two parts, the first a valuable manual on fencing with the rapier and the rapier-and-dagger; the latter half of his volume, *Of Honor and Honorable Quarrels*, is a translation of an older, standard Italian volume on the duello. George Silver's *Paradoxes of Defence* (1599) is the first half of a double volume; it is actually polemics and not fencing instruction. The second half, his excellent *Brief Instructions Upon My Paradoxes of Defence*, was prepared for publication but not published in his lifetime, even though it is a wise and forward-looking manual on the use of the short sword in duel, street-fight, or in battle.

These manuals are presented here together to facilitate the recovery of knowledge of Elizabethan fighting styles and to make them available for a fuller understanding of the references to fencing in Elizabethan literature. The three volumes reproduced here were made available through the generosity of the Folger Library, which gave its kind permission for their reproduction.

Di Grassi's *True Arte of Defence* appeared originally in 1570 in Venice, and was Englished in 1594 by I. G., Gentlemen, who remains unidentified. The book was licensed 22 March 1594. The many illustra-

v

tions are crude copies of the copperplate illustrations in the Italian editions. The translation is a reasonably accurate one and was "edited" by Thomas Churchyard. The Italian editions do not have the Preface attributed to Churchyard, nor the Advertisement found at pages 9 to 11. The Advertisement was probably provided by the translator, as is apparent from his discussion on translating the Italian word *spada* as *rapier*.

The Advertisement serves as a gentle apology for the fact that the 1570 Italian volume, in its English translation, is a bit out of date in relation to current English fencing. But the di Grassi volume provided a simple and practical system for most hand weapons. Di Grassi provides advice on nearly all weapons used on foot in the sixteenth century.

In the old but authoritative history of fencing, *Schools and Masters of Fence* (1895), Edgerton Castle judged that in 1570 the *True Arte* contained the mainstream rapier theories of Marozzo and provided some developments in rapier technique, such as clearly defining the parts of the blade (p. 21) as an aid to using the weapon in delivering cuts. We can surmise that the appearance of this translation in 1594 may have indicated the need for an up-to-date volume, and thus the di Grassi book may have encouraged Saviolo to publish his text for Englishmen in the following year.

Vincentio Saviolo's *His Practice In Two Books* was licensed 19 November 1594, and bears the date 1595. As its title page suggests, it is actually two books, with the title page of the Second Part dated 1594. The volume appears to have been well known and popular in the late sixteenth and early seventeenth centuries. The copy used for this edition is the Folger Library's copy 2, supplemented by a few pages from the Library's copy 1.

The two parts of the Saviolo volume differ markedly. The first book is in dialogue form and there is no reason to doubt that it was written by Saviolo himself. There is also no doubt that most of the second part, "Of Honor and Honorable Quarrels," is an adaptation of the authoritative Italian book on the duello, Girolamo Muzio's *Il Duello*, Venice 1551, and subsequent editions. This parallel was noted by J. W. Holme in his notes to *As You Like It* in 1914, and the parallel was explored by Ruth Kelso in 1924 (MLN, 34, 33–35). As Miss Kelso states, Saviolo translated a large part literally, sometimes omitting, but also adding a chapter deploring the fashion of secret combat. This is the chapter "Of the Duello or Combat" (pages 447 to 450). He also adds accounts of four famous quarrels and a discussion on the nobility of women, possibly intended to flatter Queen Elizabeth. A check of the Italian text suggests that Saviolo was working directly from the Italian of Muzio.

A few details of Saviolo's life can be drawn from his work and the comments of George Silver, and most of these are in DNB. Saviolo tells us he was born in Padua (*Practice*, p. 220), and he travelled in Central and Eastern Europe (DNB). Silver in his *Paradoxes* tells us that Saviolo taught rapier-fight for seven or eight years, and he refers to Saviolo in his 1599 volume as having died. The references to Saviolo in the literature of the period show him to have been a mild but successful fencing master.

Edgerton Castle gives Saviolo high marks for his rapier system. Castle calls Saviolo "a master of his art," judges that his progressions are cleverly devised, and notes that Saviolo properly teaches the superiority of the use of the rapier point over use of the edge. Castle notes that Saviolo created no major advances in fencing theory and used the traditional organization of defensive positions and cuts developed as long ago as 1536 by Marozzo. Although the non-fencer may find Saviolo's discussion of fencing hard to follow, his system is a fine one, simple and well organized and designed to protect the fencer quite as much as to harm his opponent. This editor has practiced Saviolo's sequences using reproduction Elizabethan rapiers and daggers, and finds the Saviolo system simple and effective.

Saviolo's system shows us the basic knowledge of rapier fence available to Shakespeare and his contemporaries. Jonson and others refer to Saviolo by name, although Shakespeare does not. But Shakespeare makes easy use of rapier knowledge in his plays.

Editors of Shakespeare usually note in annotating *As You Like It* that the seven kinds of lies described by Touchstone in Act V, Scene 4, satirize books on honor and good manners popular in England at this time and may have been derived from the discussion of the five kinds of lies in Saviolo (p. 346 ff.) : lies certain, conditional lies, the lie in general, the lie in particular, and foolish lies. It is possible that some of Touchstone's phrasing may be heard in such sentences as this from Saviolo's translation: "This lie cannot be avoided. . . ."

George Silver, gentleman, published his *Paradoxes of Defence* in 1599 (licensed 30 January), attempting to prove that the "short sword hath

advantage of the long sword or long rapier." This volume was reproduced in 1933 in the Shakespeare Association Facsimiles, with an introduction by J. Dover Wilson. But the *Paradoxes of Defence* is not a
fencing manual; it is an ill-tempered tract which scolds at length about
the "imperfections" of Italianate rapier fence and praises the use of
the short sword in general terms.

George Silver's actual fencing manual was not published until 1898.
Late in the nineteenth century his manuscript *Bref Instructions Upon
My Paradoxes of Defence* was discovered in the British Museum. In
1898, a British fencer, Captain Cyril G. R. Matthey, published *The
Works of George Silver*, including both the *Paradoxes of Defence* and
the previously unprinted *Bref Instructions Upon My Paradoxes of
Defence*. Captain Matthey, impressed with the techniques in the *Bref
Instructions*, believed these would be of value to his fellow officers in
Boer War fighting. *The Works of George Silver* as reproduced here is
a facsimile of the edition of 1898, including Captain Matthey's mar-
ginal comments on the *Bref Instructions*.

Most of what we know of George Silver must be drawn from his works.
He makes it clear that he was a gentlemen, but we remember him for
his scolding at Saviolo and "Italianate" teachers of rapier fence in general. It is unfortunate that the *Paradoxes* is the pamphlet on which
his reputation rests, since his sarcasm reveals little of his fencing ex-
pertness. As Matthey recognized, Silver was protesting on the basis of a
fine fencing technique.

It is apparent that his *Bref Instructions* describes an advanced
technique of short sword fencing which we would recognize as somewhat similar to nineteenth-century saber fencing. Silver was teaching a
new and radical technique of parrying with the edge of the light short
sword, and with this considerable improvement in technique had evolved
an early and effective saber style. He is surprisingly detailed and
quite correct about the importance of timing, and one is tempted to be-
lieve his claims that an expert swordsman using his advanced saber
style techniques might have been a serious adversary for a rapier man.
Of course Silver is talking not only about a fencing style suitable for a
gentleman's use in dueling; the technique he was teaching was even
more appropriate with the sword considered as a weapon for battle or
street fighting.

We have no specific date for the composition of the *Bref Instructions* but it was written after Saviolo's book appeared in 1595, since

Silver disparages the "booke wryten by Vincintio." Reading the *Bref Instructions* may be somewhat difficult at first, since Matthey did not expand contractions in Silver's manuscript.

JAMES L. JACKSON

George Mason University
Fairfax, Virginia

Di Grassi his true Arte of Defence,

plainlie teaching by infallable Demonstrations,
apt Figures and perfect Rules the manner and
forme how a man without other Teacher or
Master may safelie handle all sortes of
Weapons aswell offensiue as defensiue:
VVith a Treatise
Of Disceit or Falsinge : And with a waie or
meane by priuate Industrie to obtaine
Strength, Iudgement and
Actiuitie.

First written in Italian by the fore-
said Author, And Englished by
I.G. gentleman.

Printed at London for I.I and are to be sold
within Temple Barre at the Signe of
the Hand and Starre
1594.

*To the Right Honorable my L. Borrow Lord
Gouernor of the Breil, and Knight of the most honorable order of the Garter, T.C. wisheth continuall Honor, worthines of mind,
and learned knowledg, with increas
of worldlie Fame, & hea-
uenlie felicitie.*

Auing a restlesse desier in the dailie exercises of
Pen to present some acceptable peece of work
to your L. and finding no one thing so fit for
my purpose and your honorable disposition, as
the knowledge of Armes and Weapons, which defends
life, countrie, & honour, I presumed to preferre a booke to
the print (translated out of the Italyan language) of a gentle
maus doing that is not so gredie of glory as many glorious
writers that eagerly would snatch Fame out of other mens
mouthes, by a little labour of their own, But rather keeps his
name vnknowen to the world (vnder a shamefast clowd of
silence) knowing that vertue shynes best & getteth greatest
prayes where it maketh smallest bragg : for the goodnes of
the mind seekes no glorious gwerdon, but hopes to reap
the reward of well doing among the rypest of iudgement
& worthiest of sound consideration, like vnto a man that
giueth his goods vnto the poore, and maketh his treasure-
house in heauen, And further to be noted, who can tarrie
til the seed sowen in the earth be almost rotten or dead, shal
be sure in a boutiful haruest to reap a goodly crop of corne
And better it is to abyde a happie season to see how things
will proue, than soddainly to seeke profite where slowlye
comes commoditie or any benefit wil rise. Some say, that
good writers doe purchase small praise till they be dead,
(Hard is that opinion.) and then their Fame shal flowrish
& bring foorth the fruite that long lay hid in the earth.

¶ 2   This

This gentleman, perchaunce, in the like regard ſmothers vp his credit, and ſtands carcleſſe of the worlds report: but I cannot ſee him ſo forgotten for his paines in this worke is not little, & his merite muſt be much that hath in our Engliſh tongue publiſhed ſo neceſſarie a volume in ſuch apt termes & in ſo bigg a booke (beſides the liuely deſcriptions & models of the ſame) that ſhews great knowledge & cunning, great art in the weapon, & great ſuretie of the man that wiſely can vſe it, & ſtoutly execute it. All manner of men allowes knowledge: then where knowledge & courage meetes in one perſon, there is ods in that match, whatſoeuer manhod & ignorance can ſay in their own behalfe. The fine book of ryding hath made many good horſ-men: and this booke of Fencing will ſaue many mens lyues, or put comon quarrels out of vre becauſe the danger is death if ignorant people procure a combate. Here is nothing ſet downe or ſpeach vſed, but for the preſeruation of lyfe and honour of man: moſt orderly rules, & noble obſeruations, enterlaced with wiſe councell & excellent good wordes, penned from a fowntaine of knowledge and flowing witt, where the reaſons runnes as freely as cleere water comketh from a Spring or Conduite. Your L. can iudge both of the weapon & words, wherefore there needes no more commendation of the booke: Let it ſhewe it ſelf, crauing ſome ſupportation of your honourable ſenſure: and finding fauour and paſſage among the wiſe, there is no doubt but all good men will like it, and the bad ſort will bluſh to argue againſt it, as knoweth our liuing Lord, who augment your L. in honour & deſyred credit.

Your L. in all humbly at commaundement,

Thomas Churchyard.

4

The Authors Epiſtle vnto diuers Noble men and Gentle-men.

Mong all the Prayers, wherein through the whole courſe of my life, I haue asked any great thing at Gods hands, I haue alwayes moſt earneſtly beſeeched, that (although at this preſent I am verie poore and of baſe Fortune) he would notwithſtanding giue me grace to be thankefull, and mindfull of the good turnes which I haue receiued. For among all the diſgraces which a man may incurre in this world, there is none in mine opinion which cauſeth him to become more odious, or a more enimie to mortall men (yea, vnto God himſelfe) than ingratitude. VVherefore being in Treuiſo, by your honours courteouſly intreated, and of all honourably vſed, although I practiſed litle or nought at all to teach you how to handle weapons, for the which purpoſe I was hyred with an honourable ſtipend, yet to ſhewe my ſelfe in ſome ſort thankefull, I haue determined to beſtowe this my worke vpon your honours, imploying my whole indeuour to ſhewe the way how to handle all ſortes of weapons with aduantage and ſafetie. The which my worke, becauſe it ſhall finde your noble hearts full of valure, will bring foorth ſuch fruite, being but once attentiuely read ouer, as that in your ſaid honors will be ſeene in actes and deedes, which in other men ſcarſely is comprehended by imagination. And I, who haue beene and am moſt feruently affected to ſerue your Ls. foraſmuch as it is not graunted vnto me, (in reſpect of your diuers affaires) to applie the ſame, and take ſome paines in teaching as I alwaies deſired, haue yet by this other waie, left all that imprinted in your noble mindes, which in this honourable exerciſe may bring a valiant man vnto perfection.

Therefore I humbly beſeech your honours, that with the ſame liberall mindes, with the which you accepted of mee, your Ls will alſo receiue theſe my indeuours, & vouchſafe ſo to protect them, as I haue alwaies, and wil defend your honours moſt pure and vndefiled. VVherein, if I perceiue this my firſt childbirth (as I haue only publiſhed it to thentent to help & teach others) to be to the generall ſatisfaction of all I will ſo ſtraine my endeuours in an other worke which ſhortly ſhall ſhew the way both how to handle all thoſe weapons on horſe-backe which here are taught on foote, as alſo all other weapons whatſoeuer.

Your honours moſt affectionate ſeruant
Giacomo di Graſſi of Modena.

Ven as from our ſwathing bands wee carrie with vs (as it were) an vnbridled deſire of knowledge : So afterwardes, hauing attained to the perfection therof, there groweth in vs a certaine laudable and feruent affection to teach others : The which, if it were not ſo, the world happily ſhould not be ſeene ſo repleniſhed with Artes and Sciences.

For if men generally were not apt to contemplation and ſearching out of things : Or if God had not beſtowed vpon euery man the grace, to be able to lift vp his minde from the earth, and by ſearching to finde out the cauſes thereof, and to imparte them to thoſe who are leſſe willing to take any paines therein : it would come to paſſe, that the one parte of men, as Lordes and Maſters, ſhould beare rule, and the other parte as vyle ſlaues, wrapped in perpetuall darkneſſe, ſhould ſuffer and lead a life vnworthie the condition of man. Wherefore, in mine opinion it ſtandes with great reaſon that a man participate that vnto others which he hath ſearched and found out by his great ſtudie & trauaile. And therefore, I being euen from my childhood greatly delighted in the handling of weapons : after I had ſpent much time in the exerciſe thereof, was deſyrous to ſee and beholde the moſt excellent and expert maſters of this Arte, whome I haue generally marked, to teach after diuers wayes, much differing one from another, as though this miſterie were deſtitute of order & rule, or depended onely vpon imagination, or on the deuiſe of him who profeſſeth the ſame : Or as though it were a matter impoſſible to find out in this honourable exerciſe (as well as in all other Artes and Sciences) one onely good and true way, whereby a man may attaine to the intire knowledge of as much as may be practiſed with the weapon, not depending altogether vpon his owne head, or learning one blowe to day of one maſter, on the morowe of another, thereby buſying himſelfe about perticulars, the knowledge whereof is infinite, therefore impoſſible. Whereupon being forced, through a certaine honeſt deſire which I beare to helpe others, I gaue my ſelfe wholy to the contemtemplation thereof : hoping that at the length , I shoulde finde out the true principles and groundes of this Arte , and reduce the confused and infinite number of blowes into a compendious summe and certaine order : The which principles being but fewe, and therefore easie to be knowen and borne away, without doubt in small time, and little trauaile, will open a most large entrance to the vnderstanding of all that which is contained in this Arte. Neither was I in this frustrate at all of my expectation: For in conclusion after much deliberation , I haue found out this Arte, from the which onely dependeth the knowledge of all that which a man may performe with a weapon in his hand, and not onely with those weapons which are found out in these our dayes, but also with those that shall be inuented in time to come: Considering this Arte is grounded vpon Offence and Defence, both the which are practised in the straight and circuler lynes, for that a man may not otherwise either strike or defend.

And becaufe I purpose to teach how to handle the Weapon, as orderly and plainly as is possible : I haue first of all layd down the principles or groundes of all the Arte, calling them *Aduertisements*, the which, being of their owne nature verie well knowen to all those that are in their perfect wittes : I haue done no other then barely declared them , without rendring any further reason, as being a thing superfluous.

These principles being declared , I haue next handled those things, which are, and be, of themselues , *Simple* , then (ascending vp to those that are *Compound*) I shewe that which may be generally done in the handling of all Weapons . And becaufe, in teaching of Artes and Sciences , *Things* are more to be esteemed of than *VVordes*, therefore I would not choose in the handling hereof a copious and sounding kinde of speach , but rather that which is more briefe and familiar. Which maner of speach as in a small bundle , it containeth diuers weightie things , so it craueth a slowe and discreete Reader, who will soft and faire pearce into the verie Marrowe thereof.

For this cause I beseech the gentle Reader to shewe himselfe such a one in the reading of this my present worke, assuring him selfe by so reading it, to reape great profite and honour thereby.

And

To the Reader.

Not doubting but that he(who is fufficientlie furnifhed with this knowledge,and hath his bodie proporcionably exercifed thereunto)fhall far furmount anie other although he be indewed with equal force and fwiftnes.

Moreouer,becaufe this art is a principal member of the *Militarie profefsion*,vvhich alltogether (vvith learning)is the ornament of all the World, Therefore it ought not to be exercifed in Braules and Fraies, as men commonlie practife in euerie fhire,but as honorable Knights, ought to referue themfelues , & exercife it for the aduantage of their Cuntry,the honour of vveomen,and conqueringe of Hoftes and armies.

An Aduertiſement to the curteous reader.

Ood Reader, before thou enter into the diſcourſe of the hidden knowledge of this honourable excerciſe of the weapon now layd open and manifeſted by the Author of this worke, & in ſuch perfeſtnes tranſlated out of the Italian tongue, as all or moſt of the marſhal mynded gentlemen of England cannot but commend, and no one perſon of indifferent iudgement can iuſtly be offended with, ſeeing that whatſoeuer herein is diſcourſed, tendeth to no other Vſe, but the defence of mans life and reputation: I thought good to aduertiſe thee that in ſome places of this booke by reaſon of the æquiuocation of certaine Italian wordes, the weapons may doubtfully be conſtrued in Engliſh. Therefore ſometimes fynding this worde Sworde generally Vſed, I take it to haue beene the better tranſlated, if in ſteede thereof the Rapier had beene inſerted: a weapon more Vſuall for Gentlemens wearing, and fitteſt for cauſes of offence and defence: Beſides that, in Italie where Rapier and Dagger is commonly worne and Vſed, the Sworde (if it be not an arming Sworde) is not ſpoken of. Yet would I not the ſence ſo ſtriſtly to be conſtrued, that the Vſe of ſo honourable a weapon be Vtterly

¶¶   reieſted,

*reiected, but fo redd, as by the right and perfect
vnderftanding of the one, thy iudgement may fom
what be augmented in managing of the other:
Knowing right well, that as the practife and vfe
of the firft is commendable amongft them, fo the
fecond cannot fo farre be condemned, but that the
wearing thereof may well commend a man of valour and reputation amongft vs. The Sworde and
Buckler fight was long while allowed in England
(and yet practife in all fortes of weapons is praif-
worthie,) but now being layd downe, the fworde
but with Seruing-men is not much regarded,
and the Rapier fight generally allowed, as a wapon
becaufe moft perilous, therefore moft feared, and
thereupon priuate quarrels and common frayes
fooneft fhunned.*

*But this peece of work, gentle Reader, is fo gal-
lantly fet out in euery point and parcell, the obfcu-
reft fecrets of the handling of the weapon fo clerely vnfolded, and the perfect demeaning of the bodie vpon all and fudden occafions fo learnedly difcourfed, as will glad the vnderftander thereof, &
found to the glory of all good Mafters of Defence,
becaufe their Arte is herein fo honoured, and their
knowledge (which fome men count infinite) in fo
finguler a fcience, drawen into fuch Grounds and
Principles, as no wife man of an vnpartiall iudgement,*

10

ment, and of what profession soeuer, but will confesse himself in curtesie farre indebted both to the
Author & Translator of this so necessarie a Treatise, whereby he may learne not onely through
reading & remembring to furnish his minde with
resolute instructions, but also by practise and exercise gallantly to perfourme any conceited enterprise with a discreete and orderly carriage of his
bodie, vpon all occasions whatsoeuer.

Gentle Reader. what other escapes or mista-
kings shall come to thy viewe, either friendly I intreate thee to beare with them, or curteously with
thy penne for thine owne vse to amend them.

Fare-well.

¶¶ 2

The Sortes of VVeapons handled in this Treatise.

THe single Rapier, Or single Sworde.
   The rapier and dagger &c.
The rapier and Cloak &c.
The sword and Buckler.
The Sword and square target.
The sworde and round target.
The Case of Rapiers.
The two hand Sword.
   The weapons of the Staffe, As
The Bil, Partesan, Holberd and Iauelin.

Falsing of Blowes and Thrusts.
At single rapier &c.
At rapier and dagger &c.
At Cloak and rapier.
At sword & buckler, square target and
   round target.
At the two rapiers
At the two hand sword
At the Bill, Partesan, Iauelin, and Holberd.
At the Pike.

The

12

The true Art of Defence exactlie
teachinge the manner how to handle weapons safelie, aswel offensiue as defensiue, With a Treatise of Disceit or Falsing,
And with a mean or waie how a man may practise of himselfe to gett Strength, Iudgement, and Actiuitie.

T Here is no doubt but that the Honorable exercise of the Weapon is made right perfect by meanes of two thinges, to witt : Iudgment and Force : Because by the one, we know the manner and time to handle the wepon (how, or whatsoeuer occasion serueth:) And by the other we haue power to execute therewith, in due time with aduauntage.

And because, the knowledge of the manner and Time to strike and defende, dooth of it selfe teach vs the skil how to reason and dispute thereof onely, and the end and scope of this Art consisteth not in reasoning, but in dooinge: Therefore to him that is desierous to proue so cunning in this Art, as is needfull, It is requisite not onelie that he be able to iudg, but also that he be stronge and actiue to put in execution all that which his iudgement comprehendeth and seeth. And this may not bee done without strength and actiuitie of bodie : The which if happelie it bee

A 1. feeble

feeble, flowe, or not of power to suftaine the weight of blowes, Or if it take not aduauntage to ftrike when time requiereth, it vtterlie remaineth ouertaken with difgrace and daunger: the which falts (as appeareth) proceed not from the Art, but from the Inftrument badly handled in the action.

Therefore let euerie man that is defierous to practife this Art, indeuor himfelfe to get ftrength and agilitie of bodie, affuringe himfelf, that iudgment without this actiuitie and force, auaileth litle or nothinge: Yea, happelie giueth occafion of hurt and fpoile. For men beinge blinded in their owne iudgements, and prefuminge thereon, becaufe they know how, and what they ought to doo, giue manie times the onfet and enterprife, but yet, neuer perfourme it in act.

But leaft I feeme to ground this Art vppon dreames and monftrous imaginations (hauinge before laid downe, that ftrength of bodie is very neceffarie to attaine to the perfection of this Art, it beinge one of the two principall beeginninges firft layd downe, and not as yet declared the way how to come by and procure the fame) I haue determined in the entrance of this worke, to prefcribe firft the manner how to obtaine iudgemēt, and in the end thereof by way of Treatife to fhew the meanes (as farre forth as appertaineth to this Art) by the which a man by his owne indeuoure and trauaile, may get ftrength and actiuitie of bodie, to fuch purpofe and effect, that by the iuftruc-

tions

tions and reasons , which shal be here giuen him,
he may easely without other master or teacher,
become both stronge, actiue and skilful.

The meanes how to obtain *Iudgement.*

Lthough I haue verye
much in a manner in all
quarters of Italie , 'seene
most excellent professors
of this Art, to teach in
their Schols, and practise
priuately in the Listes to
traine vp their Schollers.
Yet I doo not remember
that euer I saw anie man so throughly indewed
with this first part, to wit, Iudgement, as is in that
behalfe required.

And it may bee that they keep it in secreat of
purpose: for amongst diuers disorderlie blowes,
you might haue seen some of them most gallant-
lie bestowed, not without euident coniecture of
deepe iudgment.   But howsoeuer it bee seeinge
I purpose to further this Art, in what I may, I wil
speak of this first part as aptly to the purpose, as
I can.

It is therefore to be considered that man by so
much the more waxeth fearefull or boulde ,
by how much the more he knoweth how t'auoid

A 2.   or

15

or not to eschew daunger.

But to attain to this knowledg, it is most necessarie that he alwaies kepe stedfastly in memorie all these aduertisements vnderwritten, from which springeth al the knowledg of this Art. Nether is it possible without them to performe any perfect action for the which a man may giue a reson. But if it so fall out that any man (not hauing the knowledg of these aduertisements) performe any sure act, which may be said to be hand led with iudgement, that proceedeth of no other thing, then of very nature, and of the mind, which of it selfe naturally conceiueth all these aduertisementes.

1 First, that the right or streight Line is of all other the shortest: wherefore if a man would strike in the shortest lyne, it is requisite that he strike in the streight line.

2 Secondly, he that is neerest, hitteth soonest. Out of which aduertisment a man may reap this profit, that seeing the enemies sword farr off, aloft and readie to strik, he may first strik the enemie, before he himselfe be striken.

3 Thirdly, a Circle that goeth compassinge beareth more force in the extremitie of the circumference, then in the center thereof.

4 Fourthly, a man may more easely withstand a small then a great force.

5 Fiftbly, euerie motion is accomplished in tyme.

That by these Rules a man may get iudgment,

it is moſt cleere,ſeing there is no other thinge required in this Art,then to ſtrike with aduantage,
and defend with ſafetie.

This is done, when one ſtriketh in the right
line, by giuing a thurſt,or by delyuering an edgeblow with that place of the ſword, where it carrieth moſt force,firſt ſtriking the enemie beefore
he be ſtroken:The which is perfourmed, when
he perceiueth him ſelfe to be more nere his enemie,in which caſe,he muſt nimbly deliuer it. For
there are few nay there is no man at all, who (perceiuing himſelfe readie to be ſtroken) giues not
back,and forſaketh to performe euerie other motion which he hath begun.

And foraſmuch,as he knoweth that euery motion is made in time,he indeuoreth himſelfe ſo to
ſtrik and defend , that he may vſe as few motions
as is poſſible , and therein to ſpend as litle time,
And as his enemie moueth much in diuers times
he may be aduertiſed hereby ,to ſtrike him in
one or more of thoſe times, ſo out of al due time
ſpent.

The diuiſion of the Art.

B Efore I come to a more perticuler de
claration of this Art,it is requiſite I
vſe ſome generall diuiſion. Wherefore it is to be vnderſtood , that as in
all other arts,ſo likewiſe in this(men
forſaking the true ſcience thereof,in hope perad-
A 3   uen-

17

uenture to ouercome rather by difceit then true
manhood)haue found out a new maner of skirmifhing ful offalfes and flips.The which becaufe
it fome what and fome times preualeth againft
thofe who are either fearfull or ignorant of their
groundes and principals,I am conftrayned to diuide this Art into two Arts or Sciences, callinge
thone the True,the other,the Falfe art: But withall giuing euerie man to vnderftand, that falfe-
hood hath no aduauntage againft true Art, but
rather is moft hurtfull and deadlie to him that v-
feth it.

Therefore cafting away deceit for this prefent,
which fhal hereafter be hãdled in his proper place
and reftraining my felfe to the truth,which is the
true and principall defier of my hart, prefuppofing that Iuftice(which in euerie occafion appro-
cheth neereft vnto truth)obteineth allwaies the
fuperioritie,I fay whofoeuer mindeth to exercife
himfelfe in this true and honorable Art or Science,it is requifite that he be indued with deep
Iudgement,a valiant hart and great actiuitie, In
which thre qualities this exercife doth as it were
delight,liue and florifh.

Of the Sword.

Lbeit Wepons afwel offenfiue as defen-
fiue be infinite,becaufe all that whatfoeuer a man may handle to offend an other
or defend himfelfe,either by flinging or kepinge
faft

faſt in his hand may in my opinion be tearmed Weapon. Yet notwithſtáding, becauſe, as I haue before ſaid, they be innumerable ſo that if I ſhold perticularly handle euerie one, beſides the great toile and trauaile I ſhould ſuſtaine, it would alſo doubtles be vnprofitable, becauſe the principels and groundes which are laid downe in this Art, ſerue only for ſuch weapons as are commonlye practiſed, or for ſuch as happely men will vſe: and ſo leauing al thoſe which at this preſent make not for my purpoſe, I affirme, that amongſt al the wepons vſed in theſe daies, there is none more honorable, more vſual or more ſafe then the ſword.

Comming therefore firſt to this weapon, as vnto that on which is grounded the true knowledge of this Art, beeinge of reaſonable length, and hauing edges and point, wherein it ſeemeth to reſemble euerie other weapon, It is to be conſidered, that foraſmuch as it hath no more thē two edges and one point, a man may not ſtrike with anie other then with theſe, nether defend himſelf with anie other then with theſe. Further all edg blowes, be they right or reuerſed, frame either a circle or part of a circle: Of the which the hand is the Center, and the length of the ſworde, the Diameter.

Whereupon he that would giue either an edg blow in a great compaſſe, either thruſt with the point of the ſword, muſt not onely be nimble of hand, but alſo muſt obſerue the time of aduātag, which is, to know when his own ſword is more
nere

nere and readie to ſtrik then his enemies. For
when the enemie fetcheth a compaſſe with his
ſword, in deliuering his ſtroke, at the length of
the arme: if he then perceiue himſelfe to be nerer
by halfe an arme, he ought not to care to defend
himſelfe, but with all celeritie to ſtrike. For as he
hitteth home firſt, ſo he preuenteth the fal of his
enemies ſword. But if he be forced to defend him
ſelfe from anie edge blow, he muſt for his greater
ſafetie and eaſe of doinge it, go and incounter it
on the halfe ſword that is hindermoſt : in which
place as the enemies ſword carrieth leſſe force, ſo
is he more nere at hand to offend him.

   Concerning thruſtinge, or the moſt perilous
blowes of the point, he muſt prouide ſo to ſtand
with his bodie, feet and armes, that he be not forced, when he wold ſtrik, to loſe time: The which
he ſhal do, if he ſtand either with his arme ſo forward, either with his feete ſo backward, either
with his bodie ſo diſorderly, that before he thruſt
he muſt needs draw back his arme, helpe himſelf
with his feet, or vſe ſome daungerous motion of
the bodie, the which when the enemie percey-
ueth, he may firſt ſtrik before he be ſtroken. But
when a man ſtandeth in due order (which ſhall
hereafter be declared) and perceiueth that there
is leſſe diſtance from the point of his ſword, vnto
his enemie, then there is from his enemies ſword
vnto him, In that caſe he muſt nimbly force on a
ſtrong thruſt to the end he may hitt home firſt.

                         The

OR asmuch as the Effectes which procede from the legth of the sword, are not in euerie part thereof equall or of like force: It stands with reson besides the declaration of the cause, that I find out also the propertie and name of ech part, to the end euerie man may vnderstand, which are the parts of the length wherewith he ought to strike, and which the parts, wherewith he must defend.

I haue said elswhere, that the sword in strikinge frameth either a Circle, either a part of a Circle, or which the hand is the center. And it is manifest that a wheel, which moueth circulerly, is more forcible and swift in the circumference then towards the Center: The which wheel ech sworde resembleth in striking. Whereuppon it seemeth conuenient, that I diuide the sworde into fower equal parts: Of the which that which is most neerest the hand, as most nigh to the cause, I will call the first part: the next, I wil terme the second, then the third, and so the fourth : which fowerth parte conteineth the point of the sword. Of which fower partes, the third and fowerth are to be vsed to strike withal. For seeing they are neerest to the circumference, they are most swift. And the fowerth part (I mean not the tip of the point, but fower fingers more within it) is the swiftest and strongest of all the rest: for besides that it is in the circumference, which causeth it to be most swift, it hath

B 1 also

alſo fower fingers of counterpeize therby making
the motion more forcible. The other two partes,
to wit, the firſt and ſecond are to be vſed to warde
withall, becauſe in ſtriking they draw litle compas, and therefore carrie with them but ſmal force
And for that their place is neere the hande, they
are for this cauſe ſtrong to reſiſt anie violence.

The

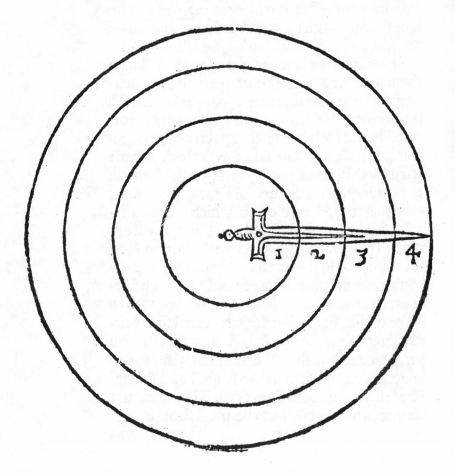

T H E Arme likewise is not in euerie part of equall force and swiftnes, but differeth in euerie bowing thereof, that is to saie in the wrist , in the elboe and in the shoulder: for the blowes of the wrist as they are more swift, so they are lesse stronge: And the other two, as they are more strong, so they are more slow, because they performe a greater compas . Therefore by my counsel, hee that would deliuer an edgeblow shall fetch no compasse with his shoulder, becaus whilest he beareth his sword farre off, he giueth time to the warie enemie to enter first: but he shall onely vse the compas of the elboe and the wrist: which , as they be most swift, so are they stronge inough, if they be orderly handled.

That

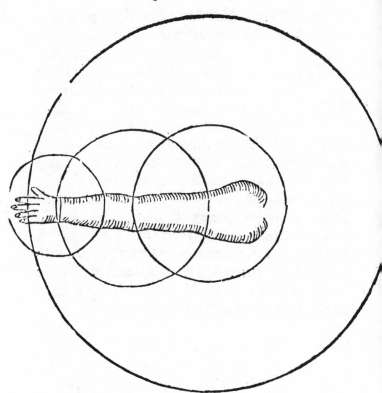

Ͻ̄ **But** *euerie blow of the point of the sword ſtriketh circulerly andhow he that ſtriketh with the point, ſtriketh ſtreight.*

Auing before ſaid and laid down for one of the principels of this art, that the ſtreit Line is the ſhorteſt of all others (which is moſt true,) It ſeemeth needfull that I make demonſtration thereof. And further hauing ſuggeſted for a troth, that the blow of the point is the

24

the ſtreight ſtrook,this not being ſimplie true,I think it expedient before I wade anie further, to ſhew in what maner the blowes of the point are ſtroken circulerly,and how ſtreightly. And this I will ſtraine my ſelf to performe as plainly and as briefly as posſibly I maie. Neither wil I ſtrech ſo farre as to reaſon of the blowes of the edg,or how all blowes are ſtroken circulerly,becauſe it is ſuf-ficiently and clerely handled in the diuiſion of the Arme and ſword.

Comming then to that which is my principall intent to handle in this place,I wil ſhew firſt how the arme when it ſtriketh with the point,ſtriketh circulerlie.

It is moſt euident,that all bodies of ſtreight or lenge ſhape,I mean when they haue a firme and immoueable head or beginninge,and that they moue with an other like head,alwaies of necesſi-tie in their motion,frame either a wheel or part of a circuler figure. Seeing then the Arme is of like figure and ſhape,and is immoueably fixed in the ſhoulder,and further moueth onely in that parte which is beneth it,there is no doubt,but that in his motion it figureth alſo a circle,or ſome parte thereof. And this euerie man may perceiue if in mouing his arme,he make trial in himſelſe.

Finding this true,as without controuerſie it is, it ſhal alſo be as true,that all thoſe thinges which are faſtned in the arme,and do moue as the Arme doth, muſt needs moue circulerlie. Thus much :oncerning my firſt purpoſe in this Treatiſe.

B3   Now

Now I wil come to my fecond, and wil declare the reafons and waies by which a man ftrikinge with the point ftriketh ftraightly. And I fay, that when foeuer the fworde is moued by the onelie mocion of the Arme, it muft alwaies of necefitie frame a cirkle by the reafons before alleaged. But if it happen, as in a manner it doth alwaies, that the arme in his motion make a circle vpwardes, and the hand mouing in the wrift frame a part of a circle downewards then it wil com to paffe, that the fword being moued by two contrarie motiõs in going forwards ftriketh ftraightly.

But to thentent that this may be more plainlie perceiued, I haue framed this prefent figure for the better vnderftãding wherof it is to be known, that as the arme in his motion carrieth the fworde with it, and is the occafion that beeing forced by the faide motion, the fworde frameth a circle vpwards, So the hand mouing it felfe in the wrift, maie either lift vp the point of the fword vpwards or abafe it downwards. So that if the hand do fo much let fal the point, as the arme doth lift vp the handle, it commeth to paffe that the fwords point thrufteth directly at an other prick or point then that it refpecteth.

Wherefore let 𝔄.𝔅. be the circle which is framed by the motion of the arme: which arme, if (as it carrieth with it the fword in his motion) it would ftrike at the point 𝔇. it fhould be conftrained through his motion to ftrik at the point 𝔅. And from hence procedeth the difficultie of thrufting or

26

ftriking with the point . If therefore the arm wold
ftrik directly at the point ᴅ.it is neceffary that as
much as it lifteth the hãdle vpwards,the hãdwrift
do moue it felf circulerlie downward,making this
circle ᴀᴄ & cariyng with it the point of thefword
downewardes, of force it ftriketh at the point ᴅ.
And this would not fo come to paffe, if with the
only motion of tharme,a man fhould thruft forth
the fword , confidering the arme moueth onelie
aboue the center ᴄ.

Therefore feing by this difcourfe it is manifeft
that the blow of the point,or a thruft, can not bee
deliuered by one fimple motion directly made,
but by two circuler motions,the one of the Arme
the other of the hand,I wil hence foreward in all
this work tearme this blow the blow of the ftreit
Line.Which confidering the reafons before alleaᵹ
ged,fhall breed no inconuenience at all.

Moſt

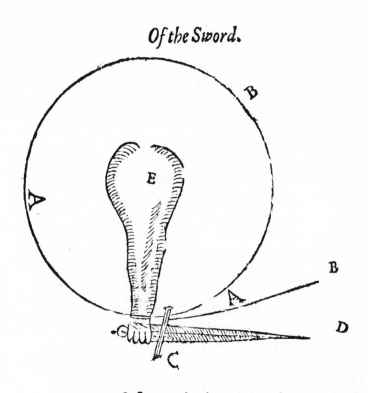

Oſt great is the care and conſiderations which the paces or footſtepps requier in this exerciſe, becauſe from them in a maner more thē from anie other thing ſpringeth all offence and defence. And the bodie likewiſe ought with all diligence to be kept firme and ſtable, turned towards the enemie, rather with the right ſhoulder, then with the breſt. And that beecauſe a man ought to make himſelf as ſmal a mark to thenemie as is poſible, And if he be occaſioned to bēd his body any way, he muſt bend it rather backwards then forwards, to thende that it be far of from danger, conſidering the bodie can neuer
greatly

greatly moue it felfanie other waie more then that and that fame waie the head maie not moue being a member offo great importance.

Therefore when a man ftriketh, either his feet or his arme are thruft forwards, as at that inftant it fhall make beft for his aduauntage. For when it hapneth that he may ftrongly offend his enemie without the increafe of a pace, he muft vfe his arm onely to perfourme the fame, bearing his bodie alwaies as much as he maie and is required, firme and immoueable.

For this reafon I commend not their maner of fight, who continually as they fight, make théfelus to fhew fometimes litle, fometimes great, fometimes wrefting themfelues on this fide, fomtimes on that fide, much like the mouing of fnailes. For as all thefe are motions, fo can they not be accomplifhed in one time, for if when they beare their bodies low, they would ftrike aloft, of force they muft firft raife them felues, and in that time they may be ftroken. So in like maner when their bodies are writhed this way or that waie.

Therefore, let euerie man ftand in that order, which I haue firft declared, ftraining himfelf to the vttermoft of his power, when he would ether ftrik or defend, to performe the fame not in two times or in two motions, but rather in halfa time or motion, if it were pofsible.

As concerninge the motion of the feete, from which grow great occafions afwell of offence as defence, I faie and haue feene by diuers examples
that

as by the knowledg of their orderlie and difcreet
motion, afwel in the Liftes as in common fraies,
ther hath bin obtained honorable victorie, fo their
bufie and vnrulie motion haue bine occafion of
fhamefull hurts and fpoils. And becaufe I can not
laie downe a certein meafure of motion, confidering the difference betwene man and man, fome
being of great and fome of litle ftature: for to fome
it is comodious to make his pace the length of an
arme, and to other fome half the length or more.
Therefore I aduertife euerie man in al his wards
to frame a reafonable pace, in fuch fort that if hee
would ftep forward to ftrik, he lengthen or increas
one foot, and if he would defend himfelf, he withdraw as much, without peril of falling.

And becaufe the feet in this exercife doe moue
in diuers maners, it fhall be good that I fhew the
name of euerie motion, to thend that vfinge thofe
names through al this work, they maie the better
be vnderftood.

It is to be knowen that the feete moue either
ftreightly, either circulerly : If ftreitly, then either
forwardes or backwards: but when they moue directly forwards, they frame either a halfe or a whol
pace. By whole pace is vnderftood, when the foot
is carried from behind forwards, kepinge ftedfaft
the forefoot. And this pace is fometimes made
ftreight, fometimes crooked. By ftreight is meant
when it is done in the ftreit line, but this doth feldome happen. By croked or slope pace is vnderftood, when the hinderfoot is brought alfo fore-
wards

wardes, but yet a thwarte or croſſing : and as it groweth forwardes , it carieth the bodie with it, out of the ſtraight line, where the blowe is giuen.

The like is ment by the pace that is made directly backwardes: but this backe pace is framed more often ſtreight then croked. Now the midle of theſe backe and fore paces, I will terme the halfe pace: and that is, when the hinder-foote being brought nere the fore foote, doth euen there reſt: or when from thence the ſame foote goeth forwardes. And likewiſe when the fore-foote is gathered into the hinder-foote, and there doth reſt, and then retireth it ſelfe from hēce backwards. Theſe half paces are much vſed, both ſtreit & croked, forwards & backwardes. And in like ſorte, halfe paces forwardes & backewardes, ſtreight and crooked.

Circuler paces, are no otherwiſe vſed than halfe paces, and they are made thus: When one hath framed his pace, he muſt fetch a cōpaſſe with his hinder foote or fore foote, on the right or leſte ſide: ſo that circuler paces are made either when the hinder-foot ſtanding faſt behinde, doth afterwards moue it ſelfe on the leſte or right ſide, or when the fore-foote being ſetled before doth moue likewiſe on the right or left ſide: with all theſe ſort of paces a man may moue euerie waie both forwardes and backewardes.

C 2

Straigt

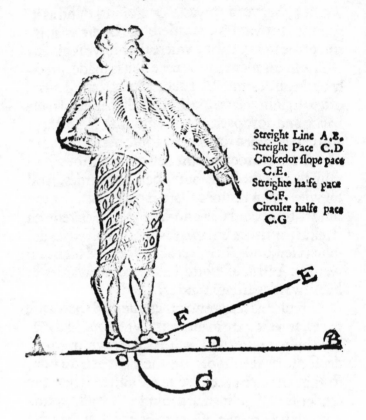

Streight Line A.B.
Strteight Pace C.D
Crokedor flope pace
   C.E.
Streighte halfe pace
   C.F.
Circuler halfe pace
   C.G

Of the Agreement of the Foot and Hand.

He right legge ougnt alwaies to be the strength of the right hand, and likewise the lefte legge of the left hand : So that if at any time it shall happen a thrust to bee forciblie deliuered, reson would that it be accompanied

panied with the legge: for otherwife, by meanes
of the force and waight, which is without the per-
pendiculer or hanging line of the body, hauing no
prope to fuſtain it, a man is in daunger of falling.
And it is to be vnderſtood, that the pace doth naturally ſo much increaſe or diminiſh his motion,
as the hand. Therefore we fee when the right foote
is behinde, the hand is there alfo : fo that who fo
ſtraineth himſelfe to ſtand otherwiſe, as he offereth
violence vnto nature, fo hee canne neuer indure
it: wherefore when he ſtandeth at his ward, bearing
his hand wide, there alfo the foote helpeth by his
ſtrength, being placed towards that parte: & when
the hand is borne a lowe, & the right foote before,
if then he would lifte his hand alofte, it is necefſarie that he draw backe his foote: And there is fo
much diſtance from the place where the foot doth
parte, to ioyne it felfe to the other foote, as there is
from the place whence the hande parteth, to that
place wher it remaineth ſtedfaſt, litle more or leſſe:
wherefore, preſuppoſing the faid rules to be true,
he muſt haue great care to make his pace, & moue
his hand at one time together : And aboue all, not
to skip or leape, but keepe one foote alwaies firme
and ſtedfaſt: and when he would moue it, to do it
vpon fome great occaſion, conſidering the foote
ought chiefely to agree in motion with the hand,
which hande, ought not in any caſe what foeuer
happen to varie from his purpoſe, either in ſtriking
or defending.

C 3   Wardes

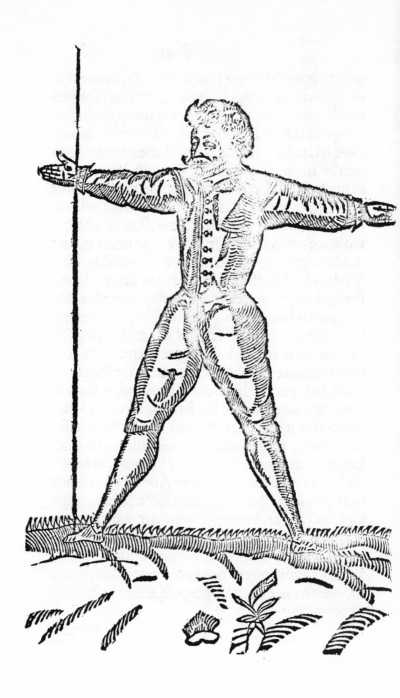

34

Ards in weapons are such sites, positions or placings which withstand the ene- mies blowes, and are as a shield or safegarde against them. For he who hath no skill to carrie his bodie and beare these weapons order lie, which either couer, or easely maie couer the whole bodie, cannot be saide to stand in warde, insomuch that a man ought to vse great diligence in the apt carriyng of his bodie and weapons, For manie times he ought to settle and repose himself in his ward, therein deliberating vpon some new deuise, or expecting when his enemie wil minister occasion to enter vpon him.

The Wards which maie be vsed with the single sword are threefold, Neither in my opinion maie they be anie more: for that one onlie straight line, which is the sword, maie not couer, defend and easelie offend after anie other maner.

The high ward.

His high warde, which also might be called the first, beeinge the very same which euery man frameth at the dra- ing of the sword out of the sheath, may so farre foorth, and in somuch be termed a warde, in how much, by turning the poynt of the sworde downewarde, it wardeth the whole

whole perſon, and for that, by gathering in of the
hinderfoote, & increſing forwardes with the right
foote, a man may diſcharge a ſtrong thurſt a boue
hande at his enemie.

In this, and in al other wardes, it is diligently to
be noted, that he beare his weapons ſo orderly diſ-
poſed, that the ſtreight lyne which goeth from the
ſwords point be ſtil bēt to ſtrike the enemy, ether in
the face or in the breſt: for if the point be ſo borne
that it reſpect ouer the enemies head, the enemie
may eaſely firſt enter vnderneth & ſtrike before the
fall or diſcend thereof: And by holding the poynt
two lowe, he may by beating it ſomewhat downwards cauſe it to be quit void of his bodie, and ſo
ſafelie come in to ſtrik, the which hath bine manie
times ſene.

The high ward.　　　　　The low ward.

His ſecond warde from the effecte
ſhall be called the broad or wide
warde, becauſe the Arme widning
and ſtretching it ſelfe directlie as
much as is poſsible from the right
ſide, beareth the ſword ſo farre off
from the bodie, that it ſeemeth to
giue great ſcope to the enimie to enter, albeit in truth
it be nothing ſo. For although the hand & the handle
of the ſworde, be both farr from the bodie, and quite
out of the ſtreight line, yet the poynt of the ſworde,
from which principallie procedeth the offence, is not

D   without

without the ſaide lyne : For it is borne ſo bending towarde the left ſide that it reſpecteth directlie to ſtrike
the enimie, and being borne in that ſorte, it may verie
well both ſtrike and defend. And when the poynt
of the ſword is borne out of the ſtreight lyne, as the
hand and handle is, then a man is in daunger to bee
hurte eaſelie by the enimie, the which happeneth not
when the poynt is bending, for in ſuch order, it is as
a barre and defence to the whole bodie.

The low Ward.

His alſo from the effect is called the baſe
ward or lock: Neither is this name impro
perlie giuen by the Profeſſors of this Art,
for that it is more ſtrong, ſure and commo
dious then anie other ward, and in the which a man
may more eaſelie ſtrik, ward & ſtand therein with leſſe
paine. This ward is framed in the Schools after dy-
uers faſhions, either bearing the hand low before the
knee, either verie much ſtretched forwardes, either
betweene both the knees. All which faſhions, (if we
regard naturall reaſon, and the motions vſed therein)
are to ſmall purpoſe : for, beſides that they are all violent, and for a ſmall time to be endured, they are alſo
ſuch, in the which a man may not ſtrike but in two
tymes, or at the leaſt in one, and then verie weakly.
Wherefore, caſting all theſe aſide, I will frame ſuch a
warde, as ſhalbe applyed, to time, to nature, and to
ſafetie : And it is, when one beareth his arme directly
downwardes neere his knee (but yet without it) and
his ſworde with the point ſomewhat rayſed, and bearing

ring towards the left ſide, to the end, it may arme and defend that part alſo, in ſuch ſort, that (being borne without violence) he may continue long. And if he would ſtrike, he may in one time, forcibly deliuer a great thruſt. But this he cannot do, if he beare his ſword directly befor him, for then he muſt ether draw backe his arme when he would ſtrike, or els ſtrike in one time, but verie weakly.

This warde therfore muſt be framed with the arme ſtretched downwards neere the knee, but yet on the outſide thereof, becauſe after this manner a man ſtandeth ſafely, commodiouſly, and more readie, both to ſtrike and defend.

The

Ithout all doubt, the thrust is to be preferred before the edge-blowe, aswell becaufe it ftriketh in leffe time, as alfo for that in the faide time, it doth more hurt.

For which confideratiõ, the Romanes (who were victorious in all enterprifes) did accuftome their fouldiers of the Legions to thruft onely : Alleaging for their reafon, that the blowes of the edge, though they were great, yet they are verie fewe that are deadly , and that thruftes, though litle & weake, when they enter but iij.fingers into the bodie,are wont to kill. Therefore I laye down this for a firme and certaine rule, that the thruft doth many times more readily ftrike, and giue the greater blowe againft the enimie. And to the end, a man may thruft it out with the greateft force at the moft aduantage,and vttermoft length that may be,he muft alwaies remember to carrie his left foote compafsing behinde him in fuch fort, that the hinderfoot fo compafsing may alwaies be in the ftraight lyne of the hand and fworde,as a Diameter in the middeft of a Circle. And in finifhing of the blowe,to drawe his hinder-foote a halfe pace forwardes , and fo by that meanes the blow is longer & ftronger, and the fhoulder and fide are onely oppofite to the enimie , and fo farre off from him,that they may not be ftrooken: and it is not pofsible for a man to frame a longer blowe than this.

VVhen

40

FOr no other cauſe, the edge is preferred before the poynt, then for the time : the ſhortnes whereof, is ſo to be eſteemed aboue all other things in this Arte, that (omitting the point and edge) it ought to be giuen for the beſt and chiefe counſell, that ſame to be the better blowe, in which a man ſpendeth leaſt time. And therfore when this happeneth and may be done with the edg, then the edg is to be preferred before the point: the which as occaſion ſerueth ſhalbe further declared.

When I reaſoned of the blow of the point or thurſt I ſaid, that a man ought to thruſt when the point is in the ſtraight line, becauſe the blowe is then performed in one time. But the edg differeth from the point, in that that being out of the ſtrait line, it indcuoreth to come into the ſame againe. Therefore when it hapneth the point to be born either on the right, either on the left ſide, either aloft, out of the ſtrait line, if then on would thruſt in the right line, he cannot performe it but in two times, whereas if he would ſtrik with thedg be it right or reuerſed, or downwards, he may do it in one time. It ſhalbe alſo verie commodious rather to ſtrik with the edg, when as ſometime a man bearinge his ſword in the ſtrait line, and the enimie therfinding it, doth with his hand beat it on this ſide or that ſide: In which caſe, if he would return it again into the ſaid line of purpoſe to ſtrik, he ſhalbe conſtrained to doe it whith great violence and much time.

For theſe reaſons I hold it better to let the ſworde ſwaie to that ſide, whereto the enemie beateth it, and to ioin vnto it ſuch force, as he may to help the motion, and (fetching withall a compas) to ſtrik with the edg.

The which blow is so readie & strong, that theni-
mie can hardly haue time to withstand it, being alredy
occupied in beating aside the sword & pretending to
strik: nothing at al expecting that thaduersaries sworde
wil strik again either so quickly, or with the edge, on
that side from which it was beaten.

The Line of the edg is from *A* to *B*,
The line of the point from *C.* to *D.*
and from *D.* to *E.*

T H E meanes of defending a blowe giuen either with the edg or point of the sword, are three. One is when the weapon is opposed to the blow, in such sort that the weapon which cometh striking either at the head or at the bodie, cannot hit home to the place whereūto it is directed, but hindered by some thing or other then set against it, be it sword, dagger, target, bil, Iauelin, or anie thing els, which at that instant a man hath in his hand. For it chanceth not alwaies ro weare or carrie weapons of purpose, or ordained to that entent . Neither happelie is it thought souldier or gentlemanlike, not to know how to strike or defend, but onely with wepons framed to that end: for which cause, it may wel be said, that the soldier differeth from other men, not because he is more skilful in handling the sword or iauelyn, but for that he is expert in euerie occasion to know the best aduantage & with iudgement both to defend himself with anie thing whatsoeuer, and therewithal safelie to offend the enimie : In which & no other thing consisteth true skirmishing.

He that perswads himself that he can learn this Art by the exercise of a few perticuler stroks of the point and edg is vtterlie deceiued: for besids , that by those perticuler triks, there is smal knowledge gotten : So the chaunces in this Arte are so daungerous & diuers, that it is impossible to deliberat suddenly, except he haue the vniuersall knowledg and vnderstandinge of all the rules and principels hereof, being grounded vpon offending & defending, and not only vpon the sword, the dagger, the target, the iauelin & the bil. For a man at al times (when he is occasioned to strike

or

or defend) doth not carrie thefe weapons about him, but is conftrained to defend himfelfe with a peece of wood from a Iavelyn, with a ftoole or fourme from a fworde, or with a cloake from a dagger, in which cafe men commonly vfe many other things not ordained for that purpofe, doing that therewith which naturall inftinct teacheth them. And this inftinct is no other thing then the knowledge of the rules before laide downe: which knowledge, becaufe it is naturally graffed in the mynde, is fomething the rather holpen and quallified by Arte, and maketh a man fo affured and bolde, that he dares to enter on any great daunger, and iudgeth (when he feeth the qualitie of the weapon, and the fyte wherein it is placed) what it maye do, or in how many waies it may either ftrike or defend. From which his iudgement fprings the knowledge of all that he hath to do, and how he hath to handle himfelfe to encounter any danger.

But returning to my purpofe, to wit, of the way how to defend, which is to carrie the weapon oppofite, this maner is commonly vfed, but is not fo profitable, being vfed as it is. And the reafon is, becaufe when men endeuour themfelues to encounter or oppofe themfelues againft the weapon which commeth to ftrike them, (neither making bolde that their weapon can, neither knowing how it fhould defend) they withdraw their bodie with their foote, and commit all thefe faultes following.

1 Firft, by withdrawing of themfelues, they encounter the enimies fworde towardes the poynt, in which place it beareth moft force, and therefore with great difficultie they fuftaine the blowe.

2 An

2 Another is, if they would strike the enimie, of force they must returne their feete and weapons thither, where they were before, and yet encreafe forwards somewhat more, if they would strongly strike him : And in this they spend so much time, that the enimie may not onely eafily defend, but also, verie well and fafely strike. To him then that woulde vfe this manner of defence without danger, it is neceffarie and needefull, when he encountreth the enimies fworde, that he do not withdrawe himfelfe, but with his left foote increafe a crooked or flope pace forwardes, the which fhall encounter the fword, which before was comming ftriking with the edge, on that parte thereof, in which it hath leaft power to offend, and fhal by that meanes eafily withftand the blowe. But if the fworde come with a thruft, he muft finde it and beat it afide : for euery litle motion is fufficient to driue the poynt farre enough from danger of hurte. And there is this aduantage gotten, afwel in the blow of the edge as of the point, that the bodie is voided out of the ftraight lyne, by meanes of the faid flope pace : and it ftandeth fo apt and fo neere to offende the enimie, that one may ftrike in the verie inftant, neither can the enimie fo much withdrawe himfelfe as is fufficient to auoyde the ftroke : For a man hath to vfe the ftraight pace of the right foote to follow the enimie, which pace is fo ftrong and fo fwift, that the enimie may not auoide it. And becaufe this maner of defence, in mine opinion, feemeth to be moft fure and fhort, I will vfe it aboue all other.

There is another waie, to wit, when one perceiueth the enimies fworde in the deliuerie of an edge-
E.   blowe,

blowe, to fetch a great compasse, he may strike him before the fall of his sword with a thrust : or els when the enimie thrusteth, (but yet spendeth many times in doing thereof) he may likewise strike him in as shorte time as may be. The which manner of defending is most profitable, & perchaunce the better of the two. For there is no man that will runne himselfe hedlong vpon the weapon, or that, perceiuing himselfe readie to be strooken, will not suddenly drawe backe and with-hold that blowe which he had alreadie prepared to discharge. And although there be some, who being strooken runne rashly on, yet generally, men wil not so do, albeit they be strooken when they are most collorick, but will, when they are strooken or wounded, giue backe and be dismayed and by reason of the bloud which goeth from them, alwaies more & more be weakened.

But yet when they be so wounded, it shall be for their profit to be well aduised, and not to discomfort themselues for the greatnes of the blowe, but to beare it paciently : for that which they doe in disdaine and furie shal turne them to much displeasure.

3 The third manner of defence is, when the bodie voideth out of the straight lyne towardes this or that side, but this is seeldome vsed alone & by it selfe, but rather accompanied with the opposing of the weapon, or with the second manner of defence aforesaid. If it be vsed alone, the manner is to let slipp the blow, and to strike the enimie in the same time that he is o-uer reached in his blowe.

The

46

*The methode which shalbe vsed in handling
the Chapters following.*

Orasmuch as I ought in the Chapters folowing to teach more particularly all the blowes and defences in euery warde, (to the end that no man doe meruaile why I do not perfourme the same, and do thinke that the instruction is therefore imperfect) I thinke good (because my purpose is now to intreat of that onlywhich pertaineth to true Arte, to the which the blow of the point, or thrustes, are most agreeable, being more readie and strong than any other) to handle them principally,

E 2

47

cipally, and yet not so, but that I will also talke of edg-
blows when in my treatise I come to that place where
it shalbe commodious to strike therewith , placing
them neere to their wardes and defenses , although
against all edgeblows this is the best defence, to strike
by the right lyne before the fall of the enimies sword,
for, being deliuered in shorter time, it withstandeth
their fall and lighting. The order I say, which I will
obserue, shalbe , to laie downe euery warde, their
blowes and defences, but principally of the poynt,
then of the edge, if neede require.

The hurt of the high warde at single Rapier.

THE truest, and surest blowe that may be giuen when a man lyeth at the high warde, is,
the thrust aboue hande, aswell for that it is
in the straight lyne, as also, because it naturally stayeth it selfe in the lowe warde : So that from
the beginning to the ending of this blowe, there is
neuer any time giuen to the enimie to enter, by reason, that the point standeth alwayes directly against
him . But in the discharging of this blowe, a man
must remember to drawe his left foote neere his right
foote, and then to encrease forwardes with the right
foote, & deliuer it as forcibly as he may, staying him
selfe in the lowe warde.

True it is, that he may also deliuer a right and reuersed edgeblowe at the head : or els, strike downwardes from the wrist of the hand : but because he is
not able to turne his wrist in so small a compasse, in
the discharge of an edgeblowe, either high or lowe,
but

but that the poynt of the fworde will be out of the ftraight lyne, by the length of a fworde, in the which (before it returne) the enimie hath fufficient time to ftrike: Therefore I would not counfell any man to vfe them either alone, or both togither. But yet betweene two thruftes, they may be verie well vfed togither, by continuing the one after the other (though they be voyded) vntill the laft thruft, the which doth fafely reft it felfe in the lowe ward. The vfe of them is on this manner.

When one hauing difcharged a thruft from the high warde, perceiueth that it doth not hurt, becaufe it was voyded by the enimies fworde, he muft turne a right edgeblowe from the wrift athwart the enimies head, fetching a compaffe with his foote behind him toward the right fide, to the ende the blowe may be the longer, which is the longeft blowe of all others. But if the enimie voide this in like cafe (which is very difficult) then he muft fuddenly turne the reuerfe from his elbowe encreafing therewithall a flope pace with the hinder foote. And it is to be noted, that in deliuering a reuerfe, the flope pace is in a manner alwaies to be vfed, to the ende he may go foorth of the ftraight lyne, in the which (if he fhould deliuer it) he may eafily be ftrooken. Hauing vfed this pace & reuerfe, whether it hit or not, the fworde in the fame inftant is fomething to be drawen or flyded: which drawing is profitable in this, that in giuing the reuerfe it doth both caufe the weapon to cut, and make the greater blowe. Wherefore it is to be vnderftoode, that all edgeblowes ought fo to be deliuered, that they may cut: for being directly giuen without any

E 3 drawing,

drawing, they caufe but a fmall hurt.

Comming therefore to my purpofe, I fay : that as foone as he hath fo drawen his fworde, he ought with the ftraight pace of the right foote, difcharge a thruft vnderneath, being already prepared, the whrich thruft is fo ftrong, both for the aptnes thereof and encreafe of the pace, that it pearceth through any impediment withftanding it. And all thefe blowes (beginning from the thruft aboue hand, till the ende of the thruft vnderneath) being roundly deliuered one after another with fuch fwiftnes as is required, are in a manner not to be warded. Befides, they haue fo great increafe of pace , that it is not almoft poffible for the enimie to retyre fo much backwarde, as thefe encreafe vpon him forward.

The defence of the thruft of the high warde at single Rapier.

ALL the furie in ftriking before fpoken of, is vtterly fruftrated, when, as here it may be feene, a man withftandeth and incountreth the firft thruft. For the defence whereof it is needefull that he ftand at the lowe warde, and as the thruft cometh, that he encounter it without , with the edge of the fword, and increafe a flope pace forward, with the hinder foote at the verie fame time, by which pace he moueth out of the ftreight line , and paffeth on the right fide of the enimie. And he muft remember to beare alwaies the poynt of the fword toward the enimie: So that the enimie in comming forwardes, ether runneth himfelfe on the fword, which may eafely happen, and fo much the rather, when he commeth refolutelie determined

termined to strike, or else if he come not so farre forwardes that he encountreth the sword, yet he may be
safelie stroken, with the encrease of a streight pace: to
which pace, hauing suddenly ioyned a slope pace, a
man must returne and increase againe though the enimie were strooken at the first increase of that pace:
For if at the first stroak and increase, the enimie were
not hit in the eye, it shall be to small purpose. Therefore as soone as he hath vsed the croked or slope pace,
he must presentlie encrease an other streight pace, the
which doth so much gather vpon the enimie, that if he
would strike him in the brest, he may thrust his sword
vp to the hiltes.

Now for the loftie edge-blowes, both right and reuersed, the rules aforesaide may suffice: To witte, the
edge-blowe sectheth a compasse. The blowe of the
poynt or thrust is the shortest, & in this blowe, he that
is nearest hitteth soonest: So then he must thrust vnder
any of these edgeblowes. And farther, for asmuch
as it is naturallie giuen to euerie man to defend himselfe, he may encounter the right edge-blowe after an
other waie, and that is, to encounter it with the edge
of his sworde, and presentlie, to driue there withall a
thrust at the enimies face, and to compasse his hinder-
foote, towardes the right side behinde, to the ende,
that the thrust may be lengthned and his bodie thereby couered, considering he shall then stand right behinde his sword.

This manner of defence, may serue to warde all
right blows of the edg, deliuered from the high ward,
and it is the best waie of all other, because it doth not
onely warde, but also in one and the selfesame time,
both

both strike and defend safely.

This manner of thrust is called the reuersed thrust. But if one would warde a reuerse, he must oppose the edge of his sword without, and therewithall increase a slope pace, & then deliuer a thrust with the increase of a straight or right pace . And this may suffice for all that which may be vsed against a loftie, reuersed, edgeblowe, as farfoorth as a man endeuoureth to oppose himselfe against the weapon . And this is the verie same also which may be vsed for the warding of the thrust,

The hurt of the broad warde at single Rapier.

THe most sure, most true & principall blowe that may be vsed in this warde is the thrust vnderhand, so that a man draw his left foote neere his right foote, and then discharge it with the increase of the saide foote, and settle himselfe in the lowe warde.

He may also in this warde with the said increase of the right foote, deliuer a right edgeblowe from the wrist of the hand, and stay himselfe in the low warde. And perchaunce he may (although with great daunger) bestowe also a reuerse : yet considering he shall do it out of the straight lyne, in the which onely he striketh safely, I do not thinke it good, that he vse either the saide reuerse, either the saide right blowe except it be verie seldom, & for the same cause, assuring himselfe in the blow of the poynt, or thrust, the which he shall not giue, except it be verie commodious, or that he be forced of necessitie, considering this thrust doth not onely easily and commodiously defend, but also,

also, at one inftant, fafely ftrike, and offend, as fhalbe
fhewed in the defence of this warde. That therefore which he may fafely do, in this warde, is to expect and watch for the enimies comming.

The Defence of the broad VVard at fingle Rapier.

IF a man would defend himfelfe from the blowes of
the forefaide broad warde, it is good that he ftande
againft the enimie in the lowe warde: for whileft he
is fo oppofite in the fame warde, the enimie may neither eafily enter, neither commodioufly defend himfelfe. So that he which is in the lowe warde may very
eafily withftand the downright blow, and the reuerfe
by giuing a thruft, for that he fhall hit him firft, And if
he would onely oppofe his fworde, and not ftrike alfo therewithall, he muft encounter the enimies fword
with the edge of his owne, and turning the fame edge
fetch a reuerfe, ftriking at the face of the enimie. And
as he fo turneth his hand and edge of his fworde, it
fhalbe good that he carrie his forefoote a halfe crooked or flope pace towards his right fide, ftaying himfelfe in the broad warde. For defence of the reuerfe,
it is to be marked, when the enimie lifteth vp the
point of the Rapier out of the ftraight lyne, becaufe
then of force he fetcheth a compaffe: And whileft he
fo doth, a man muft make a ftraight pace forwardes,
and with his left hande take holdfaft of the fworde
hande of the enimie, and incontinently wound him
with a thruft vnderneath alreadie prepared.

Now, the verie fame defence is to be vfed againft
the thruft vnderneath, which is againft the right edge-

F, blowe.

blow. Neither is there any other difference between these two defences, but that whileſt the right blowe fetcheth his compas, a man may giue a thruſt and hit home firſt: For the thruſt vnderneath, muſt onely of neceſſitie be warded, becauſe, cōming in the ſtraight lyne, it miniſtreth no aduantage or time to hit home firſt.

The hurt of the Lowe warde at ſingle Rapier.

A Man may in like maner in this ward, as in others, deliuer a thruſt, a right blowe, and a reuerſe : but the true and principall effect of this warde, is to expect the enimie, aſwell for that a man beareth him-ſelfe without warineſſe, as alſo, becauſe it is apt and readie to defende all blowes either high or lowe: For being in the middle, it is as eaſily ſomewhat lifted vp, as ſomething borne downe: So that when one ſtandeth in this warde, he may not (as for his aduantage) be the firſt that ſhall giue either the down-right blowe, or the reuerſe: for both the one and the other (departing out of the ſtraight lyne) are deadly, becauſe they giue time to the enimie to enter nimbly with a thruſt. The thruſt therefore, may be only vſed when one meaneth to ſtrike firſt, and it is practiſed either within, or without, alwaies regarding in either of the waies, ſo to beare and place his arme, that he haue no neede (before he thruſt) to drawe backe the ſame. And if the enimie warde it, by the trauerſe or croſſe motion of his Rapier, as many vſe to do, then he ought to encreaſe a ſtraight pace and lift vp his ſword hand, holding the point thereof downwards betwixt the enimies arme and his bodie, & with the encreaſe of of a straight pace to deliuer a thrust. And this manner of thrust doth easily speede, because it increaseth continually in the straight lyne in such sort that the enimie can do no other then giue backe, and especially when it is done without, for then the sworde is safe from the trauerse motion of the other sworde.

The Defence of the Lowe warde at single Rapier.

BEcause both the down-right blowe, and the reuerse are verie easily defended in this warde, I will not stand to speake of any other then of the thrust, restraining my selfe thereunto. The which thrust, if at the first it be not withstoode, may proue verie mortall & deadly. Therefore, when this thrust is giuen within, it must be beaten inwardes with the edge of the Rapier, requiring the turne of the hand also inwards, and the compasse of the hinder foote, so farre towards the right side, as the hande goeth towardes the right side. And the enimie shall no sooner haue deliuered he thrust, and he found the sword, but he ought to turne his hand; and with a reuerse to cut the enimies face, carying alwaies his forefoote on that side where his hand goeth. If the enimies thrust come outwardes, then it is necessarie, that with the turne of his hand he beat it outwards with the edge of his sword encreasing in the same instant one slope pace, by meanes whereof he deliuereth his bodie from hurt. And therewithall (encreasing another straight pace, and deliuering his thrust alreadie prepared) he doth most safely hurt the enimie.

F 2   *The*

55

HAuing as briefely as I might pofsibly fini-
fhed all that which might be faide, of true
knowledge of fingle Rapier : it feemeth
conuenient, that comming from the fimple to the compound, I handle thofe weapons firft,
which from the Rapier forwards are either moft fimple or leaft compound : And efpecially thofe which
nowe adayes are moft vfed, and in the which men are
moft exercifed, the which weapons are the Rapier &
Dagger accompanied togither , and are a great encreafe and furtherance both in ftriking and defending.

Wherefore , it is firft to be confidered , that with
thefe and the like weapons , a man may practife that
moft defired and renowmed manner of skirmifhing,
which is faide to ftrike and defend both in one time,
which is thought to be impofsible to be done with
the fingle Rapier, and yet in truth it is not fo : For
there are fome kinde of blows in the defence of which
one may alfo ftrike (as in the blowes of the edge,
downe right and reuerfed) both high and lowe, and
other high blowes which here are not fpoken of.

Wherefore feing with thefe weapons a man may
verie commodiouſly, both ſtrike and defend , for
that the one is a great helpe to the other, it is to bee
remembred, that becauſe thefe weapons are two,
and the one of lefler quantitie then the other , to
eache one bee allotted that part both of defendinge and ftrikinge , which it is beft hable to fup-
port. So that to the Dagger, by reaſon of his ſhortnes, is afsigned the left ſide to defend downe to the
knee: and to the ſword all the right ſide, & the right
and

and left side ioyntly downwardes from the knee.
Neither may it seeme strange that the onely Dagger
ought to defend all the blowes of the left side : for it
doth most easily sustaine euerie edgeblowe , when it
encountreth the sworde in the first and second parte
thereof.

But yet let no man assure himselfe , to beare any
blowe, with his only Dagger when he meeteth with
the sword on the thirde and fourth parte thereof, because that parte carrieth more force with it then may
be sustained with the onely Dagger. And yet for all
that, no man ought to accustome himselfe to defende
blowes with the Rapier and Dagger both together,
which manner of defending is now commonly vsed
because men beleeue, that they stand more assuredly
by thar meanes, lthough in trueth it is not so. For
the Rapier and Dagger are so bound thereby, that
they may not strike before they be recouered , and
therein are spent two tymes, vnder the which a man
may be strooken when he that striketh continuing by
the straight lyne, encreaseth forwards, perceiuing his
enimie to be occupied and troubled in defending of
himselfe . And albeit this is not seene to come to
passe many times, yet that is because the aduantage is
not knowen, or being known, men either are not readie to execute it, either stand greatly in feare to do it.

Therefore leauing aside this maner of defence , let
each man vse to oppose, one only weapon against the
enimies sworde, keeping the other free, that he may be
able to strike at his pleasure.

And it is diligently to be noted, that not onely the
blowes of the sworde, but also of any other weapon

F 3   be it

be it neuer so great , may with the onely Dagger be sustained and defended, when a man doth boldly encounter it towards the hand.

It is therefore to be knowen , that in the handling of these two weapons one may with lesse danger giue a blowe with the edge then at the single Rapier : For albeit the poynt of the Rapier be moued out of the straight lyne: yet for all that there is not free power giuen to the enimie to strike, considering there is an other weapon contrariwise prepared to defend : but this doth not so fall out at the single Rapier , which bearing it selfe farre off when it striketh with the edge, doth present & giue the meanes to the enimie to hit home first. And yet for all that , I would counsell no man, either in this or in any other sort of weapon to accustome himselfe to giue blowes with the edge; for that he may vnder them be most easily strooken by a thrust.

Of the Wardes.

N the handling of these weapons, men vse to frame manie wardes, all which, because many of them carrie no reason, for that they are ether out of the streight line, either vnder them a man maie easelie bee strooken, I wil cast aside as impertinent to my purpose, & restrain my selfvnto those three with the which a man may safelie strike & defend, wherunto all the rest maie be reduced.

How to defend with the Dagger.

I Haue said elswhere that the left side of the person is that part which the dagger ought to defend, that is

to

to ſaie,from the knee vpwards:the lower parts together with the right ſide ought wholy to bee warded
with the ſword.

Concerning the dagger,that which is to bee done
therewith,it is to be noted,that for great aduantage,it
would be holden before with the arme ſtreched forth
& the point reſpecting the euemie,which although it
be far from him,yet in that it hath a point , it giueth
him occaſion to bethink himſelf.

Now whether a man ought to holde his Dagger
with the edge or flatt towardes the enimie, it may be
left to the iudgement of him that handleth it,ſo to vſe
it, as ſhalbe moſt for his aduantage . I haue ſeene
ſome,who beare it with the elge towards the enimie,
alledging this to be their aduantage, that as they encounter the enimies ſworde (which commeth with
the edge or poynt)in the firſt and ſecond parte therof,
& therewithall do increaſe a pace forwards, of force
the hand turneth and placeth the edge of the Dagger
there where the flatt was firſt: So that they are to
driue the enimies ſword farre from them without any
great trouble, becauſe each little motion in the firſt
parte of the ſworde cauſeth verie great varietie in the
poynt,from whence principally proceedeth the hurt.
In which caſe,it ſhalbe very profitable to haue a good
large Dagger.

There be other ſome , whome it pleaſeth to carrie
their Dagger with the flatt towardes the enimie,vſing
for their defence,not onely the Dagger , but alſo the
guardes thereof with the which(they ſaye) they take
holdfaſt of the enimies ſword : and to the ende they
may do it the more eaſily , they haue daggers of purpoſe,

pose, which beside their ordinarie hilts, haue also two long sterts of Iron, foure fingers length , and are distant from the dagger the thicknes of a bow-string, into which distance , when it chaunceth the enimies sworde to be driuen, they suddenly straine and holde fast the sworde, the which may come to passe , but I holde it for a thing rather to be immagined then practised, the case so standing, that in the heate of fight, where disdaine bickereth with feare, little doth a man discerne whether the sworde be in that straight or no. And when he is to premeditate and marke, endeuouring and striuing in his liuely iudgement, he must aduise himselfe to perfourme it with the exquisite knowledge and perfect discerning of the enimies motions, his neerenesse and farrensse, and to resolue himselfe to strike by the shortest way that may be : for therehence springeth the victorie.

Let euery man therefore holde his dagger with the edge or flatt towardes the enimie , as it shall most aduantage him, or as he hath beene most accustomed. True it is, that by holding the edge towards the enimie there is this aduantage gotten, that with the dagger he may strike with the edge, which he may not do the other waie. But let euery man hold it as he wil, yet he ought to carrie his arme stretched out before him, with the poynt in manner aforesaide, to the end he may be able to finde the enimies sworde a great deale before it hitteth his person.

Besides this , he ought to obserue for an infallible rule, that when the poynt or edge commeth on the left side, he must beat it from that side with the dagger. And in like sort defending himselfe with the sworde,

word, to driue it from the right side, for doing otherwise : that is, if he force the blowes giuen on the left-
ide outwardes on the right side (forasmuch as the
enimies sworde hath by that meanes two motions,
the one crossing , which is alreadie giuen, the other
straight which the enimie giueth it , continuing the
one with the other) it may be, that in the straight motion, it may hit the person, before that (by the thwart
or crossing motion) it be driuen quite outwardes.
Therefore all blowes shalbe beaten outwards toward
that side or parte of the bodie which is least to the
end it may the sooner auoide daunger . And those
blowes that come on the right side must be beaten
towards the right side: and those on the left side must
in like manner be voided from the same side.

Now, as concerning the fashion of the Dagger,
thus much is to be saide : that it would be strong, able
to beare and incounter the blowes of the sword : indifferently long) that it may be quickly drawen out
of the sheath somewhat short : and those that are of
the middle size would be chosen.

The offence of the High warde
at Rapier and Dagger.

AS in handling the single Rapier, so likewise
in this , it shall not be amisse to begin with
the High warde , which in managing these
two weapons may be framed after two sortes . The
one with the right foote before , which I will call the
first : and the other with the same foot behind, which
I will terme the second . This second requireth a

G

greater

61

greater time, becaufe the point of the fworde is farther off from the enimie. The firſt (being more neere)
with the onely encreaſe of the foote forwardes, ſtriketh more readily, yet not more forcible than the ſecond, which, when it ſtriketh with the encreaſe of a
ſtraight pace, ioyneth to the force of the arme & hand,
the ſtrength of the whole bodie.

Beginning then with the firſt, as with that which
each man doth moſt eaſelie find: I ſaie, he ought if he
will keepe himſelfe within the boundes of true Arte,
to thruſt onely with the increaſe of the foote forwards,
ſetling himſelfe in the lowe warde.

In

In the second waie, which is framed with the righte foote behind, the sword alofte, and the dagger before, & borne as aforesaid, he ought in like sorte discharge a thrust as forciblie as he may, with the increase of a straight pace, staying himselfe in the lowe warde. Neither ought anie man in the handling of these weapōs to assure himselfe to deliuer edgeblowes, becaufe he knoweth that there is an other weapon which defendeth : For he that defendeth hath the selfe same aduātage, to witt, to be able with one weapon (and happelie the weaker,) to defend himself and strike with the stronger. The which stroake is painfully warded by him, who hath alreadie bestowed all his force and power, in deliuering the saide edgeblowe, by meanes whereof, becaufe there remaineth in him small power to withstand anie great encounter, let him prouide to thrust onelie.

Of all, or of the greater parte of the edgeblowes, aswell of striking as defending, I will reason at large in the Treatife of Deceite.

Of the defence of high VVarde at
Rapier and Dagger.

T O speake of the manner how to withstand the blowes of the edge, hauing alreadie saide that all such blowes may eafelie be warded by giuinge a thrust, I omit as superfluous. But for the defences of both sides of the bodie: I saie, it is greate vantage, to stand at the lowe warde, with the right foote forwardes, by the which manner of standing, the right side is put fourth towarde the enimie,

G 2   where

whereunto he will direct all his thrustes : and those may be encountred after three sortes, that is to saye: with the Dagger onely: with the Sworde onely: and with both ioyned together. But in each of them, a man must remember to encrease a slope pace, whereby that parte of the bodie which was to be strooken is voided out of the straight lyne.

When one wardeth with his Dagger onely, he shall encrease a pace, and beare his arme forwards, and hauing found the enimies sworde, he shall (with the encrease of a straight pace) strike him with a thrust vnderneath, alreadie prepared.

When he wardeth with his sworde onely , it is requisite, that making a slope pace, he lift vp his sworde, and beare it outwards, or els, as soon as he hath found the enimies sworde, that with his dagger he strike at the temples of his enimies head , staying his sworde with his owne : or els in steede of striking with the Dagger, therewith to staie the enimies sword, & with it, (encreasing another straight pace) to deliuer a thrust: but it is verie commodious to strike with the Dagger.

The thirde waie : As soone as he hath made the slope pace, and found the enimies sworde, he ought to staie it with his Dagger , and therewithall , withdrawing his owne sworde, to discharge a thrust vnderneath with the encrease of a straight pace.

The hurt of the broad warde at Rapier and Dagger.

IN each weapon and warde, I haue layde downe as a generall precept, that no man ought, (either for the

the procuring of any aduantage, either for ſtriking the
enimie more readily) deliuer blowes of the edge,
And in like ſorte; I haue ſaide, that eaſily and with
ſmall danger, one may be ſtrooken vnder any ſuch
blowe: which precepts, as in each time and place,
they ought to be obſerued: ſo in this warde principally they may not be forgotten. For a man may not
without great diſcommoditie and loſſe of time, ſtrike
with any edgeblowe, as he ſtandeth at this warde.

It reſteth therefore, that the thruſt be onely vſed,
which ought to be deliuered with the encreaſe of the
foote forwards, alwaies regarding before it be giuen,
if it be poſsible) to beate awaie the point of the enimies ſworde with the Dagger.

(The defence of the broad warde at Rapier and Dagger.

His thruſt alſo as well as the other may be
warded after three ſortes, to wit: with the
Dagger only, with the ſword only, and with
both ioyned together. But for a mans defence in
any of theſe waies, it is good to ſtande at the lowe
warde. And when he wardeth with the dagger only,
he muſt make a ſlope pace, and finding the enimies
ſworde, with his ſaid dagger, diſcharge a thruſt vnderneath with the increaſe of a ſtraight pace.

And when he wardeth with the ſworde onely
(which is the beſt of any other, both to ſtrike the enimie, and defend himſelfe) he muſt oppoſe the edge of
his ſworde againſt the enimies, and driue a thruſt at
his face, fetching a compaſſe with his hinderfoote,
both for the lengthning of the thruſt, and aſſuring of

G 3   him-

65

himſelſe.

It is poſſible to withſtand the thruſt with the ſworde and dagger ioyned together : but it is ſo diſcommodious and ſo ridiculous a waie, that I leaue to ſpeake thereof, as of a waye nothing ſafe to be practiſed.

The hurt of the lowe warde at Rapier and dagger.

N each warde, when one ſtandeth bearing the poynt of the ſworde towards the enimie, it doth much diſaduantage him to ſtrike with the edge. And if in any ſorte it be lawfull ſo to do, it is, when he ſtandeth at the lowe warde : For it is commodious, and there is ſpent but little time in the beſtowing of an edgeblowe betweene thruſtes. Or, the rather to trie the enimie, there may be deliuered an edgeblow from the wriſt of the hand, in the which as there is ſpent little time, ſo the poynt is carried but a litle out of the ſtraight lyne, ſo that the enimie may very hardly enter to ſtrike vnder either of theſe blowes. But it is better, not to vſe them, reſoluing rather to diſcharge thruſt after thruſt, then any edgeblowe.

This warde may (as the high ward) be framed after two ſortes, to wit : with the right foote behinde, and the ſame foote before : but that with the right foote behind, is vſed rather to expect the enimie than to ſtrike firſt. For although it carrieth great force by reaſon that the ſworde is farre off from hurting, and before it hitteth home, it ſpendes much time, yet the hurt thereof may eaſily be warded, either with the weapon, or by retyring a pace. I will ſpeake of that

onely

onely which is framed with the right foote before.
And in this, one may strike two waies, to wit : either
within or without : By (Within) I vnderstand, when
his sworde is borne betweene the enimies sword &
dagger. By (Without) I meane, when any one of
them is borne in the middle against the other.

When one findeth himselfe within , at the halfe of
the enimies sword, the poynt whereof, is directed to
strike at the right side, he must verie swiftly encrease a
slope pace, and in a manner straight , to the ende he
may approch the neerer his enimie , and therewithall
suddenly barring the enimies sworde in the middle
with his owne sworde and dagger, encrease a straight
pace, and deliuer a thrust.

This may be done after another plainer waie , and
that is : when he standeth at the halfe sworde , to beat
the enimies swordes point out of the straight lyne on
that side which shalbe most commodious, and in that
lyne encreasing his foote forwards to driue a forcible
thrust, at the enimies face or brest.

But standing without, he maie (with the encrease of
his foote forwards) giue a thrust at the face, which the
enimie of necessitie must defend with his sword : but
therein the sworde and the poynt thereof is commonly carried out of the straight line, in which case he may
(with the encrease of a slope pace) turne a reuerse at
the legges, and then presently something withdrawing his sworde , deliuer a thrust vnderneath with the
encrease of a straight pace.

He may also after a second manner , giue a right
edgeblow from the wrist, as short and strong as is possible, not so much pretending to strike as to finde the
enimies

enimies fworde : And it being fuddenly found hee muft with the encreafe of a flope or crooked pace, lift vp his hand and driue a thruft downwards, with the increafe of a ftraight pace.

After a thirde fort alfo, he may ftrike, and that is to deliuer the forefaid blowe from the wrift, and hauing met with the enimies fworde, to make prefently a flope pace, and ftaie the fworde with his dagger, and then nimbly recouering his owne fworde, to thruft vnderneath with the increafe of a ftraight pace.

Thefe be fufficient, concerning that which may be done in this warde with the fworde both within and without, at leaft, for fo much as may be done by true Arte.

The defence of the lowe warde at Rapier & Dagger.

ALthough in the defence of blowes in eche warde, there is great confideration & heede to be taken : yet in this efpecially is required a farr more excellent iudgement and readines in action . For this warde doth oppofe it felfe againft all others. And the grea-ter part of blowes which are of importance, proceed from this warde.

Befides, euery man doth naturally more accuftom himfelf to ftaie and repofe himfelfe in it, than in any other. Neither is it (as I beleeue) for any other caufe, then that he knoweth, by fo bearing himfelfe, he may eafilie both ftrike and defend. And becaufe in this warde, as I haue before faide , in the hurt or offence thereof, it is more commodious to ftrike with the edge than in any other warde, albeit, it is not there giuen for counfell to be good to vfe it. But yet be-caufe cause it may easily happen, there shall be here layde downe some defence for it: calling this principle before any other to remembrance, (He that is nearest, hitteth soonest,)to the ende,that knowing what way either sworde maketh , each man may resolue himselfe to deliuer a thrust vnder an edgeblowe , by the which is preuented the fall of the saide blowe.

But because none , but such as are endued with deepe iudgement,great actiuitie, and stout courage, do or may safely put this in practise : And to the end also,that those,who accustom to defend euery blow, perfourming that in two times which might aswell be done in one, may rest satisfied : I will laye downe the defence of the edgeblow.

Therefore,whensoeuer edgeblows are giuen, they are either right or reuersed, high or low.

Against the right high blowe,either the onely dagger is to be opposed , either the sworde and Dagger both together. When the onely dagger is vsed,then a straight pace must be encreased,& the dagger hande lifted vp to encounter the enimies sword in the weakest parte thereof, & being suddenly found a straight pace is to be encreased,and a thrust vnderneath (alreadie prepared)to be discharged. But if the sword and dagger be both together opposed,they both must be lifted vp , and as soone as the blowe is encountred, the enimies face is to be cut by discharging a reuerse, with the onely turne of the hand, resting & staying it selfe in the brode warde.

The right blowe,giuen beneath, or belowe, must be warded after no other manner , then by driuing a thrust at the enimies thigh,which thrust is to this purpose,

H.

pofe,that it hitteth home fafely vnder that blow, and
farther is a let, or barre, to the enimies fword, fo that
it maie not light on the legges , confidering that in
the difcharge of the faide thruft, the hinder foote muft
neceffarily go compaſsing towardes the right fide
behinde.

Reuerfes alfo, are either high or low. If high: they
may be warded with the dagger onely, therewithall
difcharging a thruft vnderneath, with the encreafe of
a ftraight pace, as foone as the dagger hath met with
the enimies fworde . Either, they may be warded
with the fworde onely encreafing a ftraight pace with
the left foote, therewithall difcharging a thruft (alreadie lifted vp in the warde) with the encreafe of a
ftraight pace of the right legge. And this manner of
warding, is more according to Arte , becaufe it hath
beene faide , That all blowes on the left fide , are to
be warded with the dagger onely.

The reuerfe blowe would be warded with giuing
a thruft which fafely hitteth, and hindreth the fwotde
to light on the legges. This blowe alfo , may be
warded after other and diuers manners, which fhalbe
declared in the treatife of Difceit : for this is not their
proper place.

There is great regarde to be taken in warding of
thruftes, to wit : to beare the bodie out of the ftraight
lyne, becaufe this is the fafeft waie that may be found
to voide them, becaufe it verie difficult to meete with
them, when they come barred and clofed in , and are
forciblie difcharged . For when a thruft commeth
within (at the verie time that the enimie ftriketh) hee
ought to encreafe a flope pace, enfuring himfelf of the
enimies

70

enimies sword with his dagger, and then to discharge
a thrust with the increase of a straight pace.

The thrust without is warded after the first maner,
to wit, when the enimie striketh, to encrease a slope
pace (whereby the bodie voideth danger) & to giue
a thrust with the encrease of a straight pace. In this
order one may warde himselfe from other wayes of
stryking.

In like case, when the enimie (onely to trye and
prouoke) doth deliuer an edgeblowe from the wrist
of the hande: let euery man be aduised, as soone as
the blowe is deliuered, to encrease a slope pace, and
deliuer a thrust with the encrease of a straight pace,
before the enimie (after his blowe giuen) do determine to discharge any more. This may suffice, for
the handling of the Rapier and Dagger truely, with
aduantage.

The Rapier and Cloake.

THat I maie continue in the weapons which
are most vsuall and most commonly worne:
After the Dagger, I come to the Cloake:
The vse whereof was first founde out by
chaunce and after reduced into Arte. Neither was
this for any other cause, then for that nature doth not
onely delight to inuent things, but also to preserue
them being inuented. And that shee may the better doe it, shee taketh for her helpe all those things
that are commodious for her. Wherefore, as men in
diuers accidēts haue casually proued, that the Cloak
helpeth greatly (for as much as they are to weare it
H 2   daily)

daily) they haue deuised how they may behaue them selues in all that, in which the Cloak may serue their turne. Which accidents, because they are infinite, & do not generally serue for our purpose, I wil restraine my selfe and speake of those onely which appertaine to this Arte, the which are such and so effectuall, that they may greatly helpe to the obteining of safe victorie, if they happen to be placed in such a man as knoweth howe to vse and handle them. And for that in true Arte it doth little preuaile, the vse thereof being in a manner altogether deceitfull, I was resolued to put ouer all this to the treatise of Deceit, as vnto his proper place. Notwithstanding, to the ende it may not seeme strange to any man, to read nothing of the Cloak in al the handling of true Art, I am minded to laye downe a certaine fewe blowes in the accustomed wardes, referring the more abundant handling thereof vnto the treatise of Deceit.

The manner how to handle the Cloake.

AS the Cloake in this Arte, hath in it three things to be considered, to wit: length, largenesse, and flexibilitie: so it is to be wayed how far each of these will stretch, to serue the turne. Of which three, one doth properly belong vnto it, and that is flexibilitie, which maie neither be encreased nor diminished: The other two, may receiue alteration. But yet it is at any hande to be prouided, that these two also be not diminished. For the Cloake is no strong thing, which of it selfe may withstand the blowes of the weapon, being directly opposed against them.

And

And therefore he shall proue himselfe but a foole, who trusting to the Cloth wrapped about his arme, doth encounter any right edgeblowe therewith. For seeing the Cloake is not flexible in that parte (which flexibilitie is his onely strength) litle preuaileth either length or largenes, wrapped about a solide substâce. But being opposite in that parte thereof, where it hath length, largenes and flexibilitie (which is from the arme downwardes) it is auailable: for all three being ioyned togither will warde any edgeblow: which manner of warding should not be so sure, if the cloake had onely length and flexibilitie: For hauing behind it litle ayre, which is the thing that doeth strengthen it, it may easily be beaten too, and cut, by any great blowe. Therefore, if a man haue so much leisure, he ought to wrapp his Cloake once or twice about his arme, taking it by the Cape or coller, and folding his arme therein vp to the elbowe, and therewithall to warde all edgeblowes from the flanke thereof downwardes, aswell on the right side, as on the left side, alwaies remembring to carrie his foote differing from his arme, for the auoyding of danger that may rise by bearing his legg on the selfe same side, neere his cloak knowing the Cloak wardeth not when there is any harde substance behind it.

Thrustes also themselues, may be giuen without, if with the Cloake, or with the hand in the Cloak, the enimies sworde be beaten off, one handfull within the poynt thereof. For the edge hauing but small power in that case, is not hable in so litle time, to cut the hand. The blowes also, aswell of the poynt, as of the edge, from the flanke vpwardes, ought to be

warded with the sworde : For to lift the arme so high
being burdened with the waight of the Cloak, which
naturally draweth downwards, as it is a violent thing
it is also perilous, least the arme be placed in steede of
the Cloake, and so rest wounded, or lest the arme or
Cloake be placed before the eyes , which by that
meanes remaine blinded.

*An Aduersisement concerning the warding and
wrapping of the Cloake.*

THere are two waies (in these daies) to wrappe
the Cloake, the one is, when one hauing leasure
taketh the Cloake by the cape or coller , and so
fouldeth it once or twice about his arme : The other
is, as often times it falleth out, when letting the Cloke
fall downe from the shoulder , it is happelie taken by
one side, & so is turned once or twice about the arme.
Nowe as concerning striking, a man ought in the
handling of these weapons as he would strike, first to
increase and carrie the one foote neere to the other,
and then farther to increase a halfe , not a whole pace,
as in other weapons : For at these weapons, it is daungerous least (making a whole pace) he entangle his
foote or feete in the Cloake and fall downe therewith.
And this must be taken heede of, in the first and second foulding, but principallie in the secoud, because
in it the Cloake is longer, and therefore doth more easilie touch the earth & intangle his feet : In the first
fold, although the cloak touch not the earth , because
the arme doth orderlie beare it, yet by reason of weri-
nes, the arme falleth & causeth the foresaid effect.

The

The hurt of the high ward at Rapier and Clok.

N thefe maner of weapons, as in others, I
will frame three wardes ; The firft by the
forefaid reafons, fhall be the high warde,
which in thefe kind of wepons more then
in anie other deferue the name of a ward. For the Rapier (fomething bending) wardeth as farre as the clok
hand, and the clokhand down to the middle legg: foe
that in this ward a man is warded from the top of the
head down to the foot.

Therefore

Therefore ſtanding at this warde, whether it be with the right foote before or behinde, he may deliuer a thruſt with the encreaſe of a halfe pace forwards, ſtaying himſelfe in the lowe warde.

The right edgeblowe ought to be deliuered from the wriſt without any motion of the feete, reſting in the lowe warde : but in deliuering of the reuerſe, it is neceſſarie to fetch a whole pace, and in a manner ſtraight. If the enimie warde it with his ſworde, then the encounter of the enimies ſworde, muſt be ſtayed ſuddenly with the Cloake-hand in the firſt part there-of, and a thruſt be deliuered vnderneath, with the en-creaſe of a ſtraight pace.

The defence of the thruſt, right and reuerſed blowes of the high warde at Rapier and Cloake.

FOr the better auoyding of the hurts which proceede from the high warde : it is neceſ-ſarie to ſtande at the lowe warde, in the which the thruſt is to be warded iiij. man-ner of waies, to wit: either with the ſingle ſworde within and without, either with the ſingle Cloake within and without. If with the ſingle ſword with-in, it is requiſite to fetch a compas with the foot back-wards on the right ſide. In like caſe to turne the bo-die the ſame waie, to the intent, to carrie it out of the ſtraight lyne (in which the blowe commeth) and to driue a reuerſed thruſt at the face, the which thruſt in ſuch order deliuered is the longeſt that is, and ſuch a one, as thereby the hurt is not onely voyded, but alſo at the ſelfe ſame time, the enimie is ſtroken in the face, If it chaunce, that the ſworde be encountred without then

76

then it is not onely profitable but also neceſſarie, to
ſtep forwardes and with the Cloake to encounter the
enimies ſworde in the firſt parte thereof. And recouering his owne ſworde, to diſcharge a thruſt vnderneath with the encreaſe of the right foote . And although it be laide down for a rule, not to vſe a whole
pace in handling of the Cloake, this ought to be vnderſtoode in ſtriking, in the which (whileſt one endeuoureth to ſtrike with his ſworde) it may be forget-
ting the Cloake, his arme may fall, by meanes whereof he may ſtumble againſt it : but in warding, it doth
not ſo happen. For nature being carefull to defende
her ſelfe (at euery litle danger) lifteth vp both her
armes, yea, although they be oppreſſed with waight
and burden.

Wherefore it is not to be feared, that in warding
this thruſt, the hand will be drawen downe by the
waight of the Cloake.

The ſame wardes and defences may be vſed with
the ſingle Cloake, in the which, one muſt likewiſe
ſtrike, with the encreaſe of the right foote. This maner of warding is not verie ſure, and therefore it requireth great actiuitie and deepe iudgement, conſidering he ought to beare his Cloake and arme ſtretched
out before him, & to marke when the enimies ſwords
poynt ſhall paſſe within the Cloakhand one handful
or litle more : and not to ſuffer it to paſſe farther, but
to beat it off, and encreaſing to diſcharge a thruſt vnderneath ; with the encreaſe of a pace with the right
foote. But as I haue ſaide , this manner of warding
hath litle certaintie and great perill in it, and yet it ſtriketh well, if it be done in ſhort time.

I.

The

The right edgeblowe may in like manner be warded with the single sworde or cloake: but when it cōmeth aloft, it shall not be commodious to encounter it with the single cloake, for by that meanes the eyes blinde themselues. How much this importeth, let others indge. But, when the saide right blowe commeth in a manner lowe, so that it may well be warded, keeping the enimie in sight, then the cloake is to be opposed, with the encrease of the left pace, & presently thereupon, a thrust to be discharged, with the encrease of a right pace.

When one opposeth the single sworde against the right blowe, he must driue a thrust at the face, & fetch a compas with his hinder foote, cutting the face with the saide thrust and staie himselfe in the broad ward. The selfe same must be done, when he defendeth himselfe with both together, to wit, with the sword and cloake.

Against the reuersed blowe, the selfe same manner is vsed in warding to wit, either with the one, or with the other, either with both ioyned together.

With the cloake, by the encrease of a pace, and by encountring the enimies sworde, as farre forwards as is possible, that thereby it may be done the more comodioutly, deliuering a thrust therewithall vnderneath, with the encrease of a pace of the right foot.

With the single Rapier, the same defence may suffice, which is layde downe in the treatise of the single Rapier, and that is, to discharge a thrust at the enimies thigh, the which withstandeth the fall of the reuersed blowe.

Nowe, if one would defend himselfe with both these

these weapons ioyned togither, he must encrease a pace with the right foot, & staying the enimies sword with his cloke, recouer his owne sworde nimbly, and then diliuer a thrust with the encrease of a pace of the right foote.

I N this warde, as well as in others, a man may both thrust and strike, yet diuersly; For he may not discharge a right edge-blowe beneath. And the reuerse is manifestly dangerous : So that, when he is to deliuer it, he ought to perfourme it in this order.

First, he shall driue a thrust, fetching a compas with his hinder foote, that by that meanes it may reach the farther, then suddenly (without mouing of himselfe) he shall discharge a right edgeblowe, from the wrist, after the which presently, the reuerse must followe, with the encrease of a pace of the right foote : and further, must follow on with the thrust alreadie prepared, and increase the like pace.

T O him that will safely warde himselfe from the hurt of the broad warde, it is requisite, that he stand at the lowe warde. And when the thrust vnderneath hand commeth, he shall thrust at the face, fetching a compas with his hinder foote towardes the right side, with which kinde of thrust, it doth lightly happen that the enimie is hit in the face:

I 2   but

but if it faile, yet for all that, the enimie obtaineth not his purpose, in the discharge of the thrust of the broad warde : For by deliuering the thrust vnderneath, and compassing of the hinder foote, the bodie is carried out of the straight lyne : So that, as soone as the thrust is deliuered at the face, and the enimie not strooken therewith, but passeth beyond his head, the reuerse is to be turned at the face, and the foote to be plucked backe, setling in the broad warde. To warde the right and reuersed blows, there is a thrust to be giuen at the thighes or some other place that may most hinder them, in the verie same time that such blowes are in their circle or compas. Although I do not beleue that there is any man so foolish, that (in this warde) will deliuer a reuerse onely.

Of the hurt of the lowe warde, at Rapier and Cloake.

His warde is so straight and perilons, that no man ought to assure himself to deliuer an edgeblow any manner of waie. For vnder any of them he may be easily strooken, and each of them may easily be warded with the Cloake. Therefore, he must diligently take heed, that he thrust onely, the which must neuer be discharged before the enimies sworde be found, and then as farre forwardes as is possible. So then finding it, he may thrust both within and without. Neither is there in this thrust any other aduantage to be gotten, then to steale a halfe pace vnwares of the enimie, which may be done verie commodiously, considering the cloak occupieth the enimies sight, And hauing drawen this halfe

halfe pace, and found the enimies sword, he must encrease an other halfe pace forwardes, and strike him, costing and forcing the enimies sworde, on that side where it may do no hurt. And this maie be vsed both within and without: But he whome it pleaseth, and who doubteth not to be entangled in the Cloake, maie (finding himselfe within) carrie his left foot making a pace therewith, and betweene his cloake & his sworde, close the enimies sworde, and deliuer a thrust with the encrease of a pace of the right foote: And finding the enimies sword without, he may vse the selfe same encrease and thrust. But if he finde not the enimies sword, he may deliuer a litle edgeblow from the wrist of the hand, in such sorte, that the enimy haue no leasure to enter in: And hauing found the Sword, to to discharge a right or streight thrust, or else not voyding the enimies sword by the encrease of a left pace, to driue a thrust from aloft downwards, lifting vp the fist somewhat high, and deliuering it with the increase of a pace of the right foote.

Of the defence of the lowe VVarde
at Rapier and Cloak.

O the ende a man may warde himselfe from all the thrustes reckned in the hurtes of this warde, he neither ought, neither happely may doe any other thing then voide his bodie from the straight line, wherein the enimie purposeth to strike, making a left pace forwards, somewhat thwarting or crossing and striking the enimie safely. The which doth not so chaunce, when one defendeth himselfe

I3   either

either with the single Cloake or single Rapier : For whilest he assaieth to defend himself, he cannot strike. And if the enimie do first moue, and strike straight, in the which, his sworde is not carried much outwardes (and it is hardly done,) I saie, the enimie may by stealing of half paces, discharge a thrust perforce. And therefore he must take heede, that (as the enimie moueth) he encrease a slope pace (by that meanes voyding the hurt) then a thwart or crossing pace next, with the encrease of a straight pace of the right foote, to strike the enimie with a thrust vnderneath.

This may suffice, for the handling of these weapons as much as appertaineth to sure plaie. All that which remaines is reserued to the treatise of deceit, in which place shall be seene manie handlings of the cloake no lesse profitable then pleasant.

Of the Sworde and Buckler.

FOrasmuch as the Buckler is a weapon verie commodious & much vsed, it is reason that I handle it next after the Cloak. For my purpose is, to reason of those weapons first which men do most ordinarily vse, then of those that are extraordinarie and lesse accustomed, discoursing vpon eache of them, as much as is requisite when I come vnto them. Therefore I will first consider of the Buckler, therewith proceeding orderly.

First his fourme , as much as appertaineth to this Arte. Next the manner how to vse it , giuing euery man to vnderstand that the Buckler and other weapons (which are said to be weapons only of warding) may

may alſo be ofſtriking, as I will declare in his proper place.

Of the Forme of the Buckler.

AS the forme of the Buckler is round and ſmall, and ought to be a ſhilde & ſafegard of the whole bodie, which is farr greater then it : So it is to be vnderſtood how it may accompliſh the ſame, being a matter in a manner impoſsible.

Let euery one therefore know, that the litle Buckler is not equall in bignes to the bodie ſimplie, but after a certaine ſorte or manner, from which ſpringeth this cōmoditie, that he which vnderſtandeth it, ſhall be reſolued of the manner how to beare and handle it, and ſhall know that in it, which ſhal not onelie aduantage him in the vſe thereof, but alſo of many other weapons.

It is to bee vnderſtoode, that the Buckler beareth the ſelfe ſame reſpect to the bodie, which the litle prike or ſighte, on the toppe of the harquebuſh artilirie or ſuch like beareth to the obiect which they reſpect and behold. For when a Harquebuſher or Gonner, diſchargeth happelie againſt a Pigion or Tower, if they behold and finde that the Prike ſtriketh the obiect, although that prike or ſight be verie litle, and of a thouſand partes one : yet I ſaie, the ſaid prike of the Harquebuſh ſhal couer the whole Pigion, and that of the Artilery in a manner the whole Tower: The effect procedinge of no other thing then of the diſtance. And it is in this manner. The eye behoulding directlie through the ſtraight ſight, as ſoone as it arriueth at the obiect, and may not paſſe through, teareth

it,

it, and sendeth through a lyne sidewise, spreading it selfe like vnto the two sides of a Triangle, the which ouerthroweth the foundation of that thing which it striketh: The which foundation, the instrument striketh with which the discharge was made. And if it worke otherwise, that commeth either of the defect of the instrument, or of that it was not firme.

Wherefore, applying this example to our purpose I saie, that the enimies sworde is as the lyne of the eie-sight, The Buckler, euen as the litle pricke or sight in the Harquebush, the bodie of him that holdeth the Buckler, as the obiect vnto the which the strok is directed: And so much the rather the Buckler shall be the more like this pricke or sight, and haue power to couer the whole bodie, by how much it shall be the further of from the thing that is to couer.

As concerning his greatnesse, standing still on the forme of the Buckler, by how much the greater it is, by so much the better it voydeth the blowes. But it is to be regarded, that it hinder not the eye sight, or at least as litle as is possible. Besides this, there is required, that about the middle thereof, there be a litle strong circle of Iron, well nayled and hollowed from the Buckler, so that betwene that circle & the Buckler the Sword may enter, by meanes whereof, a man may either take holdfast of the sword, or breake a peece of the poynt. But this is done rather by chaunce then that any rule may be giuen how a man should so take hold and breake it, for the sword commeth not with such slowenes, and in such quantitie of time, as is requisite in that behalfe.

It shall be also verie profitable, that in the midst of
the

the Buckler, there be a sharpe poynt or stert of Iron, to the end the enimie may be stroken therwith when occasion serueth.

I F a man would, that the Buckler worke the saide effect, to wit: that it may be hable with his smalnesse to couer the whole bodie, he must holde and beare it in his fist, as farre off from the bodic as the arme may possibly stretch foorth, mouing alwaies the arme & buckler together, as one entire and solide thing, hauing no bending, or as if the arme were vnited to the buckler, turning continually al the flatt thereof towards the enimie. From which kinde of holding proceed all these commodities following.

1 The first is, that the arme (standing directly behinde the Buckler) is wholy couered, neither may be strooken by any manner of thing which is before it.

2 The second, that all edgeblows are of force encountred in the firste and second parte thereof, where they carrie least force: neither can it fall out otherwise, if the enimie woulde (in manner as he ought) strike either at the head or bodie. For if the enimie would strik them, it is necessarie, that his sword come within the buckler so much as the arme is long: For otherwise it shal neuer hit home. And in this case he may well warde each great blow, and therewithal easily strike, and that in short time.

3 The thirde commoditie is, that all thrustes are most easily warded: for the Buckler being rounde,

K.   with

with th e directly flatt opposite against the enimie, &
wardinge all the bodie, the enimie will not resolue
himselfe to giue a thrust but onely against those partes
which are so well couered by the Buckler, as, the
head, the thighes, or some parte of the bodie, being
found discouered by ill bearing of the Buckler. And
seeing that these thrustes, hauing to hit home, ought to
enter so farre in, as is from the buckler to the bodie &
more (and that it is the length of an arme) they maye
easily and without doubt (making lesse motion, and
therefore in little time) be driuen outwardes by the
Buckler before they come to the bodie.

There are many other commodities to be gathered by so holding of the buckler, which at this present
are not to be recyted.

Wherefore being to finish this Chapter, I say, that
the Buckler ought not to defend, but onely down to
the knee and lesse. And reason would that it should
defend no farther than the arme can stretch it selfe,
that is to the middle thigh. In the act of fighting, a
man standeth alwaies somewhat bowing, therefore a
little more is allowed. The rest of the bodie downwardes must be warded with the Sword onely.

Of the hurt of the high warde at Sword & Buckler.

Ecause it is a verie easie matter to ward both
the right and reuersed blowes of the edge:
And for that a man may easily strike vnder
them, I will not lay down either for the one
or the other their strikings or defendings, but onely
talke of the thrust. I saye, the thrust aboue may be
deli-

deliuered in two fortes , the one with the right foote behinde, the other with the right foote before.

When the thiuft is difcharged that carrieth the right foote behinde, there muft (in deliuerie thereof) be encreafed a ftraight pace of the right foote. And it muftbe driuen & forced with all that ftrength which it requireth, and that is verie great, then fetling in the lowe warde.

When one would deliuer a thruft with the right foote before, he muft remember in any cafe, firft (vnawares of the enimie) to fteale a halfe pace , that is to faie: to drawe the hinder foote neere the forefoote, & then to caft a thruft with the encreafe of a halfe pace forwardes, setling himselfe after the deliuerie thereof in the lowe warde.

Of the defence of the high warde at Sworde & Buckler.

AS a man standeth at the lowe warde he may easily defend both those loftie thrustes . When they come, he standing at the saide warde, it shall be best to driue them outwardes, with the encrease of a left pace, and with his sword and buckler to staie the enimies sworde. And becaufe this left pace is a great increase : and likewife the enimie, driuing his thrustes, commeth with great force, it may eafily come to passe that both may approch fo neare one to the other, that he may with his bukler giue the enimie, the *Mustachio,* in the face, but that must be done when fit occasion is offered, and then further recouering his own sword to difcharge a thrust vnderneath with the encreafe of a pace of the right foote.

Of the hurt of the broad VVarde, at Sworde and Buckler.

IF a man would stepp forward, and strike as he standeth in the broad warde, it is not lawfull for him to vfe any other than the thrust, confidering the right & reuerfed blowes may not be deliuered without great perill and danger. For in the fite or placing of this warde, the sword is farre off from the bodie. And as he moueth to fetch a right or reuerfed edgeblowe, his fworde of force wil be much farther : So that it may not be done without great danger. Therefore he shall vfe the thrust onely : in forcing and deliuerie wherof, he he shall proceede first to carrie his hinder foote a halfe pace forwardes, and then to driue it on with the encrease of another halfe pace of the right foote, staying himselfe in the broad warde.

The defence of the broad warde at Sword and Buckler.

AGainst the thrust of the broad warde, the Buckler is to be opposed, standing at the lowe warde. And when the enimie commeth resolutely to thrust, then without warding it at all, he shall driue a thrust at the face, carrying the hinder foote in a compasse towards the right side aswell to lengthen the thrust, as also to carrie himselfe out of the straight lyne, in the which the enimie commeth resolued to strike, who, by this manner of thrust is easily hurt.

The hurt of the lowe warde at Sworde and Buckler.

AS this lowe warde is framed two maner of waies, that is to saie, with the right foot before & behind: So iikewise a man may strike therein after two sortes, Standing with the right foote behinde (leauing aside, the blowes of the edge, being to small purpose) he shal deliuer a thrust with the encrease of a pace of the right foote, betweene the enimies sworde and buckler, or els, if it be more commodious without the sword and buckler, setling in the lowe warde, with the right foot before, in which warde, a man may strike two manner of waies, within and without. Finding himself without hauing first met the enimies sword with his own, he shall encrease a left pace, not to the intent to auoid himselfe from the enimies sworde, but shall with his

K 3   buckler

buckler also, staie the enimies sworde, and forasmuch as he did not at the first deliuer the said thrust, he shal then continue and force it on directly with the encrease of a pace of the right foote. Finding himselfe within, the same thrust is to be vsed but more strõgly. For, with the encrease of a pace, leauing his buckler or thenimies sworde, he shutteth it in betweene his own sword & the buckler: and keping it in that strait, (wherby he is sure the enimy can deliuer no edgblow becaufe it may not moue neither vpwards nor downwards, neither forwards, but is then without the bodie,) he shal continue on, & resolutely deliuer this maner of thrust, with the encrease of a pace of the right foote.

The defence of the lowe warde, at Sword & buckler.

Or the defence of all these thrusts, it is necessarie that he stand at the lowe warde, & standing therat, whilest the thrust cometh which is deliuered with the right foote behinde, he shal do no other, than in the selfesame time, deliuer a thrust at the thigh or brest, turning the hilte of his sword against the enimies sworde, & compassing his hinder foot, withal bearing his body out of the straite line, in which the enimie striketh. And this maner of warding doth not only defend, but also safely hurt.

For the defence of the other two thrustes, the one within, & the other without, a man must take great heede, and it is verie necessarie that as the enimie encreaseth pretending to strike safely) he carrie a slope pace with the left foot & deliuer a thrust aboue hand, vpon vp on the which the enimie of himselfe shal runne & inuest himselfe. And it is to be considered, that in these thrustes, he that defendeth hath great aduan-tage: For the enimie cometh resolutely to strike, not thinking that it may in any other sort be warded then by giuing backe, But he that wardeth by encreasing, defending & drawing neere vnto the enimie, is so placed, that he may easily hurt him.

Of the Sworde & Target, called the Square Target.

IT is most manifest, that the Target is a most aunci-ent weapon, found out only for the vse of warfare, & not for frayes & peculiar quarels betweene man & man : albeit, since the finding therof, there haue beene deuised by the industrie of man a thousand waies to serue them at their neede: From whence it hath come to passe, (because it seemed conuenient vnto the pro-fessors of this Art) that this weapon was verie como-dious & profitable, aswel for his fashion, as for that it is a meane or middle wepon, between the buckler & the round Target: That they haue framed a speciall kinde of plaie therwith, although it differeth from the other two weapons in no other thing then in the fa-shion. Therefore, diuers professors of this Arte, being moued, some by reason of the forme, some by the big-nes, & some by the heauinesse thereof, haue accusto-med to beare it after diuers wayes, Those who make most account of the heauines, would for some consi-deration, that the right & proper bearing thereof, was to hold it leaning on the thigh, not mouing there-hence, but being greatly constrained therounto.

Others,

Others, who esteemed the forme & bignes thereof, because it seemed vnto them that the Target without any other motion was most apt of it selfe to ward all that parte of the bodie which is betwixt the neck & and the thigh, bare it with their arme drawne backe close to their brest. The which opinion, I meane not at this present to confute, forasmuch as by the shewing of mine owne opinion, it shall appeare how mightily they were deceiued in the holding thereof, from the true holding whereof springeth all the profite which his forme and bignes doth giue it.

The manner how to holde the square Target.

BEing desirous to beare great respect aswel to all the qualities of this Target (which are, the forme , the bignesse, and heauines) as vnto that wherwith it may either helpe or hurt, I saie (if a man would that the fourme thereof do bring him profit without hurt) it is to be holden with the high poynt therof vpwards respecting the head: the parte opposit, the low partes of the bodie : the right parte therof, the right side, and the left , the left side : from this manner of bearing spring these aduantages. First, a man may more easily see his enimie, and view what he doth by the point of the corner, which is on the one side, and that is by the high point, by which, if he woulde beholde his enimie, from the head to the feete , it is requisite that he carrie his Target, so lowe, that he discouer not too much of his bodie which is aboue it : to the warding whereof he cannot come againe , but discommodiously, and in long time.

Besides, the said commoditie of beholding the enimie,

92

mie, there is also another that is of warding: For the Target being borne after this manner (framing a triangle) the sharpe corner thereof respecteth the forehead, and the sides thereof so spread themselues, that through the least motion, any bigg man whosoeuer, may stand safe behind them. And if blowes come at the head, be they thrustes or edgeblows, al of them light vpon one of the saide sides, behinde which standeth the head safe without hindering of the eyesight. The other two sides of the Target, right, & left, with verie small motion, warde the right and left side of the bodie, in such sort, that a man may also draw back his arme: For the left side of the Target wardeth the elbowe, which it doth not do, when the high side thereof is carried equall. To conclude therefore, that in holding the Target, his bignes may the better warde, for the causes abouesaid being superfluous to be repeated againe, I counsell, it to be holden with the arme stretched forth from the bodie, not accompting the heauines to be hurtfull, because a man continueth not long in so holding it: and if the too long holding be painfull, he may drawe back his arme, and rest him selfe. The better to do this and to be able to see the enimie, I saie, he shall hold it, his arme stretched out, with the high point outwards, respecting the forehed.

The hurt of the high warde, at Sworde & square Target.

 Anie Deceites, Falses, and Wardes, may bee practised in the handling of these weapons: All which I reserue to the treatise of Deceite or falsing, as vnto his proper

L.   per

per place, traming likewife in this as in all the reft, three ordinarie wardes, vpon which, all the reft depend, and againft which they may be oppofed.

Standing at this high warde, and pretending to ftrike the enimie, it is firft of all to be prouided, that one fteale a falfe pace from behinde, and then difcharge a thruft aboue hande, with the increafe of another half pace forwards, which being warded by the enimie with his Target onely, not mouing his bodie, he may then increafe a ftraight pace of the left foote, & (fomewhat lifting vp his hand, and abafing the poynt of his fworde) force a thruft from aboue downwards betweene

betweene the Target & bodie of the enimie, with the encreafe of a pace of the right foote: the which thruft will fafely fpeede the enimie , if his bodie be not fitft voided. The felfe fame thruft may be deliuered in this high ward, ftanding with the right foote behind.

The defence of the high warde, at Sworde & fquare Target.

H E forefaid thruft may eafily be warded, if in the verie time that it commeth it be encountred with the high poynt of the Target, but yet with that fide which bendeth towardes the right hand. And as foone as the enimies fworde is come one handfull within the Target , it muft be ftrongly beaten off by the Target towardes the right hand, increafing the fame inftant a left pace. Then with as great an increafe of a pace of the right foote as may be poffible, a thruft vnderneath moft be giuen, already prepared, becaufe a man ought to ftand at the lowe warde for the warding of the thruft abouehand.

The hurt of the broad warde, at Sworde and fquare Target.

IN this warde likewife , the enimie may be inuefted on the poynt of the fworde, by going forwardes as ftraightly as is poffible, and by ftriking quickly before the enimie. For the Target (whofe charge is onely to defend) is fo great, that it may eafily warde all edgeblowes, & thofe chiefely which come from the knee vpwardes. Farther, when a blowe is pretended to be deliuered, it is manifeft, that a thruft doth enter by a more narrowe ftraight than any edgeblowe doth.

L 2 And

95

And therefore, when one woulde ftrike the enimie
ftanding at the locke or lowe warde, he muft remember that he approch as neere him as he may poffible:
and being fo neere, that with his Target put forth one
handfull more forwards, he may beate awaie the enimies fworde, then by fo beating of it, he fhal encreafe
a left pace, and prefently after it, with the increafe of a
pace of the right foote, deliuer him a thruft, if it fo
chaunce that at the firft encounter he ftrake him not
ftrongly.

The defence of the broad warde, at Sworde
and Square Target.

STanding at the lowe ward, one may warde and defend the thruft of the broad warde, diuers waies, a-
mong all which, there is one waie, verie eafie and fure
and thus it is.

For the defence of this thruft, it is neceffarie, that
he ftande at the lowe warde, his fword and arme being in their proper place: and that with his Target
fomething ftretched out from his bodie, he prouoke
the enimie, who being determined in himfelfe, and
comming refolutely to giue a thruft, hee then ought
with the increafe of a pace of the right foote, to ftrike
the enimie with a lowe thruft, vnderneath both his
owne and his enimies Target.

Of the hurt of the lowe warde, at Sworde
and Square Target.

THere are manie blowes to be beftowed, ftanding
at the lowe warde, all which I efteeme as vaine & to
no purpofe, confidering the maniford and abundant
defence of the Target. Therefore I will reftraine my
felfe

felfe vnto two onely which are verie ftrong and hardly to be warded. And they are two thruftes, the one within, the other without, with the right foote both before and behinde.

When one findeth himfelfe within, with his right foote before, and fo neere his enimie, that by the increafe of a left pace, he may with the right fide of his Target, beate awaie the enimies fworde in the middle thereof, then he ought nimblie to encreafe that lefte pace, and (clofing in the enimies fworde between his Target and his owne fworde) to deliuer a forcible thruft at the thighes, with the encreafe of a pace of the right foote. He may alfo do the verie felfefame when he findeth himfelfe to ftande with his right foote behinde, but then he muft farther increafe a pace of the right foote fitft, and then continuing ftill force his fworde and paces directly onwards, if he hit not the enimie as he would at the firft.

But if it chaunce that he finde himfelfe without, then he muft (hauing firft found out fit opportunitie to beate off the enimies fworde with his Target) encreafe a left pace, and placing the high fide of his Target vnder the enimies fworde and his owne fworde vpon it, clofing it in, in the middle, encreafe a pace of the right foote, and difcharge a forcible thruft, at the breft or face. And he may do the felfe fame, when he ftandeth with the right foote behind.

Of the defence of the high warde at Sworde and fquare Target.

FOr the warding of thofe two thruftes of the lowe warde, it is neceffarie, that a man ftande at the fame ward.

97

warde. And as the enimie commeth resolutely determined to thrust within, he must as soone, or more redily then he, encrease a left pace, and with the right side of his Target close in the enimies sword, betweene it and his owne sworde, and then to enter perforce, & thrust either betweene the two Targets or els vnder them, with the increase of a pace of the right foote.

But if the enimie come without, he must encrease the selfe same slope pace, & with the right side of his Target beat off the point of the enimies sword, & then thrust either aboue, either beneath, as in that occasion it shal be most for his aduantage with the increase of the pace of the right foote. And when in consideration of the aboundant defence of the Targer, he may neither increase his paces, nor deliuer a thrust, he must settle himselfe in the lowe warde with the right foote behinde, which ward I will largely handle in the treatise of deceite or falsing, being as it were his proper place, here ending the true handling of the sword and square Target.

Of the Sword and rounde Target.

THE round Target would require a long & a most exquisite consideration because it is of circuler forme, most capable, and most perfect of all others. But for that my purpose in this my worke, is to write that only which I know doth appertaine to this Arte, giuing leaue to euery man to busie him selfe in his owne profession. And leauing a great part of this consideration

fideration to the Mathematicians & Hiftoriographers
to reafon of his diuers qualities or paffions , either
who was inuentor thereof , either , whether it be a
weapon of antiquitie,or of this ourage, And comming to difcourfe of that , wherein it profiteth in this
our time, (being a weapon fogreatly honoured and
eftemed of Princes,Lords,& Gentlemen, that befids
thufe thereof in their affairs,as wel by day as by night,
they alfo keepe their houfes richly decked and beau-
tified therewith,) And confidering onely that thing,
in the round Target,among al other weapons which
may either profite or hurt in the handling thereof, I
faie, that the faid round Target hath beene diuerfely
holden,borne and vfed,by diuers men in diuers ages,
afwell as the other fquare Target, and other weapons
of defence, as well as of offence. And there want
not alfo men in our time , who to the intent they be
not wearied, beare it leaning on their thigh as though
that in this exercife(in which only trauaile and paines
are auaileable,) a man fhould onelie care for reft and
quietneffe. For by meanes of thefe two , ftrength and
actiuitie, (partes in the exercife of weapons, both important and neceffarie)are obtained and gotten.

Other fome, holding their whole Arme bowed togeither, haue cairried it altogeither flat againft their
bodie , not regarding either to warde their bellie , or
vtterlie to lofe the fight of the enimie, but will at any
hande ftand (as they thinke)fafe behind it,as behinde
a wal,nor knowing what a matter of weight it is, both
to fee the enimie, and worke other effects,which,(by
fo holding it)may not be brought to paffe.

Of

Of the maner how to holde the round Target.

IF a man woulde so beare the rounde Target, that it may couer the whole bodie, and yet nothing hinder him from seeing his enimie, which is a matter of great importance, it is requisite, that he beare it towardes the enimie, not with the conuexe or outward parte thereof, altogither equall, plaine or euen, neither to holde his arme so bowed, that in his elbowe there be made (if not a sharpe yet) at least a straight corner. For besides that (by so holding it) it wearieth the arme: it likewise so hindereth the sight, that if hee would see his enimie from the brest downwardes, of necessitie he must either abase his Target, or beare his head so peeping forwardes, that it may be sooner hurt than the Target may come to warde it. And farther it so defendeth, that onely so much of the bodie is warded, as the Target is bigg, or little more, because it cannot more then the halfe arme, from the elbowe to the shoulder, which is verie little, as euerie man knoweth or may perceiue : So that the head shal be warded with great paine, and the thighes shal altogether remaine discouered, in such sort, that to saue the bellie, he shal leaue all the rest of the bodie in ieopardie. Therefore, if he would so holde the said Target, that it may well defend all that part of the bodie, which is from the knee vpwardes, and that he maie see his enimie, it is requisite that he beare his arme, if not right, yet at least bowed so little, that in the elbowe there be framed so blunt an angle or corner, that his eyebeames passing neere that part of the circumference of the Target, which is neere his hande, may see his enemie from the head to the foot. And by holding

ding

ding the faide conuexe parte in this manner, it fhall
warde all the left fide, and the circumference neere
the hande fhall with the leaft motion defend all the
right fide, the head and the thighes. And in this maner he fhall keepe his enimie in fight & defend all that
parte of the body, which is allotted vnto the faid Target. Therefore the faid Target fhall be born, tharme in
a manner fo ftreight towards the left fide, that the eye-
fight may paffe to beholde the enimie without moouing, for this onely occafion, either the head, or the
Target.

M.

The hurt of the high warde, at sworde and round Target.

BEcaufe the round Target containeth in it moſt
great & ſure defence, therefore ought not any edgeblowe which may be eaſily warded with the ſingle
ſword without the helpe of the Target be deliuered.
Thruſtes alſo enter verie difficultlie to ſtrike the bodie, becauſe the Target, by meanes of the left motion
that is, ſeemeth to be, as it were a wall before the bodie. And to thruſt at the legge is no ſure plaie. That
which remaineth to be done is, to thruſt forcibly with
the ſworde: and when one perceiueth, that the point
therof is entred within the circumference of the enimies Target, it is neceſſary that he encreaſe a left pace,
and with the circumference of his owne Target, to
beat off the enimies ſworde and Target, to the end,
it ſuffer the thruſt ſo giuen of force to enter in . And
(hauing ſo beaten & entred) to continue on the thruſt
in the ſtraight lyne, with the encreaſe of a pace of the
right foote.

When he findeth himſelfe in the high ward, he ſhal
encreaſe a halfe pace with the hinderfoote, gathering
vpon the enimie, as neere as he may without danger.
And being ſo nigh that he may driue his ſword within the circumference , then as ſoone as he perceiueth
his ſworde to be within it, (his arme being ſtretched
out at the vttermoſt length) he ought ſuddenly to encreaſe a left pace, beating off with the circumference
of his owne Target, the enimies Target : and with
the increaſe of a pace of the right foote , to cauſe his
thruſt to enter perforce. This alſo he may practiſe
when the enimie endeuoureth, to withſtand the entrance of the thruſt, when it is alreadie paſt, within the
cir-

circumference of his Target.

But if the enimie (as it may fall out) ward this thrust not with that parte of the circumference, which is neere his hande, but with that which is aboue it (by meanes whereof his Target discouereth his eyes) then he may verie commodiously, encreasing his paces as aforesaid, recouer his thrust aboue, and force it vnderneath, with the increase of a pace of the right foote. And this is a more sure waie of thrusting than any other.

The defence of the high warde, at Sword & round Target.

FOr the defending of the thrust of the high warde, it is most sure standing at the lowe warde, and to endeuour to ouercome the enimie, by the same skill by the which he himselfe would obtaine the victorie. In the very same time, that he deliuereth his thrust, a man must suddenly encrease a slope pace with the lefte foote, beating of the enimies Target with his owne, & driuing of a thrust perforce with the increase of a pace of the right foote. And with this manner of defence being done with such nimblenesse as is required, hee doth also safely strike the enimie, who cannot strike him againe, because, by meanes of the saide slope pace he is carried out of the lyne in the which the enimie pretended to strike.

The hurt of the broad warde, at Sworde & round Target.

IT is verie difficult to strike in this broad ward, if first with much compassing & gathering of the enimie, a man do not assaie with the circumferéce of his Target

M 2   neere

103

neere his hand, to beate off the enimies sworde. And being so beaten, to encrease a left pace, and farther by adding thereunto the increase of a pace of the right foote, to discharge a thrust. But it shall happely be better in the handling of these weapons, not to vse this broad ward : for the hand is borne out of the straight lyne, in the which he may strike both safely and readily: And before it returne into the saide lyne, there is much time spent.

And farther, a man is not then in case with his Target to beate off the enimies sworde : But if happily he be, yet (though he be verie readie, aswell with the hand as foote) his thrust shall neuer enter so farre that it may hit home : For the enimie, with a verie small motion of his Target forwards, may verie easily driue thenimies sword out of the strait lyne. Therefore, he that would change or shifte out of this warde, to the intent to strike, must of necessitie be passing nimble & readie, and before he deliuereth his blowe, must beat the enimies sword with his Target.

The defence of the broad warde, at Sword & round Target.

BEcause in euerie occasion or accident a man standeth safe in the lowe warde, I will endeuour in this case, to place him also in the same warde, for the encountring of the hurt of the broad warde. That therefore which by mine aduise he shall do, is that he take great heede, not to suffer his sworde to be beaten off any manner of waie. And when the enimie without this beating presumeth to enter, he must in the selfesame time increase a left pace & safely deliuer a thrust vnder-

vnderneath with the increase of the right foote. And farther, when the enimie shall perfourme, that is, first finde the sworde and beate it off, (seeing of necessitie if he would enter and hit home, his sword must passe by the circumference of the Target neere the hande) then, to withstande the entrie, it is requisite that hee driue the enimies sworde outwards on the right side with his Target and with the increase of the said pace, that he enter and strike him.

The hurt of the lowe warde, at Sword & round Target.

A Man may strike in this ward, the right foote being behinde, and before, & in both waies, he may beare his sworde either within or without. If therefore he finde himselfe to stande with the right foote behinde and without, he shall assaie at any hande, before he determine to strike, to finde the enimies sworde with his owne, and as soone as hee findes it shall clap to his Target, and strike perforce with a low thrust, encreasing with the right foote. But finding himselfe to stand within, no more with his sworde, then he doth with his Target, he shall proue whether he can finde the enimies sworde, and hauing found it, shall straine it fast betweene his owne sworde and Target, & then shall deliuer a thrust with the increase of a pace of the right foote, the which thrust of force speedeth : This being perfourmed, he shall settle himselfe in this, or in either of these waies in the lowe warde with the right foote before. And as he so standeth in this warde, he may after the same sorte strike either within or without.

M 3

There-

Therefore finding himfelfe within, he fhall prouide
to meete with the enimies fword, and with the increafe
of a left pace, fhal clap to his Target, for the more fafetie, and then driue on a forcible thruft, with the increafe of a pace of the right foote. And finding himfelfe to beare his fword within in the faid ward, and
with his right foote behind, he fhall indeuour to find
the enimies fword with the Target, and hauing found
it, fhal clofe it in betwen his own fword and Target,
& with the increafe of a left pace, fhal perforce hurt the
enimie, with the increafe of a pace of the right foote.

Now, all thefe thrufts, no doubt fhall fpeede euery
time that the enimie either maketh no trauerfe mocion with his bodie, either as he ftriketh, commeth directlie forwards, or els beeing fcarefull, goeth directly
backwards, for it is not poffible that one man go fo
faft directlie backwardes, as an other may forwardes.
Yt is therefore diligently to be obferued in this ward,
neuer to determin to ftrike, either in the handling
of thefe, or of any other kind of weapons, if (with one
of them) he fhall not firft finde the enimies fworde.
The which redowneth to the great profite of euerie
man, but efpecially of thofe, who haue ftrong armes,
for that they are the better hable to beate backe the
enimies weapon.

*Of the defence of the lowe warde, at Sword and
round Target.*

AL the forefaid thrufts are warded, by not fuffering
the fworde to be found by the enimie with either
of his weapons. For the enimie (not finding it, will
not affure himfelfe, or prefume to enter, without firft
finding of the fworde) may moft eafilie be ftroken and
not

not ftrike, if a man increafe a flope pace , (to the end
he may voide his bodie from hurt ,) and with the increafe of a ftraight pace of the right foote , do alfo difcharge a thruft beneath . And after this order he may
ftrike fafelie, (not onelie when his fword is not found
by the enimie, but alfo when it chanceth to be found)
if he be readie and nimble to make his flope pace, and
to beate off, as forcible as he may, the enimies Target
with his owne fword and Target , thereby forcing a
low thruft to enter in, with the increafe of a pace with
the right foote . And thus much concerning the true
ftriking & defending of the fword and round Target.

Of the Cafe of Rapyers.

Here are alfo vfed now adaies , afwell in the
fcholles , as in the lifts , two Swordes or Rapiers, admitted, and approued both of Princes, and of the profeffors of this art , for honourable and knightlie weapons, albeit they be not vfed in
the warres . Wherfore I fhall not varie from my purpofe, if I reafon alfo of thefe, as faire as is agreeable to
to true art. To him that would handle thefe weapons,
it is neceffary that he can afwell manage the left hand
as the right, which thing fhalbe (if not neceffarie) yet
moft profitable in euery other kind of weapon. But in
thefe principally he is to refolue himfelfe, that he can
do no good, without that kind of nimblenes and dexteritie. For feeing they are two weapons, & yet of one
felf fame kind, they ought equally and indifferently to
be handled, the one performing that which the other
doth, & euery of the being apt afwel to ftrik as defend.
And

And therefore a man ought to accuftome his bodie, armes and handes afwell to ftrike as defend. And he which is not much practifed and exercifed therein, ought not to make profefsion of this Arte: for he fhal finde himfelfe to be vtterly deceiued.

The manner how to handle two Rapiers.

IT is moft manifeft that both thefe weapons may ftrike in one and the fame time : for there may be deliuered ioyntly togither two downright edge-blowes on high and two beneath: two reuerfes, and two thruftes, and are fo rich and plentifull in ftriking, that it feemeth they may be vfed onely to ftrike. But this ought not to be practifed, neither may it without great daunger For all that, whatfoeu er may be done with either of hem, is deuided into ftriking and defendinge. That this is true , it may be perceiued in the fingle Sworde, which affaieth both to ftrike and defend. And thofe who haue taken no fuch heede, but haue beene bent onely to ftrike being moued either through coller, either beleeuing, that they had to deale with an ignorant perfon, haue remained therby mightily wounded. Of this , there might be laid downe infinite examples, which I leaue to the entent I may not fwarue from my purpofe. I faie therefore that of the two Rapiers which are handled , the one muft be applyed towardes the other to ftrike, regarding alwaies to vfe that firft which wardeth, then that which ftriketh : for firft a man muft endeuour to defend himfelfe, and then to ftrike others.

Of

108

Of the high ward at two Rapiers.

PResupposing alwaies, that either hand is very
well exercised, aswell in striking as in defending, this high ward shalbe framed after two
waies, which yet in a maner is all one. The
one with the right foot, the other with the left, so working continually, that the hinder arme be aloft, the
former beneath in maner, as when the lowe warde is
framed at the single sword. And as a man striketh, he
must alwaies maintaine & continue this high warde,
which at the two rapiers, is the most perfect & surest

N.   and

and he may eafily performe & do it: for whileſt he en‑
treth to giue a high thruſt with his hinder foote, al‑
though that foot be behind yet it muſt accompanie
the arme vntil it hath finiſhed his thruſt, & ſettled it
ſelf in the low ward. The other ſword & hand(which
was borne togither with the former foote in the lowe
ward) remaining behind by reaſon of the encreaſe of
the high thruſt, muſt preſently be lifted vp, & be pla‑
ced in the ſame high ward.

Therfore it is to be noted, that whoſoeuer meaneth
to ſhift from this ward & ſtrike, whether it be with his
right or left foot, before or behinde, it is requiſite that
he ſtand without, & when he would ſtrike, he ſhal firſt
proue with his low ſworde, whether he can finde the
enimies weapons, & hauing ſuddenly found them, he
ſhal nimbly beate them back, and (in a maner) in the
ſame inſtant force on a high thruſt, with the increaſe of
a pace of the right foot: from the which, if the enimie
(for ſauing of himſelfe) ſhal haſtily and directly giue
backwards, he ſhal follow him, deliuering preſently
the other high thruſt behind, alreadie lifted vp. And
this thruſt wil ſafely hit home & ſpeede, becauſe it is
not poſsible that one may go ſo faſt backwards, as an
other may forwards.

Farther, aſwel in this ward, as in others, the warde
may be framed with the right foote before, & the right
arme lifted, & ſo côtrariwiſe. But becauſe there is ſmal
force in this ward both in the feete & handes, which
ſtand not comodiouſly either to ſtrike or defend, and
ſeeing there is required in the handling of thoſe wea‑
pons, great ſtrength and ſtedfaſtnes I haue thought
good, not to laie it downe, as to ſmall purpoſe.

The

110

THe direct opposition & defence of the high warde is the lowe ward, the manner whereof shal be seen in his proper place. That which principally is to be considered (for the lowe warde also, in like sort as the other may be framed after two sorts) is this, that of nenessitie a man stand with the same foote before as the enimie doth, to wit: if he beare the right foot before, to put foorth the right foote also, and to endeuour as the enimie doth, to stand without, for of both wayes this is of the more aduantage and safetie. Finding himselfe therefore without, in the lowe ward, he must not refuse, but rather suffer his sword to be found and beaten by the enimie: for this doth redowne much more to his owne aduantage then to his enimies because the enimie carrieth small force in his low hando wherewith he endeuoureth to finde and beat off the sword, considering it is born to farre off frō the other: for that which is slēderly vnited, is lesse forcible: wheras standing at the low ward, he bereth both his hands low neere togither and sufficiently strong. Therfore as soone as the enimie hauing beaten back the sword, shal resolue himself to giue a thrust, he must encrease a slope pace, & with his hinder low sword, driue the enimies high thrust outwardes towarde the right side, if it chaunce that he were in the low warde with his right foot before, And suddenly with the other low sword behind (which was suffered to be beatē off by the enimie, because it might turne the more to his disaduantage: for seeing the enimies sword being slenderly vnited, as I haue saide before, carried but small force, it was the rather beaten off and disappointed: So that as soone as the slope pace is encreased, and the

saide

saide high thrust warded, before the enimie place his other sworde also in the high warde, hee may with the straight pace of the right foot deliuer a low thrust continuing still to beate downe the enimies sworde with his owne lowe sworde, that is borne before: And this manner of warding is most safe and sure: for besides that it striketh the enimy with the slope pace, it doth likewise in such sort deliuer the bodie from hurte, that of force the enimie is disapointed. Neither is there any other sure waie to warde this high thrust, being so strong, and besides, hauing so great encrease of pace.

This manner of defence is most strong and sure, & is done with that sworde which is farthest off. Yet there is another waie, & that is, with the low sworde before, the which is no lesse stronger and sure than the other, but yet much shorter. For looke in what time the other defendeth, this striketh.

Therefore in the low ward it is to be noted, (when the enimie moueth, pretending to beate off the sword and there withall to enter,) that then the poynt of the sword before be lifted vpp, keeping the hand so stedfast, that it oppose it selfe and keepe outwards the enimies high thrust, and hauing made this barre, to keepe out his weapons, then & in the selfsame time, he shall encrease a straight pace, & with the low sword behind shal strike the enimie in the brest, to whome it is impossible to do any effectuall thing, or to auoid the said stroke, for that (by meanes of the point of the sworde lifted vp in maner aforesaid) both his swordes are so hindred, that they may not safely strike, either with the edge or point.

of

His broad ward, may in the selfe same maner be framed two waies, and it may deliuer the self same blows, in the one as in the other: This ward is framed with one foote before, and one foote behind, the arme (which is borne on the side of the hinder foote) being stretched wide, & broad outwards. Therfore when one standeth at this ward, and would deliuer as strayght and as safe a thrust as is possible, he shal first proue with his low Rapyer, whether he can find the enimies Rapier, which being found, he shal turne his fist outwards, and force the enimies Rapier somuch, that it may do no hurt, and then withall increasing presentlie a slope pace, shall go forewards to strike the enimie in the thigh, with the wide thrust. He might aswell also thrust him in the flanke, or in the head, but yet the other thrust is vsed, because the Rapier, which is directed to the thigh, is in place to hinder the enimies other Rapier to light on the legges.

And as in the high ward, so likewise in this, he must alwaies stand without, and hauing deliuered the wide thrust, he ought presentlie to widen the other arme, and settle himselfe in the broad ward.

FOr the defence of the thrust of the broad ward, it is necessarie that a man stand at the lowe ward, and there withall diligently obserue, the mocions of the enimics bodie, how it compasseth and passeth to and froe, by knowledge and due considerations whereof, he may easilie defende himselfe. Yf therefore the right

N 3   arme.

113

arme be ftretched out wide, the right foote alfo (being behind) fhall be in like maner widened, the which, when it increafeth forwards, fhall alfo carrie with it the right fhoulder, voyding alwayes with the left fide.

And the felfe fame muft be confidered, & practifed, when he ftandeth at his ward, the contrarie way. That therefore which he muft doe, for the defence of him felfe, fhalbe to voide that part of his bodie, which may be hurt by the enimies wide and broad thruft, and to oppofe himfelfe againft that part of his enimie, which commeth forwards pretending to ftrike: And this he fhall doe, at what time the enimie (finding the fword) would come forwards in his thruft. And in the felfe fame time, (affuring himfelf with his own low fword) fhall increafe a flope pace, thereby inuefting and incountring that part of the enimie, which came ftriking, and with the which he framed the broad ward. Neither can it be fafe ftriking at any other place, for either he fhall find nothing to incounter, by meanes of the mocion of the bodie, or els if he do not oppofe himfelfe againft that fhoulder of the enimie which carrieth the hurt, he is in hazard to be ftroken by the enimies broad thruft.

Of the hurt of the low ward at the two Rapyers.

THe low ward fhall be framed after two waies, the one with the right foote before, the other with the left, and each of them may ftrike, either within, either without. The way which ftriketh within, hath one blow, the way which ftriketh without hath two, and in all, in all, they are sixe. I will lay downe but three, becaufe they differ not from the other three, but onelie in the hand and foote, which muft be placed before, fo that they are the felfe fame, for I haue alreadie prefuppo-fed, that he who taketh vpon him to handle thefe weapons, can afwell vfe the one hand, as he can the other. He may therefore finde himfelfe to ftand with his right foote before and within, (I vnderftand by within, when he beareth one of his fwordes betwene both his enimies fwordes, and likewife when the eni-mie carieth one of his, betwene the other two. Yt is likewife true, that this alfo may be faid within, to witt, when both weapons are borne in the middle be-tweene the other two. But I fuppofe no man fo foo-lifh, who handling thefe weapons, will fuffer both his fwordes to be without, being a verie vnfure ward whereof I leaue to fpeake.

That therefore, which he is to do, (finding himfelfe with both his rapiers below, & within, with his right foote before, after the faid firft way of being within) fhalbe, that marking when he may clofe in the enimies Rapier, betwene the which the enimies rapier fhall be fo fhut in and barred, that it may do no hurt, and one of the two Rapiers, that is to fay, the right Rapier fhall paffe vnder the enimies rapier, and thurft fafelie. And his other Rapier albeit, it may thruft directly, yet (for the better fauing of himfelfe, from the enimies other Rapier that is at libertie) he fhall beare it fome-what abafing his hand, with the point vpwardes, the which point fhall fauegarde him, from the eni-mies faid Rapier, although this laft note, be fuper-fluous. For feeing the enimie muft ward himfelfe

from

115

from the thruſt that hurteth him, he hath no leaſure, nor happilie mindeth to ſtrike, but onely to defend himſelfe, either by voyding his bodie, or els by ſome other ſhift, which he ſhall then find out.

The waie of warding without, may ſtrike directlie after two waies: The firſt, by beating off the enimies Rapier, with his owne that is before, and by deliue-ring a thruſt, either at the breſt or head, with the Rapier that is behinde, increaſing therwithall a ſlope pace, and ſetling himſelfe in the low ward, with his left foote before.

The ſecond is, by taking oportunitie, which he may do, if he be nimble. And he ought with the increaſe of a ſlope pace, to driue the point of his former Rapyer directlie towards the enimie, and aboue the enimies Rapier. And his other owne rapier, which before the increaſe was behind, he muſt force on, vnder the eni-mies rapier. And thus, not giuing ouer, theſe two thruſts muſt be ſtronglie and nimblie driuen towards the enimie, by meanes whereof being ouertaken, the enimie hath no other remedie to ſafe himſelfe, then to retire backe: for he may not come forwardes, but he muſt runne himſelfe vpon the weapons, and that he will not doe. So then, the enimie retiring himſelfe may be followed, as farre as the increaſe of the right foote will beare, then, ſetling in the low ward.

Of the defence of the low ward at the two Rapyers.

AL three thruſts of the low ward, by ſtanding at the ſame ward, may eaſilie be warded, and that after one maner. If a man remember firſt to void his bodie from hurt, by the increaſe of a pace, that is verie ſlope, **or** or crooked, either before the enimie commeth thruſting, either as ſoone as he moueth himſelfe for the ſame purpoſe, or if he be actiue and nimble to trauerſe, and in defending himſelfe to ſtrike the enimie.

Therfore when any of the ſame three thruſts come, and before he perceiueth his Rapier to be cloſed, and barred in, he ſhall moue a ſlope pace, to th'entent to auoid himſelfe from hurt, and with his Rapier, which is at libertie, he ſhall go forwards and deliuer a thruſt at the enimies face, which thruſt, doth ſurelie ſpeede, if he be reſolute to enter.

Of the Two hand Sword.

HE two hand Sword, as it is vſed now a daies being fower handfulls in the handle, or more, hauing alſo the great croſſe, was found out, to the end it ſhould be handled one to one at an equall match, as other weapons, of which I haue intreated. But becauſe one may with it (as a galleon, among many gallies) reſiſt many Swordes, or other weapons: Therefore in the warres, it is vſed to be placed neere vnto the Enſigne or Auncient, for the defence thereof, becauſe, being of it ſelfe hable to contend with manie, it may the better ſauegard the ſame. And it is accuſtomed to be carried in the Citie, aſwell by night as by day, when it ſo chaunceth that a few are conſtrayned to withſtand a great manie. And becauſe his waight and bignes, requiers great ſtrength, therefore thoſe onelie are allotted to the handling thereof, which are mightie and bigge to behould, great and ſtronge in bodie, of ſtoute and valiant courage.

O   Who

Who (forafmuch as they are to incounter manie, and
to the end they may ftrike the more fafelie, and amafe
them with the furie of the Sword) do altogether vfe to
deliuer great edge blowes, downe right and reuerfed,
fetching a full circle, or compaffe therin, ftaying them
felues fometimes vpon one foote, fometimes on the
other, vtterlie neglecting to thruft, and perfwading
themfelues, that the thruft ferueth to amaze one man
onelie, but thofe edge blowes are of force to incounter
many. The which maner of skirmifhing, befides that,
it is moft gallant to behold, being accompanied with
exceeding fwiftnes in deliuerie, (for otherwife it worketh no fuch effect) it is alfo moft profitable, not properly of it felfe, but becaufe men confidering the furie
of the fword, which greatly amafeth them, are not refolute to do that, which otherwife they could not choofe
but doe. That is, either to incounter the fword in
the middle towardes the handle, when it carieth fmall
force, or els to ftand far off, watching whileft the fword
goeth, & is caried compaffing in his great cirkle, being
of the compaffe of tenne armes, or more, & then to run
vnder it, and deliuer a thruft. And thefe two waies are
effectual, when fuch men are mett withall, who are exercifed to enter nimblie and ftrike, or fuch as dare, and
haue the fpirit & courage, to fet, and oppofe theimfelues
fingle againft the two hand fword, euen as the fingle
two hand fword aduentureth to oppofe it felfe againft
many. Neither is this thing to be maruailed at, for in
thefe our daies, there be things performed of greater
actiuitie & daunger. And there be fome which dare do
this with the fword and round Target, but yet they are
not refolute to ftrike firft, but will receaue and fuftain
the

the blow, with the round Target, and then enter and thruſt, this trulie betokeneth great courage & actiuitie, although not ſuch as is required in this behalfe.

Thus much concerning that, which appertaineth to the defence of the circuler blowes, of the two hand ſword, when it indeuoreth to oppoſe it ſelf againſt ma- nie. And foraſmuch as men haue, and ſometimes do vſe, both in the liſts & other places, to fight ſingle com- bats, one to one with the ſingle two hand ſword, I wil alſo declare my opinion touching the ſame.

Of the maner how to handle the Two hand
Sword, in ſingle combat.

O thoſe, who would cunninglie handle the Two hand Sword in ſingle combat, it is prin- cipally neceſſarie that (as in other weapons) they be practiſed and haue the ſkil, to vſe the one hand aſwell as the other, and that they be both actiue in bo- die, and ſtrong in the armes, which are required in the managing of each weapon. And farther it is requiſite that they carie the principles of this Art, ſurelie fixed in their mindes and memories, by meanes wherof they may become bolde and reſolute, in as much as they haue to do, either in ſtriking or defending.

They ought furthermore to conſider, how the two hand Sword is vſed, and how it ought to be vſed.

Touching the firſt, All men vſe to deliuer thruſtes, aſwell as edge blowes, downe right, and reuerſed, with both hands to the Sword which way albeit, it be pro- fitable in the beſtowing of edge blowes, as being the better hable to ſuſtain the Sword, yet in diſcharging of thruſtes it is hurtfull, for it cauſeth them to be much ſhorter, then they would be, if in the beginning, they

O 2   were

119

were forciblie deliuered with both the handes , and then , by taking away one hand from the croſſe , they were ſpringed as farre forth,as the pomel hand,foote, and all the bodie of that ſide, may be ſtretched out. For, being diſcharged in this maner, if they hit home they make great paſſage , and if they be voyded , yet the Two hand ſword may be quicklie had againe , by the retyring of a pace , and of the hand and arme , pla-cing the other hand there where it was , and ſo ſetling in the low ward . Therefore,when one findes himſelf to ſtand in the high ward, (the which at the two hand Sword, is framed , either with the right ſide towardes the enimie , either with the left , in either of which waies , the armes would be borne aloft , and farre off fromthe bodie , cauſing the point ſomewhat to bend bothtowards the ground and the bodie , to the end it may defend both the length of the bodie, and couer it in a maner thwarting or croſſing , it being ſo farre off from the ſword.

Farther , in this ward, the hand that is towards the enimie , muſt take hold faſt of the handle neere the croſſe, and vnderneath , the other hand aboue , and neere the pomell. I ſay ſtanding thus at the high ward, he may either deliuer a thruſt , either a downe right blow of the edge.

The thruſt is diſcharged (as ſoone as the enimies ſworde is found) as farre in the beginning as he may with both armes : Then , taking away the croſſe hand,he ſhal force it farther on with the pomel hand, as much as he may ſtretch it ſoorth, alwayes in the diſcharge, increaſing a ſlope pace. And the thruſt beeing thus deliuered , hee ſhall preſentlie retyre his

saide

120

saide pace, and returne his hand againe to the croſſe,
ſetling himſelfe either in the high or lowe warde. But
if he would deliuer a down-right blow with the edge
which I counſell him not to doe, becauſe he may eaſily be ſtroken vnder it, he ſhall firſt diſcharge a thruſt
with both his handes, and then encreaſing a pace, ſhal
turne the ſaide downright blowe, ſtretching out the
arme as much as he maie. In the deliuerie of which
blowe, if he meete with the enimies ſworde, he ſhall
take awaie his hand from the croſſe, & ſtretch out the
pommel hand as much as he may, with the encreaſe
of a pace. And farther, turning the ſaid hand which
holdeth the ſworde vpwardes, to the end, to lengthen
the thruſt, he ſhall driue, and force it on, and preſently
retire himſelfe in manner aforeſaid.

Of the defence of the high ward, at the two hand fword.

THe low ward, ſhal be the defence of the high ward, and it may be framed with the right foote before & behind, in ſuch ſort, as the ſaid high warde, the which ſhal be declared in his proper place.

Therefore, regarding to place himſelfe for his defence in the low ward (and that directly contrarie to his enimie, that is to ſay : if the enimie ſtande with the right foote before, to put his left foote foremoſt, and as the thruſt or the downright blowe comes) he ſhall encounter it without, and as ſoone as he hath founde the enimies ſword, he ſhall voide his croſſe hand, and encreaſe a pace, and therewithall deliuer a thruſt, with the pommell hand, as farre as it wil ſtretch out . The which thruſt wil eaſily ſpeed, if the enimie come reſolutely in deliuering of his blowe: for he ſhal come directly to encounter the point of the ſworde, with that part of his bodie which encreaſeth forwardes. Thus much for the defeuce of the high thruſt.

The downright blowe may be warded, if whileſt the enimies ſword is in his compaſſe, he nimbly deliuer a thruſt vnder it. Or els, if he would encounter it, (as ſoone as he hath ſo done) he do voide his croſſe hand, and with the encreaſe of a pace, thruſt as farrefoorth as the pommell hand will ſtretch out.

Of the hurt of the low ward, at the two hand fworde.

BEcauſe the broad warde in handling of this weapon is painfull and vnſure, I leaue to ſpeake therof, and come to the lowe warde, which is framed two waies, to wit : either with the right or with the lefte
foote

foote before, and in either waie, one may strike both within and without. Within, is rather to warde, then to strike : for the enimie that stands without, hath the greater aduantage.

Finding himselfe therefore within, and bearing the sworde firmely, he shal force and driue on a thrust, as farre as both armes maie stretch out together, encreasing a pace and setling in the lowe warde, if he do not speede.

But finding himself to stand without, and as soone as he hath found the enimies sworde, he shall deliuer a thrust, first, at the length of both armes, then, voyding the crosse hand, encrease a pace and deliuer it out at vttermost length of the pommell hand, and immediatly after the thrust, retire his hand and pace, staying himselfe againe in the said lowe warde.

The defence of the low warde, at the two hand sword.

IT is a generall rule, that the true defence of all blows is the lowe warde. Therefore , when one standeth thereat, if there come a thrust without (because it is necessarie in this case to stand within,) he shall do no other then encounter the enimies sworde, and thrust his arme forwards, to the end he may void it from his bodie, and farther retyre his foote more backwards, & as it were, in a compasse, thereby the better sauing his bodie from the hurt.

But if the thrust come within (by reason wherof he should stand without) as soone as the enimies sword is encountred , he shall deliuer a thrust with both his hands, and then voiding his crosse hande, he shall
deliuer

deliuer it ftrongly with his pommell hand, with the encreafe of a pace. And this thruft doth fafely fpeed. Neither is it to be doubted, that by holding the fword with one hand, the enimie may take holdfaft therof, for he hath inough to do, to retyre himfelfe, and ward the thruft, neither can he perfourme fo many things in one time.

Of the weapons of the Staffe, namely, the Bill, the Partifan, the Holbert, and the Iauelin.

BEcaufe it may feeme ftrange vnto many, that I haue here placed thefe iiij. fortes of weapons together, as though I woulde frame but one only waie for the handling of all, although they differ in forme, from which form is gathered their difference in vfe. Therefore, forafmuch as I am of opinion, that all of them may be handled in manner after one waye, it fhall not be amiffe, if I declare the reafon thereof, fpeaking firft of euery one feuerally by it felfe, and then generally of all togither, holding and maintaining alwaies for my conclufion, that the skill of handling of them, helpeth a man to the knowledge of all the reft, for as much as concerneth true Arte.

Of the Partefan.

COmming therefore to the Partefan, as vnto the plaineft, and as vnto that, whereupon all the reft depend, omitting to fhewe who was the inuenter thereof, as being to fmall purpofe : I faie, that it was found

found out to no other end, then for that the foot men in the warres, might be able with them to hurt those horfemen (whome they might not reach with their fwords) afwell with their point as with their edge. Further, weapons which are to be caft, or fprong forth at the length of the arme, are for the moft part deceitfull, by meanes whereof, they might hurt afwell the Archers on horfebacke, as other horfemen.

Therefore, thefe Partefans were made bigg and of great paize, and of perfect good fteele, to the end they might breake the maile and deuyde the Iron.

And that this is true, it is to be feene in the auncient weapons of this fort, which are great and fo well tempered, that they are of force to cut any other Iron. Afterwardes, as men had confidered, that as this weapon was only to ftrike, it might in fome part thereof, haue afwell fomthing to warde withall, whereby it might be faid to be a perfect weapon, they deuifed to add vnto it two crookes or forkes, by the which, that blow might be warded, which parting from the point and continuing downe along the ftaffe, would come to hurt the perfon. And thefe forkes, or (I may faie) thefe defences were by fome men placed on that part of the Iron, which next adioyneth to the ftaffe, making them crooked & fharp, & a handfull long, & for the moft part, with the pointes toward the enimie, to the end they might ferue not only to defend, but alfo to ftrike. And to the end, the bigneffe and weight of the Partefan, (which ought to be apt and commodious to be handled) might not be encreafed, they diminifhed part of the Iron thereof, and gaue the fame to the forkes or defences : And by that meanes they

P. framed

125

framed another weapon called a Iauelin which (because the broadnes,and happily the weight and paize
thereof is diminished.) is not verie forcible to strike
with the edge, but all his power consisteth in three
thrustes. Othersome afterwards would not that these
defeces should be placed at the lower-most part of the
Iron, but in the middle thereof. And these men bearing great respect to the blowes of the edge, left the
Iron which should serue for the defence behinde, in
his bredth and waight, adioyning thereunto in the
opposite parte of the right edge, a most sharpe point
of Iron, to the end, that what way socuer it were moued, it might strike and hurt. But if any man obiect &
saie: if the said point of Iron were put there in respect
of striking, they might also as well haue left there an
edge, which being longer would strike more easily.
I answere, that the blowes of the false (that is to saye,
the hinder or backe edge of the weapon) are verie
weake, and the point doth strike and hurt more easily
then the edge. And therefore it was requisite that
there be facilitie where there was weaknes. These men
by these meanes framed the auncient weapon called
the Holberd, out of the which, men of our age haue di-
riued & made another kind of Holberd & Bill. And
these bearing also respect to some one profitable thing
or other, did maintaine the defence, and encrease the
hurting or offence. The respect was, that as they discoursed & pondred with themselues, at length they
verie warily perceiued that a man with weapon in his
hand, might make sixe motions, that is to saie, one towards the head, one towards the feete, one towardes
the right side, one towards the left, one forwards & towards

wards the enimie, the other backward & toward him selfe. Of all the which, fiue of them might verie well strike, & the laſt might neither ſtrike nor defend. Ther fore, prouiding that this laſt motion alſo ſhould not be idle & vnprofitable, they added a hook with the point turned towards the handle, with the which one might verie eaſily teare armour, & draw perforce men from their horſes. Thoſe, who framed the middle or meane Holbert, would that the ſaid hooke ſhould be placed in the ſafe or backer edge. And thoſe that deuiſed the Bill, would haue it on the right edge, leauing the edge ſo long that the hook might not altogether hinder the blow of the edge, but rather (to the end the edg might make the greater effect) they would that the hooke ſhuld beare an edg & be cutting in euery part therof. Where I gather, that the Bil is the moſt perfect weapō of all others, becauſe it ſtriketh & hurteth in euery of theſe ſixe motiōs, & his defences both cut & prick: which the new kind of Holbert doth not perform; being framed after the ſaid faſhion, & rather for lightnes aptnes & brauerie, then for that it carrieth any great profit with it: for the edge is not ſo apt to ſtrike, & the point therof is ſo weake, that hitting any hard thing, either it boweth or breaketh: neither is it much regarded in the warres, the Harquebuſh & the Pike being now adaies the ſtrength of all armyes.

Hereby it may be gathered, that with the Parteſam a man may ſtrike with the point & edge in ſuch motions: with the Iauelin, with the point onely & in ſuch motions as it may: with the Holberd and Bill, both with the point and edge, in ſixe motions. But becauſe theſe weapons for the moſt part are exerciſed.

and vsed to enter through diuers Pikes & other weapons, and to breake and disorder the battell raye, to which ende, and purpose, if it be vsed, then that manner of mannaging and handling is verie conuenient which is practised now adaies, and thus it is. The Partesan, Holberd, and Bill (but not the Iauelin, being in this case nothing effectuall becaufe it hath small force in the edge) must be borne in the middle of the staffe, with the heele thereof before, and verie lowe, and the point neere a mans head. And with the said heele, or halfe staffe vnderneath, from the hande downwardes, he must warde and beat off the pointes and thrustes of the Pikes and other weapons, and hauing made waie, must enter with the encreafe of a pace of the hinder foote, and in the fame inftant, let fall his weapon as forcibly as he maie, and ftrike with the edge athwart the Pikes. This kinde of blowe is fo ftrong (being deliuered as it ought, confidering it commeth from aboue downwardes, and the weapon of it felfe is verie heauie) that it will cut afunder not onely Pikes, but alfo any other forcible impediment. In thefe affaires the Iauelin is not vfed, bicaufe it worketh no fuch effect. But when one is conftrained to vfe it, he ought neither to beat off, neither to warde with the ftaffe, but altogether with the Iron and his defences, remembring, as foone as he hath beaten off & made waie of entrance, to thruft onely : for to handle it in deliuering of edgeblowes preuaileth not, confidering the fmall force it carrieth in that maner of ftriking. And as among all the forefaide iiij. weapons, the Iauelin in this kinde of fkirmifh, is leaft profitable, fo the Partefan is moft excellent & commodious, for

hauing

128

hauing no other defence, it is prouided in the ſtaffe, and is moſt forcible, to cut the Pikes by meanes of his heauines and waight, and the rather, becauſe it is vnfurniſhed and voide of other things, which in this caſe might let and hinder the edge blow. Therefore the Parteſan ſhalbe vſed (as in his owne proper qualitie) to enter among the Pikes, and cut them a ſunder, and other weapons alſo partlie for that cauſe, and partlie to ſkirmiſh ſingle, one to one. Which although it be not ordinarily accuſtomed, yet neuertheleſſe, becauſe both this, and the reſt of the weapons, may be handled in ſingle combate, and do containe in them, aſwell offence, as defence, Farther, to the end, the wiſe and diſcreete (happening to be in ſuch affaires) may be ſkillfull to determin with themſelues, what they may and ought to doe: I will ſhew my opinion what may be done with theſe weapons in ſingle combat, reaſoning iointly of the Iauelyn, Bill, and Holberd, becauſe there is but a ſmal difference in the Iauelyn, And the Bill, and the Holberd, are in a maner all one, and the verie ſelfe ſame.

Of Bill againſt Bill, Holberd againſt Holberd, or Holberd againſt Bill.

Foraſmuch, as the Bill and Holberd, haue the ſelfe ſame offence and defence, and be of one length: I thought it not good to make two Treatiſes thereof, becauſe I ſhould be forced to repeat the ſelfe ſame thing in both, the which, being ſuperfluous, would breed loathſomenes. I ſay therefore, that whoſoeuer would handle the Bill or Holberd, which beeing all

one, I will name indifferently, by the name of the Holberd, I say, to him that would vſe them, & ſtrike aſwell with the point, as with the edge, which bloowes at theſe weapons are mightie and forcible, it is neceſſarie, that he conſider the difficultie in ſtriking with the point, and the daunger in ſtriking with the edge. That it is difficult to ſtrike with the point, it is moſt cleere, becauſe the full courſe of the point, may verie eaſilie be hindered and tyed, by meanes of ſo many hookes and forkes which are in the Holberd.

And that it is perilous to ſtrike with the edge, hath bin declared when I intreated of the ſingle Rapier, which

which perill ought the more to be confidered in this weapon, becaufe by meanes of his length, it frameth a greater cirkle, and therein giueth more time to enter vnder it.

Therefore no man may fafelie handle the Holberd, if firft he do not confider thefe two thinges, the one, (which he may verie hardlie withftand) and that is the thruft, becaufe thefe hookes and forkes, are properlie belonging vnto it, and are impoffible to bee vntyed and taken away, when a man would, the forme being as it is. 2. The peril of the edge blow, may fome time be voided, if he be nimble and bold, performing all that in due time, which fhall heere be laid down for his inftruction.

*I*N the handling of this weapon, there fhall be framed (by my counfel) no more then one ward, bearing the hands, for the more fuertie in the middle of the ftaffe. And that ward muft be the lowe ward. The hands muft be fomewhat diftant, one from an other, and the point of the weapon directlie towards the enimie, regarding alwaies to place himfelfe with the contrarie foote before, to that, which the enimie fhall fet forth, that is to fay: Yf the enimie be before with the left foote, then to ftand with his right foote, or contrarie wife. And ftanding in maner aforefaid, he muft alwaies proue & trie (before he be determined to deliuer a thruft) to beat off the enimies weapon, which being done, prefently deliuer a forcible thruft toward the enimie. But becaufe it may lightly fo fall out, that in
beating

beating off the enimies weapon (the enimie happelie pretending to do the like) the weapons be intangled faft together . Therefore , as foone as it is perceaued that they be grappled faft, ftanding fure, and firmelie on his feete, he fhall increafe a pace towardes the enimie , lifting vp aloft the enimies weapon , together with his owne by force of the faid intangling,and then with the heele, or the blunt end of the Holberd fhall ftrike the enimie in the breft , (for which confideration it fhould not diflike me , if for that purpofe,there be faftned in the faid blunt end , a ftrong and fharpe pike of iron) and as foone as he hath ftroken with the faid blunt end,(becaufe, by meanes of the faid lifting vpp , the weapons fhall be now vnhooked) and retyring that pace which he had before increafed,without remouing of his hands , he fhall deliuer a ftrong edge blow , which then is verie commodious.

And it is to be vnderftood , that this edge blow being deliuered in this maner , is fo ftrong, that it is apt to cutt the enimies fword,if it be oppofed in his ward. Only that which is to be regarded in the deliuering of this blow , is , that he be nimble,and of ftout courage, not doubting that he fhal be ftrooken againe, becaufe he is to goe fo neere his enimie , for befides,that he is in fuch cafe , that he may eafilie ward any blowe , the enimie findeth no waie , to ftrike, except he performe it in two times, to witt, by retyring his pace and Holberd, and then by deliuering a thruft.

That this waie of ftriking is good , after the tying, and intangling of the weapons , it may be hereby vnderftood, that as a man indeuoreth to vntye, and vnloofen the weapons, either by retyring himfelfe,either

by

by carying them on the one side, to the intent to strike,
he may then go foorth of the straight lyne, by going to
one of the both sides, or els lose one time, by retyring
himselfe, vnder which two inconueniences, either he
must needes be hurt, or els defending himselfe, tye fast
the weapons againe. But these inconueniences happen not in the foresaid maner of striking.

Farther, a man may strike after an other way to wit,
as soone as by the intangling of the weapons they are
lifted vpp, to the intent to vnhooke, and vntye them,
he must chaunge his hands, and deliuer an edge blow,
either a thwart, either on high, either a low, for it is
commodious any way, so that he chaunge his hands
and retyre a pace. But this is not so commodious in
the other waie, because he may not strike but onelie
downwards. But in this maner of chaunging hands,
he may easilie strike the enimie in that place, where he
perceaueth him to be most discouered, be it aboue or
beneath.

Of the defence of the heele, or blunt ende of the Holberd.

FOr the defence of the abouesaid two blowes, it is
requisite as I haue alreadie said, that a man stand
with the contrarie foote before, to that, of the enimies.
And as the enimie (after the fastning of the weapons)
endeuoreth to lift them vpp, (being well awares therof) he ought to recouer his Holberd by the increase
of a pace, and strike with the heele at the enimies thigh
or bellie, and then chaunging his handes, he shall deliuer an edge blow, without any other retyring of him
selfe, or mouing of his hands, The which blow shall

Q   lightlie

lightlie speede, being nimblie deliuered . And when it speedeth not, yet, it will safelie ward the edge blow, which the enimie shall giue . And this may suffise for asmuch as concerneth the blowes of the Holberd in single combat, wherein there is anie difficultie to be found, the which, a man must seeke to auoide by all meanes, especiallye endeuouryng by all possible wayes to deliuer thrustes, without tying or intangling of his weapon . But although the enimies weapon, may not be tyed to any prescript law or order, (for he also vseth, all the pollicie he may to auoid daunger) yet these blowes with their fastnings are laid downe, be-cause I presuppose, that who so is skilfull to strike, not-withstanding these difficulties, will be much more ad-uentrous, in striking when he shall find little, or no-thing to hinder him, As for example, when in fight he meeteth with a weapon of the Staffe of the selfe same, or of greater length, but yet, void of hookes or forkes : For seeing his owne weapon, is onlie hable to hooke, and driue outwards the enimies weapon, he may safe-lie deliuer an edge blow, with the increase of a pace, be-ing sure, that he may not be stroken againe, but onelie with a thrust, which the enimie may not deliuer, but of force, must either retyre his staffe, either his feete, vnder which time, an edge blow may be deliuered without daunger.

Of the hurt and ward of the Iauelyn.

 He selfe same ward, shalbe framed with the Iauelyn, as with the Holberd. And because, of necessitie, the weapons will be intangled, I say,

I say, the verie same thrusts shal be giuen therwith, as are deliuered with the Holberd. But because the edge of the Iauelyn is weake, and the pacing which is made when the weapons are fastned, is onel.e profitable for the giuing of the edge blow: Therfore in handling of the Iaueling, this intangling or fastning is by al means possible to be auoided. But when a man is to strike his enimie, let him first proue, to beat off his Iauelyn, and then to force on a thrust, in this maner.

Finding the enimies Iauelyn to be within, (by within, I vnderstand, when the Iauelyn is betwene the enimies armes, or against them) then he must force it outwards, and driue a thrust with his owne Iauelyn, at the length of the staffe (without mouing of his feete) at the enimies face. Finding it without, he ought to beat it backwards, and increasing a pace, to launch out the Iauelyn at the enimies face, at the length of the staffe and arme, immediatlie retyring his pace, & hand, and afterwards settle himselfe in the same low ward.

Of the defence of the thrustes of the Iauelyn.

FOr him that would defend himselfe from those two thrusts, and strike vnder them, it is necessarie to call to remembraunce the most subtill consideration of times, without knowledge whereof, there is no man that may safelie beare himselfe vnder anic weapon: Comming therefore to the said consideration, I saie, that if the enimie would beate of the Iauelyn, (his owne Iauelyn beeing either within, either without) of force hee must enlarge and widen it from out the ſtraight lyne, if he would as aforeſaid forciblie beat off the other Iauelyn. Therefore at what time ſoeuer a man ſeeth the enimies Iauelyn wide of the ſtraight lyne, then, and in the ſame time (in the which it commeth purpoſing to beat off) he muſt nimblie deliuer a thruſt. And in like maner, finding himſelfe, either within, either without, and the enimies Iauelyn ſomething wide of the ſtraight lyne, then before it come into the ſaid lyne againe, he ſhall with the increaſe of a pace deliuer a thruſt, at the length of the hinder arme, and then retyring his ſaid pace, ſettle himſelfe at his ward againe.

Of the Partiſan.

IF any would handle the Partiſan in ſingle combat, they ſhall not ſtrike with the edge, becauſe the time is too long, and they may eaſilie be ſtroken vnder the ſame. Therefore practizing the thruſt, they ſhall vſe the ſelfe ſame offence and defence, which I haue ſhewed in the Iauelyn, to the which I referre them.

Of the Pike

AS among all other weapons, which are worn by the ſide, the ſingle ſword is the moſt honorable, as beeing ſuch a one which is leſt capable of deceit of any other: So among the weapons of the Staffe, the Pike is the moſt plaine, moſt honorable, and moſt noble weapon of all the reſt.

Therefore among renowned knightes and great Lords this weapon is highly esteemed, becaule it is as well voide of deceite, as alfo, for that in well handling thereof, there is required great strength of bodie, accompanied with great valure and deepe iudgement: for there is required in the vfe thereof a moft fubtill & delicate knowledge and confideration of times, and motions, and a readie refolution to ftrike. Thefe qualities may not happen or be refident in any perfons, but in fuch as are ftrong of armes and couragious of ftomacke. Neither may they procure to get any other aduantage in the handling thereof, then to be more quick and refolute both in iudgement and hande than their enimie is. Therefore feeing euery man may hereby knowe what is neceffarie for him fo to handle it, as he may obtaine victorie thereby: let him refolue himfelfe either to giue it ouer quite, or els to handle it as he ought, and is required.

The manner how to handle the Pyke.

THis renowmed weapon hath beene of diuers diuerfly handled, in fingle combat: (for the manner of vfing it in the warres, maketh not at this prefent for my purpofe.) Therefore it fhall not be amiffe, if (fpeaking of the manner of his vfe in thefe our daies) I declare alfo mine opinion concerning the fame. There haue beene fome (who greatly regarding eafe & little paine) would haue the Pike to be borne in the midle. Other fome, more ftrong of arme, but weaker of hart, (to the end they might be the farther off, from hurte) accuftomed to beare it at the beginning neere the

Q 3 heele

137

heele or blunt end thereof : which two waies in my iudgement are to be refused, the one being too daungerous(I meane the bearing of it in the middle) the other too difficult (I mean, the bearing it at the blunt end,) becaufe a man is not able to stande long at his ward, neither to defend himfelfe strongly, nor offend fafely, confidering, much of his force is taken away, by fufteining and bearing it at the faid end . So that, when a forcible blow commeth he hath not fufficient power to beat it off . And forafmuch as the Pike is a long straight lyne, which hath his motion in the head or beginning thereof , which motion be it neuer fo fmall, neere the hand, is yet verie great at the point, it is requifite, if he would ftrike iuft and ftraight, (when he fo holdeth it at the end) that he be greatly practifed, and haue great ftrength whereby he may be both skilfull & able to beare it fo iuft & euen, that the point thereof ftrik or hit there where the hand & eie would haue it. This is verie hardly accomplifhed, afwel beecaufe it is a thing impoffible to ftrike by the ftraight lyne, as alfo for that the armes being weakened with the paize of the Pike, do fhake and deliuer it vnftedfaftly. Therefore , for the auoyding of thefe two inconueniences, the Pike muft be born within an armes length of the faid heele or blunt end, in which place, it is fufficiently diftant from hurt, & it is not borne with much difficultie if the hands be placed an armes legth one from another of the which the hinder hand muft be ftedfaft, I meane, holde the Pike harde , and the forehand fomewhat loofe : So that the Pike may fhitt thorough it to and fro.

For

For what cause the Pike maketh greater paſſage with the point then any other ſhorter weapon.

IT is moſt manifeſt, that the Pike maketh greater paſſage with his point than any other weapon : and the twohand ſworde, more then the ordinarie ſword: & the ſword more then the dagger. And among al weapons, this is generaly true, that the longer the weapon is, the greater paſſage it maketh with the point, and the greater blow with the edge. Neither doeth this ſo chaunce, beecauſe the weapon is more heauie, neither becauſe there is applyed more force vnto it in action, as moſt men ſuppoſe, but rather through a naturall cauſe which is as followeth.

If there be two circles, the one greater then the other, and are moued by one manner of motion, the greater fhall be more fwift then the leffe : for being greater in circumference & turning round, in the fame time that the leffe turneth it muft needes be, that it goeth more fwiftly. So it commeth to paffe, that one felfe-fame hand may deliuer a greater blow with the two hande fworde than with a fingle fworde, and with a long fworde, then one that is fhorter, and with that, then with the dagger : And with a Bill, a greater blowe, then with the two hand fworde, and fo likewife in all other weapons. Wherefore it is moft cleere, that of edgeblowes that maketh the greater ftroke, which is deliuered with the longer weapon. It remaineth now to be confidered, how this falleth out in the blowes of the point. I faie therefore, the blowes of the point are alfo circuler, fo that the Pike being verie long, maketh the greater circle, and by confequence the gteater blowe of the point or the greater thruft. That the blowes of the point are circuler, may be fhewed by this reafon. The arme (being as a ftraight line, & fixed faft in one parte, as for example in the fhoulder, and mouable in the other, as in the hand, ftanding I faye, fixed as a ftraight lyne, and the one end mouing from the other) fhall alwaies moue circulerly : So that the arme cannot otherwife moue, except when it is bowed, and would then make it felfe ftraight againe, tne which motion alfo is doubtfull, whether it be ftraight yea or no. Therfore imagining that on the mouable parte of this arme, or ftraight lyne, there be alfo another thwart lvne, to wit, a Pike, a fworde, or any other weapon, then the arme mouing, carrieth alfo, circu-

lerly

140

lerly with it, the said thwart lyne: which lyne, by how much, the longer it is, by so much it maketh the greater circle, as may be seene in this figure.

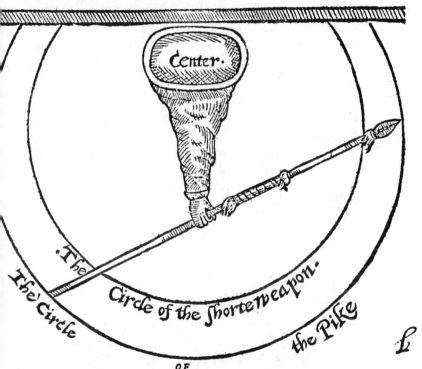

Whereby, it is manifest, that the Pike, the longer it is, it frameth the greater circle, and consequently, is more swifte, and therefore maketh the greater passage. The like is to be vnderstood of all other weapons, which the longer they are being moued by the arme, cause the greater edgeblow, and greater passage with the point.

Of the wardes of the Pike.

IN mine opinion, if a man would either strike, or defend with the Pike, he may not otherwise vse it.

then by framing of two wardes, in one of which, he shal strike the bodie from the middle vpwards, & this I will terme the low warde: the other shall striike the bodie from the middle downwards, & shalbe called the high ward. Neither shalthey be so termed for any other cause, then for that it is verie necessarie for him that striketh, first to beat off the enimies Pike, & then to deliuer his owne. But yet it should breed great inconuenience, & there would be two much time spent if finding it good & comodious to strike in the lowe warde, he would first beat off the enimies weapon, & then shift from the lowe to the high warde. For that cause I will frame the high warde, which shal bee, when one beareth his armes high, & the point of the Pike low. And the low warde is, when the armes are low, & the point of the Pike high. There is another warde which would be framed as a meane betweene these two, & that is, when the Pike is borne directly towards the enimie. And it falleth out that it is most sure & long, when it is opposed against any of the other two aforesaid, because then a man is in case both to beat off the weapon & to enter therewithall with great aduantage. But putting the case, the enimie do likewise directly oppose himselfe against this warde, then the Pikes may not beat off one another, but both parties are like to be inuested & runne through at one instant, without any defence or warding thereof.

So that this straight ward may not be vsed except it be against one of the two aforsaid. And when the enimie standeth in any of the said two, then a man must resolutly bring his weapon into the said straight ward, for as he getteth therby the greater aduātage both of length & time, so he may very easily beat off the enimies Pike.

The Pike.

Of the maner how to strike in the said wardes.

WHen the enimie is in the low ward, a man ought
always to stand either at the high or straight
ward. And contrarilie, in the low or straight ward,
when the enimie is in the high ward. And must indeuour as forciblie and as nimblie as he may, first of all,
to beat off the enimies Pike, whether it be within or
without, but yet in such sort, that he depart not much
from the straight lyne, and be therby constrayned, to
spend much time in returning thither againe, And as
soone as he hath beaten off the enimies weapon, to
thrust, bearing his bodie contrarie to his armes, to the
end, he may be the more couered from the thrustes,
and deliuer his owne thrusts with the more force, alwaies regarding in the high ward, to thrust downewards, and in the low ward, vpwards, & in the straight
ward, in the middle : for this maner of thrusting, is verie commodious, and consumeth little time.

Of the defence of the wardes.

THe hurts of these wardes, are defended in the selfe
same maner, as those of the Iauelyne are, to which
Chapter, (hauing there reasoned sufficiently) I referre
you, to the intent I may not repeat one thing often.

And it is to be considered, that there is greater regard to be had of the times in managing this weapon
then in any other, because it is not furnished with any
forkes, or other defences which may helpe a man, but
all hope of victorie consisteth in the iudgement of the
times, and in dexteritie of deliuerie.

I will not therfore at this present stand to declare

R 2

any

any more of the true knowledge of the weapon, then that, which onelie appertayneth to be spoken in this worke, but will hereafter at my more leasure, handle it more at large, at what time, it shal be knowen, that men (giuing ouer all other false & vain kind of skirmishing) ought to settle them selues in this, by meanes wherof, their iudgements are perfected, and they more insured vnder their weapons, and so by consequence are made more bold and hardie. And forasmuch as all this ought to be verified in deedes, and not in wordes, it shall be euery mans part, that will exercise himselfe in this Art, first diligentlie to learne the principles, & afterwards by exercise of the weapon to attaine to the most subtil and delicate knowledge & consideration of the times, without which (as I haue said els where) it is not possible to profit therin. For although there be happilie some, who (being strong of arme, and nimble in deliuering falses, either right, reuersed, or straight) haue bi in our time accompted for tall men, yet for al that, those who are skilfull in this true Art, ought not to giue credite vnto it, because they know assuredlie that not right or reuersed edge blowes, get the masterie, but rather the thrusts of the point, neither the bestowing of them euery way, but with aduantage and in due time. Neither ought a man to strike, therby to be stroken againe, (which is the part and point, rather of a bruite beast, then of a reasonable man) but to strike and remaine without daunger. All which things by this true Art are easilie learned.

FINIS.

THE

THE
Seccnd Part intreatinge of De-
ceites and Falsinges of Blowes
and Thruftes.

 Einge come to the end of the true Arte, and hauing declared all that which feemed conuenient and profitable for the attaynement of true iudgement in the handling of the weapon & of the entire knowledg of al aduátages, by the which as well al difaduantages are knowen : It fhall be good that I intreat of Deceite or Falfing, afwel to performe my promife, as alfo to fatisfie thofe who are greatly delighted to skirmifh, not with pretence to hurt or ouer come, but rather for their exercife & paftime:

In which it is a braue and gallant thing and worthy of commendations to be skilfull in the apte managing of the bodie, feete and hands, in mouing nimblie fometimes with the hand, fome-times with the elbow, and fometimes with the fhoulder, in retiring, in increafing; in lifting the bodie high, in bearing it low in one inftant: in breif, deliuering fwiftlie blows afwell of the edge as of the point, both right and reuerfed, nothing regarding either time, aduantage or meafure, beftowing them at randone euerie waie.

But diuers men being blinded in their owne conceites, do in thefe actions certainly beleeue that they are either more nimble, either more warie & difcreet

Aa1   then

145

then theire aduersarie is: Of which their folish opinion they are all beastlie proud and arrogant:

And becaufe ithath manie times happened them,
either with a falfe thruft, or edge blowe, to hurte or
abufe the enemie, they become loftie, and prefume
thereon as though their blowes were not to be warded. But y et for the moft part it falleth out, that by a
plain fimple fwad hauing onely a good ftomack and
ftout courage, they are chopt in with a thruft, and fo
miferablie slaine.

For auoiding of this abufe, the beft remedie is, that
they exercife themfelues in deliuering thefe falfes onlie in fport, and (as I haue before faid) for their practife & paftime: Refoluing themfelues for a truth, that
when they are to deal with anie enemie, &when it is
vpon danger of their liues, they muft then fuppofe
the enemie to be equall to themfelues afwel in kno-
ledge as in ftrength, & accuftome themfelues to ftrik
in as litle time as is posfible, and that alwaies beeing
wel warded. And as for thefe Falfes or Slips, they
muft vfe them for their exercife & paftimes fake onelie, and not prefume vpon them, except it bee againft
fuch perfons, who are either much more slow, either
know not the true principels of this Art. For Difceit
or Falfing is no other thing, then a blow or thruft de-
uered, not to the intent to hurt or hitt home, but to
caufe the enemie to difcouer himfelfe in fome parte,
by meanes whereof a man maie fafely hurt him in the
fame part. And looke how manie blowes or thrufts
there maie be giuen, fo manie falfes or deceits may be
vfed, and a great manie more, which fhal be declared
in their proper place: The defence likewife whereof
shall

shal in few words be laſt of all laid open vnto you.

Deceits or Falſings of the ſingle
Sword, or ſingle Rapier

 S I take not Victorie to be the end and
ſcope of falſing, but rather nimblenes of
bodie and dexteritie in plaie: So, caſting
aſide the conſideration how a man is either couered or diſcouered, and how he
hath more or leſſe aduantage) I ſaie that there maie be
framed at the ſingle ſword ſo manie wards, as there
be waies how to moue the arme hand and foot.

Therefore in falſinge there may bee framed the
high, lowe, and brode warde, with the right foote behind and before: a man may beare his ſword with the
poynt backewardes and forwardes: he may beare his
right hand on the left ſid, with his ſwords poynt back
wards: he may ſtand at the low warde with the point
backewardes and forwardes, bending towardes the
grounde. And ſtanding in all theſe waies, he may
falſe a thruſt aboue, and force it home beneath: and
contrarie from beneth aboue, he may falſe it without
and deliuer it within, or contrariwiſe.

And according to the ſaide manner of thruſting
he may deliuer edge-blowes, right, reuerſed, high and
lowe, as in that caſe ſhal moſt aduantage him. Farther
he may falſe an edgeblow, and deliuer it home: as for
example, to falſe a right blowe on highe, and deliuer
home a right and reuerſe blowe, high or lowe. In like
ſort the reuerſe is falſed, by deliuering right or reuerſe
blowes, high or lowe.

But it is to be confidered, that when he beareth his fworde with his poynt backewardes, he falfe no other than the edgeblow, for then thrufts are difcommodius. And becaufe men do much vfe at this weapon, to beate off the poynt of the fworde with their handes: therefore he muft in that cafe for his greater redines & aduantage, fuffer his fword to fwaie to that fide, whether the enemy beateth it, ioyning to that motion as much force as he may, performing therin a ful circuler blowe, and deliuering it at the enemie.

And this blow is moft readie, and fo much the rather, it is poffible to be performed, by how much the enemie thinketh not, that the fword will paffe in full circle that waie, for the enemie being fomwhat difapoynted, by beating off the fworde, after which beating, he is alfo to deliuer his thruft, he cánot fo fpeedely fpéd both thofe times but that he fhalbe firft ftroké with the edge of the fworde, which he had before fo beaten off.

Generall aduertifementes concerning
the defences.

Ecaufe it chaunceth commonly, that in managing of the handes, men beare no great regard, either to time or aduantage, but do endeuour themfelues after diuers & fundry waies & meanes to encounter the enemies fword: therfore in thefe cafes, it is verie profitable to knowe how to ftrike, and what may be done in fhorteft time.

The enemies fword is encountred alwaies either aboue, either in the midle, either beneath: & in al thefe

waies

waies a man findeth himſelf to ſtand either aboue, either beneth, either within, either without. And it fales
out alwaies that men finde themſelues vndernethe
with the ſword at the hanging warde, when they are
to ward high edgeblowes or thruſts: and this waie is
moſt commonly vſed: The manner whercof is, when
the hand is lifted vp to defend the ſword being thwar
ted, and the poynt turned downewards : when one
findeth himſelfe ſo placed, he ought not to recouer
his ſworde from vnderneath, and then to deliuer an
edge-blowe, for that were to long, but rather to ſtrike
nimbly that part of the enemie vnderneath, which is
not warded, ſo that he ſhall do no other then turne
his hand & deliuer an edge-blow at the legges which
ſurely ſpeedeth.

But if he finde himſelfe in defence either of the reuerſe or thruſt, to beare his ſword aloft and without,
and not hanging, in this the ſafeſt thing is, to increaſe
a pace, and to ſeaſyn vpon the enimies hand or arme.

The ſelfe ſame he ought to doe, finding himſelfe in
the midle, without and vnderneath : But if he finde
himſelfe within, he cannot by any meanes make anie
ſeaſure, becauſe he ſhall be then in greate perill to in-
ueſthimſelfe on the poynt of the enemies ſworde.

Therefore to avoide the ſaide poynt or thruſt,
he muſt turne his fiſt and deliuer an edge-blow at the
face, and withdraw himſelfe by voiding of his foote
towardes the broad ward. And if he finde himſelfe
beneath, & haue encountred the enemies edgeblow,
either with the edge, or with the falſe or backe of the
ſword, being beneath: then without any more adoe,
he ought to cut the legges, and void himſelf from the

enimies thruſt. And let this be taken for a generall rule: the bodie muſt be borne as far off from the enimy as it may. And blowes alwaies are to be deliuered on that parte which is founde to be moſt neare , be the ſtroke great or little. And each man is to be aduertiſed that when he findes the enimies weapon vnderneath at the hanging ward, he may ſafely make a ſeiſure: but it would be done nimbly and with good courage, becauſe he doth then increaſe towards his enimie in the ſtreight lyne, that is to ſaie, increaſe on pace, and therewithall take holdfaſt of the enemies ſword, nere the hiltes thereof, yea though his hand were naked, and vnder his owne ſworde preſently turning his hand outwardes, which of force wreſteth the ſworde out of the enimies hand: neither ought he to feare to make ſeiſure with his naked hand , for it is in ſuch a place, that if he ſhould with his hand encounter a blowe, happely it would not cut becauſe the weapō hath there verie ſmall force. All the hazard wil be, if the enimie ſhould drawe backe his ſword, which cauſeth it to cutte. For in ſuch ſorte it will cut mightily: but he may not giue leaſure or time to the enimie to drawe backe, but as ſoone as the ſeiſure is made, he muſt alſo turne his hand outwards: in which caſe, the enimie hath no force at all.

These maner of ſtrikings ought and maie be practiſed at all other weapons. Therefore this rule ought generally to be obſerued, and that is, to beare the bodie different from the enimes ſword, and to ſtrike litle or much , in as ſmall time as is poſſible.

And if one would in deliuering of a great edge-blowe, vſe ſmall motion and ſpende little time hee

ought

150

ought as soone as he hath stroken , to drawe or slide his sword, thereby causing it to cute: for otherwise an edge-blowe is to no purpose, although it be verie forcibly deliuered, especialy when it lighteth on any soft or limber thing: but being drawen, it doth euery way cute greatly.

Of sword and dagger, or Rapier
and dagger.

A L the wardes which are laide downe for the single sword , may likewise be giuen for the sworde and dagger. And there is greater reason why they should be termed wardes in the handling of this, than of the single sword, because albeit the sword is borne vnorderly, & with such disaduantage, that it wardeth in a maner no parte of the bodie, yet there is a dagger which continually standeth at his defence , in which case , it is not conuenient that a man lift vp both his armes and leaue his bodie open to the enimie: for it is neither agreeable to true, neither to false arte considering that in each of them the endeuor is to ouercome. And this manner of lifting vp the armes, is as if a man wold of purpose be ouercome: Therfore, when in this deceitfull and false arte, one is to vse two weapons, he must take hede that he beare the one cōtinually at his defence, and to handle the other euerie waye to molest the enimie : somtime framing one warde, somtimes an other : and in each of them to false, that is, to faine a thrust , and deliuer a thrust , to false a thrust, and giue an edge-blowe: and otherwise also, to false an edge-blowe , and to deliuer an edgeblowe

151

blowe. And in all these wayes to remember, that the blowe be continually different from the falfe : That is, if the thruſt be falſed aboue to driue it home belowe : If within, yet to ſtrike it without, and falſing an edgeblowe aboue, to beſtowe it beneath : or falſing a right blowe, to ſtrike with the reuerſe; or ſometimes with a right blowe, but yet differing from the other. And after an edgeblowe on high, to deliuer a reuerſe belowe. In fine , to make all ſuch mixture of blowes, as may beare all theſe contrarieties following, to wit, the point, the edge, high, lowe, right, reuerſed, within, without. But, I ſee not howe one may practiſe any deceit with the dagger, the which is not openly daungerous . As for example, to widen it and difcouer ſome part of the bodie to the enemie, thereby prouoking him to moue, and then warding, to ſtrike him, being ſo diſapointed : but in my opinion, theſe ſortes of falſes of difcouering the bodie, ought not to be vſed : For it behoueth a man, firſt, ſafely to defend himſelfe , and then to offend the enimie, the which he cannot do , in the practiſe of the ſaid falſes, if he chaunce to deale with an enimie that is couragious and skilfull. But this manner of falſing next following, is to be practiſed laſt of all other, and as it were in deſperate caſes. And it is, either to faine, as though he would forcibly fling his dagger at the enemies face, (frō the which falſe, he ſhal doubtles procure the enemie to warde himſelfe , either by lifting vp his armes, or by retyring himſelf, or by mouing towards one ſide or other , in which trauaile & time, a man that is verie warie and nimble, may ſafely hurt him:) or els in ſteede of falſing a blowe, to fling the

the dagger in deede at the enimies face. In which chaunce or occasion, it is necessarie that he haue the skill how to sticke the dagger with the poynt. But yet howsoeuer it chaunce, the comming of the dagger in such sort, doth so greatly trouble and disorder the enemie, that if a man step in nimbly, he may safely hurt him.

These deceits and falses, of the sword and dagger, may be warded according as a man findes it most commodious either with the sworde, or els with the dagger, not regarding at all (as in true arte) to defend the left side with the dagger, and the right side with the sword : For in this false arte men consider not either of aduantage, time, or measure, but alwaies their manner is (as soone as they haue found the enimies sword) to strike by the most short waie, be it either with the edge, or point, notwithstanding the blowe be not forcible, but onely touch weakely & scarsly : for in plaie, so it touch any waie, it is accounted for victorie.

Concerning taking holdfast, or seising the enimies sword, I commend not in any case, that seisure be made with the left hand, by casting away of the dagger, as else where I haue seene it practised : but rather that it be done keeping the sword and dagger fast in hand. And although this seeme vnpossible, yet euery one that is nimble & strong of arme, may safely do it. And this seisure is vsed aswell vnder an edgeblowe, as vnder a thrust in manner following.

When the edgeblowe or thrust commeth aboue, it must be incountred with the sword without, on the third or fourth parte of the enimies sword, and with

Bb   the

the dagger borne within, on the firſt or ſecond parte thereof:hauing thus ſodenly taken the enimies ſword in the middle, to turne forciblie the enimies ſword outwardes with the dagger, keeping the ſword ſted-faſt, and as ſtreight towards the enimie as is poſsible by meanes whereof it may the more eaſely be tur-ned. And there is no doubt but the enimies ſworde may be wrong out of his hand,and looke how much nearer the poynt it is taken,ſo much the more eaſelie it is turned or wreſted outwards, becauſe it maketh the greater circle, and the enimie hath but ſmal force to reſiſt that motion.

Of Sword and Cloke, or Rapier
and Cloke.

OR to diſceyue the enimie with the cloake,it is neceſſarie to know how ma-ny waies it may ſerue the turne, and to be skilfull how to fould it orderly about the arme,and how to take aduantage by the largenes thereof; and farther to vnderſtand how to defend, and how to offend and hinder the enimie therewith, becauſe it fales not out alwaies, that men fight with their cloake wrapped about the arme, and the ſword in hand , Therefore it is the parte of a wiſe man, to knowe alſo how to handle the cloake after any other manner.

Wherefore one may get the aduátage of the cloke, both when it is about his bodie, and when it is fol-ded about his arme: The cloke being about the arme in this maner. When it chaunceth any man to bicker
with

with his enimie, with whom he is at poynt to ioyne,
but yet happelie weareth about him at that inftant no
kind of weapon, whereas his enimie is weaponed, &
threatneth him, then by taking both fides of the
cloake as neare the coller as is pofsible, he may draw
it ouer his owne head, and throwe it at his enimies
face, who then being intangled and blinded there
with, may either be throwen downe, or disfurni-
fhed of his weapon very eafely by him that is nimble,
efpecially if he haue to deale againft one that is flow.
A man may after an other manner take the aduantage
of the cloake which the enimie weareth, by taking
with one hande both fides thereof, neere the coller;
which fides being ftrongly holden, caufe the cloak to
be a ginne or fnare about the enimes necke, the which
ginne being violently haled, and plucked with one
hande, he may fo forciblie ftrike him with the other
on the face or vifage, that he will goe neere hande to
breake his necke.

There be manie other waies whereby one may
preuaile with the cloake, to the greateft parte whereof, men of meane iudgment may eafely attaine vnto.
Therefore when one hath his cloake on his arme, and
fword in his hand, the aduantage that he getteth therby, befides the warding of blowes, for that hath bene
declared in the true arte is, that he may moleft his enimie by falfing to fling his cloake, and then to flinge
it in deed. But to falfe the flingyng of the clok is verie
daungerous, becaufe it may not be done but in long
time. And the verie flinging of the cloake, is as it were
a preparation to get the victorie, and is in a manner
rather true art then deceit, cófidering it is don by the

Bb 2   ftrenght

ſtreyght or ſome other ſhorte line : neither for any other cauſe is this the rather here laide downe, in deceite, then before in true arte, then for that when one ouercometh by theis meanes, he ſeemes not to conquere manfully, becauſe he ſtrikes the enimie before blinded with the cloake. wherefore when one mindeth to flinge his cloake, he may either do it from and with his arme, or elſe with his ſword: and in ſo doing it is neceſſarie, that he haue not the cloake too much wrapped about his arme: I ſaie, not aboue twice, neither to hold it ſtreight or faſt with his hande, that thereby he may be the better able when occaſion ſerueth to fling it the more caſelie. If therefore he would fling it with his arme, and haue it goe with ſuch fury, and make ſuch effect as is required, he muſt of force ioyne to the flinging thereof the increaſe of a pace, on that ſide where the cloake is, but firſt of all he muſt incounter, either finde, either ſo enſure the enimies ſword, that by the meanes of the increaſe of that pace it may do no hurte.

And it is requiſite in euerie occaſion, that he finde himſelfe to ſtand without: and when either an edgeblow or a thruſt comes, be it aboue or in the middle, as ſoone as he hath warded it with his ſword, he ſhall increaſe a pace and fling his cloake, how ſoeuer it be folded, either from the coller, either from any other parte, or elſe to hale it off from his ſhoulder, although it bee on his ſhoulder: and in this order it is eaſelie throwne, & is thereby the more widned in ſuch ſort, that the enimie is the more entangled and ſnared therewith.

Concerning the flinging of the cloake with the ſword

sword,I faie,it may be throwen either with the point,
either with the edge : with the poynt when one standeth at the lowe warde with the right foote behinde,
and the cloake before : In which case the cloake
would be well and thicke doubled and placed on
the arme,but not wrapped.And in steed of driuing a
thrust with the poynt which shalbe hidden behinde
the cloake,he shal take the cloake on the poynt of the
sworde, and with the increase of a pace,force it at the
enimies face.. And in this maner the cloake is so forciblie,and so couertly deliuered and flinged,that the
enimie is neither a ware of it, neither can avoyde it,
but of force it lighteth on his face,by meanes whereof, he may be stroken at pleasure iu any parte of the
bodie.

The cloake may be flong or throwen with the
edge of the sworde, when one standeth at the lowe
warde, with the poynt of the sword turned backewardes, one the left side and the cloake vpon it, fol-
ded at large vpon the arme vp to the elbowe:but not
fast wrapped about it,and whilest he falseth a reuerse,
he may take the cloake on the edge of the sword and
fling it towards the enimie , and then strike him with
such a blow as shal be then most fit for his aduantage
deliuer.

Manie other deceites there might be declared of
the cloake, aswell of flinging as of falsing it : but because I thinke these to be sufficient for an example to
frame manie other by, I make an ende.

of

Of Sword and buckler, square Target and round Target.

Eing of opinion that as touching deceite, there is but one consideration to be had of all these three weapons, and for because all the difference which may be betwen them is laide downe and declared in the true arte, in the consideration of the forme of each ofthem: Therefore I am willing rather to restraine my selfe, then to indeuoure to fill the leafe with the idle repetirion of one thing twice.

All theis three weapons ought to be borne in the fist, the arme stretched out forwardes, and this is euidently scene in the square Target and buckler: the round Target also, because by reason of his greatnes and waight, it may not be holden in the onelie fist, & forwarde, in which kind of holding, it would warde much more is borne on the arme, being stretched foorth with the fist forwardes, which is in manner all one, or the selfe same. Therefore one may false as much with the one as with the other, considering there is no other false vsed with them then to discouer and frame diuers wards, bering no respect to any aduantage. And yet there is this difference betwene them, that with the round Target, one may easely warde both edgeblowes and thrustes, and with the square Target, better than with any other, he may warde edgeblowes, because it is of square forme; and the edge of the sword may easely be retained with the streight side thereof, which is not so easely done with the buckler: for ouer and besides the warding of thrustes, the buckler is not so sure of it self, but requireth

quireth aide of the sworde. Edge-blowes also when they come a thwart (for in that case, they incounter the circumference thereof: the which if it chaunce, the sword not to encounter on the diameter, or halfe, in which place the sword is onelie staied, but doth encounter it, either beneath, either aboue the saide diameter (maie easelie slippe and strike either the heade or thighs : therfore let euerie man take heede and remember, that in striking at the buckler, either with the poynte or edge of the sword, he deliuer it crossing or a thwarte.

As concerning the falses and deceites, which may be vsed in the handling of theis weapons, as at the single sworde, they are infinite, so at theis weapons they are much more, if the number of infinite may be exceded. For besides, that with the sword one may false a thrust, an edgeblowe, on high, alowe, within, without, and frame diuers other vnorderlie wardes, There remaineth one deceite or false properlie belóging vnto theis, which is, to beare the bukler, squar Target, or round Target, wide from the bodie, and therewithall to discouer himselfe, to the end the enimie may be hindred, and lose time in striking, being therewithal sure & nimble to defend himself & offéd the enimie. And this he may practise in euerie ward, but more easelie with the square Target than with the other two, because it is bigge and large inough, & may easelie encounter and find the enimies when it commeth striking: but this happeneth not in the rounde Target, because his forme is circuler, neither in the buckler, because, besides his roundnes, it is also small: by meanes of which two things, blowes are
very

very hardly encountred except a man be very much exercised in the handling thereof. And because there are two weapons, the one of offence, and the other of defence: it is to be considered, that when by meanes of a false thrust or edgblowe, the enimies round Target, square Target or buckler, is onely bound to his warde, and his sword remaines free and at libertie, one resolue not himselfe to strike immediatly after the falsed thrust, for then he may verie easelie be hurt by the enimies sword. Therefore let him remember for the most parte, to false such thrustes, against the which, besides the weapon of defence, the sword be also bound to his warde, or else to false edgeblowes from the knee downewards: for seeing the round target, or any of the other two, may not be vsed in that place, of force the sword must be there placed at his defence, which as soone as it is found, and thereby ensured that it may do no hurte, a man may then step forwardes, and deliuer such a blowe as he best may without daunger.

*An aduertisement concerning the defences
of the false of the round Target.*

EVerie time that one vseth to false with round Target, square Target, and buckler, or as I may better saie, with the sword accompanied with them, he falseth either an edge-blowe, either a thrust, either leaueth some parte of the bodie before discouered. Against all the falses of the edge, which come from the knee vpwards, the round Target or any of the rest, must be oppressed, and then
suddenly

suddenly vnder them a thrust be deliuered, againſt that parte which is moſt diſarmed. But if blowes come from the knee downwardes, they of force muſt be encountred with the ſword, and alwaies with the falſe, or backe edge thereof, whether that the blowe be right or reuerſed: & therewithall the enimies legge muſt be cutt with the edge prepared without mouing either the ſeete or bodie. And this manner of ſtriking is ſo ſhorte that it ſafely ſpedeth. Moreouer, all thruſts and other edgeblowes, aſwell high as lowe may, naie rather ought to be warded, by accompaning the tar- get or other weapon of defence with the ſword, whoſe poynt would be bent towards the enimie, & as ſoone as the enimies ſword is encountred, if it be done with the falſe edge of the ſword, there is no o- ther to be done, then to cut his face or legges.

But if the ſword be encountred with the right edge then if he would ſtrik with the edge, he muſt of force firſt turne his hand and ſo cute. And this manner of ſtriking and defending, doth properlie belong vnto the round Target, ſquare Target and buckler, and all other waies are but vaine and to ſmall purpoſe: for to encounter firſt and then to ſtrike, cauſeth a man to ſinde himſelfe either within the enimies Target or ſword, by which meanes he may eaſelie ſtrike, before either the ſword or Target may warde againe.

But if any man aske why this kind of blowe car- rieth ſmall force, and is but weake? I aunſwer, true it is, the blowe is but weake, if it were deliuered with an axe or a hatchet, which as they ſaie, haue but ſhort edges, and maketh but one kind of blowe, but if it be deliuered with a good ſword in the foreſaide

Cc   manner

manner, becaufe it beareth a long edge, it doth commodioufly cut, as foone as the edge hath founde the
enimies fword, and efpecially on thofe partes of the
bodie which are flefhly and full of finnowes. Therefore fpeaking of deceite or falfing, a man muft alwaies
with the fword and round Target and fuch like, goe
and encounter the enimies blowes, being accompanied to gether. And as foone as he hath found the
enimies fword, he fhall within it, eute either the face
or the leggs, without any farthar recouerie of his
fword, to the intent to deliuer either thruftes, or greater edgeblowes : for if one would both defende and
ftrike togeither, this is the moft fhorte waie that is.

But when the enimie difcouereth fome parte of
his bodie, thereby prouoking his aduerfary to ftrike,
and then would beate off the blowe and ftrike withall: in this cafe, either a man muft not ftrike if he per-
ceue not that his fword is more neare the enimy, then
his owne Target is to the enimies fword, or elfe if he
ftrik and be further off, he muft recouer his fword &
void the enimies blowe, ftriking comodioufly ether
aboud ether fome wher els. And it is a very eafie ma-
ter to lofe much time, for the Target and fuch like are
heauie, And if thefe motions meete with no obiect or fteye, they paffe beyond their ftrength. But if
it fo happen or chaunce, as I haue before faide, that a
man findes himfelfe more neare to hurte the enimi e,
then the enimie is readie to defend himfelfe, then he
muft not falfe a blow firft, & then recouer his fword,
but ftrik & drive it home at the firft, as refolutlie & as
nimblie as he may poffiblie: & this mmerof ftriking
pertaineth rather to true art then to deceit or falfing.

Of

162

HEIS kind of weapons haue ſo great libertie of ſtriking or warding, and are ſo
entermedled the one with the other, as
no other ſorte of weapon is, which I may
compare with theis. There may be fram-
ed an infinite cópanie of wardes with theis weapons,
and all of them ſure, except two, which are framed
and borne without, and are theis as followeth.

To bear both ſwords with their points backward:
for this maner of warding, is as if one would of purpoſe cauſe himſelfe to be ſlaine: or elſe to beare both
aloft, which a man may hardlie ſuſtaine, conſidering
the paizes of the ſwords are naturally heauie and tend
downewardes, ſo that the armes are much cumbred
thereby. Therefore from theis two which are framed
without, ſhalbe laide downe, all thoſe which may be
founde and may be framed in the handling of theis
weapons: as for example, high wardes, lowe, wide, altered, diminiſhed, and al thoſe wards which are mixt,
as to frame with one ſworde the high warde, with
the other the broad warde, and to frame the lowe
and broad warde, the high and lowe ward, two lowe
wardes, and two broade wardes : but yet theſe
laſt two are as painfull as the two high wardes, and
therefore ſhall not be vſed. Moreouer, a man may
beare one ſworde with the poynt forwards, and the
other backewards, and he may further, verie eaſely
finde out and practiſe diuers other waies, if he conſider in how manie waies a man way moue his hands

Cc 2

his

his armes, his feete, and his whole perfon: for each of theis motions are fufficient of themfelues, to alter the warde. In all theis wardes, he may with either hande and fword, practife to falfe againft the enimie, fometimes by fayning, fometimes by difcouerie. And this is properlie belonginge to theis weapons, to wit, to falfe with one, and to ftrike home, either with the felfe fame, or with the other weapon: & likewife difcouer with the one, and ward with the felfe fame, or with the other, the which neuer yet to this daie was or might be done with any other weapon. For in the handling of other weapons, that which falceth, doth in like manner ftrike home, fo that of force, there are fpent two times : for which confideration men hold opinion, that falfing is occafion both of great hurte, and alfo of loffe of time. But yet this happeneth not in thefe weapons, which forafmuch as they are two, and are of equall power both in ftriking and defending, may be handled both after one fafhion. And prefuppofing alwaies that one is as fkilful to handle the one afwel as the other, he may difcharge at felfe fame time two thruftes, two edgeblowes, both right & reuerfed.

But if he would exercife himfelfe onelie in fporte & plaie, he fhal then continually vfe to ftrike his enimie with one, and defend his perfon with the other. Therefore when one dealeth againft an enimie that hath two fwords, one of the which maie alwaies encreafe a pace, and ftrike either with a thruft, or with the edge, from that fword he muft take heede to warde himefelfe, for it is verie forcible, and alwaies bringeth great daunger and perill with it: The other
fworde

sword which was before, maketh no increase of pace
and therefore cannot strike more then the defence &
strength of the arme will beare, and that is weake to
strike, but yet verie strong to defend: and the self same
accidentes and qualities, which are found to be in
the enimie, are incident also to our selues. Wherefore
when one findes that he standeth with his right foot
before, be it in any warde whatsoeuer, he may false
with the forsword and strik home with the same, or
else he may false with his hinder sword, & strike with
the selfe same: or else after a third waie, to wite, to false
with the one, and hit home with the other: And this
kind of false, doth more properlie belong to the two
swords then any other, but yet he must take heede
and veriewell remember that whilest he falceth with
the one, and would also strike home with the same,
that he beare the other directly opposite against the
enimie. For whilest the enimy is bound to warde the
false, and homeblowe of the one sword, he may come
in with the other and strike, if he finde any place either discouered or easie to enter: So that bearing this
rule continuallie in remembrance, which is in the
fight of two swords, to beare alwaies the one directly against the enimie, to the entent to hinder him,
that he resolue not himself to enter, he shall indeuour
to false, sometimes with the one, and sometimes with
the other sword, some times a thrust, some times an
edgeblowe, and then to driue it home, either with
the same sword that falceth, or else with the other.
But in the practise, and doing of all this, it is required
that he be of deepe iudgement, knowing presently vpon the false, what parte of the bodie the enimie disco-

uereth, increaſing thither, and inueſting the enimie with that ſword which is moſt nigh to that parte, and with the which he may moſt ſafelie ſtrike.

And it is to be conſidered, that it is a verie ſtrong & ſhort waie of ſtriking, to falſe with the fore ſworde either a thruſt or an edgeblowe, and to falſe them not once or twice, but diuers times, now alofte, now beneath, ſome times with a thruſt, ſome times with an edgeblowe, to the entent, to blinde and occupie the enimies both ſwords, and at the laſt when fit occaſiō ſerueth, to ſtrike it home with the hinder ſworde: but yet alwaies with the encreaſe of a pace. The falce which may be practiſed with the hinder ſword, is vnprofitable being made without the motion of a pace, for it is ſo ſhorte that it is to no purpoſe. Therefore it cannot buſie the enimies ſwordes in ſuch manner, that it may force him either to diſcouer or diſorder his bodie. From whence it may be gathered, that after this falſe of the hinder ſword, it is no ſure plaie to ſtrike either with theſelfe ſame hinder ſword, or elſe with the fore ſword, becauſe the enimie was neither in any parte diſcouered or troubled. The beſt thing therfore that may be don, if one would falſe with the hinderſword, is, to driue either a thruſt or an edgeblow, reſolutelie ſtriking with the encreaſe of a pace, and as the enimie moueth to defend him ſelfe, to ſtrike him with the ſame ſworde, in ſome place that is diſcouered: For he cannot ſtrike with the other ſword, for that by meanes of the encreaſe of the hinder ſword, that ſword which was before, remaineth now behinde, So that it may not ſtrike, except it encreaſe a pace, and to encreaſe againe, were to ſpende much

much time. Therefore when one endeuoreth with the encrease of a pace to force his fword within, he fhall affaie to ftrike it home, with the felfe fame fword becaufe as I haue before faid, to ftrike with the other were to long. Wherefore I wil laie downe this for a rule, in the handling of theis weapons, that if a man falfe with the forefword, he may alfo ftrik home with the fame, or elfe with the other, fo that he increafe a pace. And if he falfe with the hinder fword, he fhall prefently, and refolutely force the blow home with the fame fword, but yet with the increafe of a pace: but if he doe not fullie deliuer it, he fhall againe procure immediatly to ftrike home with the felfe fame fword, either with a thruft, or edgeblowe, be it high or lowe, as at that inftant fhall be moft commodius to ferue the turne.

An aduertifement concerning the defenfes of the two Swordes, or Rapiers.

IN fport or plaie one may ftande euerie waie againft the enimie, to witte, if the enimie be on high, to fettle himfelfe at his warde, lowe or broad. But it is more gallant to beehold and more commodius indeed to place himfelf againft thenimy in the very felf fame manner as he findeth him, with the felf fame foote before, and in the very fame fite that he is in, either high or lowe. For ftanding in fuch manner, the enimie may hardly endeuour with his falfe, to troble or bufie both fwords. And moreouer it muft be confidered, that the fore fworde is that which wardeth

both

both falses, and resolute blowes, the which it doth verie easily perfourme : For if it be borne aloft, then by the bending of the point down, it defendeth that part of the bodie, to the which it is turned. Remembring therefore these rules, which are, to stand euery way as the enimie doth, & to warde his falses with the fore-sworde, I saie, where any falses or blowes come : then as soone as he hath warded them with the fore-sword, he shall encrease a slope pace, & with the hinder sworde deliuer either a thrust at some discoucred place, either a right blowe with the edge at the legges, or els (which is better) shall fetch a reuerse, either athwart the face, or els athwart the armes, and this blowe doth most easily speede : for the enimies fore-sworde is occupied, and his hinder sworde cannot come to oppose it selfe against this blowe : neither may it so easily strike, because (by encrease of the foresaid slope pace) the bodie is moued out of the straight lyne, so that the enimie may not so commodiously strike with his hinder sword, but that he shalbe first stricken on the face or on the armes.

Wherefore, let euery man resolue himselfe, (as soone as he hath encountred the enimies sword with his owne foresworde) that he step in and strike with his hinder sworde. Neither, let him stand in feare of the enimies hinder sworde : for either it cannot hurt because the bodie is voyded (as I haue saide,) or els, if it may, it must presently prouide to stand to his defence, and thereto is so bound, that it may do no manner of hurte.

Of

168

Or the deceites & falſes of the two hande ſworde, there is no more regarde to be taken in the handling thereof ſingle, that is, one to one, then there is, when it is vſed among manie: onelie this end is to be purpoſed, to witte, to moue and handle with all nimbleneſſe and dexterity, aſwel the edge as the poynt, fetching thoſe great circuler and vnruly compaſsinges, therewith as his fourme, greatneſſe, and manner of holding requireth.

Nether ought a man ſo much to regard to fetch a ſmall or great compaſſe, or to ſtrike more with the point, then with the edg, but muſt belieue onely that the victorie conſiſteth in the nimble and actiue guiding thereof anie manner of waie. Therefore there may be framed manie wards, of al the which, beinge a thinge ſuperfluous to reaſon of, I will handle onely ſixe of them, which are moſt commodius and vſuall: wherof the firſt may be called the high warde, the ſecond the broad warde, the third, the low warde, from which there ſpringeth all other three, towardes the other ſide, making ſixe in all.

The high warde is framed by bearing the ſworde and arms lifted vp on high and wide from the body, with the poynt of ſword turned towardes that parte, as that arme is, whoſe hand is placed by the croſſe, that is to ſaie, if the right hand ſhalbe at the croſſe, & the right foote befoore, to beare alſo the ſword, with his poynt towardes that ſide.

There is an other hie warde oppoſite to this & that is, without mouing the feete at all to turne the poynt towardes the other ſide, that is, towardes the left ſide

D d   and

and to crosse the armes. And it is to be noted, that in this high warde, be it on what side it wil, the sword is to be borne with the poynt turned downewardes.

The second is the broad warde, & must be framed with the armes widened from the body, not high but straight. And from this springeth and is framed another broad warde, turned towards the other side by crossing of the armes.

The third is the lowe warde, and in this the sword would be borne with the poynt some what vppwardes. And this warde hath his opposite or contrarie, by turning the sword on the other side, and crossing the armes. There may be framed manie other wardes: As for example, to beare the sword on high, with the poynt backewardes, to the entent to driue a downe right, or cleauing edge-blowe: or else to beare it lowe with the poynt backwardes, to the entent to driue it from beneath vpwards. But in theese wardes falses are to small purpose: And if there be any one of them worth the vsing, it should be the false of an edgeblowe, the which at the two hand sworde is not to be vsed at all, because there is much time lost considering that immediatlie after the false, he must strike home with an edgeblow. For it is not commodius at the two hand sword, to false an edgeblowe, & deliuer home a thrust, because the waight or swing of the sword in deliuering an edge-blowe, transporteth the arms beyond their strength, so that they may verie difficultlie withhold the blow to such purpose, that they may be able as it were in that instant to deliuer a thrust. Therefore the false that should be vsed at the two hand sword, ought alwaies to be framed with

with a thrust, and then an edgeblow right or reuersed
to be deliuered, or else to false a high thrust, and deliuer it beneath or else where.   But yet if one would
needes false an edgeblowe, let him do it with the false
edge of the sword, then turning it in full circle, to deliuer home the edgeblowe, and in striking alwaies to
encrease a pace.   But when this false of the backe or
false edge is practised, the armes being crossed, & that
presentlie after the false, one would deliuer home a
reuerse, then he must encrease a left pace, And when
he findeth in himself any other warde; his hands not
being crossed, then if he would step forwards to strike
he must encrease a pace with the right foote. And if in
any of theese wardes he would false a thrust, which
is the best that may be ysed at the two hand sword, he
must obserue the verie same notes and rules concerning encreasing of the pace.   Further the thrust is falsed, and the edge-blowe deliuered home at the two
hand sword for no other cause or consideration, then
for that the saide edgeblowe is farre more forcible
then the thrust : For the two hand sword is long, by
meanes whereof, in the deliuerie of the edgeblow, it
maketh a great circle. And moreouer, it is so weightie
that verie litle and small strength, maketh & forceth
the blow to goe with great violence. But for as much
as the striking with the edge is verie daungerous cō-
sidering it spendeth much time, and especially in the
great compassing of the two hand sworde, vnder
which time warie & actiue persons may with sword
or other wepon giue a thrust, Therefore for the avoi-
ding of this dager, he must before he determin with
himself to strik with the edg, first driue on a thrust, ra-

                              D d 2   ther

171

ther resolut then falsed, and as farr forwardes as bo th armes will stretch. In doing of the which, he shal force the enimie to retire so much, that he may easely there-vpon deliuer his edgeblowe with the encrease of a pace, nothing douting that the enimy wil strike home first with a thrust. Therefore when one standeth at the high warde, on either side he must false a thrust, & encrease a pace deliuering there withal such an edge-blowe, as shal be most commodius to serue his turne, either right or reuersed. And further may practise the like in the broad and lowe wardes, in either of the which, it is more easye to false the said thrust, then in the other.

And it is to be considered, when the edgeblow af-ter the falced thrust, is by a slope voided, that he suf-fer not his arms and sword by reason of the waight or swinge thereof, to be so farr transported beyonde his strength, that the sword light ether on the groud or that he be forced thereby to discouer all that parte of his bodie which is before. Therefore the best re-medie is, as soone as he shal perceiue that he hath de-liuered his blowe in vaine, that he suffer his sword to go (not with a full thwarte circle, and so about his head) vntill the poynt be backwardes beneath in such sort, that the circle or compasse direct him to the high warde, in the which he may presently resolue himself and returne either to strike againe, or else defend him selfe on either side, so handling his weapon, as shal in that case be most for his aduantage.

The

He defences of the two hand ſworde require
a ſtout hearte, for that the ſuſteining of
ſuch great bl owes, by reaſon whereof, a man
conſidereth not the aduātage of time, being the moſt
principal thing of al, cauſeth him to flie or retire backe
holding for a certaintie that euerie blowe giuen therwith, is not poſſible to be warded. Therefor when he
dealeth againſt an enimie, who vſeth likewiſe the two
hand ſword, he ſhall appoſe himſelfe in the low ward:
And when a falſe thruſt commeth, if it come ſo fare
forwardes that it may ioyne home, he ought firſt to
beate it off, and then to forſe a thruſt at the enimies
face, or deliuer an edgeblow downwards at the armes
but not lifting vp the ſword in a cōpaſſe. But for that
theeſe falced thruſtes for the moſt part are farr off, &
come not to the bodie, being vſed onelie to fere the
enimie, and cauſe him to retire, that therby one may
haue the more time to deliuer an edge-blow with the
encreaſe of a pace (which pace cauſeth the blowe to
go with greater violence:)nd farther may diſcern &
iudge, by neareneſſe of the enimy, whether the blow
will hit home yea or no, for it is eaſelie knowen howe
much the armes may be ſtretched forth : Therefore
when this falſe thruſt doth not ioyne or hit home, he
ought not to endeuour to beate it off, but to expect
when his enimie deliuereth his edgeblowe, & then
to encreaſe a pace, and ſtrike him with a thruſt.

But if it happen him to deale againſt a two hande
ſworde, with a ſingle ſword or dagger, aſſuring him
ſelfe that the two hand ſword cannot ſtrike but with a
thruſt or an edgeblow , for the defence of the thruſt

D d 3 he

he may beate it off and retire himselfe, but if it be an
edgeblowe, then, as soone as the two hand sword is
lifted vp, in the same time he must encrease forwards
and deliuer a thrust, or else if he haue no time to strike
he must encounter & beare the blow in the first parte
of the sworde, which is neare the hiltes, taking holde
thereof with one hande, and striking with the other.
And this he may performe, if he be nimble & actiue,
because the two hand sword carieth but smal force in
that place.

Of the Partesan, Bil, Iauelin
and Holberde.

DEceites or falses, are all more manifest and
euident in these, then in shorte weapons
which are handled onely with one hand because both the arms are moued more slow-
ly then one alone. And the reason thereof is, that cō-
sidering they are more long, they therefore frame in
their motions a greater compasse: and this is perceiued more in edgeblowes then in thrustes. Therefore
the best false that may be practised in the handling of
these weapons, is the false of the thrust, and that the
edgeblow ought neuer or seldome to be vsed, except
great necessitie constrain, as shalbe declared. Wherefore in these weapons, I wil frame foure wards, three
of them with the poynt forwardes, of which three,
the first is, the poynt of the sword being borne lowe,
and the hinder arme being lifted vpp.

The second is, the poynt high, the right arme being
behinde and borne alowe.

The

174

The third, the poynt equall and the armes equall: And in euerie on of these a man must false without, and driue it home within, or false within and deliuer it without, or false aloft and strike beneth, & so contrariewise. But as he falseth within or without, he ought to remember this note, which is, he must alwaies to the entent he may goe the better couered & warded, compasse the hinderfoot to that parte, to the which the weapon shalbe directed to strike home after a false.

The fourth warde which is much vsed, and especially with the bill, shalbe to beare the weapon with the blunt ende or heele forwardes, the edge being lifted vpp on high. And this is much vsed, to the entent to expect the enimies blowes, and that thereby a man may be better able to warde them, either with the heel or midle of the staff, & then to enter & strik deliuering an edgblo with thencreas of a pace, the which maner of striking is most ready and nimble. The false, which may be vsed in this ward, is whē he hath warded thenimies blo with the heel of his wepon, & thē would encrease forwardes to deliuer an edgeblowe, if the enimie shall lift vpp or aduance his weapon to defend himselfe from the said blowe, then he shall giue ouer to deliuer that blowe, by retiring his weapon, and giue a thrust vnderneath, with the encrease of a pace.

And this kind of blowe is verie likely to work his effect without danger, if it be aptly and nimbly vsed.

of

THere may be vſed ſome deceite alſo in the Pike, although it be a weapon voide of any crooked forkes, and is much more apte to ſhew great valure then deceite. And for as much as it hath no other then a poynt to offend, and length to defend, for that cauſe there may be vſed no other deceit therewith, then with the poynt: & conſidering true art, is not the mark that is ſhot at in this place: I ſaie, it may be borne after diuers faſhions, as ſhalbe moſt for a mannes aduantage, as either at the ende, either in the midle, either more backewardes, either more forwardes, as ſhal be thought moſt commodius to the bearer. Likewiſe, one may frame three wardes therewith, to witte, the firſt ſtreight, with the arms equall: the ſecond with the poynt low, the third, the poynt high, falſing in each of them a thruſt, either within, either without, ether high, either lowe, and then immediatly forcing it on reſolutely, but contrarie to the falſe, and carying alwais the hinder foote towardes that ſide, to the which the Pike is directed to ſtrike. In handling of the pike, a man muſt alwaies diligentlie conſider, ſo to worke that the hinder hand be that which may rule, driue on, draw back and gouerne the Pike, and that the fore-hand ſerue to no other purpoſe then to helpe to ſuſteine it.

The defences of the deceites of the
weapons of the Staffe.

I Haue not as yet laide downe the defence of the Bil, and the reſt, becauſe they are all-one with this of the Pike. And I minde to handle them briefelie all togeither, conſidering that in theſe **a man**

a man may not either render falfe for falfe, or take holdfaft of the weapon. And although it might bee done, I commend it not, becaufe it is a verie difficult matter to extort a weapon that is holden faft with both handes. That therefore which one may doe to defend himfelfe, is to haue recourfe vnto true Art, remembring fo to warde the enimies falce, as if it were a true blowe, and to ftrike before the enimie fpend an other time, in deliuering his refolute thruft, And to take heede in deliuerie of his blowes, that he be nimble and carrie his bodie and armes fo aptlie and orderlie applied, that the weapon wherewith he ftriketh may couer it wholy.

And here I make an ende of difceit, in practifing of the which, there is this confideration to be had, fo, alwaies to falfe, that if the enimie prouide not to ward, it may reach & hit home, becaus being deliuered in fuch order, it lofeth but little time.

The ende of the false Arte.

How a man by priuat practife may
obtain strength of bodie therby

I F nature had beftowed ftrength vpon men (as manie beleeue) in fuch forte as fhe hath giuen fight, hearing and other fences, which are fuch in vs, that they may not by our endeuour either be encreafed, or diminifhed, it fhould be no leffe fuperfluous, then ridiculus to teach howe ftrength fhould be obtained, then it were if one fhould fay, he would inftruct a man how to heare and fee better then he doth alreadie by nature. Neither albeit he that becommeth a Painter or a Mufition feeth the propor-

E e   tion

177

tions much better then he did before, or by hearing ler-
neth the harmonie and conformitie of voices which he
knew not, ought it therefore be saide, that he seeth or heareth more then he did ? For that procedeth not of better hearing or seeing, but of seeing and hearing with
more reason . But in strength it doth not so come to
passe : For it is manifestlie seene , that a man of ripe
age and strength, cannot lift vpp a waight to daie which
he canne doe on the morrowe, or some other time. But
contrarie , if a man proue with the selfe same sight on the
morroe or some other time to see a thing which yesterday
he sawe not in the same distance, he shall but trouble himselfe in vaine, and be in daunger rather to see lesse then
more, as it commonlie happeneth to studentes and other
such, who do much exercise their sight. Therefore there is
no doubt at all but that mans strength may be encreased
by reasonable exersise, And so likewise by too much rest
it may be diminished : the which if it were not manifest,
yet it might be proued by infinite examples. You shall see
Gentlemen, Knights and others, to bee most strong and
nimble, in running or leaping, or in vawting, or in turning
on Horse-backe, and yet are not able by a great deale to
beare so great a burthen as a Cuntrie man or Porter : But
contrarie in running and leaping, the Porter and Cuntrie-
man are most slow and heauie, neither know they howe to
vawte vpon their horse without a ladder, And this procedeth of no other cause, then for that euerie man is not exercised in that which is most esteemed: So that if in the managing of these weapons, a man would gette strength, it
shalbe conuenient for him to exercise himselfe in such sort
as shalbe declared.

For the obtaining of this strength and actiuitie, three
things ought to be considered, to witte, the armes, the
feete and the leggs, in each of which it is requisite that euerie one be greatlie exercised, considering that to know wel
how to mannage the armes, and yet to bee ignorant in the
motion of the feete, wanting skill how to goe forwardes
and

and retire backewardes, causeth men oftentimes to ouer-throwe themselues.

And on the other side, when one is exercised in the go-uerning of his feete, but is ignorant in the timelie motion of his armes, it falleth out that he goeth forwards in time, but yet wanting skill how to moue his armes, he doth not onelie not offend the enimie, but also manie times remai-neth hurte and offended himself. The bodie also by great reason ought to be borne and susteyned vpon his founda-tion. For when it boweth either too much backewardes or forwardes, either on the on or other side, streight waie the gouernment of the arms and leggs are frustrate and the bodie, will or nill, remaineth striken. Therefore I will declare the manner first how to exercise the *Armes*, se-condlie the *Feete*, thirdly the *Bodie*, *Feete* & *Armes*, ioynly;

*Of the exercise and strength
of the armes.*

ET a man be neuer so strong and lustie, yet he shall deliuer a blowe more slowe and with lesse force then an other shall who is lesse strong, but more exercised: & without doubt he shall so werie his armes, handes and bodie, that he cannot long endure to labour in any such busines. And there hath beene manie, who by reason of such sud-den wearines, haue suddenlie dispaired of themselues, gi-uing ouer the exercise of the wepon, as not appertaining vnto them. Wherein they deceiue themselues, for such wearines is vanquished by exercise, by meanes whereof it is not long, but that the bodie feete & armes are so strengh-ned, that heauie things seem light, & that they are able to handle verie nimblie anie kinde of weapon, and in briefe ouercome all kind of difficulty and hardnesse. Therefore when one would exercise his armes, to the entent to gette strength, he must endeuour continuallie to ouercome wea-rines, resoluing himselfe in his iudgement, that paines is

Ee 2   not

179

not cauſed, through debilitie of nature, but rather hangs a-
bout him, becauſe he hath not accuſtomed to exerciſe his
members thereunto.

There are two things to be conſidered in this exerciſe,
to wit the hand that moueth, and the thing that is moued,
which two things being orderlie laid downe, I hope I ſhall
obtaine as much as I deſire. As touching the hand and
arme, according as I haue alreadie ſaide, it was deuided in
the treatiſe of the true Arte, in three partes, that is to ſaie,
into the wriſt, the elbowe, and the ſhoulder, In euerie of
the which it is requiſite, that it moue moſt ſwiftlie and
ſtronglie, regarding alwaies in his motion the qualitie of
the weapon that is borne in the hande, the which may be
infinite, and therefore I will leaue them and ſpeake onelie
of the ſingle ſword, becauſe it beareth a certaine proportion and agreement vnto all the reſt.

The ſword as each man knowes, ſtriketh either with the
poynt or with the edge. To ſtrike edgewiſe, it is required
that a man accuſtome himſelfe to ſtrike edgewiſe as well
right as reuerſed with ſome cudgell or other thing apt for
the purpoſe, Firſt practiſing to fetch the compaſſe of the
ſhoulder, which is the ſtrongeſt, and yet the ſloweſt edgeblowe that may be giuen: Next and preſentlie after, the cōpaſſe of the elbowe, then that of the wriſt, which is more
preſte and readie then any of the reſt. After certaine daies
that he hath exerciſed theſe three kindes of compaſſing
edgeblows on after an other as ſwiftly as he may poſſible
And when he feleth in him ſelfe that he hath as it were vn-
loſed all thoſe three knittings or ioyntes of the arme, and
can ſtrike and deliuer ſtronglie from two of thoſe ioyntes,
to witte the *Elbowe* & the *Wriſt*, he ſhal then let the *Shoulder*
ioynt ſtand, and accuſtome to ſtrike ſtronglie and ſwiftlie
with thoſe two of the *Elbow* and the *Wriſt*, yet at the lengh
and in the ende of all ſhal onlie in a maner practiſe that
of the *VVriſt*, when he perceiueth his hand-wriſt to
be well ſtrengthened, deliuering this blowe of the *Wriſt*,
twice or thrice, ſometimes right, ſometims reuerſed, once
right

180

right, and once reuersed, two reuerses and one right, and
likewise, two right and one reuersed, to the ende that the
hande take not a custome to deliuer a righte blowe immediatlie after a reuerse. For sometimes it is commodius,
and doth much aduantage a man to deliuer two right, and
two reuersed, or else after two right, one reuersed : and
these blowes, ought to be exercised, as well with one hand
as with the other, standing stedfast in one resonable pace,
practising them now alofte, now beneath, now in the middle. As touching the waight or heft, which is borne in the
hande, be it sword or other weapon, I commend not their
opinion any waie, who will for the strengthning of a mans
arme that he handle first a heauie weapon, because being
first vsed to them, afterwardes, ordinarie weapons will
seeme the lighter vnto him, but I think rather the contrarie, to wite, that first to the end, he doe not ouer burthen
& choak his strength, he handle a verie light sword, & such
a one, that he maie most nimblie moue. For the ende of
this arte is not to lifte vp or beare great burdens, but to
moue swiftelie. And there is no doubt but he vanquisheth
which is most nimblie, and this nimblenesse is not obtained by handling of great heftes or waightes, but by often
mouing.

But yet after that he hath sometime trauailed with a
light weapon, then it is necessarie according as he feeleth
himselfe to increase in strength of arme, that he take an o-
ther in hande, that is something heauier, and such a one as
will put him to a little more paine, but yet not so much,
that his swiftnes in motion be hindred thereby. And as his
strength encreaseth, to encrease likewise the waight by litle and litle. So will it not be long, but that he shalbe able
to mannage verie nimblie any heauie sword. The blowe of
the poynt or the thrust, cannot be handled without the
consideration of the feete and body, because the strong deliuering of a thrust, consisteth in the apt and timelie motion of the armes feete and bodie : For the exercise of which,
it is necessarie that he knowe how to place them in euerie

of the three wardes, to the ende, that from the warde he
may deliuer strongly a thrust in as little time as is possible.
And therefore he shall take heede that in the low warde, he
make a reasonable pace, bearing his hande without his
knee, forsing on the thrust nimblie, and retiring his arme
backward, and somewhat encreasing his forefoote more
forwardes, to the end, the thrust may reach the farther: But
if he chance to increase the forefoot a litle too much, so
that the breadth thereof be painfull vnto him, then for the
auoiding of inconueniences, he shall draw his hinderfoot
so much after, as he did before increase with the forefoote,
And this thrust must be oftentimes ierked or sprong forth,
to the end to lengthen the arme, accustoming to driue it
on without retyring of it selfe, that by that meanes it may
the more readily settle in the broad warde, For that is framed (as it is well knowen) with the arme & foote widened
outwards, but not lengthened towards the enimie. And in
thrusting let him see, that he deliuer them as straight as he
can possibly, to the end, they may reach out the longer.

At what time one would deliuer a thruste, it is requisite that he moue the body & feete behind, so much in
a compasse, that both the shoulders, arme & feet, be vnder
one selfsame straight lyne. Thus exercisinge him selfe
he shal nimbly deliuer a verie great & strong thrust. And
this manner of thrusting ought oftentimes to be practised,
accustoming the bodie & feete (as before) to moue in a
compasse: for this mocion is that which instructeth one,
how he shall voide his bodie. The thrust of the high warde
is hardest of all other, nor of it selfe, but because it seemes
that the high ward (especially with the right foote before)
is verie painfull. And because there are few who haue the
skil to place themselues as they ought to deliuer the thrust
in as little time as is possible. The first care therefore in
this ward is, so to place himselfe, that he stande steddily.
And the syte thereof is in this manner, to wite: To stande
with the arme aloft, and as right ouer the bodie as is possible, to the end he may force on the thrust without drawing

ing back of the arme or loosing of time. And whilest the arme is borne straight on high (to the end it may be borne the more streight, & with lesse paines) the feete also would stand close and vnited together, & that beecause, this ward is rather to strike than to defend, and therefore it is necessarie that it haue his increase prepared: so that when the thrust is discharged, he ought therevvithall to increase the forefoote so much that it make a reasonable pace, and then to let fal the hand down to the lovve vvarde, from the which if he would depart againe, and assend to the high vvard, he must also retire his forefoot, neer vnto the hinder foote, or els the hinderfoote to the forefoot, And in this manner he shall practise to deliuer his thrust oftentimes alvvaies placing himselfe in this high vvarde vvith his feet vnited, discharging the thrust vvith the increase of the fore foot. But when it seems tedious and painfull to frame this vvarde, then he must vse, for the lengthninge of his arme, to fasten his hande and take houldefast on some nooke or stafe, that standeth out in a wall, as high as he may liftvpp his arme, turning his hand as if he held a svvord, for this shall helpe very much to strengthen his arme, and make his bodie apt to stand at his vvarde. Novv when he hath applied this excercise, for a reasonable time, so that he may perceiue by himselfe that he is nimble and actiue in deliuering these blovves and thrusts simplie by themselues, then he shall practise to compound them, that is to saie: after a thrust to deliuer a right blovve from the vvrist, then a reuerse, and after that an other thrust, alwaies remembring when he deliuereth a blovve from the vvrist, after a thrust to compasse his hinderfoote, to the end, the blovve may be the longer: And when, after this right blovve, he vvould discharge a reuerse, he must encrease a slope pace, that presently after it, he maie by the encrease of a streight pace, forse on a stronge thrust vnderneath. *And* so to exercise himselfe to deliuer manie of those orderlie blovves togeither, but yet alvvaies vvith the true motion of the feet and bodie, and vvith as great nimblenesse, and in as shorte

time

time as is possible, taking this alwaies for a most sure and certaine rule, that he moue the armes & feete, keeping his body firme and stedfast, so that it go not beastly forwarde, (and especially the head being a member of so great importance) but to keepe alvvaies his bodie bovved rather backvvard than forvvard, neither to turne it but onely in a compasse to voide blovves and thrustes.

More ouer, it shall not be amisse, after he hath learned to strike, (to the end to strengthen his armes) if he cause an other to force at him, either vvith a cudgell, or some other heauie thing, both edgeblovves & thrustes, and that he encounter & sustaine them vvith a svvorde, & ward thrustes by auoyding his bodie, and by encreasing forvvardes. And likevvise vnder edgeblovves, either strike before they light, or els encounter them on their first partes, vvith the encrease of a pace, that thereby he may be the more readie to deliuer a thrust, and more easily sustaine the blovve. Farther, vvhen he shall perceiue, that he hath conueniently qualified and strengthned this instrument of his bodie, it shall remaine, that he onely haue recourse in his minde to the fiue aduertisements, by the vvhich a man obtaineth iudgement. And that next, he order and gouerne his motions according to the learning & meaning of those rules. And aftervvardes take aduise of himselfe hovy to strike & defend, knovving the aduantage in euery perticular blow. And there is no doubt at all, but by this order he shall attaine to that perfection in this Arte vvhich he desireth.

FINIS.

VINCENTIO
SAVIOLO

his Practife.

In two Bookes.

*The firſt intreating of the vſe of the Rapier
and Dagger.*

*The ſecond, of Honor and honorable
Quarrels.*

LONDON
Printed by IOHN WOLFF.
1 5 9 5.

TO
THE RIGHT
HONORABLE MY

singular good Lord, *Robert* Earle
of Eſſex and Ewe, Viſcount Hereford, Lord Ferrers of Chartley,
Bourghchier and Louain, *Maſter of*
the Queenes Maieſties *horſe,Knight*
of the moſt noble order of the Garter,
and one of her Highneſſe moſt honorable
Priuie Councell.

Auing of late,
(right Hono-
rable) compi-
led this ſimple
Diſcourſe, of
managing we-
pons,and dea-
ling in honorable Quarrels(which
I eſteeme an Introduction to Mar-

A 3 tiall

tiall affayres) I haue thought good
to dedicate the same vnto your
Honor, as vnto him whose bountie
most bindeth me : whose valour in-
forceth all soldiers to acknowledge
you the English *Achilles* : whose
fauouring good literature celebra-
teth your name for the students
Mecenas : whose benigne potecti-
on and prouision for strangers, maketh you reported off as theyr safe
sanctuary. This work, I must needs
confesse, is farre vnworthie your
Lordships view, in regard eyther
of method or substance : and being
much vnperfecter than it shoulde
haue beene, if I had had copie of
English to haue expressed my meaning as I would. But I humbly beseech your good Lordship to accept this Booke, howsoeuer it be, as
a new

The Epiſtle Dedicatorie.
a new yeeres gifte proceeding from
a minde moſt dutifully affected towards you, that wiſheth and pray-
eth, that your Honour may inioy
many good and proſperous yeres :
and is preſented by him that is and
will be readie euerie yere, daie, and
houre to liue and die at your
Lordſhips foot to
do you ſer-
uice.

Your Honors in all dutifulnes,

Vincentio Sauiolo.

TO THE READER.

HE meanes whereby men from time to time haue bene preferred euen to the higheſt degrees of greatnes and dignitie, haue euer bene and are of two ſortes, Armes and Letters : weapons & bookes, as may moſt plainly bee proued out of antique and moderne hiſtories. Let it not ſeeme ſtrange vnto anie man that I haue placed Armes before Letters, for in truth I haue found by obſeruing the courſe of times, and by comparing the occurrents of former ages with thoſe which haue fallen out and followed (as it were by ſucceſsion) in later yeeres, that the firſt Princes and patrones of people did obtaine their titles and dominions by force of Armes, and that afterwards learning & vertue did (as it were by degrees) grow and ſucceede for the making and eſtabliſhing of good orders, cuſtomes, and lawes amongeſt them. And then did common-wealths begin firſt to flouriſh, when their Princes were like Minerua, whom the Poets fained to bee the goddeſſe not onely of ſtudies but alſo of Armes, irſpiring wit into ſchollers, and fauoring thoſe that follow warres. Wherefore knowing that ſuch

B.

men

To the Reader.

men as endeuour themselues to attaine vnto the excelleneie of anie art or science, are worthie both of praise and preferment, because they seeke for that onely true nobilitie, which is in deede much more to be accounted of than birth and parentage. I haue beene induced (for the satisfaction of such, and other like noble spirites, desirous to imploie either their studies in the profession, or their liues in the practise of the arte militarie) to bestowe my paines in the writing of this Treatise concerning the Art, exercise, and manneging of the Rapier and Dagger, together with the ordering and mouing of the bodie in those actions: A thing I confesse in shewe the least peece and practise (as a man might saie) of the arte Militarie, but in verie deed to most important, excellent, and noble practise thereof. For when I consider with my selfe how some Authors doo write, that hunting, hauking, wrastling, &c. are things in some sort belonging vnto Militarie profession, for that men thereby doo both make their bodies strong and actiue, and also learne to marke the scituation of hils, woods, lakes, and vallies, together with the crooked and turning courses of riuers. It seemeth vnto mee that I may with farre greater reason saie that the Arte and exercise of the Rapier and Dagger is much more rare and excellent than anie other Militarie exercise of the bodie, because there is very great and necessarie vse thereof, not onely in generall warres, but also in particular combats, & many other accidents, where a man hauing the perfect knowledge and practise of this arte, although but small of stature and weake of strength, may with a little remouing of his foot, a sodain turning of his hand, a slight declining of his bodie, subdue and ouercome the fierce brauing pride of tall and strong bodies.

Moreuer, it doth many times come to passe that discords and quarrels arise amongest souldiers and Gentlemen of honor & accounts, the which (when they cannot be accorded & com-
pounded

192

To the Reader.

pounded by lawe, learning, and perswasion) must bee determined, and the truth thereof tried by armes and combat. And therefore he that is wise, carefull of his safetie, and provident against danger, will be at all times stored and furnished with this honorable urgent necessity, and instant shortnes of time, he shal be constrained to expose himselfe unto euident danger.

Wherefore upon these occasions, and also for that I haue bin thereunto requested by sundrie Gentlemen my good friendes, I haue endeuoured to expresse in this discourse, and to make plain by pictures all the skill and knowledge which I haue in this art: Exhorting all men of good mindes and noble spirites to learne and purchase the same, not to the end to abuse it in insolencies and iniuries, but to use it in cases of necessitie for the defence of iust causes, and to the maintenance of the honour of themselues and others. For whosoeuer will followe this profession must flie from rashnes, pride, and iniurie, and not fall into that foule falt and error which many men incurre, who feeling themselues to be strong of bodie and expert in this science, presuming thereupon, thinke that they may lawfully offer outrage and iniury unto anie man, and with crosse and grosse termes and behauiour prouoke euerie man to fight, as though they were the onely heirs of Mars, & more inuincible than Achilles: not remembring how it hath oftentimes happened, that a little wretched man of stature by skill and reason hath ouercome a vast mightie man of person, and ouerthrowen the unweldie masse and burthen of his bodie upon the face of his kind & liberall mother the earth. This manner of proceeding and behauiour doth plainely shew that these men (although peraduenture they haue learned the use of the weapon) haue not yet beene sufficiently instructed in the Arte of Armes. For by the rule and precept of this Art, men are taught by how much they are resolute in courage, and skilful of the use of the same weapon, by so much the more to shew

B 2

them.

To the Reader.

themselues vertuous, humble, and modest both in speech & action, and not to be liers, vanters, or quarrellers, for those which in this sort demeane themselues, (notwithstanding their skill or courage) do commonly carry away wounds and dishonor, and sometimes death.

I haue seene and noted in diuerse partes of mine owne countrie and in other places of the world, great quarrells springing from small causes, and many men slayne vppon light occasions. Amongest other things, I remember that in Liesena a citie of Sclauonia, it was once my chance to see a sodaine quarrell and slaughter vpon very small cause betweene two Iialian captaines of great familiaritie and acquaintance. There was in the companie a foolish boy belonging vnto one of the Captaines, who going carelesly forward, & approching neere vnto the other captaine, began to touch the hilts of his sword, whereupon the captaine lent the boy a little blow to teach him better maners: The other Captaine (the boies master) taking this reprehension of his boy in worse parte than there was cause, after some wordes multiplyed began to drawe his sword, the other Captaine in like sort betaking himselfe to his rapier did with a thrust run him quite through the bodie, who falling downe dead vpon the place receiued the iust reward of his friuolous quarrell. And to confesse the plaine truth in this point, it is not well done either of men or boyes to touch the weapons of another man that weareth them. Neuerthelesse a man ought in all his actions to seeke and endeuour to liue in peace and good agreement (as much as may be) with euerie one : and especially he that is a Gentleman and conuerseth with men of honorable quality, must aboue all others haue a great regard to frame his speech and answeres with such respectiue reuerence, that there neuer growe against him anie quarrell vpon a foolish worde or a froward answere; as it often hath and daily doth come to passe; whereupon follow deadly hatreds,

194

To the Reader.

treds, cruell murthers, and extreame ruines. Wherefore I saie and set downe as a most vndoubted truth, that it is good for euerie man to be taught and instructed in the Rapier and Dagger, not the rather thereby to grow insolent, or to commit murther, but to be able and ready in a case of iust necessitie to defend himselfe, either at the sodaine, or vpon defiance and in field assigned : for at that time it is too late to looke backe and to intend this studie, as many doo, who hauing appointed the time and place for fight, doe practise some point or other of this arte, the which being so lightly learned and in such hast, doth afterwards in time of need proue but little helpfull or auailable vnto them. But this knowledge doeth more particularly appertayne vnto Gentlemen and souldiers that professe and followe warres, for they more than other men, will (for the credite of their calling, and the honor of Armes) dispute and determine with the point of the sword all points that passe in controuersie, especially amongest themselues, who had rather die than not to haue reason and satisfaction for euerie worde of preiudice and disgrace offered vnto them. Now in this case I am to exhort and aduise men of all sortes and condition , as well the skilfull as the vnskilfull, not to bee in anie wise too suspitious, nor to catch (as they saie) at euerie flie that passeth by, for in so dooing, they purchase to themselues endlesse trouble, and enter into actions full of danger and dishonour, but rather to shunne as much as they can all occasions of quarrell, and not to fight excepte (as hath bene sayde) vpon a iust cause and in a point of honor. And to the end that euerie man may know what to doo, and bee able to practise as much as hee knoweth (at the request of certaine Gentlemen my good friends, & to make the world witnes of my gratefull minde towards them for the many curtesies which I haue receiued at their handes since my first comming into this Countrie) out of those preceptes which I haue learned from the

B 3 most

To the Reader.

*most rare and renowmed professors that haue bin of this Art
in my time, and out of that experience which I haue obserued
in diuerse fraies and fights, I haue composed aud framed this
little worke, containing the noble Arte of the Rapier and
Dagger, the which I haue set downe in man-
ner of a Dialogue, &c.*

VINCENTIO SAVIOLO
HIS PRACTISE.

 Haue long and greatly defired (my deare friend *V.*) to learne this noble fcience, and efpecially of you, who did put the firft weapons into my hands: wherefore (feeing fo good opportunitie is fo fitly 'prefented) I coulde wifhe that wee might fpende this time in fome difcourfe concerning the Arte of the'Rapier and Dagger, to the end that I might thereby, both the better retaine the title which I haue alreadie learned, and alfo adde fome new leffon thereunto.

V. Certes (my louing friend *L*) as wel for that I haue found you to be a man of a noble fpirite, as in regard of the great loue which I beare vnto you, as alfo to the end that hereafter when time fhall ferue, you may be better knowen vnto fundry Gentlemen my good friends, I am content to yeeld vnto your requeft, and therefore demand boldly any thing wherein you defire to bee refolued.

L. Sir, the loue which you beare mee I know to bee exceeding great, and therefore haue no doubt that you will fayle me in anie part of your promife, for the which fauour I acknowledge my felfe infinitly beholding vnto you. I fhall defire you therefore, according to your iudgement and skill, to refolue and inftruct mee in fuch

doubtes

197

doubts as doo occurre vnto me, for I knowe, and many noble men and Gentlemen do likewife know, that you are exquifitly able not only to refolue vs of anie doubt readily, but alfo to inftruct vs in this fcience perfectly.

V. Sir, I defire nothing more than to pleafe and fatisfie you and fuch other Gentlemen my good friends, and therefore you may expounde queſtions at your pleafure.

L. From my firſt yeres I haue liked this noble Art, but now doo much more loue it, hauing feene fuch diuerfitie of this exercife, together with the danger thervnto belonging, and (fince I came to be your fcholler) plainly perceiued how that a man in one moment may be ſlaine. And therfore I giue God thankes that in fome meafure hee hath giuen mee the knowledge of this fcience, and I hope through your good helpe to bee more fully informed therein. Wherefore I defire you to tell me, if there may be giuen anie certaine inftruction and firme rule whereby to direct a man to the true knowledge of hereof.

V. Since my childhoode I haue feene verie many mafters the which haue taken great paines in teaching, and I haue marked their diuerfe manners of playe and indangering: wherefore (both for the particular contentment & pleafure of the Gentlemen my friends, and for the general help & benefit of many) I haue changed fiue or fix fundry maner of plaies, taught me by diuerfe mafters, and reduced them vnto one by my no little labour and paine, and in this will I refolue you, and geue you therein fo direct a rule and inftruction, as that therby (being my fcholler) you may attain vnto the perfect knowledge of this fcience.

L. But

L. But tell me sir of curtesie, those which haue not bene your schollers, are they therefore debarred from the vnderstanding of your said rule .

V. In truth sir, well they may learne and conceiue much, but of those secrets which I will reueale vnto you they are not so capable as those whom I haue taught .

L. Shew me (I praie you) what may bee the cause, why this arte (being so necessarie and noble) is of so many so little esteemed ?

V. You haue moued a question whereof I am grieued to speake; when I consider with my selfe the slight account wherein this so worthy science is held, I deeme the cause hereof to be either because many which dod (peraduenture) vnderstand the same will not professe to teach it, or that many (hauing in deed no vnderstanding thereof) doe iudge the same to consist in theyr great strength and brauing courage, but they deceiue themselues. Moreouer, I am of this opinion, that many (not knowing this art to be the beginning and foundation of the art Militarie) doe therefore neglect and contemne it, because they esteeme the same to bee a thing vnto them altogether impertinent.

L. By what reason can you shew this science to be the ground and foundation of the arte Militarie ?

V. You shall heare. This word *Schermize et Scharamuzare*, to skirmish or fence, may be taken either generally or particularly. Generally, for euerie kind of sight. Particularly for single combat: and so it is taken as often as it is indefinitly set downe, and not expresly . And being taken in this sense, that it doth necessarily belong vnto the arte Militarie may many waies bee proued, for in the arte Militarie it is requisite that a man know how he

C   may

may best ouercome his enemie, and which waie to entertaine him, & as it were to dallie with him vntill such
time as he can espie some aduantage. Againe, wee doo
many times see that a great man or a Captaine doeth
wrong an inferiour person or a souldier, who for that
they are men of meaner fortune, doo seldome by lawe
recouer right or credite, wherfore the Prince or Generall (after that the partie wronged hath done his dutie;
in complaining vnto him of the iniury receiued) ought
to require and command him by whome the wrong
was done, either to make satisfaction vnto the partie
wronged, if the fact were against reason, or by waie of
disgrace, or else to fight the combat with him. Then
(being to accept one of these conditions) if hee trie the
combat, he can neuer acquite himself without danger
and dishonour, if hee haue not first learned this noble
science.

Moreouer, if a man follow the warres and conuerse
with Captaines, and incurre a quarrell, and haue no
knowledge of this arte, what shifte shall hee make? Or
how shall hee behaue himselfe beeing challenged the
combat for his Countrie or his Prince. which hath often happened, not onely in the time of the Romanes,
but in our dayes, as we may reade in the life of Charles
the fifte, and of other Emperours : *Paulus Iouius* and
Guicciardino do make mention of many combats fought
in the kingdome of Naples betweene French-men
and Italians for theyr Countrie, whereunto were required and chosen most famous and skilfull men both
of the French and Italian Nation. Wherefore a Captaine or a Generall is not perfectly accomplished in all
pointes appertaining to his place and profession, if hee
bee

bee disfurnished of this science : for admit (as it may fal
out vpon many occasions concerning his Country and
his owne honour) he bee challenged the combat, and
chance to be ouercome therein, although hee haue bin
renowmed for infinite victories, hee hath now loft in
one moment all his foregotten glorie, for both the honour of the fight, and the triumph of the victorie doth
wholy redound vnto him who hath ouercome in combat. Neither were his many victories gotten in the field
vnto him more glorious, than this one foile in single
fight is diſhonourable, for thoſe victories had many
helpes, as horſe, armour, opportunitie of time, aduauntage of place, &c. Thoſe glories many parteners, as
ſouldiers and vnder officers, but this diſhonour doeth
wholy fall vpon himſelfe, as purchaſed by ſome imperfection in himſelfe, as namely for want of this ſcience,
without the which no man profeſſing the Arte Militarie, can bee called perfect in his profeſſion, but rather
maimed in the principall part thereof, and moſt concerning the ſafety and defence of a mans owne life, for this
is a braunch of that wiſedome which holdeth the fift
place and chiefeſt preheminence in matters of warre,
for he that is deuoid of art and skill, doth raſhly encounter with his enemie, and ſo is ſlaine with ſcorne and diſhonour.

L. This which you ſaie ſeemeth to ſtande with
greate reaſon, yet neuertheleſſe wee ſee by experience,
that men vnskilfull and altogether ignorant in this arte,
haue vanquiſhed and ouerthrowen thoſe which practiſe the ſame for theyr dayly exerciſe, whereas (if your
aſſertion were true) the skilfull ſhould euermore con-
quer the vnskilfull.

C 2

V. Sir

V. Sir, you are to vnderstand, that many are called profeſſours of their Rapier and Dagger, and yet bee o-uercome by men that neuer practiſed the ſame, but how euer, not as profeſſours of this ſcience, but as baſe and vnskilfull perſons. For in him that will bee rightly cal-led a profeſſour of this arte, and in him that ſhall goe into the field to fight a combat, are required reaſon, a-nimoſitie, ſtrength, dexteritie, iudgement, wit, courage, skill, and practiſe: wherfore it may bee that thoſe which are ouercome bee men of baſe mindes, or voide of rea-ſon, and falſely called profeſſours of that arte whereof they haue no vnderſtanding, and which they doo but diſcredite. Others are ſo head-ſtrong and raſh, that they doo lyke rammes which kill themſelues by running full but at theyr enemies. But to haue recourſe vnto the firſt and higheſt cauſe, theſe actions are euermore directed by the ſecret will of God, and are the executions of his hidden iudgements.

L. Certainly ſir, when I conſider your reaſons, I am confounded in mine owne iudgement, for your ſpeech doeth neceſſarily inferre, that if a man bee able, ſtrong, actiue, wiſe, skilfull, valiaunt, and not quarel-lous, hee ſhall bee conquerour, if otherwiſe, conque-red.

V. Let vs omit therefore as a ſpeciall and extra-ordinarie cauſe, that ſometimes God ſuffereth and per-mittteth the contrarie: and take this for an infallible rule and grounde, that euerie one renounceth and forſaketh that helpe which God hath appointed, as of-ten as hee deſpiſeth and contemneth this Arte, and that God hath giuen vs wit and vnderſtanding to di-ſcerne and knowe the good and the badde: which **beeing**

beeing so, it must needes followe, that if a man will not defend himselfe nor doo his best to obtaine victorie, he must be ouercome although his quarrell and cause were most iust and reasonable, because he will not vse the meanes which God hath appointed, and therefore must blame himselfe only for his ill hap and successe. Wherefore it cannot be denied but that this knowledge and skill which groweth and riseth from this art of Defence is necessary. And therfore I say that when vpon iust ground and occasion a man shall take a quarrell in hand, and sha lhaue courage, reason, boldnes, and force to maintaine it, hauing also the meanes and helpe of this art, it will seldome or neuer chaunce but that he shall ouercome his aduersary, and vpon this reason and ground proceedeth my argument. But when he forsaketh the fauour and benefit graunted by God, in that he wil not learne how to defend himselfe: if the quite contrary happen to him he must impute the fault and blame to himselfe. And therefore I must tell you this also, that he hath most neede of this art which lacketh courage and strength, because that by this art and practise he groweth in vre with his weapon, and to haue skill and iudgement to defend himselfe. And this also I saye, that strength and valiant courage is not it which giueth victorye, but a skill and knowledge in the vse of his weapon, and a certaine nimblenes and actiuitie aswell of the body as of the hand and the foot.

L. In sooth by that which you say, it seemes to me that nature is she which worketh and perfourmeth all, and not art, because that from nature commeth courage, force, and a right frame and aptnes of the body, therefore he which shalbe furnished with these partes and shall vndertake a right and iust cause, is like to beare away the victory without hauing any or very little skil in the art of Defence.

V. Certes we may graunt, that nature may doo very much to frame a man apt and fit for this exercise, both in respect of conuenient courage and strength, but all these abilities and giftes which nature can bestow on a man, are nothing except he haue knowledge or arte, for we see that the very thinges themselues which are brought foorth by nature good and perfect, if they be not holpen by arte, by very course of nature become naught and vnprofitable. As the Vine if it be not holpen by art comes to no proofe nor profit, so likewise other trees how apt so euer they be to bring forth excellent frutes, if they are not husbanded growe wilde, and degenerate from their naturall perfection. Suppose that nature bring foorth a most goodly and beautifull tree, if it begin once to growe crooked and be not holpen it looseth all his beautye, and therefore as you see, arte is an aide and helpe to nature : so that one hauing those good partes and abilities by nature before mentioned, yet not knowing them, he can not yse them to his benefite but by the meanes of skill and iudgement; which a man by his industrie and practise attaineth vnto. And although he may strike right and crosse blows and giue the foyne and thrust, yet these being not guided by reason and skill, may as well harme him as profit or procure him any aduantage : but art which imitateth and perfiteth nature, if a man apply his minde thervnto, by many experimentes and much practise, will make him skilfull and capable of great perfection. And to proue that this is true, we see little infants which although
though

though as soone as they are borne they haue a tung, yet they cannot speake, and after when they haue learned to speake, yet they want eloquence: nature maye bestowe a gift of memory, which when it is accompanied with art and knowledge, they are able in good sorte to expresse their minde and conceipt. How can you be skilfull in riding if you haue not learned the arte, nature may helpe, but not bring to perfection: How is it possible that you should proue a skilfull Carpenter or Saylor, if you haue not by practise acquainted your selfe with those thinges which appertaine thereunto: how can a man be a professour in any art or science, vnlesse he haue learned it first himselfe: and therefore they which make so small reckoning of art, in my fancie and conceipt in this respect are worse than beastes, especially those which are practised in fight, in which a man may perceiue a kinde of reason and arte, and for proofe of this, take a young Dog which hath not been accustomed to fight, and set him on a Bull, and you shal see him assaile him with more courage and fiercenes then another which hath beene beaten and practifde in the matter, but you shall see him by and by hurte and wounded: whereas in the other you shall see the quite contrary, for before he set vpon his aduersary you shall see him spie all aduantages that maye be, and hauing found his aduantage he wil after make an assault, wherfore these braggers which without iudgement and reason will take vpon them to kill the whole worlde, at the least wise should order and gouerne themselues more discreetely then beasts: and if they being without reason can help themselues with art which is taught them, how much rather should a man which is indued with reason

reafon make his profit therof, feeke to learne it and not
to fcorne and defpife it, efpeciallye in fuch a cafe where
fo deepely it concerneth a mans life, that in the ftirring
of a foote he may be foddenlye ouertaken and flaine:
but the more skill a man hath of his weapon the more
gentle and curteous fhould he fhewe himfelfe, for in
truth this is rightly the honour of a braue Gentleman,
and fo much the more is hee to bee efteemed : neither
muft he be a bragger, or lyer, and without rruth in his
word, becaufe there is nothing more to be required in
a man then to know himfelfe, for me therefore I thinke
it neceffarye that euery one fhould learne this arte, for
as a man hath voice and can fing by nature, but fhall
neuer doo it with time and meafure of muficke vnleffe
he haue learned the arte : and as a horfe may be ftrong
and fyt for fight by nature, but can not ferue a man to
any vfe in the feelde vnleffe he haue beene firft broken
and taught, and framed to be obedient to his maifters
pleafure and minde : So much more fhould a man
learne how to mannage and vfe his body, his hand and
his foote, and to know how to defend himfelfe from
his enemy. And heereupon we fee, that how ftoute or
couragious foeuer a man be, vet when he is challenged
into the feelde he feeks then to learn the skill and practife of his weapon of fome braue and skilfull man a-
gainft the daye of the fight and combate, and for no o-
ther caufe but that he knoweth that it is neceffarye for
him, & that it concerneth his honor and life : and they
which affirme the contrary, if euer they haue occafion
to fight, fhall perceiue to their difaduantage and dif-
credit, how much they haue erred and bene out of the
way : and this which we haue difcourfed hitherto as I
                                                        thinke

thinke may suffise to proue the necessitie of this art.

L. You haue with so manye reasons and proofes
shewed the necessitie of this worthie art, that in truth I
greatly esteeme and honor it, and could wish that euery man of honour would seeke to know it and practise
it, that it might be more esteemed: but now that I
know the excellency of this art, I would gladly know
wherein consisteth the order and manner to vn-
derstandit.

V. Certes my freend *L.* I will not faile in that which
I haue promised. And therefore I wil begin this small
worke, to leaue some remembrance of me, with these
Gentlemen and my good freendes, and with you who
are desirous to vnderstand it, and especially because I
haue alwaies found you to be a louer of gentlemanlike qualities.

L. I thanke you sir for your good will and good o-
pinion conceiued of me, and therfore according to the
desire which you haue to make me vnderstand this
worthie arte, I require you to tell me with what weapon a good teacher minding to make a good scholler
ought to begin.

V. So I will, yet I must tell you, that I haue seene
many braue sufficient men teach with great diuersitie
and diuers sortes and fashions of play: and I my selfe
haue had many teachers, and found them all to differ
one from the other.

L. But I pray you of freendship tell me how there
can be such disagreement, since that all that art consisteth in down right or crosse blowes, thrustes, foynes,
or ouerthwart prickes.

V. That which you say, verilye is true, but consider
D   also

also that we see many precious stones, and yet the one to be more esteemed then the other, although they be of the same sorte and kinde: and we see many excellent men which studie the same art, and yet one is more esteemed then the other, as well ingrauers as Painters: the same is seene amongst learned men, all are learned, but one better learned then the other; and the like is to be seene in all sciences and artes, and so in this noble art God hath giuen more to one, then to another. I will begin therefore to tell you how that of many that teach, some begin and enter their schollers with the rapier and Dagger, some with the Rapier and Cloake, some with the Rapier and Buckler, and some with the Rapier alone: some after one sorte and some after another.

L. Is it not all one for a scholler to begin with the Rapier alone, or with the Rapier and Cloake, or any other weapon: may not he become a braue man, as well with one weapon as with an other?

V. Surely, they may proue well, but not so well as those which begin with the true ground, the which schollers should learne of good maisters, and teachers should with all diligence teach their schollers.

L. And what I pray you is this ground?

V. The true foundation verily and the true beginning from whence you may learne all thinges belonging to this art, is the Rapier alone, and from it will I begin, and you shal perceiue of what great importance this beginning is, and how without it hardly or neuer any commeth to true skill and perfection: yet proceed you to aske such questions as you shall thinke best, and take good heede to that which I shall say, for I will

208

willbeginne as I tolde you.

L. In truth M. *Vincent,* although as yet I haue no great skil,yet me thinkes you haue reason in your asser-tion, and that you haue got the right and true know-ledge of this science, and therefore I praye you shew me the reason why the Rapier alone is the ground and beginning of this art.

V. The reason as I take it, is because that amongst Knightes, Captaines and valiant Souldiours, the Rapi-er is it which sheweth who are men of armes and of honour, and which obtaineth right for those which are wronged:and for this reason it is made with two edges and one point, and being the weapon which or-dinarily Noble men,Knightes,Gentlemen and Soul-diours weare by their side,as being more proper and fit to be worne then other weapons: therefore this is it which must first be learned,especiallye being so vsuall to be worne and taught. In my discourse therefore of this fight of the single Rapier I will speake onelye of three wardes.

L. Tell me I pray you firste how it is best to holde a mans Rapier in his hand, and how to stand vpon his garde.

V. For your Rapier,holde it as you shall thinke most fit and commodious for you, but if I might aduise you you should not holde it after this fashion,and especial-ly with the second finger in the hylte, for holding it in that sorte, you cannot reach so farre either to strike di-rect or crosse blowes,or to giue a soyne or thrust, be-cause your arme is not free and at liberty.

L. How then would you haue me holde it?

V, I would haue you put your thumbe on the hylte,

D 2   and

and the next finger toward the edge of the Rapier, for so you shall reach further and strike more readily.

L. You haue fully satisfied me concerning this matter, but I pray you proceede and shew me how I must stand vpon my garde, or assaile myne enemy.

V. So I will, and as before I haue tolde you of diuersitie of teachers and varietie of wardes, so in this poynt also must I tell you that mens fashions are diuers, for some set vpon their enemies in running, and there are other which assaile them with rage and furye after the fashion of Rammes, and both these sortes of men for the moste parte are slaine and come to misfortune, as may be seene in many places of such like fights. Which I speak not as though those two fightes were not good for him which knowes how to vse them, becaufe that sometimes they are very necessary, according as a man findes his enemy prepared with his weapon: but then they must be doone with time and measure, when you haue got your enemye at an aduantage, with great dexteritie and readines. But as for me I will shewe you the wardes which I my selfe vse, the which if you well marke and obserue, you cannot but vnderstand the art, and withall keepe your bodye safe from hurte and danger.

L. At this present I take wonderfull delight in your companye, and nothing pleaseth me so much as this discourse of yours, to heare you giue me the reasons of those things which so much concerne the life and honour of a man: wherefore performe that which you haue promised, wherein you shall not onelye pleasure mee, but many other gentlemen and Noble men will thinke themselues to haue receiued a fauour at your handes,

handes, therefore begin I pray you.

V. That which I haue promised you I will now performe, therfore I fay, that when a teacher will begin to make a Scholler, (as for me I wil begin with the fingle

Rapier, and at this weapon will firfte enter you, to the ende you maye frame your hand, your foete, and your body; all which pattes muff goe together, and vnleffe you can ftirre and moue all thefe together, you fhall neuer be able to performe any great matter, but with great danger) I come therefore to the point and fay, that when the teacher wil enter his fcholler, he fhal

D 3   caufe

cause him to stand vpon this ward, which is very good to bee taught for framing the foote, the hand, and the body: so the teacher shall deliuer the Rapier into his hand, and shall cause him to stand with his right foote formost, with his knee somewhat bowing, but that his bodye rest more vpon the lefte legge, not stedfast and firme as some stand, which seeme to be nayled to the place, but with a readines and nimblenes, as though he were to performe some feate of actiuitie, and in this sorte let them stand both to strike and to defend themselues. Now when the maister hath placed his scholler in this forte, and that the scholler hath receiued his Rapier into his hand, let him make his hand free and at lyberty, not by force of the arme, but by the nimble and ready mouing of the ioynt of the wriste of the hand, so that his hand be free and at libertie from his body, and that the ward of his hand be directlye against his right knee: and let the teacher also put himselfe in the same ward, and holde his Rapier against the middest of his schollers Rapier, so that the pointe be directlye against the face of his scholler, and likewise his schollers against his, and let their feete be right one against another, then shall the maister begin to teach him, mouing his right foot somwhat on the right side in circle wise, putting the point of his Rapier vnder his schollers Rapier, and so giuing him a thrust in the belly.

L. And what then must the scholler doo?

V. At the selfesame time the scholler must remoue with like measure or counter-time with his right foote a little aside, and let the left foote follow the right, turning a little his bodye on the right side, thrusting with the point of his Rapier at the belly of his teacher. turning

ning redily his hand that the fingers be inward toward the body, and the ioint of the wrist be outward. In this sorte the saide scholler shall learne to strike and not be stricken, as I alwaies aduise the noble-men and gentlemen with whome I haue to deale, that if they cannot hit or hurt their enemy, that they learn to defend themselues that they be not hurt. Then to make the scholler more ready, the teacher shall cause his scholler firste to part, wherefore he shall remoue with his right foote on the right side a little in circle wise as the maister did before to the scholler.

L. What then must the maister or teacher doo?

V. At the same time that the scholler remoueth his foote, the teacher shall play a little with stirring of his body, and with his lefte hand shall beat away his schollers rapier from his right side, and shall remoue his right foot behinde his left striking a crosse blow at the head.

L. And the scholler what shall he doo?

V. When I remoue with my foote and lifte vp my hand, let the scholler passe with his lefte foote where his right was, and withall let him turne his hand, and not loose the opportunity of this blow, which must be a foyne in manner of a thrust vnder his Rapier, and let him lifte vp his hand with his ward that he be garded and lie not open, meeting with his left hand the rapier of his teacher, and let him not beat aside the blow with his Rapier for hee endangereth the point and bringes his life in hazard, becaufe he loseth the point: But I wil goe forward. At the selfesame time that the scholler goes back, the maister shall play a little, and shifting his body shall breake the same imbroccata or foyne outward from the lefte side, remouing with his left foote, which

which muft be carried behinde the right, and withall
fhall giue a mandritta at the head of his fcholler, at
which time the fcholler muft remoue with his right
foote, following with his lefte, and let him turne his
Rapier hand as I haue faide, and that the fcholler obferue the fame time in going backe as the teacher fhall,
to the end that his point maye be toward the bellye of
his maifter, and let him lifte vp his other hand with his
ward on high, that he be not ftricken on the face with
the mandritta, or in the belly with the thruft or ftoccata. Wherefore at the felfefame time that the fcholler
fhall deliuer the fore faide ftoccata to the teacher, the
teacher fhall yeelde and fhrinke with his bodye, and
beate the ftoccata outward on the lefte fide, and fhall
bring his right foot a little afide in circle wife vpon the
right fide, & fhall giue an imbroccata to the face of his
fcholler, at which time the faide fcholler fhal go backe
with his right foote a little afide with the fame meafure, and fhall beate afide the imbroccata of his maifter with his left hand outward from the lefte fide, and
withall fhall deliuer the like imbroccata of counter-
time to the teacher, but onlye to the face, and then the
maifter fhall goe backe with his right foote toward the
left fide of his fcholler, in breaking with his lefte hand
the faide imbroccata outward from the lefte fide, and
fhall ftrike a downe-right blowe to his head, becaufe
that by beating afide his foyne with his hand, he fhall
finde him naked and without garde.

    L. And what then, cannot the Scholler defend him
felfe?

    V. Yes very eafilye with a readie dexteritie or nim-
blenes, for at the fame time that the maifter fhall giue
the

the faide mandritta, the ſcholler ſhall doo nothing elſe but turne the pointe of his foote toward the bodye of his maiſter, and let the middeſt of his left foote directly reſpect the heele of the right, and let him turn his body vpon the right ſide, but let it reſt and ſtaye vpon the lefte, and in the ſame time let him turne the Rapier hand outward in the ſtoccata or thruſt, as I haue giuen you to vnderſtand before, that the point be toward the bellye of his maiſter, and let him litte vp his hand and take good heede that hee come not forward in deliue-ring the ſaide ſtoccata, which is halfe an incartata, for how little ſoeuer hee ſhould come forward, he would put himſelfe in danger of his life: and beleeue me, eue-ry man which ſhall not vnderſtand theſe meaſures and principles, incurres the danger of his life: and who ſo deſpiſeth theſe grounds which are neceſſarye as well for the ſchoole as the combat, it may bee to his confu-ſion & diſhonour, and loſſe of his life: wherefore eue-rye one which makes profeſſion of this art, ſhould ſeek to learn them and vnderſtand them.

L. For this matter I am fullye ſatisfied, wherefore I praye you proceed to teach me that which remaineth to be taught for this ward.

V. When the maiſter will make his ſcholler readye, hee ſhall practiſe him to be the firſt in going backe, by remouing his right foote a little aſide in circle wiſe, as before his maiſter did to him, and let him with great readines thruſt his Rapier vnder his teachers, and giue him a thruſt or ſtoccata in the belly.

L. What then ſhall the teacher doo?

V. He ſhall ſhift his body a little, and ſhall beate the ſtoccata or thruſt outward from the right ſide, and ſhal

E remoue

remoue with his right foote, which muſt bee conueied behinde the lefte, and ſhall ſtrike a rinuerſa at his ſchollers head, as before: and further, to the end his ſcholler may haue iudgement to knowe what fight meanes, with meaſure and time, hee ſhall teach him to giue a mandritta, and to know when the time ſerueth for it.

L. What I pray you, cannot euery one of himſelfe without teaching giue a mandritta?

V. Yes, euery man can ſtrike, but euerye man hath not the skill to ſtrike, eſpeciallye with meaſure, and to make it cutte: and heereupon you ſhall ſee manye which oftentimes will ſtrike and hitte with the flatte of their Rapier, without hurting or wounding the aduerſarye: and likewiſe many, when they would ſtrike a downe-right blowe, will goe forward more then meaſure, and ſo cauſe themſelues to be ſlaine. Wherefore I ſaye, when the maiſter and ſcholler ſhall ſtand vpon this ward, and that the pointe of the ſchollers weapon ſhall be againſt the face of the teacher, and the pointe of the teachers weapon nigh to the ward of the ſchollers Rapier, and that it be ſtretched out, thē the ſcholler ſhall remoue with his right foot a little aſide in circle wiſe, and with the inſide of his left hand barrachet wiſe ſhall beate away his maiſters Rapier, firſte lifting his aboue it, and let the lefte foot followe the right: and let him turne skilfully his body, or elſe he ſhall be in danger to receiue a ſtoccata either in the face or bellye. Therefore hee muſt take heede to ſaue himſelfe with good time and meaſure, and let him take heede that hee ſteppe not forward toward his teacher, for ſo hee ſhould bee in danger to be wounded: but let him go a little aſide, as I haue already ſaide,

L.

L. Me thinkes the maifter is in danger, if the fchollér at this time keepe meafure.

V. If the maifter ftoode ftill, hee fhould bee in danger, but when the fcholler fhall giue the mandritta, the maifter muft fhifte a littlé with his bodye, and fhall remooue with his right foote, which muftbe carried behinde his lefte, and fhall ftrike a riuerfo to the head, as I faide before, when I began to fpeake of ftoccata.

Furthermore, the Scholler maye likewife giue a mandritta at the legges, but it ftandes vpon him to playe with great nimblenes and agilitye of bodye, for to tell the trueth, I would not aduife anye freend of mine, if hee were to fight for his credite and life, to ftrik neither mandrittaes nor riuerfaes, becaufe he puts himfelfe in dagner of his life: for to vfe the poynte is more readie, and fpendes not the lyke time: and that is my reafon, why I would not aduife any of my frends to vfe them.

L. But I praye you of freendfhip tell me, if a man were to goe into the feelde with fome freend of his whome hee would bee loth to kill, fhould not thefe mandrittaes be good to wound him, and not put him in danger of his life, I praye you therefore tell mee your opinion, and how a man in refpect of his honour were to vfe and order himfelfe, put the cafe he would not kill his freend, but would willingly faue and keepe him from harme.

V. I will fpeake mine opinion of thefe things which concerne a mans life and honour, and firfte I would wifh euery one which is challenged into the feeld, to confider that he which challengeth him, dooth not require

E 2 quire

quire to fight with him as a freend, but as an enemye, and that he is not to thinke any otherwise of his minde but as full of rancour and malice towards him: wherefore when you should with weapons in his hand that will needes shoot with you, although hee were your freend or kinseman, take him for an enemye, and trust him not, how great a freend or how nigh of kin soeuer he be, for the inconuenience that may grow therby, is seene in many histories both ancient and moderne. But when you see the naked blade or weapon, consider that it meanes redresse of wrong, iustice, and reuenge: and therefore if he be your freend that will needs fight with you, you maye tell him that you haue giuen him no cause, nor offred any wrong, and if any other haue made any false report, & that he is to proue and iustifie it, that for your selfe, if by chaunce without your knowledge you haue offended him, that you are ready with reason to satisfie him and make amendes. But if they be matters that touch your honour and that you bee compelled to accept of the combat, doo the best you can when you haue your weapon in your hand, and consider that fightes are dangerous, and you know not the minde and purpose of your enemye, whome if you should chaunce to spare, afterwards peraduenture he may kill you or put you in dager of your life, especially when you vse the mandritta or right blowes: for if he be either a man skilfull at his weapon, or fierce or furious, he may peraduenture doo that to you, which you would not doo, (when you might) to him. Wherfore if hee bee your friend goe not with him into the fielde, but if you go, doe your best, because it seemeth childish to saie, I will go and fight, but I will spare and fauour

nour him. For if you were the valiauntest man in the world, and had no minde to doo him anie harme, yet when you see the furie and malice of your enemie, you shall be forced, as it were, to doo that you thought not to doo, for which you may peraduenture be sorie, and disquieted in mind as long as you liue, as well in respect of friendship, if you kill your friend, as for the punishment which the lawes will inflict and laie vppon you, whether it bee losse of goods, imprisoment, or death. And on the other side, if you be slaine or wounded, it is no excuse for you to saie afterward, that you fauoured him & did not so much as you might, for in such a case euerie man will thinke as he list: so that if your enemie were the most coward and base man that might bee, yet he shall bee counted the more valiaunt and braue man. Therefore if it happen that some friend of yours hath a quarrell against you, tell him that you will not haue any thing to doo with him: and fight with your enemie, not with your friend: neither account him your friend that will fight with you: well you may be his friend, but you shall finde him to be your enemie. Therefore whensoeuer you see anie man drawe vpon you, staie not vntill hee doo his pleasure, and trust him not, for hee hath not his weapon drawen to no purpose : and if in that sorte he will talke of the matter with you, cause him to stand aloofe off, and so let him speake : for of the inconuenience that hath growen thereby wee haue many examples, as I will shew you more at large by and by. I would wish that euerie one should beware to offend any man either in wordes or deedes, and if you haue offered offence, seeke to make amends, as a ciuill and honest man should, and suffer not the matter to grow to such extre-

mitie and inconuenience, as wee fee examples euerie
daie, whereby God is highly difpleafed. And amongſt
others I will tell you of an accident which hath happened in *Padoua,* where I my felfe was borne, of a maſter
of Fence called M. *Angelo* of *Alezza,* who many yeres
brought vp, maintained, and taught a nephew of his, in
fuch fort, that hee became a verie fufficient and skilfull
man in this art. Which his nephew, whereas by reafon
fhould haue beene louing and faithfull to him, as to his
owne father, hauing fo long eaten of his bread, and receiued from him fo many good turnes, efpecially hauing bene brought vp by him from his childhoode and
infancie, he did the quite contrarie, for his vnckle *Angelo* yet liuing and teaching fchollers, hee openly dyd
teach and plaie with many, and by that meanes came
acquainted with many Gentlemen, fo that hee fet vp a
fchoole of Fence, and beganne to teach, entifing awaie
many which were fchollers of his vnckle *Angelo.* A part
truly verie vile, and of an vnkinde vnthankfull man.
Whereupon the fayd *Angelo* complained of this iniury
and wrong offered by his nephew, to a gentleman who
was his fcholler and loued him entirely; fhewing howe
his nephew had not onely impaired his credite, but de-
frauded him of the aide and helpe which he looked for
at his hands, hauing brought him vp, as I haue faid, and
efpecially being now growen old. Which nephew (as
he fayd) in refpect of kinred, bringing vp, and teaching
of his arte and skill, was bound to haue fhewed him all
friendſhip and curtefie. Heereuppon the Gentleman,
Angelo his fcholler, promifed to feeke redreffe, although
hee was a friende alfo vnto the nephewe of *Angelo.*
And fo, by badde happe, finding the fayde nephew of
Angelo,

Angelo, tolde him that for the wrong offered to his master and vnckle, he would fight with him, and there-withall put hande to his weapon : the other refused to fight with him becaufe hee was his friend : but the Gentleman tolde him that if hee woulde not defend himfelfe hee woulde runne him thorough: as hee dyd in deede, for whileft hee ftoode vppon tearmes, and would not do his beft to defend himfelfe, he ranne him quite thorough the bodie. Therefore when a man fees anie one with a drawen weapon, let him take care to defend himfelfe, becaufe it is not a matter of friend-fhippe: But I thinke verily in this man, that the iuftice of God and his owne confcience tooke awaie all cou-rage and wit of defending himfelfe. And this was the ende of his vnthankfulneffe, which God would not leaue vnpunifhed. And if all vnthankfull and treche-rous men were fo ferued after the fame forte, I thinke there woulde not be found fo many : and truly of all vices, I take this vnthankfulneffe to be one of the grea-teft that is incident to man. Therefore to conclude this matter, I woulde counfell and aduife euerie one, to giue as fmall occafion of offence anie waie vnto a-nie as may be, and efpecially vnto his friend, to whom hee is in anie forte beholding : but when that hee is forced to laie hande on his weapon, to doe the beft he can, as well in refpect of his credite, as for to faue his owne lyfe.

L. Verily this example which you haue heere brought in, is verie good and neceffarie, as well to in-ftruct and teach a man not to truft his enimie when he feeth him comming with his weapon in his hand, as

alfo

also to warne these vnthankfull men to bee more true and faithfull. But I praie you go forward to tell me that which is behinde concerning this ward.

V. I will verie willingly, but I praie mislike not that I haue somewhat digressed from the matter which wee were about, for I haue spoken these few words not without cause, but now I will go forwarde with that which remaineth. Therefore I saie, when the master and scoller stand vpon this ward, and that the point of the scollers weapon is towarde the face of the teacher, and the point of the masters without the bodie of the scoller toward the right side, both of them being vpon this ward, the scholler must bee readie and nimble to remooue with his left foote, that the point or ende thereof bee against the middest of his masters right foot, turning his Rapier hand, and that his point be in imbrocata-wise aboue his teachers Rapier, and that his left hand bee toward the ward of his teacher: and let all this be done at once, by which meanes the scholler shall come to haue his masters weapon at commandement, and if it were in fight, his enemies.

L. This plaie which now you tell me of, me thinkes is contrarie to many other, and I my selfe haue seen many plaie and teach cleane after another fashion, for I haue seene them all remooue in a right line, and therfore you shall doe mee a pleasure to tell mee which in your opinion, is best to vse, either the right or circular line.

V. I will tell you, when you stand vpon this ward, if you remoue in a right line, your teacher or your aduersarie may giue you a stoccata either in the bellie or in the face. Besides, if your master or your aduersarie haue
a Dagger

222

a Dagger he may doo the like, hitting you with his dagger either in the belly or on the face, besides other harms which I list not to write. And therefore to proceede, I saie, that in my opinion and iudgement, it is not good to vse the right line, whereas in remoouing in circularwise, you are more safe from your enemie, who cannot in such sort hurt you, and you haue his weapon at commandement: yea although he had a dagger hee coulde not doo you anie harme.

L. But I praie you tell me whether the master may saue himselfe when the scholler makes this remoue vppon him in circular wise, without being hurt.

V. When the schollar remoueth with his left foot, the master must steppe backe; but yet in such sorte, that the lefte foot be behinde the right, and that he remoue to the right side, and shall strike a mandritta at the head of the scholler, and whilest the master shifteth with his foote and striketh the mandritta, at the selfe same time must the scholler bee with his right foot where the teachers was, being followed with his lefte, and shall deliuer a stoccata or thrust in his masters belly, turning his bodie together with his hand on the lefte side, and lifting his hand on high, to the end the master may in striking hit his Rapier, and withall shal strike at the teacher, at which time the teacher must remoue with his right foote a little aside, followed with his lefte, and shifting a little with his bodie, shall beate outwarde the thrust or stoccata of his scholler, and shall deliuer an imbroccata to his scholler, as I haue tolde you before in the beginning.

L. I praie you therefore tell me if there be any other points in this ward,

F   *V.* With

V. With all my heart, and therefore I must tell you of an imbroccata in manner of a stoccata, which is verie good and excellent, as well for practise of plaie, as for fight, but they must be most readie both with hand and foot that vse it: therefore when the scholler shall find his masters Rapier in this ward, that it bee helde vpright or toward his face, then the scholler shall winne ground a little with his right foote, beeing mooued somewhat aside, and withall let him remoue with his left foot, that it be toward the right foot of the teacher, and that your right foot be against the middest of his left, as I haue said before, and in remouing let him turne his Rapier hand, that the pointe bee conueighed vnder his masters weapon, which being done, promptly and readily his point will be towards the belly of his master, which must bee followed with the left hand, & let the scholler lift vp his hand to the ward that his fist be somewhat high, and let him take heed that he loose not his point, because the teacher may giue him a stoccata or thrust in the belly or face, for that he hath lost his time.

L. But I pray you, cannot the teacher then defende himselfe?

V. He may do the self same which I told you before, when I spake of the imbroccata deliuered aboue the Rapier, and certainly this is a verie good play when it is performed with good measure, and great agilitie and readines. But besides this, I will now shew you the man riuersa in this ward. Therfore when the scloer shal find his teacher with his point somewhat at length, that it is not towards his face, but towardes his belly, then must the scholler with his left hand beat aside his masters rapier, not at the point, but in the strength and middest of

the

the weapon, and withall muſt remooue with his leſte
foot, both which muſt be done at once: and let the ſame
foot be againſt the right ſoot of the maſter, as he did before in the foine or imbroccata, deliuered aboue and
vnder the rapier: and the teacher at the ſame time muſt
doo the like, remoouing with his right foote, as I haue
ſayd before. And as the ſcholler remoues and beates a-
ſide the weapon, let his leſt hand be ſodainly vppon the
ward of his teacher, and in giuing the ſayde riuerſa or
croſſe blowe, let the ſcholler skilfully turne his Rapier
hand, that the knuckle or ioynt may be toward the head
of the teacher, for otherwiſe he may giue him a ſlicing
or cutting blow, which we call *Siramazone*: therefore let
him performe thoſe things skilfully and at once, and e-
ſpecially let him beware that he doo not beate aſide his
teachers weapon toward the point, becauſe he ſhoulde
be in danger to receiue a thruſt or ſtoccata either in the
face or belly. Beſides, the ſcholler, ſo that he find his teacher in the ſame ward, that his Rapier bee ſomewhat at
length, & not directly vpon the face, may ſtrike the ſaid
riuerſa or croſſe blowe at his legs: but beating aſide the
Rapier with his hande muſt bee done readily, and hee
muſt remoue with his hande in ſuch ſorte, that his Rapier when the leſte hand beates it by, may be betweene
his owne hand and his teachers weapon : and with this
readineſſe muſt hee ſtrike this riuerſo, but withall, his
leſte hand muſt bee vppon the warde of his teacher.

L. But tell mee I praie you, is it not all one if I take
hold of the arme of my teacher or aduerſarie, in ſted
of laying my hande vppon his warde.

V. No in deede, for if your enemie were skilfull in
this art, whileſt you catch him by the hand or arme, hee

might

mightwith his lefte hand feize vpon his weapon &put
you in danger of your life. So that you muft take heed
to haue all aduantage of your enemie, that hee may not
in anie fort do you anie harme: in dooing of which, you
fhall alwaies be to good for him.

L. But tell me of friendfhip, if you take this ward to
be good, as well for the field as the fchoole.

V. This ward which I haue fhewed you, in my opinion, is verie profitable to bee taught, becaufe it breeds
a iudgement of the time, and a readineffe and nimbleneffe as well of the hand as the foote, together with the
body: and from this you come prepared to learne other
wards with more facilitie, and to haue a greater infight
and vnderftanding in many things, fo that for many re-
fpects it is verie commodious, good, & neceffarie. Now
alfo for fight, this ward is verie good to bee vnderftood,
and to bee fullye had and learned with beeing much
practifed therein, and made verie readie as well wyth
the hand as the foote without loofing anie time: and fo
much the rather for that we fee many Nations vfe this
ward in fight verie much, efpecially with the fingle rapier, both Italians, French men, Spaniards, & Almanes.
Wherfore I aduife euery one to feeke to vnderftand it,
learne it, and acquaint himfelfe with it, that hee may
come to that readineffe and knowledge to doo all at
once, without making anie fault or falfe point in the faid
ward: by reafon of many inconueniences which haue
chaunced, and which daily chance, which I will fpeake
of when time ferueth: but in the meane while we will
go forward with this fecond ward, in which the fcholler fhall learne to giue the ftoccata and imbroccata.

L. I thinke my felfe very fortunate that it is my hap
to

226

to finde you at this time, in so pleasant and conuenient a place, where we may passe the time in some discourse vnder the shade of these delightfull trees, and therefore according to your promise, I praye shewe me your second ward, which I shall be attentiue to marke.

V. M. *Luke,* if all men were louers of vertue as your selfe is, these things would be helde in greater account, but thorough the loue of vices, wherewith men are caried away, they are little regarded, wherefore I wil doo my best endeuour to instruct you and all other that are louers of vertue, imparting vnto them that knowledge which God hath giuen me. Therefore for your better

F 3   vn-

vnderstanding, I will first shew you how this warde is good, either to offend or defend, and cheefely with the single Swoorde and the gloue, which is most in vse among Gentlemen, and therefore I aduise you and all other to learne to break the thrustes with the left hand, both stoccataes and imbroccates, as I purpose to shewe you.

L. But I praye you tell me, is it not better to breake with the Swoorde, then with the hand? for (me thinketh) it should be dangerous for hurting the hand.

V. I will tell you, this weapon must bee vsed with a gloue, and if a man should be without a gloue, it were better to hazard a little hurt of the hand, thereby to become maister of his enemies Swoorde, then to breake with the swoord, and so giue his enemy the aduantage of him.

Moreouer, hauing the vse of your lefte hand, and wearing a gantlet or gloue of maile, your enemy shall no sooner make a thrust, but you shalbe readye to catch his swoorde fast, and so commaund him at your pleasure: wherfore I wish you not to defend any thrust with the swoorde, because in so dooing you loose the point.

L. But I pray you, is it not good sometimes to put by a thrust with the swoord?

V. I will tell you when it is good to vse the swoord: but now I will tell you how to vse your hand in that case, and cheefelye in this warde wherewith I will beginne.

Therefore if the maister desire to make a good scholler, let him begin in this sorte, causing his scholar to place his right legge formoste, a little bending

the

228

the knee, so that the heele of his right foote stand iust against the midst of his left foote, holding his swoord hand close on the outside of his right knee, with his swoorde helde in shorte, least his aduersarye should gaine the same, euer keeping the poynte directlye on the face or bellye of his enemye, and the maister shall dispose of him selfe in the same mannor, as well with his foote as with his poynt.

Moreouer, you must obserue iust distance, which is, when either of you stand in such place, that stepping forward a little, you maye reache one another, and then the maister shall make a stoccata to his scholler, going aside somewhat with his right legge, and following with the other in manner of a circulare motion towarde the lefte side of his scholler: and so hee maye haue the aduauntage if hee take it, within distance, and the scholler shall remoue his right legge in counter-time, after the same order that his maister dooth, answering him with a stoccata to the belly: but hee must take heede not to remoue too much aside, or retire too farre backewarde, for so the one shall neuer hittey and the other shall neuer learne.

Moreouer, hee must beware of comming too much within his iust distance, because if he hit his aduersary, hee may bee hitte againe by his aduersarye: wherfore I will teache you how to offend and defend in the same time. As the Scholler parteth in the counter time, hee must in the same instant breake the stoccata with his lefte hande, and iaunswere againe with an other: also the Maister to make his scholler quicke and readye, shall vse to aunswere him in the same time that his scholler deliuereth his stoccata, **going**

going aside with his right legge, and following with
the other toward the left hand of his scholler, breaking
the saide stoccata with his lefte hand, and shall aime the
imbrocata at his face, and the scholler must parte also
with his right foote toward the lefte side of his maister
circularlye, beating the thrust with his lefte hand outward toward the left side, and then he shall in like sort
make an imbrocata to the face of his maister, and the
maister parting againe with his right foote aside toward the left hand, breaking the saide imbrocata with
his lefte hande, shall thrust a stoccata, as I saide before,
to the belly of his scholler, and the scholler in the same
instant shall parte with a counter-time with his right
foote aside towards the lefte hand of his maister, breaking it with his left hand downward, and shall make a
stoccata againe to his master, and the maister therwithall shall retire a little with his body, breaking the saide
stoccata outward toward his right side, parting with his
right foote backward to the left hand, and shall answer
with a punta riuersa, to the head of his scholler, wherewithall he shall parte sodenlye, stepping forward with
his left legge before his right, turning his point quickly
to the belly of his maister, bearing vp the dagger hand,
that he be not hitte in the face with a riuerso, and so he
shalbe well garded: then the maister shall parte with his
right leg, offering him a straight stoccata to the head,
as in the first ward.

L. But I pray you why doo you vse so many stoccataes and imbroccataes?

V. Because they may learne the iust time and measure, and make the foote, hand and body readily agree
together, and vnderstand, the way to giue the stoccata

and

and imbroccata right: so that these principles are very necessarye, and will serue for the Rapier and Dagger, therefore whosoeuer will make a perfect scholler, let him shew the principles in this warde.

L. I perceiue very well, that these things which you haue spoken of, are to be doon with great agility and quicknes, but especially by the maister, if he entend to make a perfect scholler, because the maister often putteth him self in danger, and the scholler regardeth him not, neither is his hand firme: and therefore the maister must be respectiue two waies: in sauing him selfe, and not hurting his scholler: but (I praye you) are these thinges as good in fight, as necessary to be practised?

V. I haue taught you already how to place your self in this ward, with the iust distance and time belonging thereunto.

L. But I pray you instruct me a little further concerning time.

V. As soone as your Rapier is drawne, put your selfe presently in garde, seeking the aduantage, and goe not leaping, but while you change from one ward to another, be sure to be out of distance, by retiring a little, because if your enemy be skilfull, hee may offend you in the same instant. And note this well, that to seek to offend, being out of measure, and not in due time, is very dangerous: wherefore as I tolde you before, hauing put your selfe in garde, and charging your aduersarye, take heed how you go about, and that your right foot be formost, stealing the aduantage by little & little, carying your lefte legge behinde, with your poynt within the poynte of your enemies swoord, and so finding the aduantage in time and measure, make a stoccata to

G   the

the belly or face of your enemy, as you shall finde him vngarded.

L. Are there many sortes of times?

V. Many are of diuers opinions in that pointe, some hold that there are foure times, other fiue, and some six, and for mine owne parte, I thinke there are many times not requisite to be spoken of, therfore when you finde your enemye in the time and measure before taught, then offer the stoccata, for that is the time when your enemie will charge you in aduancing his foot, and when he offereth a direct stoccata, in lifting or mouing his hand, then is the time: but if hee will make a punta riuersa within measure, passe forward with your lefte foote, and turne your pointe withall, and that is the time: if he put an imbroccata vnto you, answere him with a stoccata to the face, turning a little your bodye toward the right side, accompanied with your poynt, making a halfe incartata: if hee strike or thrust at your legge, carrye the same a little aside circular-wise, and thrust a stoccata to his face, and that is your iust time: and if he offer you a Stramazone to the head, you must beare it with your swoord, passing forward with your lefte legge, and turning wel your hand, that your point maye go in manner of an imbroccata, accompanied with your left hand, so that your poynt respect the bellye of your aduersary, and break this alwaies with the point of your sword, for of all stoccataes, riuersaes, and Stramazones, I finde it the most dangerous. And re-member, that whilste your enemy striketh his madritta, you deliuer a thrust or stoccata to his face, for the auoiding of which, hee must needes shrinke backe, otherwise hee is slaine: and how little so euer your ene-mie

my is wounded in the face, he is halfe vndone and vanquished, whether by chaunce it fall out that the blood
couer and hinder his sight, or that the wound be mortall, as most in that parte are: and it is an easie matter to
one which knowes this play, to hit the face, although
euery one vnderstands not this aduantage. And many
there are which haue practised and doe practise fence,
and which haue to deale with those which vnderstand
these kinde of thrustes or stoccataes, and yet cannot
learn to vse them, vnles these secrets be shewed them.
Because these matters are for fight and combat, not for
play or practise: but I wil come back where I left. Therfore, when your enemye maketh as though he would
strike at your head, but in deed striketh at your legges,
loose not that oportunity, but either in the false proffer
that he makes, hit him, or carry your foot a little aside,
that his blow may hit the ground. So when you deale
with those which thrust their pointes downeward, at
the same time strike you at the face: and when you find
the point of your enemies weapon on high, get your
point within his, and when you haue gotten this aduantage, immediatly giue him a stoccata or thrust, or
else let it be a halfe incartata: and take heed when you
deliuer your stoccata, that you come not forward with
both your feet, because if he be skilfull at his weapon,
he may meete you with counter-time, and put you in
danger of your life: and therfore seeke to carrye your
right foot together with your hand, being a little followed with your left foote.

Moreouer, when you finde that your enemy holds
downe his pointe, and his hand alofte, seeke to stand
well vpon your garde, that your hand bee ready with

G 2   your

your right knee somewhat bending towards your enemy, and your body somewhat leaning on the left side,
because if your enemye would giue you a thrust or
stoccata, hee should come a great deale shorte of reaching your bellye with his poynte, and especiallye he
wanting that knowledge, which those haue who are
furnished with the right skill of this arte. Wherefore if
he giue you a stoccata or thrust in the bellye, you must
beat it down with your left hand, outward from your
lefte side, and withall you maye giue him a stoccata or
thrust either in the bellye or the face: and if hee make
a foyne or imbroccata to your face aboue your head,
you must be nimble with it, and may beate it aside with
your hand, the inside outwward toward your left side,
or else without beating it by, deliuer him a halfe incartata with your poynt, which must be within his, and let
it be towards his bellye, so that all these be doone with
measure and time. But if you finde your enemye with
his poynt downe, you must stand vpon a lowe warde,
and carrie your body very well, leaning vpon the lefte
side, and when you haue got him within your proportion, you may giue him a stoccata or thrust, either in
the belly or the face, and you are safe from his pointe:
for if he will make a stoccata to you, if you haue skill to
beate it aside with your hand, & to answere him again,
you must needes hit him. And if he giue a foine or imbroccata, you may reach him the incartata, as before I
haue tolde yon.

L. You haue done me a great pleasure, and I know
it will stand me in great steed if I should haue occasion
to fight, to knowe these times and proportions, which
are to be obserued: but I pray you tel me if one, who is
skilfull

skilfull and valiant should assaile me, whether this ward be good to be vsed in fight, or else whether I also should strike and answere him with the same?

V. If you will do as I will aduise you, I saie it is verie good either to assaile anie, or to tarrie and watch your aduantage, if you haue skill to stand vpon it, & to carrie your foot, hand and bodie together, holding your Rapier short, and that your point bee towarde the face of your enemie. For if your enemie haue skill in fence, and should not finde you to stand surely vpon your gard in this assault, he might deliuer a straight stoccata to your face, not purposing fully to hit him, which if you should breake with your Rapier, he might put his vnder yours, comming forward aside toward your right hande, and might giue you a stoccata in the face. Moreouer, putting the case that your aduersarie were skilfull and cunning in fight, and you not much acquainted therewith, if he should not find you vpon a sure ward, he himselfe being in proportion, and finding your pointe without his belly, he might reach you a stoccata in the belly, or an halfe incartata, especially if he know in fight how to vse his bodie.

Besides, in these assaultes, when he is without your right side with his right foot, hee might offer a stoccata from the outside of your weapon, and if you breake it with your Rapier, hee may pull his point vnder yours, and withall remoue toward your left side with his right foot, and giue you a stoccata in the belly, turning skilfully his Rapierhand, so that his fist bee toward his left side. Also if you should deliuer a stoccata to your enemie, and that he should breake it with his Rapier, immediatly you might remoue with your lefte foot, your left

G 3   hand,

hand, waiting on the weapon of your enemie, and giue him an imbroccata or foine vnder or aboue his Rapier, and may bee maſter of his weapon. But if your enemie ſtrike a mandritta at the legges, if you ſtrike it by with your weapon, he may giue you a venew either by ſtoccata or imbroccata. Therefore it is not good for anie man to vſe theſe things preſcribed, becauſe, as I haue alreadie ſayd, he had need to vnderſtand well his times & proportions, and to know howe with skill to ſhiſte and moue his bodie, & to be readie and nimble as well with his foot as hand, otherwiſe, by his owne meanes he may be wounded or ſlaine ; ſo that he had need to bee verie cunning and perfect in theſe matters, wherevpon many good maſters do practiſe their ſchollers in theſe aſſalts to make them readie. But I will let them paſſe, and will ſatisfie you concerning the skil of this ward, which you haue required to know. Therefore I ſaie, when you ſhal ſtand vpon this ward, and that you be aſſailed and ſette vpon, keep your point ſhort, that your enemie may not finde it with his, and look that you be readie with your hand, and if he make ſuch a falſe proffer as I ſpake of before, you being in the ſame ward & in proportion, may with great readines put a ſtoccata to his face, ſhifting ſodainly with your left foot, being a little folowed with the right, and that ſodainly your Rapier hand be drawen backe. But if he ſhoulde giue a ſtoccata to your face with ful force from your rapierſide outward, you may a litle ſhrink with your bodie & beat his point with your hand outward from your right ſide toward your weapon, & withall you may ſtrike a riuerſa. Furthermore, if he ſhould pul his rapier within at the ſame inſtant, to be more ſure, you muſt carrie your right foot a little aſide

toward

toward his left hand, and with great readines of coun-
tertime you must put a thrust or stoccata to his face, turning your hand most nimbly. So also in such like assalts
if your enemie shuld come to strike down right blows
or riuersi, do as I haue told you before. in mouing your
hand with great readinesse, and finding your time and
proportion. Wherefore I hold this Ward to bee verie
good, as well to assaile, as for to tarrie and watch for an
aduauntage. And you must especially take heede that
you put not your selfe in danger, because if your enemy
should finde you without your sword at length, beeing
nimble & strong, striking vpon your weapon, he might
make a passage with greate speede, and make himselfe
master as well of you as of your weapon, and put you
in daunger of your life. Whereas contrary wise,
when you doo holde your Rapier shotte, as I haue
tolde you, and that your pointe is towardes his face,
you make him affaide, especially when hee comes forward with his hand and bodie to finde your weapon
with his, he must heedes come so farre that you maye
easily hurt him without being hurt. Besides all this, if
your enemy should come to deliuer a stoccata, imbroccata, mandritta, or riuersa, you haue great aduauntage,
for hee cannot so readily strike, nor with such suretie as
you may.

L. But I pray you tel me this, if mine enemie should
charge me with his weapon at length, as putting forth
halfe his weapon in his ward, must I answere him with
the like?

V. This warde truely is verie good against all other
wards in my opinion, especially if you knewe howe to
charge your enemy, & to find time & proportiō to strike
knowing

knowing how to turne and shift your bodie as well on
the one side as the other, and vnderstanding the skill of
fight, and beeing most nimble, you may aunswere him
with it. But yet I would haue you to marke and consider well in what sorte your enemie behaueth himselfe,
and howe hee holdeth the pointe of his weapon : if
that you finde him holding his pointe alofte, that it
bee aboue yours, when that you holde it right against
his face, you must seeke to winne grounde a little wyth
your right foote before you remooue, and your hande
must be nimble and readie, & at that verie instant make
three times with your feet at once, mouing a little with
your right foot, a little with your left, and againe a little
with your right. But this must proceed from very great
skill and knowledge, for if your left foot tarrie behind,
he may giue you a pricke in the face or in the belly, or a
cut vpon the legges. Wherefore you must so come forward with your right foote at once, that you may haue
the weapon of your enemie with your hand, and your
point towards his belly. So that as you see, many & verie many things may be performed by this ward, if, as I
haue sayd, one be skilfull and nimble. But this I would
aduise you, when you would make these passages, or put
your weapon vnder your enemies, that you doe them
not in vaine nor without some aduauntage. There are
many which oftentimes by chance and hap, doe many
things in fight, of which if a man shoulde aske them a
reason, they themselues know not how they haue done
them. And sometimes men verie sufficient and skilfull
at their weapon, are hurt, either by their euill fortune,
that they suffer themselues to bee carried awaie and o-
uermastered too much with choler and rage, or else for
that

that they make no account of their enemie. Wherefore as well in this ward as in the other, take heede that you suffer not your selfe to bee blinded and carried awaie with rage and furie.

L. I perceiue verie well that the secrets of this noble arte are verie great, & that with great trauell and paines a man must come to the knowledge and skill both to rightly vnderstande and practise it, for otherwise I see, that by verie small errour a man comes in daunger of his life. But I praie you instruct me somwhat farther, as if at this present I were to vndertake a combat with some valiaunt man in defence of my credite and my lyfe.

V. In truth the secretes which are in like fightes are such, that vnlesse one haue a skilfull man in this science to instruct him, and that loues him, he shall neuer come to the right vnderstanding of them. There are manye which will thinke they knowe inough, but most commonly are deceiued; and others there are which the master or teacher loues, and shewes them faithfullie all that he can, and yet they can neuer come to knit greate matter in this science, but they who are framed of nature as it were, both in respect of abilities of bodie and minde fit to learne this arte, if they vse the help of a skilfull teacher, come to great perfection. And these abilities are the gifts of God and nature; wherefore as in others, so in this worthie arte you shall finde some more apt than others, and especiallie to giue a right thrust or stoccata, which is the chiefest matter of all. For all the skil of this art in effect, is nothing but a stoccata: wherefore if you shall haue occasion to fight, I could wish you to practise this short ward, and to stand sure vpon it, &

to seeke your aduauntage with time, which when you haue found, giue the stoccata withall, somewhat moouing your right foot, and at the same instant draw back your left, & let your rapier with your bodie shift vpon the left side, because if your enemy be cunning, he may sodainly aunswere you with a thrust, and beate aside your weapon: and therefore if you minde, to giue a right stoccata, there is no other waie to saue your selfe from harme. But if your enemie bee cunning and skilfull, neuer stand about giuing any foine or imbroccata, but this thrust or stoccata alone, neither it also, vnlesse you be sure to hit him: suffer your enemie to doo what he list, onely stand you vpon a sure ward, and when you finde opportunitie and time, deliuer the stoccata, and shift with your foot. And this also you must marke, that sometimes it is good to giue the stoccata to the right side, which must bee doone when your enemies right foot is ouer against yours, and sometimes to the lefte side. Wherefore when you will deliuer a stoccata to the right side, see that you go not aside with your foot, but giue the thrust, and then shiste backward with your left foot, as also when you deliuer your stoccata to the left side, you must shift aside with your right foot. These things must be knowen & much practised. But if your enemie vse a mandritta or riuersa, you haue had instructions already how to behaue your selfe. There are many other secrets of this ward which cannot be written nor be made plaine or sufficiently expressed to bee vnderstoode. And that it is so, many Gentlemen can witnes, who although they haue seene me doo, yet coulde neither vnderstand nor practise them vntill that I shewed them the waie, and then with much adoo and verie hardly.

hardly. Therefore I thinke I haue spoken inough concerning this ward : and if you can perfourme all that I haue tolde you, it will suffice, & this our discourse may pleasure many, which take delight to vnderstand and learne these things : but if they will repaire to the teachers of the arte, they shal better and more fully vnderstand and conceiue of all, because both knowledge and practise is required.

L. I would thinke my selfe happie, Master *Vincent*, if I coulde remember and perfourme all which you so courteouslie haue imparted vnto mee of the former fight, and as farre as I maie, I wyll doo my diligence to practise that which you haue taught, but hauing found you thus friendlie and readie to shew me what fauour you may, I am emboldned to trouble you farther, and your curtesie hath increased my longing & desire to know more in this matter, and therfore I praie you make me vnderstand the other kind of fight which heretofore you haue tolde me of, and you call it Punta riuersa.

V. I haue alredie shewed you of what importance & profit the two former wardes are, as well for exercise of plaie, as for combat & fight, if a man will vnderstand & practise them. Now also perceiuing you so desirous to go forward, I will not faile in anie part to make you vnderstand the excellencie of this third warde, which notwithstanding is quite cōtrarie to the other two. Because that in this you must stand with your feet euē together, as if you were readie to sit down, and your rapier hand must bee within your knee, and your point against the face of your enemie : and if your enemie put himselfe vpon the same ward, you may giue a stoccata at length

H 2   be-

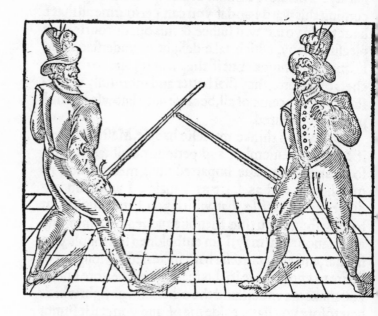

betweene his rapier and his arme, which shall bee best
performed & reach farthest, if you shift with your foot
on the right side. Moreouer, if you would deliuer a long
stoccata, and haue perceiued that your enemie would
shrinke awaie, you may, if you list, at that verie instant
giue it him, or remoue with your right foot a little back
toward his left side, and bearing backe your bodie, that
his point may misse your bellie, you maie presentlie hit
him on the brest with your hand or on the face a riuerso, or on the legs: but if your enemie would at that time
free his point to giue you an imbroccata, you may turn
your bodie vpon your right knee, so that the said knee
bend

bend toward the right side, & shifting with your body
a little, keepe your left hand ready vpon a soddaine to
finde the weapon of your enemie, and by this meanes
you may giue him a punta riuersa a stoccata, or a riuersa, to his legs. But to perform these maters, you must be
nimble of body & much practised: for although a man
haue the skill, & vnderstand the whole, circumstance of
this play, yet if he haue not taken paines to get an vse
and readines therein by exercise, (as in all other artes
the speculation without practise is imperfect) so in this,
when he commeth to performance, hee shall perceiue
his want, and put his life in hazard and ieopardie.

L. But tell me I pray you, if my enemy should firste
strike at me, how may I defend my selfe?

V. If your enemy be first to strike at you, and if at that
instant you would make him a passata or remoue, it behoueth you to be very ready with your feet and hand,
and beeing to passe or enter, you muste take heede
when hee offereth a stoccata, that you doo not put it a-
side with your weapon, because if hee should finde you
in good time and measure, you could not so readilye
put it by, as hee should be readye to giue it you. But
when that hee offereth the saide stoccata, be readye to
turne the knuckle of your hand toward your right side,
and let your point be right vpon the bellie of your enemie, and let your left foote accompanie it in such sorte,
that the pointe thereof be against the right foot of your
enemie, and let your right foot follow the left, that the
middest thereof be straight against the heele of your
lefte, the one being distant from the other, halfe a pace,
that you may stand more sure vpon your feete, and be
more redy to perform al things which shalbe required.

H 3   *L.*

243

L. But tell me I praie you, whether this warde may ferue me to any other purpofe, then for this ftoccata.

V. If you minde to deliuer a ftoccata like to the before mentioned, you muft win ground with your right foot, toward the right fide of your enemie, and as you finde the time and meafure, giue him a ftoccata either in the belly or in the face, and if your enemie fhrink at that time that you deliuer your ftoccata, it ftands vpon you to be moft readye and nimble, fhifting with your bodie and weapon, and fomewhat with your right foote, a little afide towards the right fide of your enemie, turning readilie your bodie and knee vpon your right fide, fo that your enemie himfelfe fhal come with his bodie vpon your pointe, and the more furious he commeth, the greater danger fhall he incurre, becaufe he cannot helpe nor recouer himfelfe. But remember to thruft alwaies at the face, if you may, for therby you fhall the better faue your felfe, and haue the greater aduantage. Moreouer, if your enemie fhould make a falfe proffer, or deliuer a little ftoccata, to the ende to procure you to anfwere him, that prefently hee might make you a paffata or remoue; if you be in good proportion and meafure, if he thruft at you, anfwere him, and if you will you may giue it him full and home, or fomewhat fcant and with great agilitie, whileft he maketh his paffata or remoue, turn readie your bodie with your knee, but yet vpon the right fide, and take heede you fhift not with your feete at this time, but onelie turne your bodie, as I haue tolde you, otherwife you fhould be in danger of your life, how little foeuer you fhrincke backe: and therefore I aduife you to beware that you goe not beyonde that which I haue taught you.

you. Morouer, if you can win ground on the right side of your enemie, and become master of his sword, you need not thrust a stoccata, but rather passe on him with your point aboue his sword, turning wel your hand as in an imbroccata, or else giue him a stoccata by a sincture, vnder his swoord hand, which is sooner done, remembring to passe forward with your left foot toward his right, and so let your right foot follow your left: but beware in any case that you neuer passe directly vpon your enemy, for endangering your life. If your aduersary thrust directly to your face within measure, answer him with a stoccata, in the same time that he lifteth vp his hande, but if you bee out of distance, answere not, for then you put your selfe in danger. And when your enemie offereth a stramazone or back blowe, receiue it on your sword very readilie, turning your pointe, and passing speedly with your left legge, as before taught: but if he make a punta riuersa, breake it with your leste hand toward your right side, and giue him another: and if he vse any sincture or false thrust, answer him not. Now if your enemie hold his sword out at length, and you perceiue his pointe to be anie whit without your bodie, especiallie on the left side, you must charge him, being readie with your leste hand, so that finding his point anywhit high, you shal falstfie with your sword hand vnder his Swoorde, passing forward with your leste foote in the same instant, still following your enemie without retiring, for so you shall be commaunder of his Swoord, and may vse him at your pleasure: but remember to be very redy, for you must make but on time, & take good heed that you stad not stil in doing this, for so, if your aduersary haue any skil, he may

greatly

greatlye annoye you, either with thruftes or blowes.
And oftentimes your enemy wil giue such aduantage
of purpose to haue you paffe on him: therefore you
muft well vnderftand what you doo.

L. I praie you is this all the vfe of that ward?

V. When you perfectlie vnderftand your weapons,
it maie ferue you otherwife, fo that you hold not your
fwoord hand within your knee, for if you finde your e-
nemie to beare his fwoord long, being in diftance, you
maie fodenlie beat it afide with your fwoord, and withall giue him a ftoccata in the bellie, which muft bee
done all in one time, fpeedilie turning your bodie on
the right fide, or elfe retyring with your right foote toward the right fide of your enemie: otherwife, if you
ftand vpon it, as manie doo, you might much endanger your felfe thereby, for if your aduerfarie being furious, fhould paffe on you in the fame time, hee might
put your life in ieopardie: but by the agilitie of the bodie, it is eafilie to be auoided: and againe, when you
finde his point long, you maie breake it afide with your
fwoorde, and giue him a Stramazone, or a riuerfa to
the head, but with readines of the bodie, or you maie
thruft a ftoccata, either to the bellie or face: and if your
enemie offer to breake it with his fwoorde, you maie
falfefie foddenlie aboue his fwoorde, and if he breake
it aboue, falfefie againe vnderneath his fwoorde; or if
you be readie with foote and bodie, you maie paffe on
him whilfte he breaketh your fincture with his fword,
faftning your left hand on the hiltes of his fwoord, and
you maie giue him a ftoccata, either direct, or with a ri-
nerfa: but looke that you laie not holde of his arme, for
if your enemie perceiue it, hee maie change his Rapier
                                                    foddenly

sodainly into his other hand, & so haue you at a great
aduantage, & therfore I teach you to laie hold on the
hilts, because you haue then commanded his sword
surely : and if your enemie finding your point out at
length, would beat it aside with his rapier, to passe vppon you, retire your left foote a little backward, and
with greate promptnesse in the same instant, falsifie
with a riuersa either to the face or bellye, of which
kinde of thrusts you shal often haue vse, but you must
be verie readie and well practised therein : therefore
you must labour it, that: when occasion require you
may performe it.

THE FIRST DAYES

Discourse, concerning the
Rapier and Dagger.

Luke.

F anie had euer cause to bee sorrowfull
for their departure from friends & parents, then had I iust occasion to take
our departures one from the other
most grieuous. And therfore our mee-
ting againe in so pleasant a place as this, must needes
be verie ioyfull and delightsome : wherefore among
other fauours you haue doone mee in instructions of
the single Rapier, I intreate you to shew me the lyke
touching Rapier and Dagger.

V. That which I haue heretofore shewed you, is but small in regarde of that I meane to teach you hereafter, so that hauing deliuered you the manner of the single Rapier, you may the better conceiue my discourse of the Rapier and Dagger, because it serueth much to the vse thereof: and it shall not be necessary wholye to repeate the same, but I will onelye sheiwe you how to put your selfe in garde with your Rapier and Dagger, for if I desire to make a good scholler, I would my self put his Rapier in one hand, and his Dagger in the other, and so place his body in the same sorte, that I haue before spoken of in the single Rapier, setting his right foot formost, with the point of his Rapier drawne in short, and the Dagger helde out at length, bending a little his right knee, with the heele of his right foote directlye against the midst of the lefte, causing him to goe round toward the left side of his aduersary in a good measure, that he may take his aduantage, and then I would thrust a stoccata to his bellye beneath his Dagger, remouing my right foote a little toward his left side.

L. And what must your scholler doe the whilste?

V. The scholler must break it downward, with the point of his Dagger toward his left side, and then put a stoccata to my belly beneath my Dagger, in which time I breaking it with the pointe of my Dagger, goe a little aside toward his lefte hand, and make an imbroccata aboue his Dagger, and the scholler shall breake the imbroccata with his Dagger vpward, parting circularely with his right foote toward my lefte side, and so thrust vnto mee an imbroccata aboue

my

my Dagger, in which time, with the pointe of my Dagger, I will beate it outward toward my lefte side, and answere him with a stoccata in the bellye vnder his Dagger, parting circularely with my right foote toward his left side: and in the same time he must answere me with the like vnder my Dagger, breaking my stoccata outward toward his lefte side, stepping toward my lefte side with his right foote, at which time I must mooue with my bodye to saue my face, and breake his poynte toward my right side, answering him with a riuersa to the head, and so retire with my right foote, at which time he must come forward with his lefte foote in the place of my right, and his Dagger high and straite, turning his swoorde hand, so that his poynte may goe directlye to my bellye, and he must take the riuersa on his swoorde and Dagger.

Luke.

But is it not better for the scholler to holde his Dagger with the point vpward, as I haue seene many doe to defend a riuersa?

Vincentio.

He that holdeth the point vpward, is euer in danger to be hurt on the head, or to receiue a sincture in the bellye or in the face, and likewise he is in ieoperdye to be hurt with a Stramazone, betweene the Rapier and the Dagger, because hee closeth not his weapons: therefore remember well how to carrye your Dagger, and by exercise you shall see the Dagger, for there are many that breake the stoccata inward.

L.Why

249

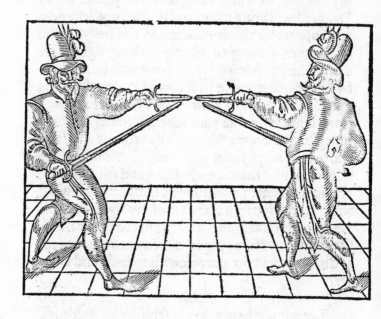

L. Why then do you neuer breake anie thruſt in-ward?

V. All ſtoccataes comming vnder the Dagger, & imbroccataes aboue the Dagger, are to bee beaten outward toward the lefte ſide, but an imbrocata by a riuerſa either in the belly or in the face, ſhould be bro-ken inward toward the right ſide, with a little retiring of the bodie, which muſt be anſwered with a riuerſa well followed, in which inſtant the ſcoller muſt paſſe forward with his lefte foote, then will I retire wyth my left foote behinde my right, and yeelding backe with my bodie, I will beate the point of his ſwoorde with

with my dagger toward my lefte fide, and fo make a direct thruft to his head : then the fcholler muft ftep with his right foote in the place of my lefte, carrying his Dagger not too high, but fo that his arme and his Dagger be held ftraight out, to receiue a blow if it be offered, and then he fhall thruft a ftoccata to my belly, which I will beat toward my left fide, and make an imbrocata aboue his Dagger, ftepping with my right foote toward his left fide, then muft he beate my imbrocata toward his lefte fide , parting with his right foot on my left fide, and fo make an imbrocata aboue my Dagger, then I parting with my right foot on his lefte fide, will beate his imbrocata towarde my lefte fide, and make a blow to his head : in which time hee muft do the halfe incartata, that is, he muft bee readie while I lift vp my hand, to put a ftoccata to my belly, bearing out wel his dagger to receiue the blow, turning fodainly his body on the left fide, fo that the heel of his right foot be iuft againft the middle of his left, and this is the true halfe incartata.

L. I pray you why do you make your fchollers vfe fo many ftoccataes and imbrocataes?

V. To make my fchollers apt and readie with rapier, dagger, and foot, that they may accompany one another in one inftant, whereof there is great vfe in fight. But one that would teach thefe principles and cannot plaie with his body, putteth himfelfe in great danger to be hit on the face, efpecially if the fcholler bee anie thing readie, and thruft a long ftoccata, for if the fcholler anfwere readily, his dagger cannot faue him. Therefore hee that wil exercife thefe rudiments

3   muft

251

muſt haue a very apt and well framed body, ſo that if you deſire to bee made readye and perfect, practiſe theſe principles, learning well the time and meaſure, and therby you ſhall open your ſpirites in the knowledge of the ſecrets of armes: neither do as many do, who when they are to fight, playe like children that runne to learne their leſſons when they ſhould repeat them, therefore learne, that in time of peace you may vſe it for a good excerciſe of the bodye, and in time of warre you may knowe how to defend your ſelfe againſt your enemies: and do not as many, that when they haue iuſt occaſion to fight, withdraw thēſelues, deſpiſing knowledge and vertue, not conſidering that almoſt euery little prick killeth a man, and I haue ſeen which thorough a fooliſh conceite of their owne abilitie, haue been wounded and ſlaine : therfore if you will preuent the fury of ſuch, you muſt be well practiſed in your weapons.

L. As farre as I can perceiue, the rules of the ſingle rapier, and of Rapier and Dagger, are alone, and I ſee well, that to learne firſt the Rapier alone, is very neceſſary to bring the body, hand, and weapon to be readye together in one inſtant, but one difference I finde betweene the ſingle Rapier and the other, becauſe in managing the Rapier alone, you cauſe the ſcholler to hold his left hand ſhorte, and in the other to holde out his hand and Dagger as ſtraight as hee may, whereof I would gladly know the reaſon.

V. At the ſingle Rapier if you holde ſoorth your lefte hand at length, your enemye maye wound you thereon, becauſe you are not ſo well garded as if you
with

withdrew it shorter, neither so readye to put by the swoorde of your aduersarye as with a Dagger, and therefore remember this well.

L. I see it standeth with good reason, but I praie you shew how I must assault mine enemie in fight? or how being assaulted by him, I must defend my selfe?

V. There are many that when they come to fight, runne on headlong without discretion, because finding themselues iniured, they holde it their partes to assault first.

L. Why? is it not the challengers parte to bee the first assaulter?

V. Yes, if you finde time and opportunitie, for (I pray) tell me why goe you to fight?

L. To defend mine honour and maintaine my right.

V. What is to defend your reputation, but so to hurt your enemye, as your selfe may escape free? for when you goe to fight, put on this resolution, either to take away his life, or to cause him to acknowledge his faulte, with seeking pardon for the same, which is more honorable then a blody victory: neither do like children, which in their wanton fighting stand farre a sunder, and make semblance to beate one another: therefore note it well, for if your aduersary be a man of iudgement and valour, and you be the first in offe-ring, you bring your lyfe in ieopardye: for either of you being within distāce obseruing time, the first of-ferer is in danger to be slain or wounded in the coū-ter time, especially if he thrust resolutelye: but if you be be skilfull and not the other, then may you gain time and meafure, and fo hit him, fauing your felfe, & then the more furiouflie your enemie commeth on, the more he runneth headlong vpon his owne danger. Some are of opinion that they can hit him that fhall hit them firſt, but fuch as haue neuer fought: or if by chance in one fight they haue beene fo fortunate, let them not thinke that Summer is come becaufe one fwallow is feene. Mee thinketh more commendable for a man to defend himfelfe, and not offend his enemie, than to hurt his enemie and bee wounded himfelfe, for when you fhall perceiue the danger that infueth by euery affault without time and meafure, you wil change your opinion: and fome others there are that hold it a fhame for a man to retire.

L. In deede it is accounted difgracefull to giue ground, becaufe therein a man feemeth to feare his enemie.

V. There is difference betweene retiring orderly and running backward, for to hit and retire is not difcommendable, though the other be fhamefull; & hee that holdes the contrarie, vnderftandeth little the danger of weapons.

L. And I praie you what good doth retiring?

V. If you be affaulted on the fodain, your enemy hauing gained time and meafure, fo that you are in euident danger to bee flaine, had you rather die than retire a foot?

L. Some are refolute rather to die than yeelde an inch.

V. But if fuch knew they fhould bee flaine, & that
fo

254

so small a matter would saue their liues, I doubt not but they would retire with both feete rather then faile. Many talke as they haue heard, and not as they know: whereupon I will recite a Combate perfourmed by a great Captaine called Signior Ascanio della Cornia.

L. Truly I haue heard of one such, but I know not whether it were he that was a master of the Campe in that great armie of Don Iohn d'Austria against the Turke.

V. He was the very same, but to come to the matter touching the opinion of the ignorant: this Captaine being entred the listes against his aduersarie in the presence of many Princes and great men (which listes enuironing the circuit appointed for the Combate, and being touched by either of them, the same person is helde vanquished, as if he had beene driuen out) was very furiously charged by his enemie, and sought at the first onely to saue himselfe by retiring, which the other perceiuing, began to scoffe at him, bidding him beware of the listes, wherewithall the Captaine espying aduantage, made a resolute stoccata cleane through his bodye, and so slew him, now whether of these think you wonne most honour?

L. In my iudgement Ascanio, who entertained the furie of his aduersarye, till in discretion hee found oportunitie to execute his purpose.

V. I am glad to heare you of that opinion, for wee see the like in martiall policye, where oftentimes retraites are made of purpose to drawe the enemye either into some imboscata or place of aduantage, and

such

such as are most infolent and prefumptuous, are eafieft drawne into thofe plots, who runne headlong on their death like beaftes. In like forte, hee that vnderftandeth the true vfe of his weapons, will fuffer his aduerfarye in his rafhnes, vntill he finde time and aduantage fafely to annoy him. And fithens I haue begun to fpeake of combates, I wil recite one other perfourmed in Piemont, in the time of Charles the 5. betweene two Italians, and two Spaniards, as I haue heard it deliuered by diuers Gentlemen prefent at the action. A Spanifh Captaine, more braue in fhew then valorous in deede, to infinuate himfelfe with the Emperour, began in fcornfull forte to finde fault with other nations, and among the reft, with Italians, where the Spaniard had neuer had foote of ground, if the Italians themfelues had not beene made inftruments of their owne conquefte : but to let that paffe, this Spaniard hauing in woords difgraced the Italian nation, it came to the Italians eares, whereupon two Italians, the one of Padua, and the other of Vicenza, wrote a cartell vnto the Spaniard, which was carried by him of Vicenza, who finding the Spaniard accompanied with diuers Gentlemen, deliuered him the cartell, which he receiued, faying that hee would go to his Chamber and read it, whereunto the Vicentine replyed, that he fhould read it ere hee departed, and that it was a cartel. Which the Spaniard hauing read in prefence of the whole companye, asked the Vicentine whether he or his fellow would maintaine the cartell, to whome the Vicentine anfwered, that the woords repeated in the cartell was a lye, and

that

256

that hee was present to auouch it: wherewithall hee offered to draw foorth his sworde, and so the Spaniard and his companion accepted the combat against the two Italians, of which matter the Emperour hauing aduertisement, conceiued displeasure against the presumption of the Spaniard, and so, place of combate was prepared in presence of many great personages: the combatters being entered the listes, one of the Italians (who were both in their shirts onely) rent of the lefte sleeue of his shirt, which the Spaniard beholding, saide hee needed not take so muche paine, for he meant to haue cut of his arm sleeue and all: to whom the Padouan replyed, that he meant to haue cut of the Spaniards head firste, and therefore prepared his arme for the purpose, wherwithall they encountred all very furiouslye, so that the Vicentine was first wounded, who crying out to his fellow that he was hurt, the Padouan comforted him with hope of better successe to come, and began warely to keep his garde, but the Spaniards presuming on the victorie, charged them so much the harder without regarde, till at length the Padouan finding his time, with a resolute stoccata ranne the one through the bodie, and with a sodaine riuersa, cut the others neck almost quite in sunder, and so they were both slaine together: I haue induced these examples for two causes, the one, for that many contemne this art, and make no account therof, and the other because there are some so insolent, as they seek nothing but to sowe discension between frendes and allies, which if they were restrained, it might saue the liues of many men:

for as wee fee in the laft example, there wanted not much to haue caufed a generall mutiny between the Spaniard & the Italian, through the infolencie of the Spaniard, if the Emperour had not drawne the matter to a fhorter triall, by forbidding any one to offer the firft blow amongft them, vpon paine of death: pronouncing the Italians victors, that had acquited themfelues in fo honourable forte. Therefore you may fee how dangerous the company of thefe quarrelfome perfons is, who doe leffe harme with their fwordes then with their tungs : for as the Italian prouerbe is, *La lingua non ha offo, ma fa rompere il doffo*, that is, the tung hath no bones, and yet it breaketh the backe : ill tunges are occafions of much debate. But to returne from whence I haue digreffed, you muft neuer be too rafh in fight, account of your enemye, yet feare him not, and feeke all meanes to become victor, and fo you fhall maintaine your reputation, and not endanger your felfe in vnaduifed haftines.

L. I haue taken great pleafure in thefe difcourfes, which in my opinion importe very much the knowledge of Gentlemen, and truely the Spaniards were iuftly punifhed for their pride, in fcorning other nations : you fhall fee manye of that humour, that will blame other nations, who deferue to be reiected out of all ciuile company : for if one man haue a faulte, his whole countrie is not ftraight to bee condemned thereof. But fhew me I befeech you, how I muft behaue my felfe when I am to fight, you haue alreadye taught mee the time, meafure, and motion of my body, and now I would learne fomething of refolution.

V.Ha-

V. Hauing taken weapons in hand, you muſt ſhewe boldnes and reſolution againſt your enimy, and be ſure to put your ſelfe well in gard, ſeeking the aduantage of your enemie, and leape not vp and downe. And beware in charging your enemie you goe not leaping, if you be farre off, but when you approch, gard your ſelfe well, for euerie little diſorder giueth aduantage to your aduerſarie, therefore learne to knowe aduantages, and thruſt not at your enemie vntill you bee ſure to hit, and when you haue giuen meaſure, note when it is time to thruſt : then finding your enemie out of garde, make a ſtoccata reſolutely, or elſe not at all : for although you be in time and meaſure, and yet your enemie bee well garded, he may verie eaſily hurt you though his skill be but ſmall. As may be ſeene in many, which altogether ignorant in the vſe of weapons, will naturally put them ſelues in ſome gard, ſo that if one looke not well about him, he ſhal be much endangered by ſuch a one, not becauſe he knoweth what he doth, but by reaſon that not foreſeeing the danger, hee followeth his purpoſe wyth reſolution, without being able to yeelde a cauſe for that he hath done. Therefore (I ſaie) you muſt ſeeke to gain not meaſure onely, but time and opportunitie as wel to ſaue your ſelfe as anie your enemie, if you will do well, & then if it happen not well vntoyou, thinke that God doth puniſh you for your ſinnes : for wee ſee often that at ſome one time a man will doo excellent well, & yet afterward he ſhall ſeeme as though he had neuer taken weapons in hand. And to make it the more apparant : There was a ſouldier in Prouence for his valor in many exploites before ſhewed, generally reputed a verie gallant man, who on a time being in a town beſieged, was so suddenlye stricken with the terrour of the batterie, and dismaide therewith, that hee could no longer refraine from seeking some caue to hide himselfe: who afterward taking hart agresse, came foorth againe, and beeing demaunded of the Captaines where hee had been, who told them the truth of the whole matter, and afterward behaued himselfe very valiantly.

In like sorte Marco Querini a gentleman of Venice, Captaine of the Gallies belonging to the signorye of Venice, in the sea Adriaticum, liuing delicatelye in all carelessenes, suffered the Turkes to run ouer the gulfe, spoyling and robbing at their pleasure, not daring to make resistance, which the Generall of the Signory vnderstanding, repaired thither with all expedition, thretning Querini Captaine of the gulfe, if hee perfourmed his office no better, the whole shipping should bee taken from him, & he sent home to Venice on foot. The shame whereof moued him so farre, that afterward hee became famous for his exploites.

Moreouer in the time of the Venecians warres with the Turke, the Generall of the Turkish forces beeing come into the Sea Adriaticke, neere vnto Schiauonia, Allibassa & Carracossa, who afterward died in the battaile of Pautou, would needs inuade the Isle Cursolla with some forces, and batter a towne there, where the men dismaied with the soddainnes of the attempt, betooke themselues to flight, and left the place to the defence of the women, who quitted theselues with such vndaunted courage, that one of them betaking her self to a peece of artillerie, plaied the gunner so artificiallie, that she directed a shot cleane through the ship where Allibassa was, much spoyling the same, which hee perceiuing, presently commaunded the ancker to be waied, and hoifing vp failes, retired all his forces, by which meanes the women faued the cittie: fo that heerin we fee the difference of mens difpofitions in courage at diuers times, and yet I commend it not in any man to want valour at any time. But to come to the purpofe, albeit one be not fo well difpofed to the managing of weapons at one time, as at fome other, yet hauing the practife and vnderftanding thereof, he fhall euer be fufficient to maintaine his parte.

L. It may well be that you haue faide, and I thinke that hee that hath the perfect vfe of his weapons, may very well defend himfelfe againft any man, though hee finde his body but ill difpofed: but feeing you haue begun to difcourfe of time, I pray you teach mee fomething concerning the difference of time.

V. You know what I haue faide concerning the fame, in my difcourfe of the fingle Rapier, and in like forte I muft inftruct with Rapier and dagger: therefore you muft at the firft charge your enemye, and hauing gotten aduantage of ground on the lefte fide, you muft make a ftoccata vnder his dagger, if he hold it too high, retiring immediately a little with your lefte foote, accompanied with your right, but finding his dagger low you muft make a fincture vnderneath, and thruft aboue his dagger, & that is the iuft time, in doing whereof you muft remember to carry your right foote a little afide, following with the left toward the left part of your aduerfary, and if he offer you either ftocata or imbrocata, you may anfwer him with a half incartata, turning your hand as in doing the ftoccata: or otherwife if hee beare his dagger low, you may thruft to his face, which is les danger for you, becaufe euerye little blowe in the face

stay-

ftaieth the furie of a man more than anie other place of
his body, for being through the bodie, it happeneth often times that the fame man killeth his enimy notwithftanding in the furie of his refolution : but the bloud
that runneth about the face, difmaieth a man either by
ftopping his breath, or hindering his fight: and he fhall
oftner find aduantage to hit in the face than in the belly
if he lie open with his weapons: but marke wel how he
carrieth his rapier, if long & ftraight with his Dagger a-
loft, you muft charge him lowe on your right foot, and
hauing gained meafure, beate downe the pointe of his
fword with your dagger, and make a ftoccata vnder his
dagger without retiring, but beware that in breaking
his point you put not downe his dagger arme, but hold
it firme, neither draw it in, leaft your enemie hit you on
the face, or giue you an imbrocata aboue your dagger:
but bearing your dagger firme and ftraight, if your enemie fhould anfwere your ftoccata, he might be in daunger to receiue a thruft. If your enemie carrie his fword
fhort, in an open ward, you maie come ftraight on him
and giue him a punta riuerfa either in the belly or face,
with fuch readines, that your fword be halfe within his
dagger before hee can breake it, turning nimblye your
hand toward your left fide, fo that in offering to breake
he fhall make himfelfe be hit either in the face or in the
belly : and forget not to retire an halfe pace with the
right foot, accompanied with the left.

Moreouer, if your enimie lie with his fword alofte,
and the point downwards, you maie charge him foure
waies, firft on the right fide, clofing your weapons in a
lowe gard, and your right foot within the right foot of
your enimie toward his left fide, and then being within
distance

diftance, giue him a ftoccata, fudenly drawing home
your point againe, or you may play with your bodie,
but hold your dagger firm, marking (as it were) with
one eye the motion of your aduerfarie, and with
the other the aduantage of thrufting.

Secondly, you may make a ftoccata to his bellye,
not refolutely, but to caufe him to anfwere you, and
then you muft playe with your bodye toward your
lefte fide, and bearing the thruft on your right fide,
paffe a little on his right fide, and make a riuerfa a-
bouc his fworde.

Thirdly, you may come vpon his point with your
dagger, clofing well your weapons, and then beating
away his point with your dagger, in the fame inftant
put a ftoccata either to his face or bellye, but in anye
cafe ftirre not your dagger arme, leaft hee falfifie and
giue you an Imbroccata aboue the dagger: therefore
remember to beare your arme ftraite, and only your
wrift higher or lower.

Fourthly, you may charge him on the right fide in
the fame warde, but contrariwife, for where before
you bent your body on the right fide, you muft now
turne on the left, fo that his pointe may ftill be without your body, and hold your dagger at length, then
being within meafure, you may fuddenly paffe with
your left foot, carrying the point of your dagger vpward, and turne your point vnder his Rapier, that it
goe directly to his belly, in manner of an imbroccata, in doing whereof you muft turne your body well,
lifting vp your fworde hand, and with your Rapier
and Dagger, affure your felfe of his, otherwife your

wea-

weapons lying open, if your enemye bee skilfull, and
know how to turn his hand, hee might hit you either
in the bellye or face with a riuersa, or cut you on the
head, for euery disorder endangereth a mans life.

Furthermore, if your enemy carry his sword low,
charge him directly, turning your body on the right
side, with your dagger at length, the pointe hanging
something toward the ground, and then as you finde
his dagger, so make your thrust: if high, to his belly, if
lowe, to his face: if his head be aboue, put a stoccata
to his face by a trauersa (as it were) vnder his dagger,
and forget not to retire withall with your right foot:
and if hee hold out his sword with the the pointe vpward when you are toward his right side, you shall
put your self in the ward aforesaid, bending your body on your lefte side, and so gaining ground, make a
stoccata vnder his sworde, so that your dagger be vnder his rapier, and keepe it without your bodye from
your left side, and your point in his belly: and remember alwaies that in taking your enemies pointe, you
stir not your dagger arme, because hee may then endanger you, as I haue before said. Moreouer, if your
enemie put himselfe in the same gard, with his rapier
at length, and you in your gard with your right foot
formost and your point held short, so that your right
foot be opposite to his, you shall little and little steale
ground with your right foote, and followe with the
left, till you are within distance, and then with agilitie thrust either to his belly or face: and this is a notable thing if it bee well vnderstoode, for beside the
knowledg it requireth practise, that you learne not to
approche neerer to your enemy then you may saue
                                                    your

your felf:otherwife you may charge him on the right
fide, bending your body to the left fide, and then hauing gotten the aduantage, you muft fuddenly paffe
with your left foote, turning withall your pointe vnder his fworde, that it afcend to his bellye, and clap
your dagger as neere as you can to the hiltes of his
fwoorde, all which together with the motion of the
body, muft be done at one inftant. I fhall not need to
difcourfe much of your enemies holding of his dagger, but as your enemy carrieth it, either high or low,
fo (I fay) you muft with difcretion thruft either to his
face or belly: but you muft bee verye well exercifed
in thefe paffataes, for perfourming them with quicknes of the bodye, albeit you happen to faile of your
purpofe, yet your enemie fhalbe able to take no aduantage therof, but you fhalbe ready to anoy him ftil
either aboue or beneath, wherein you muft followe
him in mouing his body: fo fhall you ftil holde your
aduantage, and hit him where you will, & if he thruft
again, you fhall break toward your right fide, and reply with a riuerfa to the face. Againe if your enemie
beare his rapier long and ftraight, you may charge
him, and beating away his fworde with your owne,
fudenly turn in your point to his face or belly, which
is a verie good thruft, being done with great agilitie,

If you perceiue your enemies rapier farre out, &
that he go about to falfifie vpon you either aboue or
vnderneath your dagger, then put your felfe in your
ward, with your weapons clofe together, and as low
as you may, holding firme your dagger hande, and
whatfoeuer falfifieng he maketh, neuer moue awaie
your Dagger hande , neither lifte it high or lowe

to get your enemies Rapier, and if you lye belowe in
the ward when he falsifieth, remaine so without styr-
ring any higher, (for otherwise hee might at that
time finde fit opportunitie to hit you, if he be skilfull
in wepons) but follow him close, for if he once thrust
resolutely, be it aboue or beneath, he must needs lose
his whole Rapier, and you may easily hit him: and in
your thrusting stand firme with your body and dagger. Also if he holde his dagger straight vpward, and
that the point of his rapier be at the hiltes of his dagger, as you shall finde occasion, so doe, that is, if his
dagger hand be high, thrust a stoccata to him vnder
his dagger: if lowe, make a stoccata to his face, either
close by the hand, or by the middest of his arme, and
and if you will thrust as you are in your warde you
may, or else with retiring. Moreouer, if your enemie
turne his dagger point toward his right side, charge
him on that side, with a punta riuersa to his face, remaining in your warde, or retiring as you please. A-
gaine, if he lying in that warde, carry his point out of
the warde of your dagger any whit a little too high,
charge him close, and holding forth your Dagger,
you may suddenly take his point with your Dagger,
or if you will you may by remouing the right foote a
little forward, giue him a stoccata, but keepe stedfast
your dagger hand, as I taught you before, least otherwise he make an imbroccata to your face. Againe, if
he carrye his point any whit too much toward your
right side, turn your body on your left side, in a good
ward, charging him on the right side, and bring your
right foote cleane without his right foot, and hauing
so doone, thrust your rapier vnder his about the middle,

dle, and so, make a passata vpon him, or you may charge with a riuersa to his throte, or such like, either abiding in your warde, or suddenlye scaping away with your body. If you perceiue he holde his rapier farre out, and not turned, charge him below, turning your body on the right side, and turne your dagger point somewhat lowe vpon your enemies point, and hauing gotten this aduantage, being within measure, thrust either to his bellye or face, as you shall best see cause.

L. I finde now that after a man hath the arte, hee must also haue great exercise and practise to bring his bodie to a true frame. But as you haue hetherto shewed me to charge mine enemie in due time, so now I praie you teach me to defend my selfe when my enimie chargeth me.

V. If your enemie charge you, and haue gotten anie aduantage of you either with his foot, or turning of the bodie, or rapier, or dagger, or by what meanes soeuer, seeke to put your selfe in a sure warde, and retire a little, keeping your selfe still in gard, least else by retiring, if you moue vp your bodie or dagger, your enemy might by dexteritie and quicknes offend you greatly: but whilest hee chargeth you, couer to turne your bodie to one side or other, as you find the point of your enemies rapier, and euen at that instant that he moueth his foot in charging you, as you finde him open in any place, so seeke to offend him, and beware (as I sayd before) in what sort you retire: for somtime there is a fit time, when you thrust to retire, and some times not, therefore take diligent heed thereunto.

Moreouer, when he hath gotten aduantage, being

in

in his ward, if he wold thruſt a ſtoccata to you vnder your dagger, you ſhall be nimble to auoide it by turning your daggers point downward, & you ſhall anſwere him with a ſtoccata, or imbrocata, or punta riuerſa, as you ſhall finde opportunitie : but if he make an imbrocata aboue your dagger, you may auoide it by lifting vp a little the point of your dagger, and by turning the wriſt of your hand to the left ſide, for that his imbrocata ſhall go cleane without your left ſide, & you may make a thruſt to him, as you ſhall finde him open in anie place. Againe, if hee make an imbrocata to your bodie, you may giue backe a little with your bodie, and beat it awaie with your right ſide, & may make to him a punta riuerſa to his bodie or face: likewiſe if he be towards your right ſide, & thruſt at your face, you may yet beat it awaie, & anſwere him with a punta riuerſa or a paſſata. Againe, if he make an imbrocata aboue your dagger, beware that your rapiers point be within his, and make vnto him a meza-incarta, turning the pointe either to the belly, face, or throate: but you muſt with greate agilitie turne your point & bodie on your right ſide. Againe, if he make a blow to your head, at the inſtant that he moueth his hand make you ſodainly a ſtoccata vnto him, and (if you be in a good ward) you may make a punta riuerſa to his thigh, but if he make a blow to your leg, ſtand faſt in your warde with your bodie farre out, and in his thruſting come forwarde with your right foote, whereby you ſhal cauſe him to leeſe the greateſt part of his rapier, and turne your dagger point low, receiuing the blow on the ſame, and you may make vnto him either a ſtoccata to the face, or a riuerſa to his
necke

necke or arme. Again, when he thrusteth to your leg, remoue your right foote to your right side, as it were making a circle, & so offend your enimy: as if he make a riuersa to the head, you may take it vpon your rapier & dagger, passing with your left foot, turning your rapier hand & making a stoccata: and if you will you may by passing receiue the riuersa vpon your dagger onely, but looke you carrie your dagger point aloft, as I haue told you before. Againe, if hee make the riuersa to your leg, you may sodeinly passe with your left foot to his right, & take the riuersa on your dagger, for thereby you get the strength of his rapier, and are master of it, and may easily strike him. Again, if he make anie violent blow at your head, retire a litle on your lefte side, & receiue it with your rapiers point, passing with your left foote, & turning your point to his face, & clapping your dagger on his rapier: all other blowes and riuersaes you may easily receiue on your dagger, but it behoueth you to receiue thē with the point of your rapier, otherwise your enemie might thrust his rapier between your rapier & dagger especially if he cast his hande vpward, and his pointe downward, therefore take heed how you thrust, for these are all good times. If your enemie come furiouslie vpon you to assault you, keep you still in your gard, and in his comming neere to you, thrust at him, for he is neither in ward nor yet standeth firme, and the more resolutely he commeth vpon you, the more he is in danger, and the woorse is it for him, because hee may easily with a little pricke bee slaine: but courage ioyned with skill and knowledge is verie good.

Againe,

Againe, if a tall man fhould affault a little man, this ward is exceeding good for the tal man, becaufe if he charge the other, & the tall man thruft, being within rech, he lofeth his point, & the litle man may giue him a ftoccata, or make a paffata at him, but if the tall man know how to put himfelf in ward & thruft, he might haue great aduauntage by the length of his reach, in thrufting a ftoccata, and retiring with his bodie. Againe, if your enemie woulde make a paffata on you with his left foote, when you finde him to remoue, & woulde beate your weapons awaie with his dagger, moue your right foote a little backward, and fodeinly turne your point ouer his dagger, and make an imbrocata to him, for in his paffing he loofeth his dagger, and whileft he paffeth, you may retire a little into your ward, and make a ftoccata to his face, and fuche like, whereof I cannot now ftand to write.

THE

foddenlie into his other hand, and fo haue you at a great aduantage,& therfore I teach you to lay held of the hilts,becaufe you haue thē commanded his fword furelie : and if your enemie finding your pointe out at length,wold beat it afide with his rapier,to paffe vpon you,retire your lefte foote a little backeward,and with great promptnes in the fame inftant, falfifie with a riuerfa, either to the face or bellie : of which kinde of thruftes you fhall often haue vfe,but you muft be verie readie and well practifed therein : therefore you muft labour it,that when occafion requireth you maye performe it.

I   THE

271

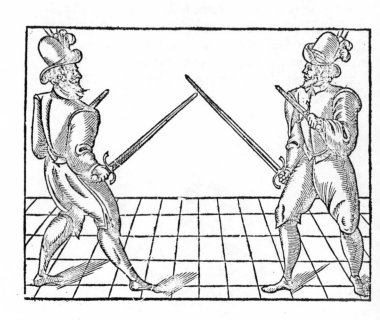

THE SECOND DAYES
Discourse, of Rapier *and* Dagger.

Luke.

Haue been so well satisfied with this first ward of Rapier and Dagger, that I should thinke my selfe verye happie, to put in practise, as much as you deliuered vnto me in precept: but I will not spare any labour to exercise all. But now you shal doe me much pleasure, if you will teach mee the other warde, which you call Puncta riuersa.

V. I haue discoursed vnto you, how profitable the former wardes bee, as well to learne as to fight, beeing well vnderstoode and practised: and euen so will I now make you acquainted with the worthines of this ward, and of what importance it is, notwithstanding that it is quite contrary to the other: especially, in learning of it. Therfore he that will teach that warde, must place his scholler euen as at single Rapier, that is, that his feete stand both equall with toe and heele, euen as if hee were to sitte downe, and that his Rapier handle be held within side of his right knee, and that somwhat shorte, and that his Dagger be helde out at length with his arme stretched out, holding the point of his rapier

I 2   continu-

continuallie vpon the face of his maister, who ought to set him selfe in the same ward, and to giue a stoccato in the middle of the Rapier, in punta riuersa to his schol-ler, or else betweene the arme and the Rapier, or in the bellie, or in the face, escaping a little backeward with his right foot, accompanied somewhat with his left, to-wards his lefte side.

L. What shall the scholler doe in the meane while?

V. While your maister giueth you the thrust, you shall not strike it by with your dagger, but onelie tur-ning your Rapier hand, passe with your lefte foote to-wards his right side, and the point of your Rapier being placed aboue his, and thrust forwarde, shall enter right into his bellie.

L. And what shall the maister doe to saue himselfe?

V. When hee giueth the thrust, and you passe to-wards his right side, hee shall with great nimblenes re-coyle a little backward with his right foot, accompani-ed with the left toward the left side, bearing his bodie backward, and pearching your Rapier with his dagger, shall strike it outward from his left side, and giue you a Mandritta at the head.

L. Then what remaines for me to doe?

V. You shal come with your right foote, to the place where your maisters right foot was, and shal giue him a thrust in the belly or in the face, receiuing the mandrit-ta vpon your Rapier and Dagger, and the euent will be no other then the same of the former ward : and by this meanes you shall become very nimble and quick, both with foote, hand, and bodie : otherwise, if you haue not all these partes readie and perfect, by offering the stoccata, you hazard your self gretly & dangerously.

For

For while you thrust, if your aduersarie surpasse you in nimblenesse, and bee readie, he may enter with his lefte foote and put you in great danger, bringing your weapon into his owne power. Therefore when you wyll giue this thrust either in the bellye or face, passe wyth your right foot towardes the right side of your enemy, so that your right foote bee somewhat on the out-side of your enemies right foote, and so being in right measure, you may giue him the said thrust either in the bellie or in the face with great celeritie and aptnesse, recoiling somewhat with your left foot, accompanied wyth the right : and if your enemie enter with his left foote, you shall speedily turne your bodie on your lefte side, whereby, the more secretly your enemie commeth vppon you, and the more forcibly hee entereth, the more hurt shall he doo himselfe, and the more easily shal you be able to master him, and become Lorde of his owne weapon.

Besides, if you place your right foot a little towards your enemies right foot, you may make a thrust toward his right side, but in thrusting, see you bring your right foote towardes your enemies left side : if you see that hee goeth about to enter with his left legge, turne your bodie well on your right side, for then if hee enter witn his left legge, the point of his Rapier will go by the out side of your bodie, and you may giue him a riuersa vppon his legge with your Rapier, and stabbe him with your dagger in the bodie. All which you must do with great celeritie and quicknesse, turning your bodie with great nimblenesse on your left side, and recoiling somwhat with your left foote, being accompanied with the right, and so you shal deliuer your selfe and your rapier

I   3   with-

withall out of the power of your enemie, but if you bee not paſsing readie with your foot, and in turning your bodie wel and fitly on your right ſide, your enemie entering maye thruſt you in the bellie with his Rapier, and giue you a ſtabbe with his Dagger beſides. Therefore I aduertiſe you to exerciſe your ſelfe continually, that occaſion beeing offered you to fight, you maie perfourme the ſame with much readineſſe, and without daunger, otherwiſe, if you onely faile in one and euen the leaſt point, you endanger your life. For it is not maine force that doth the deede, but readineſſe, dexteritie, and vſe of knowledge and arte. You muſt therefore labour and take paines, which beeing ioyned to the greate deſire and loue you beare to this arte, will bring you to the perfection therof. Inſomuch that you ſhall bee able to turne and winde your bodie which waye you will, and therewithall know how and which waie you ought to turne it.

Againe to the purpoſe : If your enemie make towardes your right ſide, and offer a thruſt, happilie preſſing too much forward, you ſhall immediatlie turne your bodie on the left ſide, ſo that the point of his Rapier paſſing beſide your bodie, you maye giue him a ſtoccata : or you may plaie with your bodie, and beate his Rapier pointe outward from your right ſide wyth your Dagger, and giue him a punta riuerſa ouer his Rapier in the belly or face. Or alſo while hee thruſteth, you may beate it by with your Dagger, and carrying your right foote towarde his right ſide, giue him the ſame thruſt. Or againe, whileſt hee doeth thruſt, you maye ſtande firmelie, turning your bodie a little vpon your lefte ſide, and ſtrike by his Rapier pointe with

your

276

your Dagger, and therewithall giue him a riuersa vpon the legge. And if hee bee skilfull in managing his weapon, take heede in anie cafe that you let him not get within you, or winne grounde of you, but feeke ftill to growe vppon him with your foote, that is, that your right foote bee without fide of his right foote, and when hee giues the forefaide thruft, take heed you ftrike neither with your Rapier nor Dagger, if you meane to enter vpon him with a paffata, becaufe hee hauing once gained of you both opportunitie of time and meafure of grounde, you endaunger your felfe verie much: but you fhall onelye turne your Rapier hande inwarde, paffing fpeedelie with your lefte foot to his right foote, placing the middeft of your right foote iuft at the heele of your lefte foote, holding your bodie on the left fide.

As for your Dagger, that muft bee helde vp with the pointe alofte, to the ende that it maie bee mafter of his Rapier: and fo fhall hurte him either vnder or aboue his Dagger. But you muft beware and take greate heede, not to paffe directlie right vppon him, when you make your paffata with your lefte foote towarde his right foote, for if that he bee anie thing skilfull, hee maie giue you a ftoccata or imbroccata. Wherfore whē you make towards him, fee you throw your felfe wholie on the lefte fide, accompanying your left foot with your right, in the manner aforefaid.

Furthermore, if you perceiue your enemies Rapier pointe to bee borne towardes your right fide, hauing gotten vppon him with your right foote, paffe with your lefte foote verie fpeedilie and quicklie to his right foote, and carrying your Dagger, as
in

277

in the manner aforesaid, and giue him an imbroccata vpon his Rapier: But if you finde his Rapier point born vpon your bodie, you shall turne your bodie on your lefte side, and with great celeritie drawe your point vnder his Rapier, that the point therof be vpon his bellie, and your left foote by the right, your dagger being readie with the point vpward, to command his rapier, resting your bodie on your right side.

Furthermore, if you perceiue his Rapier to be long, and the point thereof borne somewhat high, you shall neuerthelesse answere him in this ward: now not holding your Rapier hand on the inside of your knee, but carrying your dagger straight out, and winding your bodie on your lefte side, you shall make semblaunce to beate by his weapon with your dagger, and with great quicknesse you shall draw the point of your dagger vnder his Rapier, readily turning your bodie yppon your right side, and carrying your right foote together with your left somewhat towards his lefte side, &c. But beware how you vse this passata, vnlesse you bee well practised in it, and see you holde stiffe your dagger hande, for if you suffer your hand to swarue anie thing downward, your enemie maie giue you an imbroccata in the face.

Moreouer, in your passata lift not your dagger too high, because (if he bee skilfull with whome you fight) whilest you lifte vp your dagger, or holde your Rapier and Dagger too open, and not inough closed, hee maie retire a little, and so giue you a stoccata or imbroccata, insomuch that you must haue an especiall care of all, or or else you cannot auoide daunger of death. Againe, when you make this passata, see that you remaine not

with

278

with your lefte foote, hecaufe he may giue you a mandritta vppon the legge, or elfe a ftoccata in the bellie.
Alfo in the fame paffata, fee that your bodie reft not
wholie vppon your lefte fide, becaufe that fo dooing,
you fhall your felfe beare your enemies Rapier pointe
vpon your face.

Befides this, when you lie in this warde, and make
vppon your enemie towardes his right fide, if you perceiue that hee holde his Rapier hande fomewhat
high and farre off from his bodie, followe you well in
this warde, and getting fufficient grounde of him, you
maie giue him a ftoccata in the bellie : and in giuing it,
fee that the pointe of your Rapier enter vnder the middeft of his, being your felfe readie to winde awaie with
your bodie.

Furthermore, in charging him, if you finde that his
pointe bee carried to the ground-ward, turne fteadfaft-
ly vppon your lefte fide, and holde your dagger out in
length towards his right fide : and if you can beate the
middeft of his Rapier with your Dagger, at the fame
inftant giue him a ftoccata. You maie alfo in the fame
warde make a paffata with your lefte foote. But if perhappes your enemie when you lie in this warde, fhould
make femblaunce to thruft you, not meaning fo to do,
but onelie for vauntage, fo you bee in equall meafure, anfwere him, and loofe not that time: but if you be
not in equall reach, thruft not earneftly, nor make a
paffata vppon him, for fo you fhoulde endaunger your
lyfe : but in aunfwering him make but a fhort thruft
at him, to the ende that if your enemie or aduerfarie
afterwarde make a true thruft, or elfe come forwarde

K   with

279

with his lefte foote, to make a paſſata vppon you, you
maie ſodainly turne your bodie on your lefte ſide, and
place your Dagger-hand right with your right knee.
And ſo you maie giue him a ſtoccata in the bellie, or
elſe a riuerſa vpon the legge, and become maiſter of his
weapon : and by howe much the more ſtrongly hee
thruſteth, and the more furiouſlie hee entereth with
the paſſata, by ſo much the more eaſilie may you hurt
him : but haue a great and ſpeciall regarde to doo it
with much nimbleneſſe and dexteritie both of bodie
and hand.

Furthermore, if you finde his Rapier long, in charging him you maie ſtrike the middle of his Rapier
with yours, and ſodainely giue him the punta riuerſa:
but it muſt be done with great quickneſſe of the hand,
beeing readie with your right foote to ſteppe towardes
your enemies right ſide, or elſe to recoile ſomewhat
with your bodie backwardes as ſwiftly as you canne :
for elſe if your enemie at that inſtant ſhoulde enter
with a paſſata ſomething fiercelye, your lyfe were in
greate hazarde, and eſpeciallye if you ſhoulde make
your thruſt ſtraight, carrying your foote right towards
his, as manie doo : but if you ſteppe with your right
foote aſide, you maie verie eaſilye auoide the daunger.

Againe, if you finde his Rapier point out at length,
you maie ſtrike his Rapier with yours, and giue him a
greate mandritta or riuerſa at the head, but with greate
ſwifteneſſe of hand and bodie. Alſo lying in the ſame
warde towardes the right ſide of your enemie, you
may

may giue a falſe ſtoccata at his bellie, and if your enemie doo happe to ſtrike it backe with his Rapier, you
ſhall ſodainely put the pointe of your Rapier ouer his,
and giue him a ſtoccata or punta riuerſa vpon his face,
or his bellie, if hee ſhoulde too much hang downe his
hand, at which time you muſt beare your right foote a-
ſide towardes his right ſide. You maie alſo offer a
falſe thruſt at his face, and if hee go about to ſtrike it
by with his Rapier, you maie put your pointe vnder
his Rapier, and carrying your right foote ſide-waie,
giue him a ſtoccata in the bellie: or in both theſe falſe
thruſts, when he beateth them by with his rapier, you
may with much ſodainneſſe make a paſſata with your
lefte foote, and your Dagger commaunding his Rapier, you maie giue him a punta, either dritta, or riuerſa.

Moreouer, if your enemie finding you with your
Rapier point borne out in length, ſhould ſtrike by your
rapier with his, in the verie inſtant that he ſtriketh, you
maie paſſe with your right foote towards his right ſide,
and with great quicknes putting your Rapier ouer his,
giue him a punta riuerſa in the face. and if hee bee not
verie ſkilfull at his weapon, you may ſodainly make a
paſſata vpon him, and this maie happen vnto you verie
often : but you ought to bee well exerciſed in theſe
pointes, which may make you verie nimble and quicke
with your foot, body, and hand, leaſt for want of knowledge and practiſe in this facultie, you fal not into ſome
inconuenience and diſhonour, for in the verie leaſt
point conſiſteth life and death.

K 2   There-

281

Therefore neglect not these thinges, but rather take pains and trauaile in the knowledge of them, honoring and esteeming them both excellent and profitable: neither haue I entered into this charge, to discourse and explaine these pointes for their sakes that hate valour and knowledge, for vnto such doo I not directe my speech, but vnto those that loue, regarde, and honour vertue: who beeing worthie of this knowledge, may alwaies commaund my seruice.

But to returne to our purpose: if your enemie find you in this sayde warde, holding your bodie towardes your lefte side, and towardes his right side, and giue you a mandritta at the head, you shall speedilye and with greate agility turne your bodie on your right side, and receiuing his mandritta vppon your Dagger, retourne him a stoccata either in the bellie or in the face. Likewise, if hee giue you an imbroccata ouer the Dagger, you shall (turning your bodie vppon your right side) aunswere him with a stoccata. But if hee when you lie in this warde, giue you a riuersa at the heade, you may immediatlye make a passata with the lefte foote, and so presentlye requite him with a stoccata.

If you thinke it not conuenient, and therefore will not passe with your lefte foote at the same instaunce that hee giueth the riuersa, you shall turne your bodie on your lefte side, and so haue your choice eyther to giue him a stoccata in the bellie, or a riuersa at the legges: and if you bee thoroughly exercised and practised in charging, you maye giue him a dritta or a riuersa at his legges, being the first to strike.

Many

Many things more may you doe in this warde, according as your enemie fighteth : and you maye vſe this warde after many manners, ſo you be throughlye acquainted with it, and haue by continuall practiſe brought your foote, hand and bodie to it.
But this ſhall ſuffiſe vntill another daye.

K 3   THE

THE THYRDE DAYES
Discourse, of Rapier *and* Dagger.

Luke.

IKnow not certainly, whether it hath been my earnest desire to encounter you, that raisde me earlier this morning than my accustomed houre, or to be assertained of some doubtfull questions, which yester-night were proposed by some gentlemen and my selfe, in dis-
courfe

284

courfe of armes: for they helde, that although a man learne perfectly the dritta, riuerfa, the ftoccata, the imbroccata, the punta riuerfa, with eche feuerall motion of the body, yet when they hap to come to fingle fight, where the triall of true valour muft ende the quartell, they vtterly forget all their former practifes. Therefore would I requeft of you, (if you fo pleafe) to know your opinion, whether in fingle fight a man can forget his vfuall wardes, or vfe them then with as much dexteritie and courage as he accuftomed in play.

V. It is very likely, that many are of this opinion, for there are fewe or none that in caufe of quarrell when they come as we tearme it to buckling, but fuffer themfelues to be ouercome with fury, and fo neuer reméber their arte: fuch effect choller worketh. And it may be fome being timerous and full of pufillanimity, (which is euer father to feare) are fo fcarred out of their wits, that they feeme men amazed and voide of fence. Or fome may be taken in the humor of drinke, or with diuers other occafions, that may enfeeble their vnderftanding. And by thefe reafons well may they forget in fight, what they learned in play: but in them in whome no fuch effectes are predominant, neither are affailed with fuch accidentes, they behaue themfelues difcreetely, and are not diftempered with any fuch perturbations: and befides this, I haue feen many that being fearfull by nature, through dayly practife haue become couragious, and alwaies fo continued. Neither is it poffible, but in practife he fhould obtaine courage and encreafe his valour more then before.

L. But to what end doe you teach fuch skill, if it be fcarfe fecure, and hard to performe.

V.

V. To this I anſwere, that this vertue or art of armes is proper and behouefull to euerye one for their liues, becauſe that no man on earth, but hath had or hath in preſence ſome difference or contention with ſome of his companions, which moſt commonly is decided by fight. To them that are of an hautie courage, this skill addeth aduantage: to them whoſe nature is fearful, the vſe of weapons extenuateth a great parte of feare: and theſe, both the one and other, ought as much as in them lyeth, to auoide all cauilling, and ſuch diſordered ſpeeches as procure contention: but eſpeciallye, let ſuch men take heede, to whome nature hath not giuen a valorous ſpirite: as for others, whoſe courage is hot, it importes them very much, to haue great skill in their weapon, for being ouer-maſtered with heate and courage of their harts, if in managing their armes they wāt a skilfull dexteritie, they ſoone ſpoyle themſelues: for through wante of knowledge, they come to be ouerthrowne, where rather it behoueth them with aduiſement and diſcretion, not onely to ſpy their own faults, and ſoone to amend them, but alſo thorough his enemies ouer-ſights, to take his owne aduantage.

L. True it is I confeſſe what you haue ſaide, for ſure, who ſo wanteth courage, muſt of neceſſitie forget his cunning. But tell of curteſie, were it that a man were to combate, and through breuitie of time it were not poſſible to be perfect in the depth of this knowledge, what order would you take, to inſtruct him that he might be ſafe and dangerles.

V. I wil tell you, I would acquaint him with one only warde, which amongſt all other is the beſt for fight, to him who will vnderſtand it: of which I meane now

to

286

to entreate, to the end I may entttuct you in it, that being throughly practised in that onely warde, you maye combate securely. Therefore to make my scholler perfect in that manner of lying, I would place him with his lefte foote and dagger before, extending his bodye far, and I also would lye so, then would I haue him trauerse towards my left side, and I circularly would passe with my right foote, thrusting a stoccata eitherat his face or brest.

L. And what shall the scholler doe then to defend himselfe, and offend you?

V. Whilste I thrust my stoccata at him, and that I passe about towards his lefte side, in that moment that I parte from him and thrust, hee shall likewise in that counter-time passe circularly towards my left side, and then shall thrust a stoccata at my brest or face, winding his body vpon his left side.

L. And how will you saue your selfe?

V. In that instant, wherein both my selfe and he doe passe thrusting at me in that counter-time; if I be not very prompt, with the motion of my bodie, hee maye easilie strike me in the brest or face: therefore whilest that I thrust at him and he at me, I will break it with my Dagger from my lefte side, turning the pointe either high or lowe, according as hee thrustes; and I would helpe my selfe with drawing my body backwards, and in that time I would carry my right foote towards his lefte, and then would I thrust an imbroccata about his Dagger.

L. And what can he doe?

V. Hee shall doe the like, guiding his right foote to-
L ward

warde my lefte, and i fhall breake my Imbroccata outwarde from his lefte fide, and thruft an imbroccata at mee aboue my Dagger: and I wil retire afide, as I haue tolde you in the former wardes, and make at him with a dritta, or riuerfa, or an imbroccata with the dritta, as in the others;

L. I am of this minde, that whofoeuer would perfome this warde, had neede to be perfectlie inftructed and throughly exercifed, and that hebe of good knowledge: for certainly this I thinke, it is an excellent ward for him that knowes to doe it well, but very dangerous for a raw fcholler or imperfect. And if you would mamifeft fome lying to counter-check this warde we haue fpoken of, I fhould thinke my felfe highlye beholding for fuch a fauour.

V. Obferue this firfte, if you were in fight, to vfe this warde, and that your enemie in like forte fhould garde him felfe with the fame lying : marke this cheefely and firft how hee beares his weapons and his bodie, high or lowe, and how hee holdes his Rapier and Dagger, and according to his lying, affaulte and offer to him. Therfore in the encounter that you fhall make, charge him towardes his lefte fide, keeping your felfe fafelye in your warde, and haue this regarde, to keepe your poynte within his. And if he lye high with his bodye and Dagger, keepe your poynte vnder his Dagger hande, and thruft your ftoccata at his brefte: but if you fee him lye with his Dagger lowe, thruft an imbroccata at his belly with great celeritye, or at his face, auoiding with your right foote circularlye towardes his lefte, turning quickly your body vpon your
lefte

lefte fide, in manner of an halfe wheele: but it behoues
you to be verye readye, otherwife, in ftaying in your
paffage, if hee auoyde in that counter-time, hee maye
put you in danger of life: the like is, if you paffe directlye, you are both of you in danger of death: or
if you fhould paffe directlye, and hee keepe him felfe in
fafe warde, or that he auoide in compaffe, he may well
faue him felfe and endanger you. Therefore finding
your enemie in this warde, euer obferue to carrie your
felfe in compaffe.

Moreouer, if you affaile your enemie with this
warde, and hee lye with his right foote formoft, if hee
holde his Rapier far from him, you may directlye take
his pointe, keeping your dagger long out, and your bodie lowe: and if he thruft either aboue or belowe, keep
your Dagger ready to break his thruft, and offer home
to him vpon the lefte foote, or paffe towards him with
your right foote, as you fhall finde beft. And in your
caricado fee if you can commaund his fwoorde with
your Dagger, either from your lefte or right fide, and
then thruft your ftocceta or punta riuerfa. If you fee
him lye difplaied, followe him, bearing your Dagger
within his fword, and you maie well thruft your ftoccata either at his face or breft: or elfe make a paffata refolutelie, wheeling halfe about, keeping your felfe prefentlie in a good warde, vpon your right foote.

Moreouer, in this warde you maye eafilie giue
him a mandritta or riuerfa vpon his legges, or you
maie vfe a caricado vpon his right fide, keeping your
warde, and carrying well your bodye, that the halfe
of your right foote garde your lefte heele, and guiding

L 2   your

289

your body directly vpon your left side, make forwarde directly vpon his right foot, thereby to commaund his fwoorde, and then may you ftrike him vpon the lefte foote. Againe, if you fee hee keepes his Dagger pointe vpon you, thruft a ftoccata at his face: if you finde him not well commaunding his point, charge him vpon his right fide, bearing the dagger long, and break his thruft outwards, offring your ftoccata at his face or breft, Like-wife, if you fee he commaund not his point, and being aduantaged vpon his right fide, you maye with great readines put your pointe vnder his fwoord, lifting your fwoord hand and your dagger, when in the mean time you may giue him a ftoccata or imbroccata, and be ma-fter of his fwoorde with yours and your Dagger. And in charging him vpon his right fide, you may giue him a riuerfa vpon his legge.

Againe, if hee offer a mandritta at your head, in the lifting of his hand aduance your felfe with your right foote, and receiue it vpon your Dagger, giuing him a ftoccata at his breft or face: fo if hee thruft a riuerfa at your head, you fhall lift vp the point of your Dagger, & receiue it on your dagger & fworde, & in the fame time thruft an imbroccata at his belly, or elfe taking the riuer-fa vpon your Dagger, you fhall giue him another ypon the legges, or a ftoccata in the belly. Likewife, if your enemie fhall giue you a mandritta vpon the legge, you fhall nimbly paffe circularly with your right foote to-wards his lefte fide, for fo hee cannot offend you, and you may hit him either in the belly or face.

Moreouer, if your enemie thruft an imbroccata a-boue your Dagger, you muft readilye paffe with your right

right foote before he retire with his point, and you may well hit him in the face, breaſt, or legges. Again, if when you charge him towardes his right ſide, you ſee his point be farre out and ſomewhat high, keepe your bodie vppon your lefte ſide, and lie lowe couered in your ward, bearing your dagger at the length of your arme, keeping good meaſure: and in your cariage, make ſhew to put by his Rapier with your dagger, and ſodainly fal your point vnder his ſword, trauerſing with your right foot round, turning your bodie vppon your right ſide, & ſo thruſt your ſtoccata at his face, or breaſt. And if he hold his point high, you may charge him directly with his point, for if hee thruſt either aboue or below, in the time of his thruſt aduaunce your left foote, extending your dagger, and by that aduancing hee ſhall looſe his point, and you maie hit him with a dritta or riuerſa at your pleaſure. And if he thruſt at you, and you paſſe about with your right foote, then you maie likewiſe hit him.

L. Truly you haue giuen mee to vnderſtand excellently of this ward: but let me intreate you to teach me how I maie defende my ſelfe if one aſſaile mee in that ward, and how I may beſt offend my enemie, keeping my right foot formoſt.

V. I haue tolde you many things concerning this ward, if you know how to doo them and practiſe them. Beſides, there bee diuerſe other thinges which I cannot ſhew you with ſpeaking: but for this time it will bee ſufficient if you can performe what I haue declared. And I will tell you: if you lie with your right foote formoſt, and he keepe his left foote forwarde, according as you marke his lying, ſo do, charging him either on the lefte

L 3
or

or right side. And although you hit him not, and that he passe vpon his right foote, doe you but change your bodie to your left side, lifting vp the point of your poniard, firming your hand on your righr knee, so shall you be master of his sword, and maie easily strike him, and the more fierce he is, the more shall you commaund his weapon and endanger him: neither can hee strike you either within or without your dagger, or on the legges. And if you seehe keepes his dagger winding towardes his right side, thrust a riuersa at his face, so that your point may enter in the midst of his dagger, and sodainly recoile, and if he likewise parte, turne your bodie, as I haue tolde you, vpon your left side, and as you see him lie, so guarde your selfe, bearing your bodie on which side you thinke best.

And surely beleeue mee, the first warde I taught you of Rapier and dagger, is absolutely the best both against this and anie other kinde of lyings. Therefore I woulde wish you to learne it perfectly, and exercise it thoroughly, that if occasion happen, you may be both skilfull and well practised. But take heede of one fault, which many incurre, who if in plaie they receiue one or two stoccataes, they inforce themselues to giue one to be reuenged. But this is neither fit for a scholler, nor orderlie, since in plaie we shuld behaue our selues friendlie, both to learn and passe the time, and also to exercise our selues in stirring our bodies, and vse this arte for the right effect. Wherein wee ought especiallie to auoide choler and anger: For where occasion happens to fight, in deede, rapiers are not as foiles, which cannot doo much hurt, but a small pricke of a Rapiers pointe maie either kill, or at the least maime. So that in anie wise a-
uoide

uoide ſo daungerous an ouerſight. And if you happe to wound your enemie, though verie ſmallie, yet by the ſight of his blade, hee heeing kindled with furie, ſhall both enſeeble his ſtrength, and fall from his right bias. Therefore I wiſh you take good heede, and if you ſee your ſelfe apte to incline to ſuch a faulte, amende it, and learne perfectlie to defende your ſelfe well, to the end that if perhappes you cannot hurt your enemie, either for that he ſurpaſſeth in ſkil, or you want ſtrength, yet you maie auoide danger of beeing hurt your ſelfe, which will bee both honorable and profitable to you, conſidering that euen the verie firſt thruſt is ſufficient to ende the whole controuerſie. Therefore bee heedfull and wiſe, and remember I haue tolde you ſoundly for your owne ſafetie.

L. I aſſure you I will followe your aduiſe, which I ſee grounded on ſuch reaſon, as euerie wiſe and reaſonable man ought to followe it, eſttaunging himſelfe from all furious fellowes, who thinke to purchaſe honour by running headlong on their death. Therefore will I ſequeſter my ſelfe from their acquaintance. But I praie you proſecute and go forward with the reſt of this ward.

V. Sithence I ſee you conceiue ſuch pleaſure in it, I will proceede on and goe forward a little farther. Manie there bee which exerciſe this warde vppon theyr leſte foote, but therein they differ. Therefore it importes to bee well inſtructed in the diuerſitie: for if your enemie lie in that warde, and you vppon your right foote, and hee beare himſelfe and his Dagger highe, charge him towardes his leſte ſide, and in the approche, ſee you parte with greate readyneſſe

with

with your right foote towardes his left, and speedilie
thrust you a stocata in his belly, & in the thrusting, look
you enter vnder his arme or hande, turning your bodie
on the right side, and the back side of your sword hand
toward your left. If he hold his dagger low, charge him
towards his left side with your right foote side-waies,
and thrust either a stoccata or imbroccata, as you shall
thinke best, aboue his dagger, and for your owne safe-
gard, turne your bodie vpon the right side. And if you
see him lie displaide, carrie your bodie on your right
side, and trauerse to his lefte, and then thrust your stoccata betweene his sword and dagger.

Moreouer, you maye thruste your stoccata either at his face or breast, but doo it with greate
promptnesse, and in the same time recoile with your
left foot drawing after your right, and be quicke in the
retire to recouer your rapier, that if your enemie make
forward, you may be readie againe to thrust: therefore
be quicke and vigilant, otherwise if in your thrusting
you be not readie, in that selfe same time your enemie
maie well hit you: but retiring with your feete, and e-
scaping with your bodie, you shall shunne all daunger.
Againe, if you finde his rapier point high, charge him
lowe vpon the left foot, and directlie with your dagger
at his Rapiers point, bearing your Dagger as I haue
taught you: so you maie thrust either at his face or brest
without retiring, but being sure to lie wel in your ward,
for in the time whilest you retire or withdraw your feet,
you shall be in danger, but keeping that ward sure, you
are without perill, for whether hee thrust aboue or belowe, you beeing in that ward are safe, and more ready
to winde your pointe aboue or belowe his dagger, or

you

294

you maie giue him a mandritta on the legs: neither can
he hurt you in his circular or turning, if he should so recoile. Againe, if you see him lie vpright, lie you so likewise, but euer keepe your Dagger readie, and you maie
seigne a stoccata at his face, and whilest he goeth about
to breake it, winde your pointe quicklie vnder his dagger, and wheele with your bodie halfe compasse, auoiding with your right foote side-waies, as I haue tolde
you. And if hee charge you lowe and lie open, comming directlie on your pointe, giue backe your bodie a
little, and thrust a riuersa or a stoccata like an imbroccata, and readilie remoue with your right foot backward:
or if hee lie as manie doe, with his sword vpon his dagger crosse-wise, you may redilie thrust him in the face,
and retire backeward towards his leste side. Againe, in
that maner of lying, you maie charge him towardes his
right side, and thrust a stoccata at his face, betweene his
Rapier and Dagger, euer remembring that your sword
passe by the middest of his Dagger, and giue him a riuersa in recoiling backward towards his right side. And
if you fortune not to hitte him, and that he passe vpon
his right foote, doe you but change your bodie to the
leste side, lifting vp your poniard, and holding your
hand firmelie on your right knee, so shal you be master
of his swoorde, and maie easilie hit him : and the more
fierce he is, the more you shall commaund his weapon,
and mangle him, neither can he strike you, either within or without your Dagger, or with a dritta or riuersa
vpon the legges. Againe, if you see him holde his dagger with the point turning to his leste side, thrust at his
face a riuersa, guiding your pointe to enter in the middest of his dagger, and soddenlie recoile: and if he like-

wife parte, doe as I haue alreadie tolde you, winding
your bodie well vpon your lefte fide: if you finde him
lying open, vfe your caricado toward his right fide, and
lye lowe in your warde, carrying your bodie on your
lefte fide, bearing your Dagger out at length, as I haue
taught you in the firft warde : but let your hand beeing
directly with your knee, turne with your bodie, and in
this manner you maie offer a thruft: and if hee thruft
firft, beare your dagger readie to defend your felfe, and
your rapier to offend him. But in this be very heedful,
as I haue often tolde you, neither eleuate nor abafe
your dagger hand, nor beare him ouer the one fide or
the other, for if your enemy haue good skill in his weapon, and withall a readie hand, he may eafilie beare his
pointe compaffe and hurt you : or many times feigne a
thruft to deceiue you. Therefore be alwaies aduifed to
keepe your hand firme, not abafing or lifting vp your
pointe, or turning your wrift on the one fide or other:
and if he thruft at you, you maie well readilie both defend your felfe, and offend him.

Moreouer, if he abafe his point, lie in your lefte foot
warde, and vfe your caricado vpon his right fide, and if
hee thruft either an imbrocca aboue your Dagger, or a
mandritta at your head, remouing his right foot, turne
readilie your bodie on your right fide, lifting vp your
Dagger, and turning your wrifte. Againe, if you finde
his pointe farre out, charge him in your left foot warde
towards his right fide, and charge him with your Dagger clofe to his fworde, and letting fall your pointe vnder his, you maie eafilie thruft a ftoccata or imbroccata, but euer keepe firme your Dagger hand, and lift not
vp your bodie, and in breaking his thruft toward his
                                                    left

left side,you maie giue him a riuersa either in the brest or on the legs. Besides this, many more practises there be,which with good exercise of body,and readines of hand,might easilie be effected. But because it groweth somewhat late,and our discourse hath lasted so long, I will take my leaue of you,retiring my selfe to dispatch some busines before my going home.

L. I am infinitely beholding vnto you for these good instructions,and to morrow I wil meete you, to vnder-stand somewhat more,for my farther skil,and auoiding of idlenes.

V. God be your guide,and to morrow I will expecte you.

M 2   THE

Vincentio Sauiolo his Practise.

THE FOVRTH DAYES
Discourse, of single Rapier.

Entreating how a lefte handed man, shall plaie with one that is right handed.

Luke.

Ffter your departure yesterdaie in the after-noone, I was in an honorable place, wher vpon occasion of some ielousie of loue of certaine gentlewomē two gentlemen of the companie fell at words, and from words to deeds, but they were not suffered at that time to proceede to any further action, neuertheles they gaue their faithes the next morning to trie it with their weapons. and so accordinglie they met, and brauely perfourmed their combate: in the execution whereof I tooke great pleasure to be a beholder, not that I had anie delight to see them kill one another, but for another cause, (and that was) to see by experience the truth of that which I haue heard manie affirme: and seeing there is so good an opportunity offered, I wil entreat you, hauing troubled

298

bled you in a greater matter, that you will aſſoyle me certaine doubtes, which I ſhall demaund of you, and make me rightly vnderſtand them, whereby I ſhall remaine greatly bound vnto you.

V. I praie you tell me, what were theſe gentlemen which fought, and whether anie of them be hurt: after, be bolde to declare to me your doubtes, and I will not faile to reſolue you the beſt I can.

L. Sir, I doubt not of your curteſie, which I haue found you alwaies willing to ſhewe to euerie man, but cheefely to your freends: but to tell you the truth, I haue forgot the gentlemens names, but this I can well ſaie, that in the handling of their weapons they behaued themſelues very manfullie, neither of them receiuing any wound, for they were both very quicke with the rapier to offend, and with their daggers to defend: but the greateſt reaſon that led me to be preſent there, was to ſee how well they managed their weapons, one of them being right handed, and the other left handed: becauſe I know many of opinion, that the left handed haue great aduantage of the right, yet I ſee both doe their vttermoſt this morning, without any hurt of either partie, and in beholding both the one and the other diligently. I could not diſcerne anie iot of aduantage betweene them: therefore you ſhall doe me great fauour, if you diſcourſe vnto me, whether the left hand can haue any aduantage of the right, or the right of the leſte: withall inſtructing me, both how to defende my ſelfe from ſuch a one, and how to offend him.

V. Of this queſtion, I haue heard many times much reaſoning, and many there are indeede which ſo think, but beleeue me, the left hand hath no aduantage of the right hand, nor the right, of the lefte no otherwise than you your selfe finde your owne aduantage.

L. Tell me therfore, if you would teach a left hand, how would yon begin?

V. I would teach him first with the single rapier, making him to stand with his left foote forwardes, and that his heele should be right againſt the middle part of his right foote, & I would put my selfe with my right foot forward, as I told you before concerning the single rapier, & I would that the scholler should hold his sword out at length, that the point thereof bee directlie at my face, and that he holde his sword-hand, as it were in a line, from his bodie, & outwards of my sword towards my right side, passing withal with his left foot towards my left side, putting his rapier vnder mine, and to giue me an imbroccata in the belly, by turning the knuckle of his hand downwards towards his left side.

V. It seemeth that you doo all contrarie to the right hand, because in teaching the right hand, hee vseth the stoccata, but the left hand, you make him to begin with the imbroccata. But what will you doo to defend your selfe in the meane time?

V. I will auoide somewhat with my body, and with my hand beate downe his imbroccata without my left side, and carrying my right foot after my left foot, giue him a riuersa at the head.

L. What shal the scholler doo in his defence, both to hurt you and saue himselfe?

V. He shal doo quite contrarie vnto him that is right handed, because the right hand, when I offer him a riuersa at the head, passeth with the left foote, and giueth me the imbroccata vnder my rapier: but the left hande, whilest

whileſt I go backe with my right foot, and that I liſt my rapier to giue him the riuerſa, he ſwiftly paſſeth with his right foot before his left, and giueth me a ſtoccata, liſting his hand from behinde: & ſo in the paſſataes which he ſhall make, ſtanding with his left foote forward, and paſſing with his right foot to ſtrike his enemie, whereas the right hand paſſeth with his left foot when he giueth a ſtoccata to his enemie, the left hand cleane contrarie, in paſſing giues the imbroccata to his enemie: & wheras the right hand ſhal giue the imbroccata, the left hand quite contrarie ſhall giue the ſtoccata, and that which I ſaie, is for the left handes inſtruction againſt the right. But nowe I will ſpeake no further of this warde, for ſo much as no other thing foloweth but that which I haue tolde you alreadie concerning the firſt warde of the ſingle rapier, and I will declare vnto you the warde of the rapier and dagger, both to inſtruct the lefte handed how to deale againſt the right hand, and how the right hand ought to behaue himſelfe againſt the lefte hande, which ſhall be our next diſcourſe. And for this time I praie you pardon me, hauing occaſion to go a little way hence, to take vp a matter betweene two of my friends, vpon certaine differences happened betweene them, & by and by we will meet againe. Farewell.

The leſte handes Warde at Rapier and Dagger.

L. Seeing you haue alreadie declared howe a leſte hande is to bee taught at ſingle Rapier, I praie you alſo tell mee, how you woulde likewiſe inſtruct him at Rapier and Dagger, and afterwardes the defence againſt him.

Y. I

301

V. If I should make a good lefte handed scholler, I would place him with his lefte foote forward, and his lefte heele, againft the middle of his right foote, making him to holde his Rapier shorte, and his Dagger out long.

L. In what warde would you put your felfe?

V. I would put my felfe in the firfte warde of Rapier and Dagger, carrying my bodie in good ward towards my left fide, and I would giue him a ftoccata vnder his Rapier, bearing my right foote towards his lefte fide, turning well my bodie circularlie vpon my right fide, and he in the fame time turning the point of his dagger downe, shall beate by my ftoccata from his lefte fide, and withall pafsing with his lefte foote towardes my lefte fide, hee shall giue me an imbroccata vnder my Dagger: I in the meane while will auoide a little with my body, ftriking by his imbroccata from my left fide, and carrying my right foote againe towardes his lefte fide, I will giue him an imbroccata vnder the Rapier: then he shall turne his Dagger pointe vpwarde, and ftrike by my imbroccata from his lefte fide, going with his lefte foote circularly towards my left fide, and shall giue me a ftoccata in the face ouer my Dagger, and I will beate by his ftoccata outwards from my lefte fide, going againe with my right foote circularlye towards his lefte fide, and giue him another ftoccata vnder the Dagger, and hee shall beate it by as before, going afide with his lefte foote towards my lefte fide, and shall giue me an imbroccata vnder the Dagger, as before, and I auoiding a little with my bodie, will beate his imbroccata outwards on my right fide, parting at the inftant with my right foote, and carrying after my lefte: and

giue

302

giue him a riuerſa at the head, and if I ſhould not bowe backeward with my bodie when I did beate by his imbroccata towardes my right ſide, I my ſelfe ſhould receiue it in mine owne bellie, or the face: and whileſt I goe with my right foote, and giue him a riuerſa, he ſhal goe with his right foote where my right foote was, and giue me a ſtoccata in the bellie, whereas he ſhal receiue the riuerſa vpon his Rapier and Dagger.

L. Theſe thinges would ſeeme very ſtrange to ſuch as vnderſtand them not, becauſe when you offer that riuerſa to the right handed man, you teach him to paſſe with the leſte foote, and to giue you the imbroccata, contrarilie you in the ſame caſe make the leſte handed man, to paſſe with his right foote, giuing you the ſtoccata.

V. Did I not tell you that the leſte hand had no aduantage of the right, nor the right of the leſte? onelye vſe and knowledge giueth the better either to the right or the leſte: and oftentimes you ſhalbe occaſioned to doe manye thinges, dealing with the left handed man, which you muſt do cleane contrary to that which you would doe, dealing with the right handed man: wherfore ſeek to learne and to practiſe your ſelfe, that when occaſion ſhall be offered, you maye knowe how to behaue your ſelfe, and contemne the opinions of theſe *Spaca montagne*, which deſpiſe arte, becauſe ignorance was euer the enemy of knowledge. Is it poſſible that he which neuer ſaw the warres, can be better knowledged then he which hath ſpent his life wholye therein, and borne honorable charges? can hee which neuer made ſhot in anie peece of artillerie or hargebuſe, or bow, be more perfect, or at leaſt know ſo much as they which

of

of long time haue made profession therof? so it is in the
vse of weapons, and in euery other facultie : for example, take a Cannoneer which well vnderstandeth his
arte, and he will charge his Peeces in such good forte,
that it shall be a hard matter, or almost impossible for
them to break: afterward take one of these contemners
of arte, who with their blinde iudgement presume to
be able to doe all thinges, to such a one giue the handling of a Peece of ordinance, and let him not want pou-
der, shot, or any necessaries therto belonging, and let
him charge according to his vaine knowledge, you shal
see him presentlye breake all and kill himselfe. The like
falleth out in the handling of armes, the ignorant will
doe one thing for an other, which shall turne to his
own confusion, for by the mouing of his bodie or foot
onely out of time and order, he may easilie ouerthrow
him selfe, and hasten his owne death.

C. It hath been seene neuertheles, that many altogether vnexperienced in the hargebuse, haue made as
good shot as they which haue long practised the same.

V. It is an olde saying, that one flower maketh not a
spring, for although this vnskilful man haue made, or
may make at any time some good shot, assure your selfe
it is to be attributed to chaunce or fortune, or as it is
said, to his good hap, and if he should bee demaunded
at what thing hee made his leuell, if hee wil confesse a
truth, hee will not denie, that his leuell was set at an
other marke, and in truth it may not be otherwise: for
triall wherof make him shoote again, and you shall see
hauing no more knowledge then before, nor practising
the said exercise, that scarse euer hee will make the like
shot againe. But they which are wel instructed and exercised

ercifed therin, will feldome make one fault. In like fort,
in the vfe of other weapons, one maye giue a cunning
ftroke, but it fhal be by fortune, and no cunning: fo that
thinking to giue the like blowe againe, he will occafion
his owne death, and that onely by not knowing what
time to ftrike: after the fame manner hee that will take
vpon him to charge a Peece of artillerie, not knowing
the charge thereof according to the waight of her bullet, will foone breake all, and murder him felfe: but he
which truely hath his arte, you fhall fee him with dexteritie charge & difcharge, without any encombrance,
hauing his fecrets readie to coole the Canon when fhe
is ouerheated, and other artificiall feates which hee can
make to ferue his turne: fo that it is no meruaile that he
which is guided onely by prefumption, and will thruft
him felfe into matters which hee knoweth not, if hee o-
uerthrowe him felfe and fuch as rely vpon him: and e-
fpecially certaine harbrainde wits, who vfe to defpife e-
uery thing, with whom I exhorte you to haue no dealing, feing they are men void of al reafon, which ought
to be the rule of mans life, and without which a man is
no man, but the outward fhape of a man onely.

L. Truly I know you fay the truth, and of force the
knowledge of al good fciences muft come from God,
which is of a diuine nature. But let this paffe, I pray you
refolue me in this: wherfore vfe you not to ftrike at the
poniard fide, as wel as at the right fide, and by what reafon ftrike you at the fworde fide? tell me alfo which is
the better fide to ftrike, either the poniarde fide or the
fworde fide, and which of them is more fafe?

V. When you goe to charge a lefte handed man in
your warde, looke firft in what ward he lyeth, and how
hee holdeth his weapons, anfwering him in the fame

forme: and touching your demaund, to knowe wherfore I ftrike not at the Dagger fide, I wil tell you: when I finde him in this ward carrying his lefte foot formoft, if I fhould make at his Dagger fide and ftrike firfte, I put my felfe in danger to hurt my felf, becaufe in thrufting I runne vpon the pointe of my enemie: but making at his lefte fide, I am out of danger of his pointe, whereof making to his Dagger fide I am in perill: for if you ftrike firfte and the lefte handed man haue a good Dagger, and be quicke with his fworde, he will alwaies put you in hazard of an imbroccata: and in truth there are fewe lefte handes which vfe ftoccataes, but for the moft parte imbroccataes. Now if he offer you the imbroccata firft, being towards his dagger, and you being nimble with your bodie, whileft hee ftrikes at you, you fhall a little bow afide with your body, and beat by the pointe outwards from your left fide, and you may eafilye giue him a ftoccata or an imbroccata: but if you ftrike, firft you endanger your felf: and if you will ftrike the firft, you fhall go towards his left fide, to be in more fafetie, and offering your blowe, feeke to be without his pointe, ftriuing to faften your ftoccata at his face, and retire your lefte foot back with great fwiftnes, your right foot accompanying your left: but finding him in his ward, to beare his fwoorde out at length, if you be well aduifed, you fhall carrie your right foot after your left, and lye in the third ward I taught you concerning the left foot: and regarde wel whileft you are in warde vpon the right foot, and if you wil, out of the firft ward of Rapier and dagger, enter into the third: be fure that you paffe not forward with the left foot firfte, for in fo doing he might giue you a ftoccata in the belly or face:

therefore

306

therefore carie your right foot after your left, and in the said ward, charge him towards his left side, who lying with his left foot forward, as you do, if you charge him on the left side, vnles he be verie ready and perfect at his weapon, you shal haue great aduantage of him, & make your selfe master of his weapons, and greatly indanger his life. Neuerthelesse if he be skilful, and know how to plaie with his bodie, he maie auoide the foresayd dangers, and hazard your life, if you bee not the more skilfull, albeit you finde him, as I said before, lying with his left foot forward. Wherefore it is necessarie that you vnderstand and practise well your selfe, seeing the least errour you maie make, may be your great hurt.

L. But suppose that one be altogether ignorant, and haue not these turnings of his bodie in a readinesse, you tolde mee there was no difference betweene the right hand and the left hand, neither of them hauing aduantage of the other. And now you tell mee, that the right hand, in case he lie in the third ward, trauersing toward the left side of his enemy, hath great aduantage of a left hand. I praie you therefore shew mee if there be anie other ward, wherein the lefte hande may so lie, that the right hand shall haue no aduantage vpon him.

V. You know how I saide there was no aduauntage betweene them, besides that which vse and knowledge giueth to either partie, wherefore if the right hande change from the first warde into the third, to assault the left hand, then the lefte hand shall carrie his lefte foote after his right, so lying with the right foote fowarde in good ward, and the right hande lie in the third warde, with his lefte foot forward, and so shall neither the one or the other haue a iote of aduantage, except that which

he

he can giue by true obferuation of time and meafure, and his better knowledge: fo that if the lefte hand be well inftructed, finding his aduerfarie with his right foote forward, and with his owne right foote forward chargd toward the right fide in good warde, then fhall he haue the aduantage vpon the right handed, and be able to make him felfe maifter of his enemies armes. But if the right hand bee well knowledged and bee acquainted with the turnings and windings of the body, and be quick and readie with the rapier and dagger, he maie auoide thefe hazards, and endanger the left handed man. And this is one of the fpeciall points which either the one or the other can learne. This which I haue tolde you (efpeciallie if either of thē haue to deale with one that is ignorant) will giue him the aduantage againft his aduerfarie. Furthermore, if you fhall lye in the firft warde with your right foote formoft, bearing your felfe fomewhat towards the right fide of your enemie, and hee offer a mandritta at your head, be you readie with your dagger bearing the pointe high, and turning your bodie vpon your left fide, for fo you fhall giue him a ftoccata, or imbroccata, or punta riuerfa, in the belly or face, according as you fhal finde your beft aduantage, & your enemie moft difcouered: you may alfo ftanding ftedfaft in good warde, giue him a riuerfa at the legges. But if you fhould offer to auoide it by turning of your bodie, and be not quick therein, your aduerfarie might giue you a mandritta vpon the face or head: for there are many who in auoiding with their bodies, lofe their daggers, and put themfelues in great danger: alfo the efcape which you make with your bodie vpon the lefte fide, is clean contrary to that which you vfe againft the right handed man, becaufe
that

that when the right handed maketh a mandritta at your
head, you do not raise the point of your dagger much,
and turne your bodie vpon your right side, but dealing
with the left handed, you turne your bodie vpon your
lefte side: also when he giueth you a riuersa, you shall
turne your bodie vpon the right side. Moreouer, if you
shall haue occasion to make a mezza incartata, you shal
do it in a forte clean contrarie to that which you make
dealing with a right handed man, for you make your
mezza incartata to the right handed man, giuing him a
stoccata, but to the left handed by an imbroccata,
playing well with your bodie: if you be well skilled in
your weapon, exercising your selfe in the first, second,
and third wards, you shall do many thinges more then
I speake of. Likewise the left handed, if he practise well
these foresaid wardes, shall be able to defend himselfe,
and to deal against any other ward. And for this time I
wil not discourse to you any farther, onely I aduise you
to exercise your selfe in all these points I haue set down
vnto you, because besides the knowledge, you shall
make your practise absolute in such sorte, that when
occasion shall serue to speake of such matters, you maie
be able to giue a sufficient reason therof, & also defend
your selfe against such as will offer you iniurie, for the
worlde is nowe subiect to many wronges and insolencies. But you shal therby make your selfe most perfect,
and know far more in this behalfe then I haue vttered
vnto you, for it is not possible in this art to expresse all
by words, which by your own experience and diuersitie of occurrences you shall finde. But for this time e-
nough, let vs pray to God to defend vs frō all mishaps.
   L. Amen, saye I, thanking you hartilye for your
curtesie and fauour shewed me in these matters, and I
will

Vincentio Sauiolo his Practise

will not faile heereafter to vifite you nowe and then, that our friendfhippe maie dailie grow greater, offering at all times my fmall power to doo you feruice in acknowledgement of this your goodnes.

V. And I alfo thanke you for your kindneffe and louing offers. *Adio.*

L. Adio.

The end of the firft Booke.

OF
HONOR AND
HONORABLE
Quarrels.

The second Booke.

LONDON,
Printed by IOHN WOLFE.
1594.

THE PREFACE.

Orafmuch as diuers and sundrie persons haue heretofore
treated of the matter of single combats (whereof I haue
also framed this present discourse) and
haue not only grounded their opinions vppon deep iudgment and exact considerati-
tion of the subiect they were to handle, but
also with all furniture of wit and wordes
commended the same vnto the view of the
world: I might iustly doubt (as being in-
wardly guiltie of mine owne weaknes and
insufficiencie) to go forward with the enterprise I haue presently taken in hande:
But for that my purpose heerein is rather to discharge my duetie and zeale to
the Nobilitie & Gentrie of England,
and by publishing of this Treatise to
yeelde a testimonie of my thankefull

O 2   minde

313

The Preface.

minde for their manifolde fauors, than by froth of speech to make my matter saleable, or to purchase either credit to my selfe or acceptance of the Reader: my hope is, that such persons to whose ranke it belongeth to manage Armes, and to know the vse of their weapon, will no lesse fauorably conceiue of my indeuors, and with their curtesies supplie my defectes, then I haue bin redy by my painful & liberal diligence to deserue their likings, & do now present my labors in the most humble degree of reuerence.

A
DISCOVRSE
OF SINGLE COM-
B A T S:
WITH SOME NECES-
sarie confiderations of the caufes
for which they are vn-
der-taken.

Hen I enter into due examination, of the firſt original ground and occaſions of this kinde of encounter, and with-all conſider the corruption of mans nature thorough whoſe ambitious and inſolent humors theſe violent trials haue beene often practiſed : I cannot but allowe of the iuſt complaints framed againſt man by Philoſophers, and wiſe men of former times : as that beeing by his induſtrie and knowledge able to ſearch out and attaine vnto the amplitude of the aire, the hidden ſecrets of the earth, and the reuolutions of the heauens: yet is ſo diſguiſed and masked in the iudgement of him ſelfe, ſo

retchles

retchles in his own affayres, as that he neuer effectual-
ly confidereth of his own proper nature and inclinati-
on, much leſſe endeuoureth to reforme, what by the
eye of reaſon hee might finde controllable and blame-
worthie in his diſordered affections. For if as euerye
man is by nature capable of reaſon and vnderſtanding,
ſo he would diſpoſe and order the conueigh of his life,
as he might be reported no euil ſpeaker, no lyer, no de-
ceiuer, no quarreller, no traitor to his freend, or iniurious to his neighbour: they which haue written of
this ſubiect might well haue ſpared their labour, and
this rigorous kinde of congreſſe had beene either not
knowen at all, or much leſſe practiſed then it is. But ſi-
thence it is a thing common in experience, and vſually
ſeene, that through want of gouernment in ſome perſons (who giuing themſelues to the ful current of their
diſpoſition, making their wil their God, and their hand
their lawe,) matters are carried in a contrarye courſe: it
is neceſſarye that ſomething be written of this action,
euen as muche as ſhall bee conſonant to reaſon and
iudgemente, at leaſt to limit and reſtraine the manner
of proceeding in quarrels, if not vtterlye to remoue
the occaſion of ſo vnneceſſarie ſtrifes and fruitleſſe
contentions. Otherwiſe, in ſteede of order, we ſhould
followe confuſion, and depriue both our owne
actions and all thinges elſe of their due and iuſt
endes.

The premiſes conſidered, it is no meruayle if diuers perſons giuing themſe ues wholye to the bent
of their owne indiſcretion and wante of iudgement,
eſteeme of thinges cleane contrarye to their nature
and qualitye. For if a man frame himſelfe to leade
a ciuill

ciuill and temperate courſe of life, ſome will ſaie
hee is a foole: if hee be not quarrell-ſome, hee is a
cowarde: if no gameſter, hee is of baſe education:
if no blaſphemer, an hipocrite: if neither whore-mon-
ger nor baude, hee is neither man nor courteous, but
altogether ignorant of the rules of humanity and good
fellowſhip. A lamentable ſtate is that, where men are
ſo miſled by ignorance and ſelfe-loue, as thus to ouer-
ſmoothe and colour their vices and imperfections
with the names of vertues, and to thinke any action currant that is doone by them, and authoryſed
by their vnreſiſtable ſwaye, and diſtempered ap-
petites.

What is become of the gentilitie and inbredde
courteſie of auncient noble Gentlemen? where is
the magnanimitye of the honourable Knightes of
fore-going times, whoſe vertues as they are recorded
in hiſtories wherin we read of them, ſo ought to haue
beene lefte to their poſteritye, that in them we might
ſee the image (now forgotten) of auncient true
Nobilitye? But ſince all thinges fall to decaye, it
is no meruaile though vertue (I ſpeake with all
due reuerence and fauour) bee not found but in few:
for ſurelye there be many in whome nothing remaineth but the bare tytle of nobilitye, in that they be
Gentlemen borne: who in their manners wholy degenerate from their aunceſtors, and make no account
either of honour or diſhonour, giuing themſelues
to ſuch pleaſures, as their vnbrideled appetite leadeth them vnto. Neither can I aſcribe any reaſon to
this their ſlyding from vertue vnto vice, contrarie
to the courſe taken by their honourable aunceſtours,

but

but this, that whereas while their fathers liued, their bringing vp was committed to tutors of good gouernment and discretion, their parentes beeing dead, they withdrawe themselues from their vertuous kinde of life, leauing and reiecting the sage counsailes of their instructors, and cleauing to their owne deuises. To whom, if they amend not and take a better course, will lighten shame and destruction.

Wherfore by way of aduise, I wish all men to auoid euill companie, which for the most part is the cause of great and infinite losse, as well of honor and life as of goods and possessions: and to followe vertue, bearing themselues with a sweet and curteous carriage towards euery man; by which course they shall gaine commendation and credite, and shall be esteemed of all men: and auoiding all such occasions of dislike as may be offered, obtaine a good and honorable reputation. Doth not God forbid a priuate man to kill his neighbour? as it is manifested in sacred scriptures against *Caine*, to whome God saide, that the bloud of *Abel* his brother cryed from the earth for vengeance against him, shewing therby that he abhorreth murder, and wil reuenge it in due time.

Moreouer, he created vs naked, without anie thing naturally giuen vs, wherwith to offend or hurt: wheras other creatures haue some of them hornes, others clawes, others strong and sharpe teeth, and others poyson: And thus were we created of almightie God, to to the end we might liue in peace and brotherlye concorde, as the sonnes of God, and not as the children of the Deuill, who are the inuentours that found out the vse of weapons, therewith to offend their neighbours,

and

and to maintaine the authoritie of their father the Deuill: who was a murderer from the beginning, and taketh pleasure in the deftruction of men, raifing difcention between families, cities, prouinces, and kingdoms. Vpon which occafion, the neceffary vfe of armes hath gotten fuch credit in the worlde, as Kings and Princes haue nobilitated fome with the name of Knights for their excellencie therein: which name is made noble, and that vpon great reafon, for fuch men as haue purchafed nobilitie, by conquering kingdomes for their Princes, more refpecting their honour and countries good, then any other thing, and efteeming leffe of life then of death, in regarde of preferuing that honor vnblotted, which belongeth to Knights, ought not in any wife to be deftitute of high reward. In fo much, that armes being doubled by fo many valorous men, it were a great fhame for one of noble of-fpring, not to be able to fpeake of armes, and to difcourfe of the caufes of Combats, not to know how to difcerne the nature and qualitie of wordes and accidents which induce men to challenges, not to bee acquainted with the manner of fending cartels and challenges, and how fitlye to anfwere the fame: and in a word, not to haue fo much experience in thefe affaires, as to accorde the parties challenging and challenged, bringing them from their hoftile threates, to louing embracementes: and of quarreling foes, to become louing freends, al caufes of difcontent beeing taken away on either fide. The ignorance wherof, hath in thefe times bred great mifcheefe, for many thinke that an iniurie being offred in deed or worde, the matter may not with their credits be taken vp before they haue fought, not regarding if they bee

P   iniured

iniuried indeed, that they ought firſt to examine what
hee is that hath doone it, and vpon what occaſion hee
might doe it: if in woorde, what qualitie the perſon is
that ſpake iniuriouſly, and whether hee deſerue an anſwer or no. For a man beeing carried away with chol-
lor or wine, maye chaunce to vtter that, for which (his
fury being paſt) he will be willing to make any ſatisfaction: wherfore it were fondly done by him that would
fight vpon euery worde. Neither can I be induced to
thinke, that there is any iniury (which is not accompanied with villanie) for which with due ſatisfaction, all
cauſe of fighting may not be taken away. But if the iniurie be ſuch, that either murder be committed by tre-
cherie, or rape, or ſuch like villanies, then is it neceſſarye to proceede in reuenging it; as in due place I will
more largely declare.

In the meane time, I thinke it neceſſary to ſet foorth
ſome conſiderations of circumſtance belonging to this
ſubiect of quarrels, not becauſe I take vpon me to teach
or correct any man, (for that belongeth not to me) but
onlye by way of aduertiſement, to warne gentlemen
to auoide all dangerous occaſions, growing for want
of fore-ſight.

And firſte conſidering the little vnderſtanding
and ſmall diſcretion of manye, with the dayly danger
which ſuch men runne into by indiſcretion, it is fitte
for a man to conſider his owne eſtate; for if hee bee
a Gentleman borne, hee ought euen for that reſpect
with great regarde abſtayne from any acte whatſoeuer, whereby his woorthye calling may be ſtayned,
hee ought to embrace myldenes and curteſie, as one
that hath a hart of fleſhe, not of ſtone, more encly-
ned

ned to clemencye, then to crueltye : to the ende his
conuersation bee acceptable, by reason of his sweete
and louing behauiour, he must also be in minde mag-
nanimous, not base or abiecte, as one ill borne, and
worse brought vp : for so will hee easilye be discerned
from that rascall sorte of lose minded companions, vn-
furnished of all ornamentes beseeming a gentleman,
whose repaire into companye is commonlye without
vsing any curtesie or salutation, where hauing intruded
themselues among honest gentlemen, if chaunce they
are acquainted with any of them, without crauing
leaue either of him or the reste of his companye, they
take him by the sleeue, vrging him to goe with them,
without any consideration of the person so taken, or of
offence therby offered to the rest of the company, who
in all likely-hoode might be offended with his vnadui-
sed follie, in playing so vnmannerlye a parte : thinking
themselues if not altogether wronged, yet at least dis-
curteoufly dealt withall, in that their company should
be so neglected & little set by : insomuch that through
such ill demeanour, they often-times purchase vnto
themselues muche iniurye. For it maye happen, that
some fantasticall madde conceited fellowe, taking this
kinde of discurtesie in euill parte, will fall a reasoning
with him that offereth it, and so by multiplying of
speeche, they may fall from words to blowes, whereby
some or other may be spoyled vpon a matter not worthy the talking of : for all men bee not of one minde,
and a mad brainde fellow may easilie light vpon another as fond or fondlier fantasticall then himself, whet-
by both of them may fall into diuers vnlooked for inconueniences and mischeefes on the sodaine.

P 2   More-

Moreouer, at weddinges or great feaftes, where is great reforte both of gentlemen and gentlewomen, it may happen that a company of gentlemen retyre afide from the reft of the companye, taking with them fome gentlewoman or other to deceiue the time with talke, or difcourfe on fome other paftime: where if fome one of thefe mannerles gentlemen fhould chance to come and folicite the gentlewoman fo retyred, to dance with him, without crauing either her good liking, or the gē-tlemens with whom fhe was difcourfing, or otherwife paffing ouer the time: vndoubtedlye, if fome of the gentlemen of the fame company fhould happen to be mad conceited, hee might chaunce to be well beaten for his pleafure: whereof alfo further inconuenience might arife, and perchaunce the whole mariage might therby be difturbed, and quarrels might grow among the frends & kinsfolk of either party, wherupon much hurly-burly maye enfue: and experience teacheth vs, that diuers men of account haue lofte their liues, vpon like diforders. Whereupon I conclude, that modeftye and curtefie are moft conuenient ornaments, as wherby men fhall auoide many dangers and quarrells.

There be alfo certaine vndifcreet men, whofe groffe fault I cannot ouerflip without blaming: thefe men vfe as they either ftand or go in ftreets, fo to ftare and looke men paffing by them in the face, as if they woulde for fome reafon marke them: which breedeth fuch an offence vnto fome men fo marked, that they cannot take it in good part, and therefore it is verie dangerous. For it maie happen, that a man may looke fo vpon one that either is by nature fufpitious, or by reafon of fome fecret thing knowen to himfelfe, maie fufpect, that hee is there-

therefore looked vpon. Wherevpon great quarrels may
arise, for the man so looked on maie fall a questioning
with him that looketh on him, who perhaps answering
him ouerthwartly, may both moue him to choler, & be
moued himself also, & so bring the matter to some dangerous point. Whereof I haue my selfe seene a notable
example, passing through the Citie of Trieste, in the
vttermost part of the territories of *Friule* in Italy, where
I sawe two brethren, one a most honorable Captaine,
and the other a braue and worthie souldier, who walk-
ing together in the streetes, were verie stedfastly eied of
certaine young Gentlemen of the Citie, who stared the
Captaine and his brother in the face something vn-
seemely, and (as they tooke it) discurteouslie: whervp-
pon they asked the Gentlemen in verie curteous manner, whether they had seene them in anie place before,
or whether they knew them. They answered no. Then
replied the Captaine and his brother, Why then doo
you looke so much vpon vs? They aunswered, because
they had eies. That (sayd the other) is the crowes fault,
in that they haue not picked them out. To bee short, in
the end one word added on the other, and one speech
following the other, the matter came from saying, to
doing: and what the tung had vttered the hand would
maintaine: and a hot fight being commenced, it could
not be ended before the Captaines brother was slaine,
and two of the gentlemen hurt, whereof one escaped
with the rest, but the cheefest cutter of them all was
hurt in the legge, and so could not get away, but was
taken, imprisoned, and shortly after beheadded: he was
very well beloued in the Cittie, but yet could not e-
scape this end: being brought therto by following his

P 3   mad-

mad brained conceits, and by beeing misled by euill company: the rest of his company were banished their country. Now if these gentlemen had more curteouslie and wiselye demeaned themselues, no more hurte had followed that bad beginning: euerie man therfore shall doe well, to haue a great regarde in this respecte, least like disorders be to their danger committed.

Furthermore, I like not the custome which some men haue in medling with other mens weapons, especiallye with theirs that professe armes, neither can I thinke it an ouer-wise parte for men to be viewing one the others Rapiers, whereof may this inconuenience rise, that a man may so take occasion to kill his enemie, towards whome in outward appearance hee carryeth him selfe as his verye freende: for all is not golde that glistereth, and you may think a man to be your freend, whose hart as it is hidde from your eyes, so also is vnknowne vnto you: all which mischeefe may by discretion and fore-sight be auoided, in offering no occasion or opportunity for the effecting therof.

Moreouer, when men light into the companye of honorable Gentlemen, they ought to haue a great regarde of their tung, to the end they say nothing which maye be euil taken or mis-constred: and in talking or reasoning to girde at any man, or finde fault with him, howbeit you may doe it neuer so truly, for it is ill playing so as it may pricke, and it is not good iesting to the disgrace of another.

It is no lesse behouefull for men to beware that they entise or suborne not other mens seruants, which of it selfe is odious, and purchaseth naught but shame and reproche to the performers of such base practises.

I

I muſt alſo miſlike them that offer wrong to other mens ſeruants, for beſides this, that they bewraye their baſenes of minde, they ſeeme alſo to reſemble him of whom the prouerb ſaith, that being vnable to ſtrike the horſe, beats the ſaddle, which ſignifieth as much, as whē he is not able to deale with the maiſter, he wreaketh it on the ſeruant: I hope therefore that gentle men will conſider how baſe a thing it is to doe this, and alſo how that often-times much hurt enſueth: for one houſe is by this means ſtirred vp againſt another, and whole families are turned vp-ſide downewarde: for whoſoeuer ſeeth his ſeruants abuſed, wil think him ſelfe wronged: and will therefore endeuour to reuenge ſuch wrongs, as offered vnto him ſelfe: according to the prouerbe, loue me and loue my dogge.

Alſo Gentlemen ought to abhorre carrying of tales, and reporting of other mens ſpeeches, for that is a very vnchriſtianly actiō, vnworthy to proceed from a braue and free minded man: for ſuch as vſe tale-bearing, often-times thinking to reporte but wordes, reporte that which cauſeth a mans deſtruction: on the other ſide, if any man chaunce to ſpeak euil of you in your abſence, you ought not to ſeeke meanes to bee reuenged of him that ſo doth, deſpiſing and contemning him. For a common ſaying it hath been of olde time (be it ſpoken with reuerence) he that ſpeketh of me behinde my back, ſpeketh with that which is behinde my back: And ſure it is that no man of value or vertue will ſpeak any thing of a man in his abſence, but rather to his face: neither muſt a man eaſilye giue credite to all thinges which he heareth, for whatſoeuer hee bee that carryeth tales, hee dooth not nor can not truely deliuer a mans ſpeeche wholie

wholie without addition or substraction : for a word or
two is easily adioyned, which notwithstanding is of efficacie sufficient to alter the whole state of the speech.
Which may moue anie man to thinke it a vaine matter
for to go about to maintaine anie quarrell vpon no better grounds : and it may fall out, that by giuing credite
to tales, one maie indanger himselfe and his friends. E-
uerie man shall therefore doo well to bridle his owne
tongue, and to consider of other mens speeches before
he credite them, and not report vnto his friende euerie
thing he heareth spoken of him, except it concerne his
life or reputation : for in such a case a man ought to
warne his frend, to the end he may be prouided against
the wrong which is intended against him. And in this
case also I wish this obseruation to be kept, that the partie grieued first go to him which spake the wordes, and
aske him in curteous manner (not without courage)
whether he haue reported or spoken such wordes, &c.
Which if he denie in presence of credible persons, then
is he that reported it to bee charged with the iniurie :
who if he acquite himselfe by prouing that to bee true
which he reported, yet considering that the partie accused hath denied them before witnesse, you are to rest
satisfied and contented : for by denying them he recal-
leth them.

Furthermore, let euerie man take heed he maintain
not anie dishonoured or infamous persons quarrell, of
what condition or calling so euer he bee.

Also it is wisedome for a meane man not to deale
with men of great calling, for he shall be sure howsoeuer the matter go, to get little by it. And if chance, some
occasion of quarrell being offered, he let it slip, suffering

the

the matter to be taken vp, he shall doe well to retire into some place further of: for it is better for men to liue as freends asunder, then as enemies together: whereas else euerye small matter that might happen, would renue the olde quarrell. Hence commeth it that this prouerbe was vsed. That the eye sees not, the hart greeues not.

Contrarilye, a man of great calling and authoritye ought not to wrong any man of the meaner sorte, for there be many who, howbeit they be but poor and of no authoritie, yet they wante neither valour nor courage, and will rather dye, then take any iniurie. Wherof I will rehearse two or three examples, which I haue my selfe seene.

There is a certaine village about a mile distant from the famous Cittie of *Padua* in *Italye*, where the *Boggiarini* dwelt, men well to liue for their calling, wanting neither hart nor courage: and as it is a custome throghout all *Lombardie*, in Sommer-time there be many places, where in Castels and in Villages also, great markets and wakes be kept, vpon the daies of such Saints as the parish Churches are dedicated vnto: whither resorte merchants and Cuntry-men of all sortes, from places farre and neere, to make merrie and good cheere, hauing good Countrie musicke: the yonger sorte after dinner and supper vse all exercise and pastime, dauncing with their loues on a fair greene, kept for the purpose. To which dauncing diuers gentlemen would resorte, onely to see the cuntrymen and women sporting and vsing their rurall pastimes: among which gentlemen were two nephewes to the Duke, who espying two maidens among the cuntry wenches surpassing all

Q   the

327

the reſt in beautie and comelines, being ſiſters to the *Boggiarini*, fell into ſuch liking of them, that within ſome fewe daies they went vnto the houſe of the ſaide *Boggiarini*, accompanied with certaine gallant youths, thinking by giftes and faire ſmoothing ſpeeche, to per-ſwade and entice the maidens to become their para-mours, & to follow them home to their places: but the maidens father and two of their Bretheren, came to the gentlemen, hauing had an inckling of their intent, and tolde them that they were very poore, and not able to entertaine them according to their calling, yet that notwithſtanding ſuch was their honeſtie, that they greatly regarded their reputation: wherefore if it plea-ſed them to come to their houſe with honeſt intent, they would ſtretch their power to the vttermoſt to ple-ſure them, and their gratefulnes of minde towardes thē for their curteſie in vouchſafing to come vnto them: but if they came to any other intent then vertuous, then they beſeeched them to departe. Heereupon the madde youths that accompanied the Gentlemen, be-gan to drawe vpon the countrymen, who being leſſe in number farre then the gentlemen, were forced to re-tyre and ſaue themſelues in their houſe, and for that time the matter was ſo ended. But not long after the *Boggiarini* chaunced to meete with ſome of theſe gal-lants, where two of them were ſhrewdly handled: for which cauſe the two *Boggiarini* were committed to cloſe priſon by the Maieſtrates, and remained ſo for the ſpace of eleuen or twelue moneths, and then were releaſed: the gentlemē vnderſtanding that they ſhould be releaſed, departed ſoddenlye the next day from Ve-nice, with ſeauen luſtie fellowes well armed, intending

to

to kil the *Boggiarini*, and so went to Padua: on the other side, the *Boggiarinies* kinfemen being informed of their cofins releafe out of prifon, haftened to Padua to bring them home, and carried them their weapons : they therefore hauing difcharged all duties, after they were fet at libertie, tooke their iourney in hand and went homeward, but the gentlemen meeting them at a place called *Seruy*, rufhed violentlye vpon them on the foddaine, crying all with a loud voice, kill, kill, kill: they not knowing what they ment at firft, but quickly after perceiued who they were, would not willinglye hauehad to do with them, as by othes and proteftations they declared, defending themfelues as well as they could, and retiring backe to efcape them: but beeing compaffed round about, and feeing no way to efcape death but by the death of thofe that affailed them, when they perceiued that neither intreatie nor proteftation, nor anye thing could moue the reuengfull Gentlemen to holde their handes, euen after fo many iniuries before that by them offered, as hauing gone about to violate their fifters, hauing beaten their father, and hauing obtained punifhment for themfelues by the Maieftrates, with a yeeres imprifonment, being content with nothing but their liues, at length after they had retired much, and fought all meanes to auoyde the fight, they began to fet aparte all refpectes, abandoning their liues: whervpon laying about them with all ftrength and no leffe courage, in fhort fpace they flew the Dukes Nephewes both, and another Gentleman, and hurt diuers of the others that accompanied them, onely one of the *Boggiarini* beeing harmed with the loffe of three fyngers. The fight being ended, one of the *Boggiarini* getting

Q 2   on

on a Millars horse escaped, the other three purposing
to saue themselues in a Monasterie, were taken and put
in prison: afterward their cause being brought before
the Councell of *Venice*, an vncle of the gentlemen that
were slaine, vnder-tooke the patronage and defence of
the poore cuntrymen, (they beeing in truth guiltlesse)
and making a speech for them, obtained so much that
they saued their liues, howbeit they were banished out
of all the territories of the *Venetian* seignory. The ende
of these gentlemen that were so pittifully slaine, maye
be an example to all others how to behaue themselues
towards men of meaner degree.

In the same cittie of *Padua*, happened another cause
not much vnlike to this, between a Gentleman of *Bres-*
sia and a Baker. This gentleman hauing many houses
in that cittie, (in one of which a baker was tenant) vpon
some small occasion, gaue the baker warning to prouide him another house: the baker being an honest man
got all his neighbours to intreate the gentleman to let
him continue his tenant, but their intreatie serued not,
and the poore man to his vtter vndoing, was thrust out
of his house, which so greeued him, that hee vowed his
Landlords death : who hauing had some notice thereof, tooke as great heed as he coulde, continually comming home before night, least by his late being abroad
he might be endangered. Thus two yeeres being past,
hee began by little and little to wexe more carelesse,
thinking in that space a man might forget any wrong :
but the poor baker had not so forgottē that great iniury, for I haue heard many say, that the offender writeth
in the sand, but the offended in marble : & so this baker
meeting the Gentleman late in the night, hastilye runneth

neth into a fhoppe where Cheefe and fuch like thinges were folde, where borrowing a knife, maketh after his olde Landlord, and ouertaking him, cutteth his throte, fo that the Gentleman within fewe howers dyed, and the Baker was bannifhed by the Maieftrates, becaufe they could not otherwife punifh him, he being fled.

I haue read in the hiftorie of the laft warres in *Perfia*, how *Mahomet Baffa* Generall of the Turkifhe Empire, tooke a certaine penfion from a Souldier (who for his valour had well deferued it) and beftowed it on fome other whom he better thought of: wherupon the fouldier being with great reafon offended, feigned himfelf madde, and the better to effect his purpofe, feemed to think that he had entred into fome order of Mahometan religion, and fo came dayly into the Baffaes chamber mumbling out his praiers, whereat hee and all the reft about him laughed, but the fouldier vfed this fo often, till efpying fit opportunity he flew the Baffa, and being taken and brought before the great Turke, was by him giuen to the Baffaes flaues to do their pleafure with him, for hee had confeffed the whole matter vnto the Turke.

Before the ouerthrow of the Turkifh Nauie, which was in the yeere 1571. the Sates of Venice had a little before fent *Sfortia Palauifino* their Generall into Slauonia by land, and into other Eafterne partes, with that authoritie as in time of warres Generals vfe to haue: he being arriued in thofe places, efpied opportunity to take a certaine Cittie called Margarita, in a countrie: wherefore hee leauyed an armye with all fpeede, and marching towarde the Cittie, planted his ordinance, and began to batter the walles of the fame Cittie. At

Q 3   the

the affaulte wherof he bare in his hand a kinde of pick-axe, with a thing like a hammer at one end, and a long pike at the ftaffe ende, able to pierce any bodie armed with a curats: which kinde of weapon is much vfed by the Sclauonians, Croacians, Turkes, Albanoies, and Hungarians: with this pickaxe did *Sforcia Palauicino* encourage his fouldiers to ftrike thofe that returned from the affaulte, or were not fo forward as they ought to haue beene, and among others would haue ftricken a certaine Venetian Gentleman, whofe feruant pre-fently ftept before his maifter to *Sforcia* with his peece in his hand, and bad him holde his hand, for that hee whom he went about to ftrike was a gentleman of Ve-nice and his maifter, and therefore willed him to take heede of touching him, purpofing, if *Sforcia* had not re-tired from his maifter, to fhoote him through with his Peece. *Sforcia* noting and admiring the fellows valour and fidelitie, in hazarding his owne life to faue his mai-fter from wrong, earneftlye requefted the Gentleman, to let that his feruant bee his, promifing to fhewe him much fauour, which the Gentleman both to gratifie *Sforcia* and to aduaunce his man to preferment, did: and *Sforcia* made him a Captain, and wonderfully en-riched him, infomuch that in fewe yeeres after he be-came a great man.

It is a groffe follye for men to fcoffe and ieft at o-thers, in what cafe foeuer it be: neither ought thofe men who by nature are framed comely and tall, to be girding at thofe vnto whome nature hath not been fo beneficiall. There be many that being carried away with plaufible conceite of their owne manhoode and ftrength, by reafon of the propernes and greatnes of
their

their well shapen bodies, despise men of lesse stature, thinking that in respect of themselues they be nothing, and that if occasion were offered them to fight with them, they thinke they were able to minse them as smal as pye-meat, not knowing that men are not measured as woollen Cloth by the yarde, or that little men haue oftentimes ouerthrowen great fellowes. In considera-tion whereof, I will recount vnto you what happened in Italye, in the Cittie of Boulogna.

When the Emperour *Charles* the fifth, came to be crowned by Pope *Clement* the seuenth. This Emperour had in his traine, a great Moore like a Giant, who be-side his tallnes wanted no valour and courage, beeing wonderfull strong: he enioying the fauour of so great an Emperour, was respected of all men, and particular-lye of diuers Princes which accompanied the Empe-rour: which brought him to such a proud conceite of himselfe, and his owne worthines (ascribing the good fauour of all the Princes and gentlemen that followed the Emperour to his own deserts, and not to the good will that they sawe the Emperour bare him) that hee laughed al men to scorn, thinking none able to encoun-ter with him.

Whereuppon hee obtained leaue of the Empe-rour, that proclaimation shoulde bee made, that if any one in all that Citie being so ful of people, would wre-stle with him, hee would challenge him: which being published, euery man was sorelye afraide of his huge-nes, strength, and eager countenance. Insomuch that none could be found that durst vndertake the match, saue the Duke of Mantuaes Brother called *Rodomont*, who though he was but of an ordinary stature, yet was he he both very ſtrong and nimble withall, and (as it was credibly thought,) all his breſt was wholy made of one bone: he was very valiant, and by reporte could break at one courſe ſeauen ſtaues tyed together, inſomuch that if he had not had a good horſe, he ſhould break his backe: but for many raſh enterpriſes, he was banniſhed from all tylt-yardes and iuſting. This *Rodomont* ſeeing that no man elſe durſte vndertake to bee matched in wreſtling with the proude boaſting Moore, notwithſtanding that his brother the Duke and the reſt of his kinred vſed all meanes to diſſwade him, would neuertheleſſe himſelfe wreſtle with him, to make it knowen vnto all the worlde, that he would not ſuffer ſo beaſtlie a creature, to ſtaine the honor of Italian Gentlemen, and to giue the Emperour (who was a ſtranger) occaſion to laugh at the Italians, ſeeing them put downe by a monſtrous Moore. *Rodomont* therefore buckling with the Moore in preſence of the Emperour and all the Princes, behaued himſelfe in ſuch ſort, that the Moore could not foyle him with any fall, inſomuch that hee was brought only to touch the ground with one knee, howbeit the Moore ſtrained himſelfe to the vttermoſt ſtrength : and ſo the night drawing on, after they had tryed their force a long time, the Emperour cauſed them to ceaſe till next daye, at which time *Rodomont* came to meete the Moore againe with great courage, and hauing now had good triall of his ſtrength, and knowing what he was able to doe, as ſoone as he ſawe fitte opportunitie, nimblye tooke the Moore about the middle, and claſped him hard againſt his owne breſt, holding him ſo vntill he perceiued him to be breathleſſe, and then letting him ſlippe out of his armes, the

Moore

Moore fell down dead fo heauilie, that the whole place
fhaked, as iffomefteeple had beene caft downe: which
Rodomont perceiuing, prefentlye got from the whole
company, and taking pofte horffe fled, fearing leaft the
Emperour fhould haue doone him fome difpleafure:
but hee wente not about it, confidering that the challenge was publiquelye proclaimed by his owne leaue
and authoritie. Howbeit hee was greeued for the loffe
of his ftout Moore.

One example more will I recount concerning info-
lencye, efpeciallye becaufe this *Rodomont* of whome I
fpake, was an actor in the tragedie. It happened that the
Duke of *Mantua* and his brother *Rodomont* being in the
fame Emperour *Charles* his Court about certain affaires
of their owne, they on a time walked in a great chamber, expecting that the Emperour fhould fend for them
when his Maieftie were at leafure: into which chamber at the fame time, came a certain Spanifh Captaine,
who without any greeting or falutation, came by them
and brauely walked, euen betweene the Duke and his
brother, nothing refpecting the greatnes of that prince,
and fo braued them three or foure times: wherewith
Rodomont being greatlye offended, with the difcurtefie
of this proud and infolent Captain, went to a window
which he perceiued to be open, and ftaying til the captaine came that way, tooke him by the coller with one
hand, and putting the other vnder his breeche, thruft
him out at the windowe, and brake his necke: Wherevpon he fled from the Court with all fpeede he could.
But the Emperour being enformed of the matter, blamed not *Rodomont*, confidering the Spanifhe Captaine
had fo infolently behaued himfelfe to *Rodomonts* bro-

R ther

ther the Duke of *Mantua*. It were an endlesse thing for me to rehearse all the examples that I haue heard, concerning this vice of insolencie, which are infinite, and happen dayly in all countries, by reason of the little regarde that is had in the bringin g vp of yong men : and so I will only exhorte euery man to take heed least him selfe fall into like follie.

    I will not omit to speake of a certaine vice, and parte not to be vsed by a gentleman, seeing it proceedeth of meere cowardise : which is, when a man hauing fallen out with one or other, and wanting courage to deale with him in single fight, procureth base and cowardlie meanes by the help of some of his freends, with whom he plotteth how they may circumuent his enemy. And so watching him at some time or other, will draw vpon him, as if hee had mette him by chaunce, who thinking vpon no villanie, without any suspition at all, likewise draweth to defende himselfe, as a man ought to doe, which when the other plotters espie standing a far off, drawe neere as strangers to them both, and vnwilling any hurt should be done on either side, whereas they most traiterouslie will either themselues impart a thrust by the way, or so strike his weapon, that his enemy may take occasion to hurt him : which villanie (for I thinke no term bad inough to expresse it by) you may escape, if you take heede when any one draweth vpon you, that none else come neere you, willing them to retire, with protestation, that you will take them as your enemies, if they doe not: for by reason that you knowe them not, they cannot but like of your protestation, if they meane you no euill, seeing that you not knowing thē can not assure your self of their good affection to-

wards

wards you, and care of your safegarde. Therfore in any cafe, at fuch time as you fhal happen to be enforced to defende your felfe on the fodaine, let no man come neere you, for it is very dangerous : and I fpeake this becaufe I haue feene the like doone verye often, and found it confirmed by great experience. And to faye fome thing of parting, I will by the way declare thus much. That hee that will parte two that are fighting, muft go betwixt thē both, hauing great regarde that he nether hindreth one more then the other, nor fuffereth the one more to endanger his enemie than the other: and if more come to parte then one, they muft deuide themfelues, and fome come on one fide, and fome on the other, taking great heede that neither of them be any way either preiudiced, or fauoured : wherefore I doe not miflike with the great Duke of *Florence* his o-pinion, who vpon paine of great forfeiture, forbad all men to parte thofe that fhould fight, for hee would haue them fuffered to fight til they parted themfelues, and if any one chaunced to be hurt, they fhould blame themfelues, feeing they were the onelye caufe there-of.

If the like were vfed in all places, I thinke we fhould not haue fo muche quarrelling by halfe as wee daylye fee among Gentlemen: for furely manye will be ve-rye readye vpon no occafion to drawe vpon a man, onely becaufe he knoweth that he fhall not be fuffered to fight.

Some others there be, who to wreake themfelues vpon their enemies will doe it by a thirde meanes, by giftes or promifes, perfwading fome needy fellow to picke a quarrell, with their enemy, whom either the

R 2

poore

poore fellow hurteth or killeth, and fo encurreth danger of death: or at the leaft is hurte or maimed himfelf.
Therfore I could wifh euery man to meddle with his
own quarrels only, neither reuenging his own wrong,
by another, nor wreaking other mens iniuries by himfelfe, vnleffe he haue good reafon to the contrarie, as in
diuers cafes a man may honeftlie and honorably both
intreat others to reuenge his wrongs, and be alfo intre-
ted of others.

There be alfo fome gentlemen fo careleffe, that beeing in companye with honeft gentlemen, thinke that
whatfoeuer follie they commit, the companye will be
ready to defend them, and fo will either fcoffe or gybe
with them that paffe by, or vfe fome knauifhe tricke toward fome one that is not of their companye, or fall a
quarrelling with one or other whom they think good,
and fo hauing fet manye together by the eares, they
are the firft that will runne awaye, or hide themfelues
in fome corner till all be done. By my counfel therfore
fhall no man be fo fond as to backe anye, or take parte
with any that are fo void of difcretion or gouernment.

Like vnto thefe you fhall fee others, who will inuite
their freends to fome dinner or paftime abroad, onely
to ferue their turnes in reuenging their wronges, hauing plotted meanes for the execution thereof, wherby many times much harme hath beene doone, fufficient to caufe any man to beware of falling into like inconueniences.

All which I haue heere fayde, becaufe I haue my
felfe had experience thereof. And thefe bee the things
whereof quarrelles proceede; which beginning but
betweene two or three, fomtime are fo farre increafed,
that

hat whole families are wrapped in quarrels and broils, which oftentimes are not ended without great hurt & bloudshed. Euerie man ought therefore to know how to behaue himselfe in these cases, and not to presume vpon his owne skil or knowledge, but to learne how he ought to proceed in matters of combats or quarrelles: For a man maie dayly learne more than he knoweth, & especially they that want experience: seeing it is a matter seldome seene, that he shall be able to know what is good, that hath not had some triall of that which is euill. According to a verse of Petrarke, Euerie one must learne to his cost: which saying pertaineth especially to young men, who for the most parte can neuer learne to gouern themselues aright, vntill such time as they haue had experience of some mishappe or other, concerning either their goods, life, or credite. But as nothing is so daungerous but maie bee preuented, so in this pointe, that men take good heed and arme themselues with the sure shield of sound counfell and aduice, that they may easily auoide such errors as I haue in these my aduertisements discouered and made
knowen for their profit
& commoditie.

R 3   A

A Difcourfe moft necefſarie for all Gentlemen that haue in regarde their honors touching the giuing and receiuing of the Lie, where-vpon the Duello & the Combats in diuers fortes doth infue,& many other inconueniences,for lack only of the true knowledge of honor,and the contrarie:& the right vnderſtanding of wordes, which heere is plainly ſet downe, beginning thus.

A RVLE AND ORDER
concerning the Challenger and Defender.

 L L iniuries are reduced to two kindes, and are either by wordes or deedes. In the fiſt,he that offereth the iniurie ought to bee the Challenger : in the later, hee that is iniuried:Example, Caius ſayth to
Seius

Seius that hee is a traitour : vnto which Seius aunſwereth by giuing the lie : whereuppon enſueth, that the
charge of the Combat falleth on Caius, becauſe hee is
to maintaine what hee ſayd, and therefore to challenge
Seius. Now when an iniurie is offered by deede, then
do they proceed in this manner. Caius ſtriketh Seius,
giueth him a boxe on the eare, or ſome other waie hurteth him by ſome violent meanes: Wherewith Seius
offended, ſaith vnto Caius, that hee hath vſed violence
towardes him, or that hee hath dealt iniuriouſlie with
him, or that hee hath abuſed him, or ſome ſuch manner
of ſaying. Wherevnto Caius aunſwereth, Thou lyeſt :
whereby Seius is forced to challenge Caius, and to
compell him to fight, to maintaine the iniurie which
hee had offered him. The ſumme of all therefore, is in
theſe caſes of honour, that hee vnto whome the lie is
wrongfullie giuen, ought to challenge him that offereth
that diſhonour, and by the ſwoorde to proue himſelfe
no lyer.

There bee manie that delighting to finde faulte
with that which is ſette downe by others, bee it neuer ſo truely and exactly perfourmed, will in this caſe
alſo ſeeke to ouerthrowe the rules which I haue a-
boue alleadged concerning Challenging and Defending, oppoſing manye Argumentes and obiections,
which I thinke friuolous to trouble the Reader
withall, and therefore wyll neyther rehearſe them
heere, nor ſpende ſo much labour in vaine as to aunſwere them, conſidering that men but of meane capa-
citie will bee able to diſcerne and iudge of the ſmall
reaſon that they are grounded vppon. For who is
ther that ſeeth not, howbeit ſome men finer witted than
endued

endued with valour and courage, will by multiplication of fpeeches giue caufe of greater offence, and therby giue the other occafion to challenge the combat, rather than to do it themfelues. Yet that notwithftanding
the true and perfect manner of proceeding in cafes of
honour is, that whofoeuer offereth iniurie by deede, as
ftriking, beating, or otherwife hurting anie man, ought
prefently without anie further debate or queftioning,
to be challenged to the Combat, vnleffe hee refufe the
fame by making fatisfaction for the offence or offered
iniurie.

And in iniuries offered by worde, no refpect ought
to bee had of all the wordes which by aunfweres and
replies are multiplied, (as when one faith, Thou lyeft,
the other anfwereth with the fame wordes, and the firft
replieth, with thou lieft alfo, and fo maie perchaunce
make a fraie with wordes only, which foolifh and chil-
difh manner of proceeding cannot but bee mifliked of
by Gentlemen of reputation) but to whom fo euer the
lie is vniuftlye and wrongfully giuen, vnto him fhall it
belong to become Challenger, by Armes to maintaine
what he fpake or did, whervpon the lie was giuen him.

What the reafon is, that the partie vnto whom the lie is giuen, ought to become Challenger: and of the nature of Lies.

SOme men maruell why that hee vnto whome the lie
is giuen, ought rather to challenge the Combat, than
he

hee that is called a traitor or a villaine, or by some other
iniurious name, seeing that it woulde seeme more reasonable, that hee which is most iniuried, ought to become Challenger, and not the other, and that this is a
greater iniurie to saie vnto a man, Thou art a theefe,
thou art a villaine, & a traitor, than this, Thou lyest. But
the lawes haue no regarde of the wordes, or of the force
or efficacie of them, but prouide that the burthen of
the challenge shall euer fall on him that offereth the iniurie: for it is thought that euerie man is honest, iust,
and honourable vntill the contrarie bee proued. And
therefore as in common triall by ciuill iudgement and
order of lawe, whosoeuer is accused of anie crime, is by
simple denying the saine deliuered from condemnati-
on, vnlesse further proofe thereof be brought agaynst
him: euen so in this case, whosoeuer speaketh of another man contrarie vnto that which is ordinarilie presumed of him, it is great reason that the charge of proof
should lie vppon him, to make that manifest vnto the
worlde by force of Armes, that such a man is guiltie of
such and such thinges as hee hath laide to his charge.
Heereuppon some maie cauell, and aske howe that hee
that is iniuried by deede shall becolme challenger, (as
I haue sayde) if that the lawes prouide that the burthen thereof shall belong vnto him that offereth the
iniurie.

Wherevnto I aunswere, that if I beate or strike anie
man, thereof proceedeth no cause of proofe, it is manifest that I offend or hurt him, and I know no cause why
I shoulde proue that I doo so. But if the other saie vnto
mee, that I did not as a Gentleman worthie to beare

S

Armes,

Armes, or that I dealt not honorably, or any such thing, I repell his sayings with the Lie, and force him to maintaine what hee hath spoken : whereof I am acquited with sole deniall, till hee make further proofe.

And now as concerning the nature of Lies, I saye that euerie deniall, bee it neuer so simple, beareth the force of a Lie, beeing altogether as much in effect. And I see no other difference betweene a simple denyall and the lie, than is betwixte a speech more or lesse curteous. Wherefore although the names of deniall are diuerse, as Thou lyeft, Thou sayeft vntruly, Thou speakeft falsely, Thou spareft the truth, Thou telleft tales, Thou regardeft not how falfely thou reporteft a matter, Thou art wide from the truth, This is a lie, a tale, a falsehood, &c. Yet all these manners of speech import the Lie, whether hee vnto whome they were spoken spake iniuriously or no. For though I saie not anie euill thing of anie other, but chance to discourse of some matter, or rehearse some tale or historie, or reporte any thing, as occasion of speeche may bee offered mee, if some one that ftandeth by telleth mee that I saie not truely, or vse anie of the foresayde formes or manner of speech vnto mee, furely hee bringeth my truth in queftion, and causeth mee to bee reputed for a lyar, and so consequently offereth mee iniurie. And forasmuch as euerie iniurie offered by wordes, maie be the firft time wreafted and returned vppon him that offereth the iniurie, I maie lawfullie repulfe that iniurie with a seconde denyall, which shall beare the force of a Lye, where his firft shall bee accounted of the nature of an iniu-

iniurie, by which meanes the burthen of the challenge
shall rest wholie vpon him. But if hee chaunce to saie
onely thus, or after this manner vnto mee, This is not
so, or the truth heereof I take to bee otherwise, &c. I
cannot take anie such speech iniuriously, for it may be
the thing whereof I spake is not true, and yet I doo not
lie, and therefore such a speeche so spoken cannot anie
wayes burthen mee, vnlesse I shall make some iniurious replie thereunto, which hee repealing with the
lye, maye laye the burthen of challenge on mee: for
a worde commeth sometimes to bee iniuryous, and
sometimes not, onelye by beeing sometimes iniuriously spoken, and sometimes not. As for example: If one
man doo saye vnto another, Thou sayest not true, hee
dooth thereby make him a Lyer, and so hee doth iniurie him. But if hee doo replye and saie in this manner,
That which thou sayest is not so, or it is not true, &c.
No such manner of speech or saying can bee iniurious,
for that, as I haue aboue sayde, the thing may bee false,
and yet hee no Lyer, by reason that hee eyther maye
bee euyll infourmed, or else not vnderstande the matter as it was, or some suche other thing might happen, whereby hee might bee mooued to reporte and
speake that agayne which is not true: wherefore anie
such aunswere whatsoeuer cannot in anie sort fall bur-
denous vnto him. One case excepted, which is, if hee
saie that hee dyd suche a thing, or that hee dyd saie
such a thing, or that hee had beene about such a matter, or that hee dealte in suche a case, &c. And another
answere him that he did not, or that the same which he
sayd was not true, &c. For so hee is burdened beeing

accoun-

accounted a lyer, becaufe a man cannot bee mifinformed in anie thing which he fayd or did himfelfe, which injurie hee is to repulfe with the lie, and ſo the charge of challenge remaineth on the other, vnleffe hee in faying that hee dyd or fayde ſuch or ſuch a thing, doo thereby offer ſome man iniurie, who by giuing the Lie maie repulfe the fame iniurie, and ſo caſt the charge of challenge vpon him. To conclude, by all this which is fayde it manifeftly appeareth, that whofoeuer taketh heed that hee offer no offence in his wordes or ſpeech, ſhall neuer bee endangered to bee iniuried with the lie.

Of the manner and diuerfitie of Lies.

T O the enae that the nature of Lies may the more eafilye bee knowen, and when the Lie ought to bee giuen and when not, and in what cafes, it is requifite I fhould particularly difcourfe thereof : For ſome Lies bee certaine, and ſome conditionall, and both the firſt and the later, ſome of them are generall and ſome of them fpeciall. Vnto which two fortes, I will adde a third kind of lies, which may be tearmed Vaine-lies.

Of Lies certaine.

L Ies certaine, are ſuch as are giuen vppon wordes fpoken affirmatiuely, as if anie man ſhoulde faie or
write

346

write vnto another. Thou haſt ſpoken to my diſcredit, and in preiudice of my honour and reputation, and therefore dooſt lye. And in this reſpect is this a lye certaine, becauſe I affirme that ſuch a one hath ſpoken euill of me: yet becauſe I doe not particularly mention wherein or how he hath offended me by ſpeeche, the lye which I gaue him is generall, and therefore of no force. For to haue the lye giuen lawfully, it is requiſite that the cauſe whereupon it is giuen, be particularlye ſpecified and declared. Wherefore lyes ſpeciall, and ſuch as are giuen vpon ſure and expreſſe wordes, are ſuch as aſſuredlye binde the parties vnto whome they be giuen, to proue the ſame which they haue ſpoken, when as they cannot deny that they haue ſaid, whereupon the lye was giuen them, as for exemdle: *Alexander* thou haſt ſaid, that I being imploied by his highnes in his ſeruice at *Pauia*, haue had ſecret conference with the enemie: wherfore I ſay that thou haſt lyed. This is a ſure & a ſpecially, and by conſequence lawfully giuen.

Of conditionall Lyes.

Onditionall lyes be ſuch as are giuen conditionally: as if a man ſhould ſaie or write theſe woordes. If thou haſt ſaide that I haue offered my Lord abuſe, thou lyeſt: or if thou ſaieſt ſo heerafter, thou ſhalt lye. And as often as thou haſt or ſhalt ſo ſay, ſo oft do I and will I ſay that thou doeſt lye. Of theſe kinde of lyes giuen in this manner, often ariſe much contention in words, and diuers intricate worthy battailes, multiplying wordes v-

pon

pon wordes whereof no sure conclusion can arise : the reason is, because no lye can bee effectuall or lawefull, before the condition is declared to bee true, that is, before it be iustified that such words were certainly spoken. For the partie vnto whom such a lye is giuen, may answere according as he findes him selfe guiltie or not: if chaunce he haue so saide, he may by generall wordes seeke meanes to escape the lye which is giuen him: and withall vpon those words which the other hath spoken or written vnto him, he may happilie finde occasion of a meere quarrell, and giue him a lye certaine. And on the other side, if indeed he haue not spoken those words wherupon the lye was giuen him, then may he saye absolutelye, that hee spake them not: adding therto some certaine or conditionall lye, as for example: Whereas thou chargest me that I should say that thou art a Traitor, and thereupon saiest that I lye : I answere, that I neuer spake such words, and therfore say, that whosoeuer saith that I haue spoken such wordes, he lyeth. Yet notwithstanding I cannot like of this manner of proceeding, because therby men fal into a world of words.

Some holde an opinion, that such an answere might be framed : Thou doost not proceede in this case like a Gentleman, neither according to the honorable custome of Knights : which when thou shalt doe, I will answere thee. Vnto whom I cannot giue applause, considering that the other maye replye, that hee lyeth, because hee saith hee did not as a Gentleman, &c. alleadging that many Gentlemen haue obserued and vsed that manner of proceeding, and so shall the other haue occasion by his ignorance, in not knowing how to answere the lye conditionallye giuen him, to giue him a
certain

certain lye: therfore not to fall into any error, all such
as haue any regarde of their honor or credit, ought by
all meanes possible to shunne all conditionall lyes,
neuer geuing anie other but certayne Lyes : the
which in like manner they ought to haue great regarde, that they giue them not, vnlesse they be by some
sure means infallibly assured, that they giue them rightly, to the ende that the parties vnto whome they be giuen, may be forced without further Ifs and Ands , either to deny or iustifie, that which they haue spoken.

Of the Lye in generall.

He lye in generall is considered in two
sortes, the one hauing respect to the person, and the other to the iniurie. That
which toucheth the person, is termed generall, when no especiall person is named
to whom the same is giuen: as if one should say, whosoeuer hath reported of me that I haue betraied my lord,
doth lye falsely. And to this lye it is holden of braue
men of reuerence, that no man is bound to answer the
same: which seemeth to me to be excellent well vnderstoode, because this charge or imposition maye seeme
to touche manye, beeing that manye haue spoken the
same, and so one with many should be bound to fight:
which were to graunt an inconuenience directly, for
it is not allowed that any man should enter into combat more then once for one quarrell, and that no man
shal put his honor vpon another mans sword or valor:
so might it come to passe that such a one might take the
quarel, that the lie was neuer meant vnto. wherupon, to
auoid such disorders, the best meane is, that this lie so gi-
uē be not adiudged lawful, nor approued for sufficient.

The

The other lye which we haue termed generall in respect of the iniury, is this: *Antony* thou hast spoke ill of
me, or thou hast saide somewhat in preiudice of my reputation, and therefore I say that thou hast lyed. This
lye for that it is vpon words in which the lye especially
declared not what is the thing from whence the slaunder was, or speeche preiudiciall to reputation spoken
is, for that in many sortes a man maye be ill spoken of,
and ones reputation preiudiced: happening verye often, that hee whosoeuer talketh of another man, in diuers matters speaketh that which hee of whome they
were spoken, might esteeme them to his shame and
disgrace: and therefore it is most necessary to expresse
the point whereupon he holdeth himselfe offended: to
the end that it may be considered, whither hee wil take
vpon him to proue his sayings, or whither he wil proue
it with his weapon, or ciuillye by the lawe. And thus
for these causes this lye cannot be accompted no waies
of value nor lawfull: and he that hath giuen the same,
if hee will come to the definition or determination of
quarrell, must write the particular and declare it: for in
right hee is bound so to doe, if so much time bee permitted.

Specification
of the quar-
rell.

And this I say, a lye giuen in this sorte, doth not only
binde, but is verye dangerous to bee wrested, and the
danger whereof I speake, is thus: as by this case following you may easilie see. *Paul* vnderstandeth that *Nicholas* hath saide of him that he is an Vsurer, and hauing
vnderstanding of these wordes, writeth vnto him: *Nicholas* thou hast spoken ill of mee, and therefore I saye
thou lyest. *Paul* peraduenture knowing many defaults
more then this in *Nicholas*, maye answere him thus: I
confesse

confesse that I haue spoken ill of thee, but I specified the particularitie of that which thou hast doone, and I saide that long since thou committedst such a fault, and such another, and shew how. and thus bring foorth the ground of his speech, without making mention at all of that particularity of which *Paul* charged him with: and this maye adde more, that so thou lyest thy selfe, saying that I speaking ill of thee doe lye. Heere if *Paul* returne to write, should reply, I say that thou lyest in saying that I am an Vsurer. Not for all this shall his lye make him guiltie, because the generall lye permitting an exception, it maye be well wrested, being apparant that in speaking ill of *Paul, Nicholas* did not lye. And after the first lye is accompted false, it is to be presumed that also the second containeth a kinde of falsetie: for whosoeuer is accounted once naught, is alwaies esteemed naught in the same kinde: and the presumption being against *Paul*, it behoueth him to be the actor, so as for the effect in the generalitie of the lye, he shal fall into this inconuenience. Besides, such may be his default as the same by lawe might be proued against him, that neither as Defendant or Plaintife, he may enter the duello or combat. I conclude therefore, for the small validitie of the generall lye, that it hath qualitie to put an other man to the paines of proofe: as for the danger that it bringeth with her, all cauilieres, and braue men ought to take heede of it altogither. Although there were no other thing, then to auoide the multitude of cartelles, being a thing more comely for gentlemen to binde themselues to the action, then lay themselues open with many words.

T

Of the Lye in particular.

He speciall lyes are those which are giuen to speciall persons, and vpon expresse and particular matter, and the example is this: *Siluano* thou haſt ſayde that at the daye of the battaile of *S. Quintin* I did abandon the Enſigne, whereof I ſaye thou lyeſt: and this is that lye, that before wee tearmed aſſured and lawfull. It is verye neceſſarye that hee that goeth thus to worke, muſt haue ſuch profes, and witnes of the ſpeech of that hee which intendeth to beginne the repulſe with the lye, that the other maye not denye it : for if I haue not proofes conuenient, hee maye anſwere that I haue lyed my ſelf in ſo giuing him the lye, and in ſuch a caſe I ſhall not onely be driuen to prooue that I abandoned not the Enſigne, but proue that he hath laid that blame vpon me vniuſtly : but if he cannot iuſtly denye it, then there is no doubt but that he muſt alſo proue it. But when he ſhall deny that he ſpake theſe wordes, and I haue proued them by iuſt circumſtance, if then he ask the combate to prooue his ſaying that way on me, the ſame then is to be vtterly refuſed, for the deniall of his ſpeeche commeth ſo to be an vnſaying of his worde: and thereupon it is to be preſumed, that as well in his accuſation as deniall, hee was a lyer. And in theſe quarrels, wherein appeareth manifeſt falſitie, thoſe who commaund (as ſoueraigne Lords,) ought not to permit the

The office of great Lords. The office of Caualieres.

T

the combat, nor braue men (I meane caualieres) ought not to be aſhamed in ſuch caſes to refuſe the battaile, being more honorable to auoide it with reaſon, then to enter it againſt all right, and all bond of duetie. Now this true and lawefull lye beeing that wee would in this chapter ſpecifie, with which onelye braue men ought to giue the repulſe vnto all iniuries, wherewith they finde themſelues offended with any body, and wil either by mouth or writing giue it, they muſt ſo perfectlye manifeſt themſelues in the words wherein they finde themſelues outraged, and in ſuch ſort build their intent, that no one of their words may be denyed nor wreſted: if they determine not afterwards to haue queſtion or doubt of the Challenger or the accuſed, which is in engliſh Plaintiſe and Defendant.

Of fooliſh Lyes.

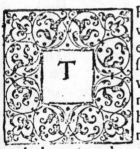

He common opinion is, that he who giueth the lye, looſeth the election of weapons, ſo that hee ſaie vnto another that he lyeth, without hauing regarde to the manner how he doth it, wherby he thinketh to haue done great matter. And heereupon it commeth, that euerye daye there riſeth from the common ſorte new and ſtrange fooliſhneſſes, as he who wil giue the lye ere the other ſpeake, ſaying : if thou ſaye that I am not an honeſt man, thou lyeſt in thy throate.

The lye before the other ſpeakes.

T 2　　　　And

And this is a changing of nature, for the lye beeing bu
an anſwere, in this manner it commeth to anſwere tha
which was neuer ſpoken. Here let vs put a caſe, it is tru
that ſometime one hearing that another hath ſayd tha
he is a theef, will anſwere : If thou ſaie that I am a theef
thou lyeſt : this Lie is generall, helde incontinentlye to
charge another. But the forme of this giueth (as it ſee-

**A lye that gi-
ueth meanes to
be repented.**
meth vnto me) meanes and waie to the ſpeaker thereof
to reſolue with himſelfe well whether he will continue
therin or no, as though hee would ſaie to himſelfe, take
heed if thou wilt affirme that which thou haſt ſpoken
that auouching it I pretende to giue thee the Lie, and
hee not returning to ſaie the ſame, that lye doeth not
binde, for that a man maye ſometime repent himſelfe,
ſaying ſomewhat in choler or with little conſideration.

**A lye at plea-
ſure.**
But now to returne to our fooliſh Lies, whoſe faſhion
will giue cauſe of laughter. If thou wilt ſaie that I am
not thy equall, thou lyeſt : where he doth not onely anſwere himſelfe before the other hath ſpoken, but alſo
putteth himſelfe vppon his pleaſure , that ſaie I what
I canne, till I haue ſpoken it I doo not lie : as I cannot
ſaie that I am going into France, vntill that I am in the
waie, and that I am imbarqued. And of ſuch lyke Lyes
I haue heard ſome good ſtore amongeſt no common
men. There are not anie of theſe more right than this,
which is much vſed, in that thou haſt ſpoken ill of mee,
thou lyeſt : and if thou denie the ſame thy ſaying, thou
lieſt alſo. That if I haue ſpoken il of thee, or if thou canſt
proue that I haue ſpoken it or no, if thou canſt proue
it, it behoueth thee to tell it. Let this bee an example,
thou haſt ſaid that I am an heretike, and ſhew plainelie
that I haue ſayde it, and vpon the expreſſe and particu-

lar

lar iniurie, giue me a certaine and especiall lye, if thou canst not proue that in such words I haue iniuried thee, and wilt enter into quarrell with me, then it is thy part to lay before me that I haue spoken ill of thee: so it toucheth me to answere and repell the blame that thou doost giue me. It is no reasonable matter that thou wilt lay vpon me the title of a slaunderer, and yet take away the meanes both of my answere & repulse, and be both Challenger and Defender in one matter. But these are certaine fashions of writings or challenges, found out eyther of men which thinke themselues too wise, or those which vnderstand very little. These kinde of lyes I esteeme not onely to be vnlawfull, but that they may bee turned backe with a lye in the throate: that I who know that I haue not iniured him, may safelie answere him that he lyeth, that I denying that I haue spoken ill of him doe lye.

And I maye speake of the other, that one meeting with his enemie saith : holde or giue me thy hand, that I may tell thee that thou art a lyer, & he answereth that thou lyest: and so not vsing any otherwise his handes, thinketh sufficiently that he hath discharged himself of his aduersaries charge, and dooth not vnderstand that these wordes, hold thy hands, will signifie, I will proue it if thou holde thy hand: and not holding his hand, he is not bound to goe any further. It is sometime seene that one asking another a thing, as a man should saye: hast not thou saide such wordes? wast thou not such a day in such a place? in stead of answere yea or no, it is answered by a lye: of all such, and such like, I doe not intend to mencion or remember, being to great a labor

to

to gather them together, for that they are woorth no more, than as he that had loſt his girdle, ſayd that whoſoeuer had taken awaie the ſame lyed. Or he that heard another breake winde behinde, ſayd, if you ſpeak to me ſir, you lie in your throate. To theſe I will ioyne others as vaine and fooliſh, whereof I will giue examples. I ſay to you, like to lyke, whoſoeuer you bee, that hee is an whoremonger, and hee then not giue them one word, but another daie with aduantage of weapon or companie, will tell me that I lyed. The other beeing himſelfe lykewiſe iniuried, wil make no anſwere, and afterwards out of audience will ſaie vnto the giuer of the iniurie, that hee lyed, or will publiſh a cartell full of giuing the lie. Theſe I ſaie, and ſuch lyke are of no woorth, for that they are not giuen like Gentlemen or Caualiers, In diſgrace giuen and receiued in the preſence of others with out aduantage, there muſt no aduantage bee ſought in the anſwering of them, but vnto the iniuries preſently giuen, preſent anſwere muſt bee made. To thoſe a farre off giuen, farre they are to be anſwered: and ſuch as are writ, written anſweres are allowed. Neither muſt that lye be called lawfull which is giuen with more aduantage, than the iniury was giue, becauſe no reſpect ought to withdrawe me to anſwere him who doeth iniurie or hurt, ſo that he be not armed, or ſo accompanied, that I anſwering him, hee might doo me wrong in oddes of weapon, in ſuch maner iniuring me, I ought not vnſaie my worde in ſeeking my aduauntage, yet it is certaine, that if anie perſon, I hauing meanes to doo ſuperſticery and wrong, ſhould charge me with infamy, I ought not to ſtaie from giuing him the lie therefore, for ſo is my dementie or lie lawfull. Neither can he alledge, that my

challenge

A lye giuen wout cauſe,

A lye giuen after an ill ſorte.

356

challenge therein was superfticery, the fault being to be giuen by him who sawe me so aduantaged vnder him, & would come to outrage me. But Gentlemen out of this case must obserue, that the lie or dementie ought to be giuen in more honest manner than the iniuries are done. And if that one far off thee haue spoken ill of thee thou straight maist giue him the ly, & maist write to him that he lieth in his throat, and so likewise present. And if he haue written anie thing in preiudice of thy reputation, thou by writing maist answere him, and very honorably thou maist also giue it him present. And seeing now mention is made of writing to him who farre of speaketh ill of another, I will adde this, that I know that of some it is said, that whosoeuer is the first that writeth he is accounted Chalenger, which opinion is in no sort to be allowed, for the Challenger is he that moueth the quarrell, and he offereth the quarrell that giueth the iniurie, whether it be by worde or deede present or farre off: and for that the other shall not preiudice the matter with the maner of writing, the writing first or last is no matter at all. But I haue seene it disputed amongest the wisest sorte of Gentlemen, that cartelles of dementies or giuing the lie, beeing heere and there cast abroad, euery one did defend for themselues to bee the first that published, pretending amongest themselues, that he who was the first that wrote hast the best aduantage.

And because wee haue spoken of superfticerie, which is not onely considered in respect of the aduantage of weapons or of persons, but for respect of priuiledged places, or the sight of the prince, where it is not lawfull for one that he maye freely shewe his griefe.

Heere

Heere one may aske me what hee ought to do, if in the preſence of the Prince, one will giue mee outragious wordes? To this I will alwaies thus aunſwere, that neither he ought to let paſſe the repulſe by the lye, nor the Prince ought at all to take it in diſdaine, for hee ought rather to bee tollerated that giueth another a repulſe of an iniurie, then he who doth it. and hee that beareth that in his preſence an iniurie ſhould be done me, of a greater reaſon ought to beare that I defende the ſame: but yet ſo, and with ſuch reuerence muſt he anſwer the ſame by aduenture, as the ſame may ſeeme full of modeſtie. And this I will now ſaye, that ſo much the more I holde my ſelfe bound to anſwere, by how much that I know that he that did me iniurie, is accounted of the Prince, before whom I may be accuſed: but heerein I preſcribe no lawe to any body, but onely ſhewe mine opinion, which whoſoeuer followeth, ſhall doe honorably and for his reputation: whom it ſhall not like to followe, let cuſtome ſtand in ſtead of lawe. And now turne to ſaye, that Princes ought more patiently comparte the diſcharge, then the charge that another hath giuen in his preſence.

A

A concluſion touching the Chal-
lenger and the Defender, and of
the wreſting and returning
back of the lye, or De-
mentie.

O come to the ende of this Treatiſe of Dementies or giuing the lie, and to conclude
the queſtion of the Challenger & the Defendant, ſeeing alreadie wee haue determi-
ned, that hee to whome the lie is giuen for repulſe of an
iniurie, he is properly the Defendant. To the ende that
more cleere contentment therein may be giuen, we are
verie diligently to examine the lawfull dementies or
lies, and by this examination remember our ſelues (if it
be conuenient) of thoſe things which before wee haue
treated of, and of their manner, and principally of the
proper nature of the Lie, the which is to put backe the
iniurie: and when it doth not this office, it becommeth
of it ſelfe an iniurie, and with another lie the ſame may
be repelled: and vpon this conſideration, I ſaie that the
Lie maie be giuen in the affirmatiue, and ſo vppon the
negatiue, and ſometime it falleth out, that vpon the aſ-
firmatiue it cannot be giuen, and ſometime vppon the
negatiue it hath no place , and ſo conſequentlye both
heere and there beeing giuen, it maie bee wreaſted and
ſent backe, and yet it may bee giuen both in the affirmation and negation in the ſame quarrell, without that

V.   it

it may bee fubiecte to anie repulfe of either of the parties.

And heere of each my opinion, I will giue an example,
The Lie lawfully giuen vpon the affirmatiue, is fuch as
before wee haue fet downe more than in one manner.
One fayth of another, that he is a rebell vnto his Lorde,
he who anfwereth, fayth that he lyeth. This lie cannot
bee auoided, beeing that it is giuen in the repulfe of the
flaunder which is layed vpon him. But if I fhoulde faie
of anie man, that he were an honeft man, & one fhould
giue mee the Lie vpon thefe wordes, in this it requireth
not repulfe but an iniurie, and I may faie, that he fhould
lie that thinketh that I fhoulde lie. Now is it his parte to
proue that he is not an honeft man, as well by reafon I
gaue him caufe of iniurie, as alfo that it is prefumed of
euerie one that hee is honeft, if the contrarie cannot be
apparently proued : and whofoeuer fayth that another
is vnhoneft, muft proue his fault therin committed, for
the which hee ought not to bee efteemed an honeft
man.

Now let vs paffe ouer to the Lies which are giuen
vpon the negatiue, whether they bee lawfull, or lawfully maye bee turned backe or no : as if one fhoulde
faie of mee, that in fome matter of armes or fighting I
did not my duetie, and I fhoulde aunfwere him wyth
the lie, the fame fhall bee a moft lawfull aunfwere : for
that in that fpeech, that I had not doone my duetie, hee
putteth on my backe no fmall burthen of infamie,
wherein it fhall bee moft lawfull and conuenient that
I fhoulde difcharge my felfe with the lye, and heere
the repulfe of an iniurie beeing the lye, and the prefumption beeing in my fauour, and that a man muft
not

not prefume of another, but that hee doeth his duetie in all refpectes, whofoeuer goeth about to giue mee that blame, to him it appertaineth to bee efteemed Challenger. But if one faie that hee hath not fayled in his loyaltie to his Lorde, and I fhoulde aunfwere him that hee lyeth, hee maye faie vnto mee, thou lyeft in that thou fayeft I lye, and with great refon it maye bee fayde, hauing aunfwered mee fo, for hee not dooing iniurie vnto anie bodie with thofe wordes, nor anie man ought to prefume that another fhoulde bee difloyall, that with the lye which I giue him, I doo not defende my felfe nor anie other of anie iniurie, but go about to outrage him, when hee maye lawfully returne backe that lye, and I come directly to bee dementied, and fo confequentlye mufte become Challenger.

Now it refteth that wee fhewe vnto you the examples of thefe cafes, in which in euerie and the felfe fame quarrell, both vppon the affirmation and negation you maye giue the lye, that neither of the one fide nor the other there is anie meanes or waie lefte to giue them the repulfe, and it is thus.

Two Gentlemen or Caualiers are brought to the fteccata to fight, there are weapons prefented vnto them, vppon the which they reafon and debate betweene themfelues whether they be to bee refufed or no, fo long that the daie is paffed with out comming to the battaile or fight, there dooth arife a queftion heerevpon amongeft them, whether they bee refufed or no.

This man whofoeuer hee bee fayth, that wyth reafon they might bee refufed, doeth charge him

that brought them, and hee who sayth that they maye
not be refused in reason, chargeth him that refuseth to
fight with them, and therefore the taske being giuen as
well on the affirmatiue as negatiue, the lie may accordingly bee giuen, and no more the affirmatiue than the
negatiue may it be wrested or sent backe, being both in
the one and in the other manner giuen for repulse, and
not of anie iniurie. And thus much maye suffice to bee
spoken of this subiect, seeing that of the other manner
of Lies, how they ought to be giuen, & which of them
may be wreasted, and which not, therby appeareth that
they are fully demonstrated which are lawfull. & those
knowen, it followeth consequently to knowe who
ought to be accouted chalenger. And so (God be than-
ked) we finde that almost we haue dispatched this matter, no lesse vneasie (as it is sayd before) to be handled &
vnderstood, than necessary to be knowen of all caualiers
and Gentlemen.

Of iniuries rewarded or doubled.

Eere yet there resteth a new question,
yea, euen in the Challenger and De-
fendant, which wee will not let passe
without some declaration, and this is
in such cases, as when on the one parte
they speake, and on the other they an-
swere with iniurious wordes, and that either they reply
the same, or doo adioyne vnto them others, of which I
haue made this title of requited iniuries or redoubled.
For

For requited inimies I vnderstand, when one replieth only the iniury that was giuen him, and doth adioyne nothing thereunto : as thou art a theefe, a theefe thou art. The redoubled I call those, when one is not contented to haue saide to his aduersarie the selfe same wordes of outrage, but doth ioyne thereto an other or more, as if I should say to another, that he is a false monie maker, and he should say to me I am so, and an homicide withall: vpon these causes the writers of Duello moue manye questions, whither vpon them there should be any fighting or no : and if they should fight which should be Challenger and which the Defendant: heerein to shew you that which I think, before I will speake thereof any thing at all, I do adiudge him an ill brought vp gentlemen, who feeleth himself to be charged with any blot of infamy, shall not be as wel attetiue to take away that, as to seek with like or greter iniurie to slaunder his aduersarie, that he ought with a lye put backe that which shalbe spoken to him, rather then either reply the same, or multiplie any other in words: and so doing, two commodities will followe him, the one that with the lye he shall charge his enemye with that dutie to bee Challenger : the other that hee shall make himselfe knowne a person farre from iniurious intention. But if the case happen in any of the formes aforesaid, there is somewhat to be marked how a man must behaue himselfe therein. I say therfore when one calleth me traitor, and I say thou art a traitor, & do not thereto only ioyn any word that hath not the force of the lye, no combat is to follow : and if hee come to replye the same iniurie many other times, it shalbe as

An iniurie not thought.

V 3   much

much as if an iniury once repulſed, there is no more repulſe to be ſpoken of.

But if it ſhould be anſwered, thou lyeſt that ſayeſt I am a traitor, for that thou art the traitor: I doe not ſee wherefore the combate ſhould not followe heere, for with theſe words I haue diſcharged my ſelfe with that he charged me, and laide vpon him the ſlaunder of traitor, which is that I ſend back the injurie done to me, and iniurie him with the repulſe thereof, binding him to his proofe: and although he ſhould replye, but thou lyeſt thy ſelfe that I am the traitor, for all this hee is not diſcharged, but anſwered to that iniurye that I gaue him : and becauſe the lye was giuen of me in time, it will haue the greater reaſon, and is required at his hand to proue the truth of his ſpeech: but hauing called me traitor, I ſhould anſwere him, thou art the traitor, and hee afterwarde ſubioyne thou lyeſt: now the caſe of Challenger will come vpon me, becauſe he dooth not ſtaye himſelfe vpon the firſte iniurye, but anſwereth to that I ſaide to him; and now to me there remaineth no more meanes to binde him to the proofe, beeing alreadie with the lye giuen me made Challenger. Neither can it be ſaide, that that anſwere, thou art the traitor, hath ſo much the force of a repulſe, as of an iniury: for that the repulſe ſtandeth in the negatiue, and if the negatiue haue not the force of a lye, it chargeth not : and that being anſwered Traitor, the iniurie with a lye may be put back lawſullie, that although it be true, that an iniurie once wreſted will not permit any more writing : it is to be vnderſtoode, that there is great difference betweene the wreſting & repulſe: with the wreſting

sting

364

sting, I say to thee that thou saiest of me, but with the repulse I giue thee not that blame that thou giuest me, but onely doe free my selfe thereof, charging thee with no blame at all, but with the dutie to prooue that thou hast saide, and that that which I say should be so: if one should say that I am a theefe, and I should answere him that he lyeth, this shalbe tearmed iniurie, and not wrested, but repelled: and if to one of these lyes which we haue shewed before, which haue the nature of an iniurye, an answere should be made to them by another lie, this shalbe called wresting. And this is a true resolution, and so to be approued and followed according to the stile and order of Gentlemen and Caualiers. And that which I haue saide of rewarded iniuries, I saye the same of the redoubled, that hee must not bee tearmed Challenger by the multiplication of iniuries, but must be ruled by the lye, hauing saide to you before that about question of words, the proofe of the lawes are appointed to the iniuryer, and not to the iniured: true it is, that when neither of the one side nor the other the lye is, hee shall not remayne without some blame to whome the same was firste spoken, how manye or great soeuer they be.

Nor that is not to bee taken for good aduise which is set downe by some writer, that if I should call another Traitor, and he shoulde answere that I am a Traitor, a Theefe, a robber by the highway, I shoulde subioyne I will prooue it to thee with my weapon, that I am neither Traitor, Theefe, nor robber by the high waye, but that thou art the traitor thy selfe.

What

What a foolish enterprise shall this be of mine, that hauing the meanes to make me Defendant, will make my
selfe Challenger, and offer my selfe to the proofe. Besides, what an ill kinde of proceeding should mine be,
to come to the determining of so many quarrels with
one battaile or combat, the same not being to be granted for diuers things together: for it may come to passe
in the one they maye be true, in the other false: and so
fight for the one with reason, and the other without: a-
bout which, those that will forme quarrels ought to be
wel aduised: and if they be not rightly framed, the Lord
before hee giueth licence for the fielde, must reforme
them, or at the least prouide that when the gentlemen
or caualieres bee conducted thither, that their godfa-
thers in capitulating, giue them a conuenient forme.

Quarrels must be simple. (margin note)

That straightwaies vpon the Lye, you must not take armes.

Ow if in the discourse about the lyes
which we haue made, it is concluded
that the lyed, which is he that hath the
lie giuen to him, is to be Challéger, we
doe not say therefore that is to be vnderstoode, that presently for the lye a
man should runne to his weapon: for the triall of the
sworde being doubtfull, and the ciuile certaine, the ciuile is that way by which euery man of reckoning and
reputation ought to iustifie himselfe. For he ought to
be

The sword and ciuile proofe. (margin note)

366

be esteemed honorablest, who with certain proofe approueth his honor, then the other that with an incertaine testimonie, doth think to answere his reputation. But I see amongst Gentlemen to be noted such an abuse that they thinke themselues to haue committed villanye, to attempt any other meanes than by the sworde: wherein how much they deceiue themselues which thinke so, I will say nothing else at this present, but that the ciuile profe is the profe of reason, & fighting but the proofe of force: and that reason is proper vnto man, and force of wilde beastes. Leauing the ciuile proofe and taking the armes, we leaue that which is conuenient for men, to haue recourse to that which is belonging to brute beastes: which peraduenture Gentlemen would not doe very often, if they vnderstoode wel their dutie, and when they would wel consider that it is no lesse the parte of a Caualier to know, to put vp well his sworde, then well to drawe it out.

Those therefore which think they haue the lye duly giuen them, ought if they haue meanes by the way of reason to proue their saying, they ought by the same I say, proue it, and not follow the other way of armes, if thereto they be not constrained by necessitie, and so as they could not by any other meanes iustifie themselues.

Those other which are offended for that they haue not the lye duelye giuen them, those maye wrest the same, or by some meanes lightly reproue it.

X   Of

Of the forme of Cartels, or Letters of Defiance.

Hen Cartels are to be made, they muſt be written with the greateſt breuity that may be poſsible, framing the quarrell with certaine, proper, and ſimple wordes: and ſpecifying whether the cauſe was by woord or deed, you muſt come to the particulars of the ſame, ſhewing well the perſons, the thing, the times and places, which doe appertaine to the plaine declaration thereof, ſo that one maye well reſolue to the anſwere: for the Duello being a forme of iudgement, as in the ciuile, criminall, and in action of iniury, a particular ſetting downe is required: no leſſe can be ſaide of the iudgement belonging to Gentlemen and Caualiers, theirs being of no leſſe force. And he that ſhalbe Challenger, ſhall call his partie aduerſarie to the field, hee that ſhalbe the Defendant, ſhall ioyne thereto his lye.

And in ſuch manner of writing, the leaſt eloquence and copie of woordes that maye be muſt be vſed, but with naked and cleere ſpeeche muſt knit vp the concluſion.

And this I ſay principally of the Defendant, which with ſuperfluous ſpeeche moſt commonlye confound themſelues, and in that they are not content to haue repelled the iniurie with the lye, and will ſet downe the field, and ſaye that they will defend their ſaying with their weapon: which thinges are not onelye ſuperfluous,

368

ous, but dangerous, becauſe when one hath giuen the lawfull lye, ceitaine, and particular, ſo incontinent is he to whom the lye is giuen made the Challenger, and the proofe belonging vnto him, it is in him to chuſe what way beſt liketh him to proue his ſaying: whether it be ciuile, that is by law, or by armes: and mine aduerſary chooſing the proofe by armes, the choyſe of them commeth vnto me.

Now if I giue the lye, and afterward ſet downe the proofe of armes, I enter into his iuriſdiction, and doe the office of Challenger : whereupon it is moſt reaſonable that mine appertain to his, and ſeeing that I haue elected the proofe of armes, the election of them doth not remaine to him : for it is no reaſon nor honeſtye, that I both call him to armes, and alſo take the choiſe of them.

And here I muſt adioyne another thing, that albeit that ordinarily he that hath the election of armes, is accounted the guiltie or Defendant, I ſhould ſaye that the ſame ſhould ceaſe in this caſe, that if peraduenture by ſpeaking of armes I happen to preiudice my ſelfe in the election of them, for all that the quarrell dooth not alter: but he that hath accuſed me of any default, is to proue his ſaying, & not I to proue my repulſe: & therfore we ſay that by the force of the iniurye done vnto me, and by me put back, he is to be Challenger, and I for hauing called him vnto armes, do loſe the election of them: wherupon it followeth that he muſt be forced to proue his intention with thoſe armes which ſhal be elected by himſelfe.

And although it ſeemeth to me ſuperfluous to remember it, yet for that it is a thing not to be paſſed in ſilence, for that it is oft to be confidered, becaufe there muft be alwaies had in regard, what words they vfe euery time they fpeake of the fight: and the proofe and maintayning are taken in the fame fenfe or fignification, and do appertain to the Challenger: where the Defendant ought not to put forth himfelfe, but to defend and fuftaine: and if he fhould offer to maintaiaine or defend, he fhould become prefentlie vpon the fame to be challenger. Of the anfweres which are to be made vnto the cartels, there is no more to be faide, but fo much as is fpoken alreadie. In the giuing of the lye, the anfwers yet may be ruled and ordered, and that when vpon the lye there happeneth no difputation vnto him that receiueth it, there refteth nothing but his iuftification, either vnto the proofe, or fatisfaction of the iniurie.

And heere I will not ftay to tell you, that it feemeth vnto me a moft gentleman-like thing, in all manner of writings to fpeake honourably of his enemie, for fo a Gentleman or Caualier doth honor to himfelte, fhewing thereby to haue quarrell with an honorable perfon: whereas otherwife, hee difhonoreth himfelfe, and fheweth himfelfe rather to haue minde to fight with the pen then with the fworde.

Of

Of the manner of sending of Cartels.

Entlemen were wont to send a gloue for a defie, and with fierce wordes did difpatch the fame, when they came vnto the fight : for it was not then amongft them efteemed peraduenture any aduantage to bee Defendant, not vfing that (I cannot tell what to tearme it) wittie or cauelling kinde in election of Armes, which in thefe our daies are accuftomed. Afterward came the cuftome of sending of Cartelles, in which manner of proceeding there was much difficultie and newneffe, and diuerfe offences to bee carried. Laftly, the publication is taken vp, the which is more fure and more readie, chiefely the Lordes hauing feene the multiplication of quarrelles, haue prouided that in their ftates no cartels maye bee prefented, which beeing fo effectually brought to paffe that euerie one of them doth vfe it, it leaueth no occafion to fpeake many wordes vpon it : Thus much I faie, that as Cartels are publifhed, & in affurance thereof the daie intimated and notified, then there is no place lefte of excufe or alledging of ignorance. And by this means all manner of hiding the matter, and all other euafions that might haue beene vfed in the time of apprefentation are cleane taken awaie.

The election of Armes is verie cauelling.

This I fhal faie more, which I haue touched before fpeaking of the foolifh lies, that when anie man whofo-

euer fhall giue me a lie prefent, and without aduantage
of weapons or of men, if then I do not anfwere him, to
come afterward to publifh a Cartell with the Lie, I can
not hold my felfe fatisfied : for not being charged with
out anie fuperfticerie, and I not anfwering the fame, &
going about a farre of to anfwere him, I do in a manner
confeffe that I am not a man to ftand face to face wyth
him, and thus by my deeds confent that he is fuperiour
to mee, howe fhall I by writing equall my felfe to him,
and my opinion is, that fuch a lye fhall neuer be counted lawfull. Truth it is, if I doo not aunfwere prefently
the iniurious wordes, I am not of opinion that therfore
another time I fhal be barred to make my anfwer to the
fame, and to him that gaue them mee, onely this, that I
muft fo holde the fame, that thereby I take not any aduantage in the doing of it. And if one fhall bee fo lame
or weake, that anfwering it is feene manifeftlye that the
other without anie paine may hurt or offend him : to
this man it may bee lawfull to feeke affured meanes to
aunfwere. And fo in all matters of iniurie which are
committed with fuperfticerie, although they be fpoken
to a mannes face, it is a thing cleere, that aunfwering by
writing, and by the waie of publication, is an anfwering
to one moft legitiuely, and when the other with another fuperfticerie fhould aunfwere him it, that anfwere
fhall alfo be lawfull.

After

After the defie it is not lawfull that the one Gentleman should offend the other, but in the steccata, which is the place of Combat.

Fter that the one hath called the other to the battel, as well in the requirer as the required, it is not lawful that either may offend his aduersarie anie more, for that that request or calling bindeth gentlemen to the ordinarie waie : and although there shoulde arise amongest them questions or strife, they must obserue this rule, for whilest this question doth hang, no other thing is to be innouated. And if either of them should assault his aduersarie in this time, he is to bee esteemed, adiudged, and declared a breaker of faith, and amongest other Gentlemen from henceforth, in anie other quarrell to bee refused and put backe. And this censure is so vniuersally approued, that I neede not endeauour my selfe to confirme it anie farther.

When

When one doth call another for an offence done vnto him by a third perſon.

IT happeneth ſometimes that one offended with another mans words, or otherwiſe, maketh another ſtrike him, or gaue him the baſtonado, ought he that is ſtriken to bee called Challenger, or elſe the ſtriker? vnto which demand we haue a readie anſwere. That as the ciuill laws doo proceed as well againſt the one as the other, ſo in ſuch caſe the combate beeing permitted, a Gentleman ought to proceede as well againſt the one as the other of them.

True it is, it is ſayde, that when the one hath to endure, and the other endured, that when the thing is no more but manifeſt, hee that is offended ought not to leaue the certaine for the vncertaine. And beeing aſſured that he is oppreſſed of ſome body, his doubt or preſumption doeth not make him apte to require another perſon of eſtimation before he doo diſcharge himſelfe of him that oppreſſed him, and be offended againſt him that hath with hand offended him, and ouercomming him, it is cleere that hee, remaineth diſcharged. But to kill or ouercome him that required him as principall Challenger, I doo not ſee how hee is relieued or eaſed, for the other may alwaies ſaie that hee ſtrake me, for his

owne

owne particular interest, that the proofe of Armes is an vncertaine proof, but the stroke is certaine, in such case the blame or griefe will still remaine vpon himselfe. Wherevpon I resolue to saie, that the manifest deed of the offence, and not the occult author of the same is to be called. And this assure againe, that although there are some shewes of them, a man maye also doubt whether they may be false, but there is no doubt of him that is the offender.

What is to be done if question rise vpon the quarrell, or vpon the person of the Challenger.

Any times it falleth out , that one calleth another vnto the fielde, and therefore must accept the defie, but aunswereth the same with some exception, obiecting either that he did not vnderstand the quarrell, or that it doth not touch him, or that the caller is infamous, or hath other charge, or is not of lyke condition, or such lyke. In which case there is nothing to say, but that it is necessarie before wee passe anie further, that such difficulties bee made cleere, and the meane to cleer them is, that the gentlemen submit themselues to the iudgement of some prince or noble man trusted

Y

fted

375

sted on both partes, and chosen of both the parties, and accordingly as they do censure it, so the quarrell to be left or followed. And be it that the one wil not accept the proposed iudgment, the opinion of gentlemen shall bee of him, if he were Challenger, that the oppositions made were iustly made to him, and if he were Defendant, that hee had an vniust quarrell to defend. And when the Challenger should be the man that shoulde refuse the iudgement, to the Defendant remaineth nought else to doo, but to stand ypon it firmely: truely yet when the Defendant shall auoid the determination, then it appertaineth to the Challenger to proceede further, hauing shewed or sent him the letters patents or of the fielde, hee hath more to do, he must send them him, & notifie them, requiring him that either hee accept the one, or send backe the others, or else let him choose one of them with protestation that if hee do not accept the same, or refuse to send, hee doeth cause him to vnderstand that she shall auoide it, and is to accept such an offer, specifieng one of his patents and letters, and that in conuenient time hee shall finde him in that place or field to make an end with his weapon of the quarrel if hee shall bee there, otherwise with all disdaine and contumacie hee shall proceede to his infamie, wyth those clauses which shall bee necessarie for such an effect. And this is both a Gentlemans course and reasonable order of proceeding, for if there were not such an order of proceeding fonnde out, for euerie one that woulde finde out meanes to auoyde all calling into the fieldes, most men would refuse all
fighting

fighting, & iudgement, & the required shall remaine mocked without anie remedie. And this remedie is lawfull to be vsed when the Defendant doth flie the iudgement thereof, that the same shoulde be chosen of both the parties by cōmon accord: for when the quarrell is contested and cleere, no matter now stan-deth to be determined on, for there remaining anie one Article to be determined on, they cannot binde another to accept it, nor to send patents or letters of the fielde, for that hath his time and place when all controuersie is past, and that done, then there resteth nothing but to come to blowes.

Whether the subiecte ought to obey his Soueraigne, being by him forbidden to Combat.

 His doubt is often moued by them that write of this matter, concerning which Gentlemen are resolued, that for their Prince and Soueraigne they will glad-ly hazard their liues euen into greatest daungers, but their honour will they not in anie case suffer to be spotted with disgrace or cowardise, wher-by they are growen into this custome, that beeing challenged to the combate, or vnderstanding or perceiuing that others meane to challenge them, or else intending and resolued wyth themselues to

Y 2 challenge

challenge others, they will retire into some secrete place, where it shall not consist onely in theyr Princes power to forbidde, or staie them from it, and so laying aside all respect either of their Princes fauour or losse of goods, or bannishment from their Countrie, they take the combate in hande. And whosoeuer shoulde doo otherwise amongst men professing Armes, shoulde bee iudged to haue greatly empayred his credit and reputation, and dishonoured him selfe in high degree.

Also he should bee esteemed vnworthie to conuerse with Gentlemen, and if chance he should challenge anie man afterward, he might deseruedly bee repulsed, & lawfully. Which manner and order being confirmed by long custome, and vniuersally approued and helde for sterling among knightes and Gentlemen of all sortes, I thinke it needles heere to trouble my selfe with aunswering all such friuolous obiections as diuerse make that haue written of this subiect whereof some alleadge the ancient description of warre, wherein it was not lawfull for anie souldier to combate against the commandement or without speciall leaue of the Generall: for they consider not the difference of the cases, which is greate, seeing it is another matter to be in an armie, where a man is bound to attend to especiall enterprises, and to bee idle at home. Besides this, there is also muche difference betweene the defiances vsed in auncient times, and oures, which being in no vse or custome, & scarse knowen vnto the Romanes, how could they make any lawes or take any order concerning them.

Further-

378

Furthermore, those Gentlemen or Souldiers that in ancient time challenged one another to the combate, beeing of contrarye armies, and enemie one to the other, (whom these writers alleadge against vs) were induced to seeke the tryall of armes, for one of these two causes: either for that the decision of the whole warre was agreed vpon by both parties, to be committed to some fewe of eche armie, as it fell out when the *Horatij* and *Curatij* tried their valour for the whole armies : and in this case it is most necessarye that the election of cōbatants should apertain to the superiors & cheefe gouernours: neither can it by any reason be lawful for eche one to take any such enterprise in hand that is willing to doe it, or else for profe of their valour: in which case also no Souldier ought to goe to the combate without licence, neither doth any burthen or charge remaine vpon him, if he deny the combate, for that hee is to vse his valour in that warre not according to his owne pleasure, but his vnto whome hee hath sworne his seruice and obedience, without any respect of particular interest: yet it may so fall out, that a Souldier being burdened with some especiall quarrell concerning his reputation, ought so much to regarde the same, that he ought to abandon both the armye, his countrie and naturall Prince, rather then to suffer it to passe vnanswered. Concerning which point, I will say as much as I can presently call to remembrance.

True it is, that if there rise any quarrell betweene two gentlemen of two aduersary armies, they ought not either to challenge, or answere a challenge without the authoritie of their Generall : for that without his leaue, it is not lawful for any man to haue any intelligence or dealings whatſoeuer, with any in the enemies Campe : but if that the quarrell were ſuch, that either of the parties ſhould be diſhonored either by delaying the challenge, or not aunſwering the ſame, then ought he whoſe honor and reputation is in danger of ſtaine, to enlarge himſelfe as much as in him lyeth, from that ſubiection hee is in, and bring himſelfe into the waye whether the ſafegarde of his honor inuiteth him. Inſomuch that among Gentlemen this opinion is currant, that if a man were in ſome Cittie beſiedged by the enemie, and could not obtaine leaue of the Gouernour to come foorth, hee ought to leape ouer the walles, to goe and defend his honor. Yet will I not deny, but that if a mans country or naturall Prince ſhould be intereſſed in the matter, he ought to haue a reſpect both of the one and the other: and eſpecially when a great parte of the quarrel ſhould concerne either his Countrie or Prince : for that the the maner of proceeding therin, ought toibe platted by their counſaile and aduiſe. But in all other caſes, when the matter onely concerneth a mans own intereſt, then ought not any gentleman be backward in challenging, or anſwering the challenger: and in no caſe either ypon commaundement, or vpon any penaunce whatſoeuer, refuſe the combat.

Neither according to my ſimple conceite, ought any prince to look for any thing at his ſubiects hands that may empaire their reputation, or woorke their diſhonour.

How

How Gentlemen ought to accept of any Quarrell, in such manner that they may combat lawfully.

Hey that maintaine any quarrell, vse most commonly to vndertake the combate with such intent, that howbeit the cause of their quarrell be iust, yet they combate not iustly, that is, not in respect onely of iustice and equitie, but either for hatred, or for desire of reuenge, or for some other particular affection: whence it commeth to passe, that many howbeit they haue the right on their sides, yet come to be ouerthrowen: For that God whose eyes are fixed euen on the most secret and inner thoughts of our harts, and euer punisheth the euil intent of men, both in iust and vniust causes, reserueth his iust chasticements against all offenders, vntill such times as his incomprehensible iudgement findeth to be most fit and seruing to his purpose.

Wherfore, no man ought to presume to punish another, by the confidence and trust which hee reposeth in his owne valour, but in iudgement and triall of armes, euery one ought to present himselfe before the sight of God, as an instrument which his eternall maiestie hath to woorke with, in the execution of iustice, and demonstration of his iudgement.

If

If therefore any man violate the chaſtitie of my wife, ſiſter, neece, or kinſe-woman, I ought not or may not call him to the trial of the ſworde, to the end that I may be reuenged of him. Nor if any one ſhould proue diſloyall to his Prince or Countrie, ought I challenge him to the combate in reſpeɛe of the hatred that I beare him, or to obtaine fauour at the Princes handes, or to purchaſe honour in my Countrie, or if any of my kinſemen or freends were ſlain, maye I challenge the murderer to the fielde, in reſpeɛ of the kinred or freendſhip I had with him, but my intent ought to be ſuch, that howbeit I had not beene eſpecially offended, and no particular affection or reſpeɛ ſhould induce me thereunto, yet for loue of vertue, and regarde of the vniuerſall good and publique profite, I was to vndertake ſuch a combate. For I ought in all particular iniuries preſent vnto mine eyes, not the perſons either offending or offended, but rather fall into cõſideration how much that offence diſpleaſeth almightie God, and how much harme may enſue vnto humaine kinde thereby. And for adulterie ought a man to combate, not as to reuenge the wrong done to one particular perſon, but in regarde of all, conſidering how holye and religious a bond matrimonie is, being a lawfull coniunction inſtituted and ordained by God, to the end that man and woman therein ſhould not as two, but one perſon, liue together in ſuch manner, that nothing except death only might ſeperate and diſſoyn them. Wherfore perpending the dignitie and worthines hereof, and how that by adulterie this deuine ordinance and inſtitution is violated, matrimonyall

con

coniunction infringed, and lawfull procreation corrupted, euerye Gentleman ought to vndertake the combate, not so muche to reuenge himselfe, or his freends, or to chastice or punishe the offenders, as to preserue and keepe from violence a bond so sacred and inuiolable, with sure hope, that God, who (as *S. Paul* saith) will iudge the Adulterer, will by means thereof giue most seuere iudgement.

In like manner, if some man haue mis-behaued himselfe in any matter concerning his prince or cuntrie, each Gentleman ought to thinke, how that God hath ordained and authorised Princes to be aboue vs, to the ende that vnder him they may as his ministers and officers gouerne vs his humble flocke, how that nothing beeing more gratefull and acceptable vnto God, then good gouernment among men (who assembled together, and liuing vnder the same lawes, beare themselues orderly, gouerning their liues and manners aright) we are not so much bound in dutie towardes any, as towards them that are as it were lieutenantes vnto almightie God in earth, for so I call our princes and gouernors: and towards that assemblie & congregation of mankind, vnder whose lawes we are borne and bred, I meane our Countrie, and how that no greter wickednes can be committed than for a man to rebel against him whom God hath ordained Lord and gouernor ouer him, or to wrong him vnto whome he hath giuen his faith, or to betray that citie vnto which hee is both for his liuing, bringing vp, & many benefits besides infinitly beholding. In respecte whereof, I saie each Gentleman hauing

Z   conside-

confidered and weighed all this, ought as a publique
plague, and not as a particular enemie, to perfecute
him that committeth any of thefe odious exceffes:
calling him to the triall of the fwoorde, confidentlye
hoping and trufting with affured faith, that God will
chaftice and punifh him that hath fo greeuouflye offended both him and his people, violating his facred
ordinances and conftitutions. And for the fame reafon, if fome man haue committed murder, hee that
will combate with him, muft not doe it to this ende,
onely to wreake the death of him that is murdered,
in refpect that he was his freend or kinfeman, but he
ought to call to minde what a noble and excellent
creature man is, who being taken away and brought
to naught by murder or flaughter, the faireft and no-
tableft woorke which almightie God hath framed, is
marred, and fpoiled. Infomuch that whofoeuer committeth murder, dooth diffolue and breake the moft
perfect peece of woorke that the creator of heauen
and earth hath made, and defaceth the image and
likenes of God. And for that God in his facred law
ordeined, that man-flayers fhould be carryed from
his alter and put to death, the partie that will combate, knowing how greatly his diuine maieftie is offended with this finne, ought not to vndertake the
combate, becaufe he would kill him, but becaufe hee
might be as it were, the minifter to execute Gods deuine pleafure, and moft holy commaundement.

By thefe examples maye a Gentleman perceiue
what ought to be doone in all other cafes, fo that it
fhall be needles for men to feeke examples for eache
offence,

offence, troubling both my selfe and the Reader. In the meane time, take this by the way, that whatsoeuer I haue heere saide of the Challenger, is also in the same manner to be vnderstoode of the Defendant: insomuch that both the one and the other ought to regarde the preseruation of their honour and innocencie by iust meanes: the one neuer challenging but with iust cause and vpright meaning, and the other neuer accepting any challenge, vnlesse hee know himselfe to be guiltles : and in such sorte, that he may take it with a good conscience, as to doe or performe any action that concerneth his honor, to liue and dye in defence thereof. For, as it is shamefull to doe any dishonorable act, so is it more shamefull and opprobrious to maintain the same, and stand in defence of it.

And againe, a man finding himselfe innocent and wrongfully dishonored, ought not to feare any danger, but to venter his life at all times, for the righting either of priuate or publique wronges: in all things, considerations, and circumstances, hauing a speciall regarde vnto iustice. For God giueth right vnto him that is iust, and ouerthroweth the vniust: whosoeuer therefore shall take armes for iustice to repell vniust iniuries, may be assured to preuaile, and with an vndismaied courage goe about what he vndertaketh.

Z 2

Of

OF INIVRIE, OF
the Charge, and of the
ſhame.

Hereas I haue before ſufficientlye intreated vppon the qualitie of Lyes, and ſhewed the nature of them to bee to returne iniuries, per-aduenture ſome wyll meruaile why I ſhould againe ſpeak thereof in this place , ſeeing that the iniurie muſt needes be before any returne, which (though I confeſſe) bee out of order to reduce it vnder this title, yet in diuerſe reſpects I haue bene mo-ued thereunto, as namely, for that I finde a verie ill cuſtome generally followed in quarrelles, where by contempt of right courſe and law it ſelfe, Gentlemen are raſhly carryed to take weapons in hand, not con-ſidering firſt if it bee a lawful quarrell, or ſuch as may deſerue a Combat, nor doo they euer deſire to bee directed by an orderly proceeding. But Gentlemen of diſcretion ought firſt before they enter into armes rightly to examine the quality of their quarel, if it be worthie the proofe by weapons, and by this meanes
make

make a right introduction to the truth, so as men bee not rashly lead on to the slaughter. Again, the ground of all quarrels betwixte Gentlemen is this, that they thinke themselues iniuried or charged, whereof my purpose is chiefly to intreate, so farre forth as I shall thinke it needfull.

To beginne then with iniurie, it is nothing else but a thing done without reason, as (as we vse to say) wrongfully. And Charge is no other but an inforce-ing of a man to returne, or to prooue or reproue anie thing alledged, which is so tearmed by this name, be-cause that the lawiers affirme, that the charge of pro-uing resteth on the Challenger. Whereby it appea-reth that the man charged ought to be the Challen-ger : and touching these two wordes, it is to be vn-derstood that sometime both iniurie and charge are at one time done, and sometime charge without in-iurie, and a man maye also iniurie and not charge. Touching the first thus it is, I am charged by one with an offence I neuer committed, wherin he doth me iniurie, because hee doth vnlawfully seeke to de-fame me, and then laieth the charge on me, in that he forceth mee to seeke to returne the iniurie, and make answere to his opprobrious wordes, vnlesse I would suffer my selfe to be shamed. Whereupon I giue him the lie, and so discharge my selfe and come to charge him, which setteth me free, & bindeth him to main-taine his wordes, which is as much as to vrge him to challenge. Wherefrom we are to note, that I onely charge him without iniuring, because my answere is but reasonable, and so the charge resteth on him, as I

Iniury.

Charge.

He that is char-ged.

Iniury charge.

Charge with-out iniurie.

Z 3　　　　sayd

fayd before. Iniurie without charge is of two fortes,
viz. of wordes and of deedes. Of wordes thus, if one
man fhould fpeak anie thing of another, which were
manifeftly knowen to bee falfe, to this he fhould not
bee bound to aunfwere, becaufe the firft 'without a-
nie returne woulde bee accounted a falfe accufer and
a lyer: and in mine opinion, it is a more honourable
reputation for a man to bee filent in fuch a cafe, than
by aunfwering to feeme to make any account of the
wordes : as a noble worthie man fayde vnto a Gentleman that had flaundered him, that hee would neither holde him a friende nor an enemie, not yet anfwere his wordes, reckning him vnworthie to bee
wel fpoken off by an honeft man, and too bafe a fubiect for a man to fpeake euill off. But if in cafe of
fuch fhamefull and falfe wordes, a man fhoulde bee
vrged and giue the lie, it is more than is requifite, as a
thing whereof a quarrell ought not to be taken, for
quarrels are to teftifie a truth, and where that is once
manifeft, the quarrell is not required.

Iniurie by deeds without charge is, when a man
by aduantage or fuch lyke meanes offereth a wrong,
and it is euident that fuch a facte was villanouflye
doone, and this iniurie I account doone without
charge, in fuch lyke forte as that was by wordes, becaufe that if hee that is iniuried woulde demaunde
the other a reafon of his villanie, howe coulde he o-
therwife maintaine it vnleffe by alleadging that the
other had taken aduauntage of him, or doone him
fome wrong. And if this bee fo, what needeth farther proofe ? But perhappes fome man wyll aske me
if

388

if in this cafe hee fhoulde put vp this iniurie without
reuenge. To whome I aunfwere, that Combat was
ordayned for iuftifieng of a truth, and not to laye o- *Combat not*
pen a waie for one man to reuenge him of another, *ordayned for*
for the punifhment of fuche thinges refteth in the *reuenge.*
Prince for the maintenance of peace in the realme,
which if it fhoulde bee feuerely executed, no doubt
but there woulde bee fewer quarrelles by many degrees. And in troth, the offence is the greater in this
Realme, where wee knowe God, and heare his Go-
fpell dailie preached, which expreflie forbiddeth
manflaughter : by howe much that hee that killeth
maketh a maffacre of the verie true image of the liuing God.

Wherefore we ought onelye to feare, reuerence,
and obey him, and not follow our owne vaine appe-
tites, which carrie vs headlong into vtter ruine and
deftruction. But to returne to reuenge, he that needs
will followe it, ought to take another courfe then
combate, albeit many no doubt will aduife a man to
returne like for like, which in no cafe I would not
wifh fhould be followed. But many perhaps that are
rather ledde by an ill cuftome than reafon, wil won-
der at this I haue alreadie alleadged, becaufe heerafter I will alfo affirme, that where an iniurie is fhame-
fullye doone, not onelye the iniuried is free of the
charge, but the iniurier refteth wyth the fhame, for
in matters of chiualrie, where a man committeth
no fhamefull, difhonourable, or vile facte, hee cannot truely bee fayde to haue doone vnlyke a Gentleman : and mee thinketh it an vnpofsible thing
to

to auoide receiuing iniurie from another, therefore when anie thing happeneth which a man cannot escape, it ought to be iudged shamefull. For a shamefull thing is, where a man committeth villanie which was in his power not to haue done : as for example, I haue power in my selfe to refraine from iniuring another, from committing wicked facts, from breaking my promise, from committing treason, which things if I obserue not, I bring vpon my self the greatest infamie and shame that possibly anie man may bring on himselfe: his then ought the shame to be that hath doone this beastly act, and not his to whome it was done. Which may be yet farther confirmed by this argument : that where a man proceedeth not lyke a Gentleman, he sheweth a cowardly feare in himself, not to dare to maintaine it in equalitie against him whome hee sought to haue wronged. And touching this opinion, auncient men before vs haue sayd, that the iniurie is not his to whome it was doone, but his who doeth it. Againe, my opinion is that in case of some former quarrell, he that doth anie dishonest iniurie may be denyed the Combate, as one that hath before committed a defect, and hee that receiueth it ought (as the case may be) to bee receiued alwayes, supposing alwayes that this defect of him that iniurieth is manifest. And I wyll not omit in this place to speake of an ill custome vsed nowe a daies, which ought no lesse to bee confuted by reason, than it is commonly followed with great affection, which is, that when a man knoweth himselfe to haue rightly receiued the lye, by and by to auoide the proofe, hee

seeketh

From what a man ought to refrayne.

The iniurye is his who doth it.

Hee is dishonored that doth any ill act.

seeketh to giue the baſtonado, or ſuch lyke fact, and
many times turnes his backe and runnes his waie, to
the ende that hee that is iniuried may not preſently
take reuenge, and in this ſort he thinketh to be valy-
antly diſcharged, which lykewiſe the common ſorte
doo verily iudge, and doo not perceiue their errour,
and how groſly they are deceiued. For firſt of all, if
for honour ſake I would doo anie thing, I am to doe
it honourablie and lyke a Gentleman, and not villa-
nouſly and lyke a traitour : nor muſt I thinke that a
ſhamefull fact can grace or diſgrace me, but muſt reſt
aſſured, that the charge don me by another is yet ſtill
vpon me, and that I bring a greater ſhame vnto it by
this diſhonourable deede. Next, if I cannot commit
a more odious thing in combat than to runne away,
how may I thinke to haue done honourably by running awaie? And wherefore ſhould not hee bee accounted of all ſorts of Gentlemen more honourable
from whom I runne, than I who runne, albeit I haue
done him ſome great diſgrace: for to iniurie another
is no honour, and to runne awaie is a ſhame. Therefore I will neuer be perſwaded, that a man that hath
iuſtly receiued the Lie, can by anie ſuch act diſcharge
himſelfe, or that hee is not bounde to prooue that
whereon hee receiued the Lie, but that hee ought to
bee the Challenger: and this opinion do I holde vppon the reaſons before alleadged, which mee thinketh a Gentleman ought ſooner to followe, than a
blinde opinion of the vulgar ſorte, which hath in it
neither lawe nor reaſon. And I woulde wiſhe Gentlemen by theſe rules to examine the cauſes for

The reuenge ought to bee done honorably

Who he is that offendeth in an ill ſorte.

A a   which

which a man intendeth to fight, & first to vnderstand
the nature of quarrels if they deserue Combat, or if
they maie otherwise be answered than by the sword,
and not to be perswaded by intreatie or fauour of a-
nie, to agree to vnnecessary quarrels, because that besides the offence towardes God, it is an iniurie to a
man to draw him to fight that is not bound, and it is
also a wrong to the magistrate before whome such
controuersies ought to be decided, intruding themselues into their office and function. Nor yet may we
allowe a quarrell vppon euerie Lie, as I haue at large
shewed in my discourse of Lies : and wee maye also
note here that a Lie lawfully giuen, is that which maketh the charge, whereby the other is bounde to the
proofe simply, and not to the proofe of Armes, because (as I haue sayde before) in such a case where o-
ther proofe may bee made than by weapon, the Lye
doth not onely not binde a man to the Combat, but
euerie Gentleman is bound to desist from the triall
by Armes, and to relie on the triall by reason.

    I must also adde heereunto, that euerie Lie where-
of a man cannot make iustification by ciuill lawe,
doth not yet by and by deserue combat. For I would
not haue anie thinke that there is such efficacie in a
Lie to binde a man to fight, as it seemeth some holde
opinion, which in deede proceedeth from a corrupt
vse of certaine that haue beene before vs, who for
Duello is not want of vnderstanding, without law, reason, or right
necessarie vp-
on euerie Lie course of Chiualrie, in the beginning dyd giue ly-
bertie to infamous persons, to require the Combat,
(as men desirous and willing to beholde others in
fight)

fight) as if it were at the baiting of a bull, or some o-
ther wilde beaft, whose succeffours imitating theyr
predeceffours, haue brought these thinges to this
paffe, as generallye it is holden, that whosoeuer hee
bee that receiueth the Lie, bee it vppon whatsoeuer
occasion, hee is presentlie bounde to discharge himselfe thereof onely by his swoorde, and not by anye
other meanes . Which disorder beeing thus farre
proceeded, ought no doubt to bee carefully redres-
sed, that Gentlemen maye bee reduced from theyr
erronious opinion by the selfe same waie and means
that they fell first into it. And to the ende that men
maye bee rightly perswaded, I saie that the Lye is
not the thing that induceth fight, but the occasion
whereupon it was giuen, and if there were no proofe
of the defect whereof a man is blamed, that hee can
in no sorte binde the other to fight, becaufe the regarde ought to bee to the qualitie of the iniurie, and
not to the Lie.

The Lie doth
not leade a
man to fight.

But I am sure some will account this opinion
newly vpstart: to whome I aunswere, their custome
and opinion is farre more newe, and that mine is rather to bee proued auncient, becaufe no law can bee
found, that commandeth a man for the receiuing of
the Lie to fall presentlie to fight . but all those lawes
whereon the Combat hath beene graunted, haue expreflie reiected the occasions, amongeft which, no
mention is made of the Lie : and this is the true and
auncient custome approoued by the lawes of the
Lombardes, and by the institutions of the Emperours.

Aa 2

And

And if a man ought prefently to fight vpon the Lie, it is vaine that the Lombards and other Princes after them, haue taken paines to fet downe the particular caufes for which a man ought to fight, and thofe alfo for which it is not lawfull to fight: fo as I conclude that in all cafes a man ought with greate iudgement and circumfpection behaue himfelfe wifely.

For what caufes Combats ought to bee graunted.

O greatly different is our cuftome now a daies, from the orders & laws of the firft inftitutors of Duello, as if a man fhoulde go about to reduce them into particular cafes, it were not onely a trouble to fome, but a verie impoffible thing : for which caufe I will onely treate of that which I fhall iudge meeteft by a generall rule to bee obferued, and include all combats vnder two heads.

The caufes of Duello.

Firft then, I iudge it not meet that a man fhould hazard himfelfe in the perill of death, but for fuch a caufe as deferueth it, fo as if a man be accufed of fuch a defect, as deferue to bee punifhed with death, in this cafe Combate might bee graunted. Againe, becaufe that in an honourable perfon his honor ought to be preferred before his life, if it happe him to haue fuch a defect laid againft him, as in refpect thereof he
were

were by lawe to be accounted dishonorable, and should therefore be disgraced before the tribunall seate: vpon such a quarrell my opinion is, that hee is not to be denied to iustifie himself by weapons, prouided alwaies, that hee be not able by lawe to cleere himselfe thereof, And except a quarrell be comprehended vnder one of these two sortes, I doe not see how any man can by reason or with his honor, either graunt or accompanye an other to the fight.

Moreouer, such Gentlemen as doe counsaile or accompany a man, ought to be iudges of the quarrell, for vnto them it belongeth cheefely to knowe if the quarrell deserue triall by armes or no, if the person be suspected of the defect laide against him, and if there be presumption thereof. But if these thinges be not well iustified and proued, the combate ought not to be admitted, because that the profe by armes being ordained, as a meanes to sift out the truth, as in ciuile iudgement, where the proofe is reasonable and certaine, no man can be put to torture without due information, and sufficient witnes, much lesse ought it to be doone in the iudgement of weapons, which perhaps may fall out to be as little to reason, as very doubtfull. *The dutie of gentlemen.*

Againe, those Gentlemen are to vnderstand if the quarrell haue been vndertaken heretofore by any of the parties to be proued by lawe, or otherwise: and then whether it be proued or no, it is not lawfull afterward to bring it to combat: besides, they are diligently to consider, if it may be iustified by any other meanes or no. And if in case it may be done by law, *The quarrell assayed at the ciuile law.* *Ciuile Proofe.*

wea-

weapons are not to be allowed: for if by ciuile caufe cotrouerfies are remitted from one iudge to another, as actions more belonging to one then to another, much rather is the like to bee doone, from the iudgement of armes, to ciuile law, feeing the inequality is much the greater : and vpon thefe two laft articles thefe gentlemen ought to take oath of him that demaundeth the fielde, and without iuftification thereof, there is no reafon to graunt it to any man: which thing is fo muche the more to bee obferued, by how much it is a common cafe, that men are moued to fight vpon fuch quarrels as might be ended by ciuile law, and whofoeuer is once challenged the fielde, it is accompted a fhame for him to refufe it: in which cafe the vulgare opinion is, that it is not manlynes in a gentleman to ftand vpon reafons.

Moreouer, if happilie in cartels there be any mention made, that notwithftanding he could proue his intent by ciuile teftimony, yet he intendeth to doe it by weapons, this I fay is a very great abufe, and Gentlemen ought to take oath of infamy, that is, that they doe not require the fielde maliciouflye, or with a minde to infame another, but onely for proofe of the truth, and this oath hath beene ordeined and put in practife of men long agoe. And we muft alfo adde, that thofe gentlemen ought fullye to bee fatisfied by oath, from the that demaund the fielde, if that which they pronounce, be their true quarrell, becaufe many times fome men will not ftick to determine to themfelues one pretence of their fight, & yet make known to the world another, which abufes gentlemen ought diligently to take heed of, becaufe many times fuch malice

malice hath been diſcouered. Touching all ſuch matters whereon anye controuerſie or diſſencion maye
growe, men ought ſpecially to beware, not to be ſelf-
willed, but are rather to take counſail and aduiſe both
of their freends and experienced men, and if there
be cauſe to iudge this courſe neceſſarie in anye matter, it ought cheefelye to bee in ſuch caſes, wherein a
mans life and honour is touched, for we ſee that euen
the wiſeſt ſorte to ſtudy and endeuour by all meanes
poſſible to furniſh themſelues with men experienced
and ſeene in chiualrye and armes, that they maye bee
counſailed and aduiſed by them, and may in ſuch ſort
wiſh them to the field, as may beſt ſtand with reaſon,
which office may onely be executed by learned men
and gentlemen, wherof the firſt are tearmed counſai-
lors, and the ſecond Padrini: but if happily one man ⟨Padrini, are
be ſeen in both, hee maye very well ſuffice to execute ⟨thoſe that are
both offices, but becauſe the charge conſiſteth princi- ⟨choſen by the
pally on the Padrini, we will ſpeak ſomwhat of them. ⟨combators on
⟨either ſide.

    Firſt then my opinion is, that they were ſo called,
either becauſe ſuch gentlemen as had remitted themſelues vnto them, ought to account of them as their
fathers, or els that this mutation of letters is deriued ⟨Patrones,
from the latine, which termeth thoſe patrones, which ⟨Padrini.
take vpon them the defence of another: ſome alſo cal ⟨Pattini.
them not Padrini, but Pattini: which if we wil allow,
it muſt be, for that they do make the matth of the cō-
bate: but howſoeuer they be called, or whenceſoeuer
their denomination be deriued, they are very neceſſary, and their very office is to defend, as aduocates do
their clients: and as this is their duety, ſo me thinketh
they deſerue no leſſe priuiledge then aduocates doe.
                                    And

And therefore as in ciuile controuersies aduocates are not to satisfie or paye anye parte of that wherein their clyents are bound or condemned, so in reason the other oght not to be charged to the field in those quarrels, wherein they are but as it were proctors, for the iniuries, the lyes, the cartels, and challenges, that are alreadie past betwixt the principalles, and the Padrini speake but as procurators, which is as much as if the principalles themselues speake : and if happilie the principals should haue any words together after the quarrell concluded, yet new charge or lies should be of no force, which if it be betwixt the principals grã-ted, much more ought to be to them that speake for them, which as it is reasonable, so is it to be obserued for the better conseruation of the right vse of chiual-ty, and to the end euery man may freely execute his function, which thing I note, because it happeneth sometimes, that such men take vpon them to be Pa-drini, who doe it more to take holde of a newe quar-rell, then for the defence of their gentilitie. And this is a wonderfull abuse, as it hath been shewed before, as also for that the nature of Duello is rather to re-straine a man, than to giue him libertie, beeing verie vnmeete : then vpon one combate should still ensue another. In which respect gentlemen ought strictlye to obserue this rule before: and as oft as it happeneth to growe anye quarrell betwixt Padrini, gentlemen ought to condemne it as vnlawfull, and seeke by all meanes possible to preuent such dishonest actions.

There ought no controuersie to arise betwixt the Padrini.

The dutie of gentlemen.

That

That men should not fight without weapons of defence.

He opinion of our ancients is, that whēsoeuer any man is licensed to the Combate, in al other cases, except for infidelitie, hee is to fight with a staffe and a Buckler, wherby I conclude, that duello was not instituted for the honor of chiualrie, as our late combators haue wrested it, but onely for the sifting out of the truth, which was not doone with the weapons of a Gentleman, but with a staffe: and therfore to goe about to reduce our customes now a daies, to those of former ages, were more ridiculous then possible to be done: but I will onely treat of the weapons belonging to Gentlemen, which I thinke meetest for Combats.

Firste therefore it is to bee vnderstoode, that the wisedome and discretion of a man, is as great a vertue as his magnanimitie and courage, which are so much the greater vertues, by how much they are accompanied with wisedome: for without them a man is not to be accounted valiant, but rather furious: neither is hee valiant that rashly and without aduise hazardeth himselfe in great matters, or endaungereth himselfe most: but hee that aduisedly behaueth himselfe in actions belonging to a gentleman, and where

B b 2

a publique benefite or his owne honor requireth it, doth not retire himfelfe from danger: for (as a Philofopher well faith) neither is hee valiant that is afraide of euery bugge, nor yet he that doth not temper his feares.

Againe, as the courage of the minde imboldeneth a man to affault his enemy, fo wifedom teacheth him likewife how to defend himfelfe : fo as I will neuer holde him couragious, that will be led to fight without fufficient weapons of defence. And albeit the common forte thinke the fingle Rapier in the fhirte, or the poniard or fuch like weapons, wherein there is a manifeft iudgement of death to one, moft honorable, neuertheles I am not of that opinion, nor will I account them that enter the combate in fuch forte more honorable, then wilde beaftes that wilfullye run vpon their own death.

And touching fuch as think it an honorable thing not onely not to efteme their life, but voluntarilye to runne on their death, I will account their life at a very lowe and bafe price, feing they themfelues fet no greater reckoning on it.

It is helde a moft fhamefull matter, if when the cuftodie of a Caftell fhall be committed to a man, hee fhall without licence forfake it : and fhall wee that haue our liues lente vs in keeping from our creator, haue no refpect of fo goodly a receptacle of our foules, but wilfully deftroye it, making our felues as it were, rebels vnto God, and fo bring both bodye and foule to perdition?

Moreouer, if a Gentleman goe to the warres, wee

fee

see him so esteemed of as hee is in shewe of his armour: and therefore I see no cause at all that a man should in publique matters seeke to be well armed, and in priuate quarrelles come naked: and me thinketh a man should at all times and in all places shewe him selfe valiant and desire the victorye: which if it be granted, they should likewise in al matters of moment prepare themselues armed.

And if Gentlemen will haue this respect of curtesie towarde their enemie, as to giue him weapons wherewith he may end the controuersie: I thinke it reason they should be such as may arm him, and not burden him.

The dutie of euerye Gentleman, is to temper his courage with wisedome, that it may be knowne, that neither he setteth so highlye by his life, that for safegarde of it, he will commit any vile fact, nor yet that he so slightlye regardeth it, as that without iust cause he will depriue himselfe thereof: albeit I doe not account it a dishonourable act, to come armed like a man at armes, if the weapons be such as belong to a Gentleman, and hurt not a man priuilie.

Again, I would that armes should incontinently be vsed, and that a man should not then enter the combate, when the time is for him to leaue: and aboue al, that the weapons of defence, were both weapons of armes and warre: and if so be a man would fight with weapons only of defence, the gentlemen should in no case admit it, but that they should fight like gentlemen, as it hath been many times done.

Touching the choice of your weapons, and of the

inequalitie of them, and the imperfections of the bodie, the Defendant hath great aduantage, and it is not without iuſt cauſe, for ſeeing hee is both accuſed and conſtrained to fight, it is great reaſon that hee ſhould haue all the honeſt fauour that might be, and it is no little honor to him that in caſe he onely be not ouercome, hee is accounted the vanquiſher: where contrarily, the Challenger is to ouercome, vnles hee will altogither looſe the quarrell, whereof there is great reaſon, becauſe to the one it appertaineth to prooue, and to the other it is ſufficient onely to defend.

Likewiſe, it is as great a fauour that hee hath to chooſe the weapons, which is alſo very meete, for if a man chooſe to call me to fight, the election of the weapons is mine.

In this choic it is certain, that there is not the liberty giuen, as is thought: for this parte alſo, as all other partes of duello is grounded vpon reaſon, and if wee will be nyce to ſee how a man is authoriſed to make the choyce, wiſe men are of opinion, that gentlemen ſhould receiue their ſentence of weapons from diuine iudgement, if in caſe the iuſtification cannot by other meanes be made: and if they will haue the benefite of that, it is neceſſary that they abandon all violence and deceite, which (as *Cicero* ſaith) are the properties of the Lyon and the Foxe, and farre from the nature of man.

Now if theſe things ſhould in the whole courſe of our life be helde and perfourmed, much more ſhould they be deſired in the ſifting out of a truth, and in the direction of iudgement.

And

402

And touching violence, me thinkes the law hath well prouided, by giuing the aduantage of the weapons to the Defendant, which if it were not so, euerie naughty man would embolden himselfe to make wrong accusations, and vrge euerie man of lesse strength to fight, perswading himselfe to be able to beate him downe to the ground. But seeing the law hath so well prouided against this, seeing that deceit (as the same *Cicero* likewise affirmeth) is worthie of much hatred, it is a commendable thing that it is so. For in the choise of weapons, it belongeth to vs to make some lawe for the Defendant, which should be such, as he should not vse anie deceit in, nor graunt such wepons as fit not with the disposition of a mans bodie. For albeit a man maie saie that wee are natuly apt in all exercises to vse both handes, yet it is manifest, that vse dooth ouercome nature, to make vs right or left handed. And therfore if I shall be knowen to be right handed, I cannot force my aduersarie to fight with a weapon for the lefte hande, seeing the disposition of my bodie is not such. And if I haue no defect in my arme, or my thighe, or legge, I cannot come to fight with vambraces or such lyke harneis, for those partes, which hinder the bending of the elbow, or of the knee, for this is an apparent deceit and ought to bee refused in the Combat, and the Padrini ought not to admit such weapons.

If in case I be lame or hurt in one of mine armes, or my hands, or want an eie, I may verie wel appoint my enemie such weapons as maie in lyke sorte bind his legge, his arme, or his hand, or that may hide one of his eies, but yet if he bee lame of one arme, I maye sure appoint him such armour as may hinder the other that is sound.

And to conclude, if it be lawfull for me to appoint such weapon or armour to mine enemie as may hinder him in the same sort that I am hindred, yet I must not hinder him vnlesse my selfe be also hindered : as thus, If I be blinde of my right eie, and he of his left, I must not therefore also hinder his right eie, for this is not to make equalitie of my wants, but to take his whole sight from him.

Likewise a right handed or left handed man, or a man weakned or maimed so of his hand as he cannot well close it, or that wanteth a finger, whereby hee is not able to holde his weapon in his hand, in my opinion, is not to be constrained to fight with his imperfect hand, but may lawfully and iustly denie the challenge, which is also to bee vnderstoode of all other members and lims, so as it is requisite that all things be guided with reason and iudgement for both parties, that it doo not appeare that that which is done, is done for reuenge or to infame another, but onely for the iustifieng of the truth.

Of

Of the time for Duello.

He time appointed for Duello hath alwaies bene twixt the rising and setting of the Sunne, & whosoeuer in that time doth not prooue his intent, can neuer after bee admitted the Combat vppon that quarrell. And in case the day be spent without any combat, it cannot be remitted to the daie following without the consent of the Defendant, who being challenged for that daye, and appearing there, hath performed all partes of his honour and dutie (vnlesse thorough anie default of his the combat was not attempted) and is farre from all matters touching that quarrell. But it is not sufficient for the Defendant onely to consent, except like wise the Lord that granteth the field do condescend thervnto: for hauing once admitted the field in a prefixed daie, that being past, he is discharged. Againe, such may the case be, as the first daie being gone, the combat may bee lawfull on the second daye, but without newe conditions, in ordinarie course wee are to obserue that which we sayd before.

Of

Of accidents that happen in the Combat.

S I haue alredie begun for to treate of Duello, so I doo meane to prosecute it, according to our vse now a daies. First then after that the Combatters are entered the lists, if they haue no further agreement betwixt them, which of them so euer shall happen to touche the railes or bounds, or shall haue anie part of him out of the lists, is not to be accounted neither prisoner, or ought he to haue that member cut off, but the fight is to continue to the death or flight, or til it be forbidden. But if any of them go out of the lists, he is become prisoner: if his horse be wounded or slaine, or if anie part of his armour breake, he is not to be supplied. And if he let fall his weapon out of his hand, it is lawfull for the other to wound him vnarmed, I saie lawfull in this respect, that it is accounted an honour to the other to bid him take vp his weapon, and to staie from hurting him til he haue recouered it again: albeit that in case the victorie should afterwarde happen to the other, whereas hee might first safely haue ouercome,

hee

he fhoulde bee accounted a foole, and verie well ferued.

Thefe things I account ordinarily to be obferued
vnleffe it were otherwife agreed vpon, which conditions are to bee helde inuiolable vnder the paine appointed: and albeit no punifhment were alotted, who
fo euer fhouid doo contrarie to the agreement, were
to be helde a traitor: which agreement lykewife is to
bee with confent of both parties, wherein one man
cannot binde another to accept anie condition that
is without the limit of the lawe. I thinke it neceffarie
to fet downe that the Chalenger is to giue the firft affault, for whereas he is to proue, and the other but to
defend, it is plain, that if he begin not, the other is not
bound to ftirre a foot, yea, and whatfoeuer he fhould
attempt before hee fhould perceiue the Challenger
comming to affault, were meere fuperfluous. Again,
at the enterance of the Combatters within the liftes,
let it bee proclaymed, that no man vnder paine of
death fpeake a word, nor make anie figne, which if it
happen to bee done, ought feuerely without fauour
to bee executed, as one that intermedleth in a matter
of life and honor of other men.

C c   If

407

If Gentlemen beeing in the Lifts may repent them of the Combat.

A Nother queftion is held, whether Gentlemen brought into the field may repent them of the combat, which I perfuade my felfe wil neuer happen twixt honorable perfons : for howe canne a Challenger repent him of the ending his quarrell without perpetuall fhame and difhonour, and neuer to be allowed to require battel of anie other, becaufe he proued not that to be true for which he once vndertooke weapons. I woulde wifhe euerie one that thought his quarrell vniuft, not to take it vppon him, and rather than fight againft a truth, make full fatiffaction to the iniuried, which fhould bee doone in a zeale and loue of vertue : for the ftanding obftinate in his purpofe vntil the time that he come to haue his weapons in his hand, and then recant, mee thinketh, it argueth a moft vile and wicked mind. And I do not fee how this repentance can come from the Defendant, except he bee content to giue ouer the quarrell and acknowledge himfelfe fuch as hee was accufed for. Which (as I fayde of the Challenger) hee might doo with leffe fhame before hee tooke weapons than after. And whenfoeuer without farther fatisfaction they

they fhould come to agreement, doubtles the Challenger fhould receiue the fhame : fo as I fee not how fuch a cafe fhould happen: but if it fhould be, my opinion is, that if the quarrell were of a matter belonging to the Prince, or in another mans intereft, the honour ought to conftraine them to fight, or to make manifeft the truth of the fact : but if it were touching their particular caufes, it might bee licenfed without Combat, but not without fhame.

Whether Gentlemen may in the Liftes chaunge theyr Quarrell.

I Cannot paffe ouer another doubt, which is this: Two men fighting together, the one faith, Defend thy felf traitor. And the other aunfwereth, I grant thee the firft quarrell, and I do now fight with thee vppon the fecond. In which cafe I think it cleere, that he to whom the quarrell is refufed, is the victor, & yet if the other ouercome in the fecond, he is lykewife to be accounted victor. But notwithftanding, my opinion is, that

C c 2

neither

409

neither of them can with honour depart the lifts, but
that they are both blame-worthie as difhonourable
Gentlemen, taking vpon them to fight in vniuft quarels, which muft needes bee prefumed by both their
loffes, for the victorie of one cannot take awaie the
loffe of the other: wherefore in this lyke cafe, hee that
would take holde of a new quarrell, fhould not faye,
I remit thee the firft, but onely thou lyeft in faying I
am a traitour, and vpon this heereafter I will defende
my felfe, and then if he chaunce to ouercome in this,
it cannot bee faide that he hath loft the other, but the
prefumption fhoulde bee fauourable on his fide, for
if his aduerfarie haue had the worft in one, it is to bee
prefumed the like in the other: but he to whom it belongeth better to fight on the firft quarrell, fhuld not
condifcend to the fecond, but anfwere, that hee wyll
make an end of the firft, and afterwards fpeake of the
reft And where the other hath remitted him the firft,
he is to take aduantage therof, and to demand of the
Lord of the field the patent of his victorie, and not to
fight anie more, nor fhould the Lorde himfelfe fuffer
him to fight againe. And this is as much as I thought
good to fpeake of that which appertaineth to the
Gentlemen.

Now will I come to the office of the Lordes of
the fielde, who if after the Letters of the field are dif-
patched, the gentlemen wil either in the field or with
out it change their quarrell, may at their pleafure reuoke thofe letters, & forbid them the battell, becaufe
they are not bound to grant the field but vppon that
fpeciall quarrell which was referred vnto them, and
where-

whereupon they graunted their letters, whereby alſo for this cauſe it ſhould not be, vnles the quarrel were expreſſed in the patents.

Againe I ſay, that if the Gentlemen change their quarrell in the liſtes, without aſſent of the Lords, and that one be ſlaine, the Lords ought to puniſh this fact in the ſlaier, as man-ſlaughter, hauing kilde a man in his iuriſdiction, without the priuiledge of a free field, for the fielde is not to be accompted free and priuiledged, but onely for that ſpeciall quarrel wherupon it was graunted: except ſome men may ſaye, that the Lord perceiuing them to vndertake a newe quarrell, and not forbidding them, ſeemeth by his ſilence to conſent: which I will neither affirme, nor deny.

Who is not to be admitted to the proofe of Armes.

Oraſmuch as Duello is a proofe by armes, which appertaine to gentlemen, and that gentry is an honourable degree, it is not meet to admitte proofe by armes to any but to honorable perſons, and therfore as before ciuile iudges it is not permitted, that infamous perſons can accuſe anye other, ſo in the iudgement of gentrie, an honourable perſon cannot bee accuſed but by an honourable perſon: for how ſhal he be able to accuſe another of any defect of honour,

nour, that in the like is faultye himfelfe: and whereas
the vfe of weapons hath been ordeined to an honorable end, for to punifh the wicked, how can they be
receiued to this office, that are worthy themfelues of
punifhment?

Therefore it is to be concluded, that they are not
to be admitted proofe by armes, who haue committed any treafon againft their Prince or Countrie, or
fhall haue had conference with enemies, which may
be preiudiciall to any of them, nor they who hauing
beer taken of the enemie, hauing meanes to returne
doe not returne, or being fent as fpyes, doe remayne
with the enemy, or haue become fpies on both fides,
or fuch as hauing taken oath, or haue not ferued out
their full pay, do runne to the enemie, or not hauing
taken oath, doe go to the enemie, at fuch time as both
parties are in armes, for this fact is of the nature of
treafon, becaufe that thou making femblance to bee
in my fauour, and I trufting thee, when time is that
I ftand moft in neede of thee, thou becommeft a rebell againft me.

Moreouer, fuch are to be denyed the fielde, as
in battaile haue abandoned their leaders or enfignes,
or either by night or day fhall haue forf ken the gard
of the enemye or Prince, that was committed vnto him,

To thefe we may alfo adde freebooters, and all
fuch as for any military diforder are banifhed.

Likewife, all theeues, robbers, ruffians, tauerne
hunters, excommunicate perfons, hereticks, vfurers,
and all other perfons, not liuing as a Gentleman or a
Souldier,

Souldier: and in conclusion, all such as are defamed for anye defecte, and are not allowed for witnesses in Ciuile lawe, are comprehended in this number.

And of these I saye that not onelye they are to bee refused vpon challenging another man, but all honourable persons or Gentlemen should abandon their companye, and whosoeuer should fight with them, should iniurie himselfe, making himselfe equall with dishonourable persons.

But it is very meete that hee that will refuse another vpon his infamye, should be sure that the other is faultie thereof, or that it is so apparant, as hee cannot deny it: for otherwise he should turne the quarrell vpon his owne backe, and then shalbe forced to proue it.

And as it is not lawfull for such manner of men aboue recited, to challenge another, so if they be once challenged, aduantage cannot be taken againſt them of infamie: nor is it meete to accept a mans excuse, that should say, he knew it not before, for whosoeuer will challenge another, ought aduisedly to consider, that he bindeth himselfe to such matter as hee must not repent himselfe of.

But I do not include in this, that if after the challenge, he should commit any infamous act, whether he were Challenger or Defendant, he should not yet be refused. Moreouer, if an honourable person, should challenge a defamed person, or contrarywise he being challenged by a base person, should accept of the challenge; which is not onely an act of priuate
                                    interest,

413

intereſt, but a preiudice to the degree of gentrye: in this caſe it is the office of the Lord of the field, not to ſuffer this combate to proceede, nor to graunt them letters of combat.

Touching thoſe that doe not an-ſwere, or doe not appeare in the field.

Hen a man is challenged to the fielde, he is to anſwere by wepons and not by words, vnles the challenger bee ſuch as with reaſon he is to be refuſed, prouided alwaies that a man cannot by ciuile lawe defend himſelf, & that the quarel deſerue combate. But where theſe reſpects want, whoſoeuer being challenged doth not anſwer, or without cauſe, dooth not accept the letters of the fielde, or accepting them, not hauing a ſufficient excuſe, doth not appeare, is to be reputed diſhonourable in euerye man of woorths iudgement: and the challenger at a conuenient time is to appeare in the fielde, to vſe the accuſtomed ſolemnities. For the day before the combat, the Padrino is to come before the
Lord

Lord of the fielde, and tell him that his champion
is come to proue his quarrell, and for that cause hee
as his procurator doth appeare, to see if the contrarie
party be come, and if he intend to capitulate or bring
to passe, that they may be in the greater readines, a-
gainst the next day, protesting that his Champion is
in readines, and is to beseeche the Lord of the fielde,
to cause enquirye to bee made, if either hee or some
bodye for him be present, and that if there be no notice of his comming, he will make open proclamation, that whosoeuer is there for the contrarye parte
should appeare: for if hee doe not appeare, it shall
proceede against him, as one contumacious, and that
hath fayled of his dutye, which the Lord of the field
is not to denye the other: and on the day appointed,
hee is to appeare in the lists at a conuenient hower,
where his Padrino offering him to the Lord, and
shewing that his Champion is come to fight, is to
make a newe instance, for a new proclamation touching the quarrell, which hee is likewise to doe at
noone and at the euening, and withall shall make
shewe of his armour and of his horse, wherewith he
came furnished to fight: whereby hee shall haue
cause to accuse his aduersarye of contumacye, and
to demaund that his Champion bee admitted to run
the fielde, and to bee pronounced victor, and that
the other bee condemned of contumacy, of failing,
and vanquished in the quarrell.

And that hee pronounced vanquisher, maye vse
such tearmes against him, as by the order of gentrye
is permitted: all which thinges the Lord ought to

D d graunt

graunt him: and the Gentleman shall go about the fielde three times, with an honourable pompe of his Horse and armour, and sound of Trumpet, and shall carrye with him the letters: which being done, hee maye likewise carrye the portraiture of his aduersarye.

And whatsoeuer hath beene saide of the Challenger, may the Defendant in like case doe.

What is to be doone vpon the alleadging of any impediment, for not appearing in the fielde.

WE are now to consider what course is to be taken, if any gentleman do not appear in the fielde at the appointed time, nor doe not prooue a lawfull impediment that hindered him: in which case I affirme, that first

if

if the impediment happen, at such time as notice
might bee giuen thereof, before the contrarye party
should appeare himselfe to the fielde, it is then to be
admitted, vpon defraying the others charge and
paines, and vpon the iustification to him of his lawfull excuse, offering himselfe also at conuenient time
to procure a new field, and to satisfie any losse which
the contrarye party should suffer by meanes of pro-
longing of time.

But if this let should fall out so suddenly, as in no
forte there could any knowledge be giuen of it, before the very day appointed, yet is the excuse to bee
approued, so as the impediment be lawfull, and then
is hee likewise to defraie the charges of him that appeared: for if I make agreement with thee, to meete
thee on such a daye at such a place, and for such a
cause, and I be there present and thou bee hindered,
whereby I am put to a new charge, there is no reason
that thy commoditie should returne a discommodi-
tie and a losse to me. But excuses of lawfull impediment, should be great infirmities, tempestes, or waters,
that maye stoppe passage, the warre of a mans countrie, or Prince, or against infidels, and such like accidents, which any indifferent iudge may think lawful.
Imprisonment also is a lawful excuse, vnles it be such
as a man at all times may be freed of: for Gentlemen
that are to goe into the field, ought by all meanes to
auoyde euery occasion, that may hinder them from
their intent, for whosoeuer in matters of honour
dooth not seeke all that hee can to salue his honour, or hath other respect at all than to his honour,

maketh a great breach of his honour : and therefore whofoeuer fhould procure himfelfe to bee commaunded to ftaye by his Prince, is to bee adiudged as one that procureth his owne imprifonement.

Againe, I doe not allow it as a lawfull meanes to prolong time, if after a quarrell be once concluded, a man fhould take vpon him any newe charge of office, for I would thinke this fought after to that end, and is not to be approued good, becaufe that being bound in honor, hee is firft to fatisfie that, before hee goe about new matters.

And yet I graunt, that if in this meane time (be it by fucceffion or good fortune) any lordfhip or great title fhould befall a man, by meanes whereof, his aduerfarie that before was his equall, is now become farre his inferiour : in fuch cafe this accident is to be taken for a newe and iuft impediment, not fo much to winne time, as to fight in his owne perfon : for in this cafe the quarrell begunne, fhould bee perfourmed by a fubftitute or Champion, as wee tearme him.

In

In how many cafes a man may ouercome in the Lifts.

He fucceffe of fighting in the Liftes may happen diuerflie, for fomtime it may be that the Combat enduring to the Sun fet, the Challenger may neither ouercome the Defendant, nor yet bee ouercome by him, in which cafe the Defendant is to bee adiudged the vanquifher, and to be abfolued of the blame obiected him by his aduerfarie, and the Challenger fhall bee accounted the vanquifhed, and an ill Combatter, and maye be refufed if afterward hee challenge anie man vpon anie other quarrell, but yet hee fhall not bee the Defendants prifoner, vnleffe hee fhall ouercome him. And in this one cafe onely the Defendant fighting and not ouercome, doth ouercome the other. Other cafes are common both to the Challenger & Defendant, whereof one is in killing his aduerfarie, another is, when a man yeeldeth, bee it in whatfoeuer kinde of wordes. A third is, when a man dooth expreffelye difclaime from the quarrell, confeffing himfelfe eyther trulie accufed, or to haue falfelye accufed: and

D d 3 laft

laſt of all is the running out of the Liſtes. Of which
ſortes of looſing the fielde, euerye one is by ſo much
the more ſhamefull, by howe much the more I
haue placed and ſet him downe in his loweſt place
or roome: and to bee ſlaine in the fielde, as it is leſſe
ſhamefull, ſo it is farre more daungerous and hurtfull.

It may alſo happen, that a man by ſtrength
maye ouercome his aduerſarie or his enemie, and
binde him, or in ſuch ſorte holde him in his owne
power, as euerye one that ſeeth maye iudge, that
if he will he may kill him, and thereby end the fielde:
for holding him in ſuch ſorte, and requiring him to
yeeld, and the other not agreeing, it is certain he may
lawfully kill him: but if hee ſhoulde not kill him, and
thereby the daie bee ſpent, it may bee doubted what
iudgement ſhould in this caſe bee giuen. But if the
Defendant bee the better, there is no queſtion to
bee made, but hee is to bee pronounced vanquiſher,
although there coulde not bee ſo full a iudgement
giuen of his ouercomming, as we haue ſpoken of before. And if the Challenger ſhoulde bee hee that
ſhoulde chaunce to haue the Defendant in his power, the matter coulde not ſo eaſily bee determined
of. But in this caſe theyr Articles are chiefely to bee
conſidered, which maye bee drawen in ſuch manner, as without anie adoo at all the matter maye bee
reſolued. For if in them it bee expreſſed and ſette
downe, that the Challenger is not to bee helde vanquiſher, vnleſſe hee either kill, or make the Defendant denie his accuſation, in this caſe hee cannot
bee

bee accounted vanquisher: but if it bee concluded, that the Defendant bee not accounted vanquished except hee bee slaine or denie his wordes, I woulde not then condemne him as vanquished: and yet I woulde saie that the Challenger had well discharged his parte, beeing in his power to haue killed his enemie. And if the Defendant woulde renue this quarrell on anie other daie, I doo not thinke it in anie wise lawfull that it shoulde bee graunted him. And if in case there shoulde not bee anie wordes in their Articles touching this pointe, the one holding the other in his power, (as I haue sayde before) mee thinketh hee is lesse to bee adiudged and taken to bee his prisoner than if hee had yeelded himselfe vnto him, and so voluntarilie to haue become his prisoner, but that hee shoulde bee sentenced to bee vanquished and ouercome, and the vanquisher were deuoutly and reuerently to bee esteemed and honoured, as one that onely satisfieng and contenting himselfe wyth the victorie, dyd not seeke or desire cruelly to imbrue his handes in his enimies bloud.

Touch-

Touching accidents that happen to the victorie of the Lists.

HEE that is ouercome in the Listes, is thereupon the others prisoner, and hee is to haue both his armor, garmentes, horse, and other furniture whatsoeuer, which hee brought with him into the Listes, as ornaments for his fighting: and this is the right case in this matter, for the spoiles of the vanquished are the vanquishers Ensignes.

The person of the vanquished by an honourable custome hath ben giuen by the vanquisher either to the Lorde of the field, or to some other prince or noble man whome he serued or followed . Which custome albeit I commend, and wish euerie one to follow it, yet I must confesse that the vanquisher maye if hee list, vse his owne discretion, and hold his prisoner, which no man canne denie him, because hee is to serue him, but not in base offices, nor in anie other but such as belong to a gentleman: and the prisoners taken in the Lists may bee constrained to discharge the expences of the Combat, and they maye be ransomed for money, euen as Gentlemen taken in the warres.

The

The diuerſitie of olde and new cu-
ſtomes concerning the
vanquiſhed.

Muſt not omit to tell you, that that which I haue before ſpoken of priſoners, hath rather ben brought in by cuſtome of Gentlemen ſince they began to enter quarrels vpon their honor, than by anie auncient inſtitution of Duello. For by the lawe of the Lombards, he that was ouercome in fight, was not geuen as priſoner, nor yet pronounced infamous for euer performing any after-quarrel, but diuerſly ſentenced for that fault whereof hee was accuſed. For, as it appeareth plainelye in writing, whoſoeuer accuſed for manſlaughter was ouercome, loſt one of his handes: and whoſoeuer was condemned of adultery, was adiudged to die. And touching the witneſſes, who for conſummation of their wordes did combat, the vanquiſhed loſt his hand, and his other companions dyd redeem their liues by mony: ſo ſeuerely did they execute the iudgement of their Duello. And our learned men alleadge, that becauſe this proofe is vncertaine, albeit a man ſhoulde in the Liſtes bee founde in fault worthie to receiue puniſhment, yet hee were not to ſuffer death, but a mittigation ought to bee v-

Ee ſed,

fed, giuing him fome eafier punifhment. VVhich as
they alleadge truelye and verie commendably, fo is
that cuftome of theirs to bee condemned, who in cafe of Duello caufe galowfes to be fet vp neere to the
place, and doo immediatly hang vp the vanquifhed.
But what greater punifhment can there be, than that
which our lawes do inflict vpon the vanquifhed, they
doo not chaften them in the purfe, nor in cutting off
anie member, nor in theyr lyfe, but in that which to
euerie wife man is more deare than all the reft, for
they depriue him of his honour, for loue whereof
there is no noble mind that will not fpend his bloud.
Thofe that iffue vanquifhed out of the Lifts, carrie a-
waie fo much the more fhame, by howe much they
came thether defirous of honour, and that not becaufe one man ouercame another, for of necefsitie,
two fighting together, one muft be the victor, & (as I
haue fayde before) the Challenger not loofing doth
loofe, fo as hee is not difhonourable for beeing ouercome, but becaufe he is accounted a badde man that
would take vpon him an vniuft quarrell, and that hee
would fight againft the truth, which hee is chiefelye
bound to maintaine. And therefore weighing and
confidering the greate daunger thofe men incurre
that commit thefe things to the proofe of the fword,
Gentlemen ought to bee more flowe in fighting, except great occafion vrge them, and vnleffe they bee
certaine to fight vppon iuftice, fo as they may haue
great hope to obtaine Gods fauour in it.

Touch-

Touching the vanquished, and of the restoring of Honor.

AS I sayd before, so I will here again say, that the chalenger that doeth not ouercome his aduersarie in the Lists, doeth remaine the looser, not hauing proued so much as hee ought, and that hee may neuer after challenge anie: which is confirmed with this reason, that whosoeuer prooueth not his woordes true, is to bee thought a false accuser, and consequently is regarded and esteemed a badde man. And the lyke is also of euerie other man whether hee bee Challenger or Defendant, that is ouercome by force, or made to yeelde, or denie his wordes, or runne awaie, for hee can neuer after that time demaunde Combat nor bee allowed it.

But I knowe some that are of opinion, that if I ouercome one in the Listes, and afterwardes release him, if a newe quarrell or controuersie befall him wyth another, by my leaue hee maye challenge his aduersarie the Combate, whereto no man of anye reason or vnderstanding ought to consent. For if I ouercomming him shall haue condemned him

Ee 2   as

425

as infamous, how can I allowe him fit to fight with a man as good as my felfe? And if hee challenge me, I fhall refufe him. I cannot take awaie his fault that hath beene ouercome by mee, vnleffe that I confeffe I ouercame him wrongfully, and fo condemne my felfe of infamie: and if I cannot take awaie his blotte from him, I cannot make him equal with an honorable perfon: and therefore this opinion is wholye to be reproued of euerie Gentleman.

And as this reftoring of a man to his honour, is by occafion giuen mee to fpeake of, it bringeth mee in remembraunce of the reftoring which Princes were wont to make of treafons and rebellions doone againft them, and fuch lyke faults. Wherein, to fpeak my opinion, I thinke well that albeit the Prince may after my treafon committed, graunt mee fauour and pardon of my lyfe and goods, and giue mee honour, and a thoufande other fauours, yet fhee cannot make, that that which is doone fhoulde bee vndoone, or that the ill fact paft bee not an ill fact, or that I committed not anie treafon, or that my foule is not defiled, and that I am not anie notorious vilaine. And that Prince whatfoeuer that fhall reftore mee, ought neuer to truft mee, but fhoulde rather ftill prefume, that whereas I was once inueigled and drawen to betraye my maifter, I will eafilye be perfwaded againe to the like : and euery honourable perfon fhould conceiue ill of me, and auoyde my company. And it ought rather to be faide, that I am reftored to my goods, and the fauour of my Prince (if happilye fhe will take me into her fauour) than

426

than to my former honour, becaufe that albeit my Prince reftore me to all thofe degrees that fhe may, yet fhe cannot reftore me to my firfte innocencie : as for example: if I be good, fhe cannot make me bad, for it is not in her power to reforme my minde. Princes cannot take from good men their goodnes, nor from the wicked their wickednes : for their power extendeth on their goods and perfon, but not on their mindes: my Prince may make me poor or rich, but not good or bad, for God onely hath power ouer our affections. I conclude therefore, that if one that is reftored from fome notable and manifeft villany, would challenge another to combat, and that this other refufe him, I would iudge him to haue behaued himfelfe honorably, and that in reafon he might refufe him: for if (as I haue faide before) a Princes reftoring to honor is not lawfull, I will leffe think that a gentleman by licenfing one ouercome by him in combate, can make him lawfull to fight with an honorable perfon.

But returning to the reftoring which I fpake of before vfed by Princes, my opinion is, that it ought to bee good in the children of traitours, and in the reft of their difcent, as in thofe that ought not beare the punifhment of others offences, efpecially feeing that thofe that are baptifed, are by Gods lawes freed from the finnes of their fathers.

E e 3   Whe-

Whether one once ouercome and afterward being vanquisher, may challenge another.

Ome men doubting whether one once ouercome in the listes, and afterward challenged to fight, doe ouercome, be to be saide that he hath recouered his honour, and if after that hee may challenge any man to the field: it hath been thought that by the honour of his second combating, he hath taken away the blotte of the first, but yet for the better conclusion, wee are to think that the first losse cannot be recouered by any new combate.

And vpon this question I haue seene the iudgement of *Alfonzo d' Auolos* Marques of *Vasto*, which was this. The dutie of gentlemen is to preferre their honor before their life, and he whosoeuer goeth the looser out of the listes, sheweth that hee accounted more of his life than honor, and therefore albeit hee should afterward enter combate and ouercome, yet it is not to be saide that hee hath recouered his honor, because it may be presumed, that hee came thether with an intent to trye his fortune if hee could ouercome, and yet with a minde in all accidentes, to

saue

saue his life, becaufe worfe could not befall in honor then had done before, which hee had once loft. And whereas fuch prefumption may be had of him, and that a man maye well thinke that hee came into the fielde with intent to do any thing, rather than dye, he is in no forte to be faide, to haue reuiued his honour, that was before dead in the duft : but if afterward he would challenge any man, he ought to be refufed.

This was the opinion of that gentleman, and this holde I for a gentlemanlike opinion, which euerye wife man ought to allow and follow: and this expofition is to be vnderftoode, not onelye of thofe who confeffe themfelues the loofers, or run away, but of thofe alfo who hauing had the charge of proouing, haue loft, by not fatisfying the proofe : becaufe that they being befpotted with blame of falfe accufers, by meanes of their loffe, cannot be forced from fault of falfe accufation, for that they were afterward falfelye accufed: nor can they take away from themfelues the prefumption, to be accounted falfe accufers, if they fhould accufe any man, feeing they haue beene once before condemned in the fame: fo that in what forte foeuer a man goe out of the lifts loofer, hee is fubiect to the iudgement before giuen.

Againe, after that a man hath beene once ouercome in the lifts, euery honourable perfon ought to beware not to enter into proofe of weapons with him, as alfo with all other infamous perfons : and the like is alfo to be obferued, albeit being challenged by an other the fecond time, hee fhould yet then ouercome.

After

After the challenge, for fome cau-
fes the Combate may bee
refufed.

F after an agreement of Combate betwixt two, one of thē fhould commit fome default, which fhoulde bring him into fuch infamy, as who foeuer were ftaind therwith, could not challenge another to the field, in this cafe he that had committed this fault, might bee refufed by his aduerfarie, as one that was growen worfe in his condicion, and that had changed his nature from that which he was, when their quarrell was firft be-gunne betwixt them.

But here is to be vnderftoode, that this new occa-fion for which a man may be refufed the field, fhuld be infamye, which a man by his owne faulte was fal-len into, as treafon, falfe oath, or other notable mat-ter, and not any iniurie or charge done him by fome other, which might require reuenge by weapons : for in fuch cafe, as the firft which had a quarrell with him, might refufe him, as become worfe in his con-dition,

dition, for the second fhould not refufe to come to combate with him with whom he entered into quarrell, albeit he had receiued charge from any other. And there is no reafon that a man fhould remaine charged of all handes, without any meanes to difcharge himfelfe. Therfore he is to take vpon him the fecond quarrell, and perfourming that with honour, he may and ought to follow the firft.

But this is to benoted, that the refufal of a man for beeing become worfe in condition, appertaineth to the Defendant, and not to the Challenger : for they that are charged ought to feeke to difcharge themfelues, and not fuffer that another man doe in any forte take from them fuch occafion: and to be able to do this the better, let them follow this rule of reafon, that whofoeuer is firft in time, is alfo to be preferred in way of reafon. And becaufe that many times one contrary is to be gouerned by another, I will alfo affirme, that if a quarrell depending betwixt two, or the challenge being feene, and the letters of the field fucceeding, if the on of them fhuld come to fuch degree of eftate & fignorie, that the other were now no longer his equal, then might he refufe to be brought to the profe by weapons in his own perfon amongft the other: but yet hee is to perfourme that by his Champion, for the inequality of condition, is no occafion to break of the definition of the quarrell.

F f   Of

Of the inequalitie of noble men, and cheefely of commaunding Lords.

Orasmuch as this subiect of challenging and defending, and of refusing and not refusing the fielde, is very large, and hath need of much consideration, I doe not see how a man may truly and fully determine of it, without speaking of the degrees of nobilitie, wherin I will not call in question what true nobilitie is, because I holde it vndoubtedly to be vertue, and that he is truly noble that is vertuous, be he borne either of great or meane parentage, and that whosoeuer hath not this nobilitie of vertue, of whatsoeuer stock hee proceede, by how much hee descendeth from a more noble kinred, by so much will I account him the more base, not being able to maintaine and keep the honor left vnto him by his ancestours: for nobilitie is seated in the mind, and by the mind it is shewen. But (as I saide before) I intende not to dispute hereof, for hauing alreadie before shewen, that such as are defiled with infamie, maye bee refused from proofe by weapons: it is alwaies to be vnderstoode, that nobility is not without vertue, and my discourse is to be in this subiect, that I speake now of Duello, what

what the degrees of nobilitie are that maye exercise weapons, by which knights come to be equall or vnequall: for albeit that vnder the title of Knightes, Kinges and Emperours, Gentlemen and Souldiers, be comprehended, yet there is such an euident inequalitie betwixt them, as euery man knoweth that a Gentleman cannot compare with a King, nor a souldier with an Emperour: and albeit this matter hath been diuerslie handled by manye, yet I purpose to speake now thereof after a new and particular manner, according to the custome of degrees and worship of our present time. First then I alleadge, that there are many waies, whereby we may consider the diuersitie of degrees: for concerning the places of dignitie, I will firste place those Princes that are not subiect to any other, which I will call soueraigne Princes: next to them feodatory Kings, and them I will call most excellent: thirdly, men right honourable, and after them such as are titled noble men, vnder which title I will comprehend all the degrees of worship. These then we are vndoubtedly to account superiours to priuate Knights, and therefore as they are superiours to them, so are they twixt themselues vnequall: for both noble men are to giue place to the right honourable, and the right honourable to the most excellent, and the most excellent to the free and absolute Princes. Besides that, betwixt them of one and the same title, there may also be great inequalitye, forasmuch as there is a great difference, for one right honourable or noble, to depend on a free Prince or a Prince feodatorie.

F f 2   And

And the like confideration is to bee had of feodatory nobility, forafmuch as one man may affume vnto himfelfe the abfolute power of a Prince, and another man can haue no greater authoritie, than as an
ordinary iudge.

Befides, it is not the leaft regarde that wee are to
haue, to their other qualities and mightines of fignorie, as, if they haue vaffales noblemen, or no: if they
hold Citties, and multitudes of fubiects, and great
port, for all thefe thinges are to be refpected, whether
they be free Princes or feodatorye: whether they be
mofte excellent, or right honou rable, or noblemen:
whether they haue this honour of free Princes or of
feodatory Princes: if they haue noble and honorable
men feodatories, and if they poffeffe noble and great
ftate: and if wee finde them not in fome of thefe di-
ftinctions to be much different, wee are rather in the
controuerfie of armes, to efteeme them equall, then
to admit one of them, to refufe the other. And becaufe there can be no greater difference, than one to
be free, and the other fubiect: and for that foueraign
Princes are onely truely free, and all the reft in fome
forte fubiect, we muft conclude, that as a foueraigne
cannot be challenged the fielde by any man of ano-
prince ther degree, likewife, thofe which wee haue
tearmed mofte excellent, are not to refufe combate
with thofe that are tearmed right honorable: if they
be equall in feodatory nobility, and not vnequall in
other qualities.

The like is alfo to be held betwixt right honourable and noblemen, fo as their condition, as the greatnes

nes and nobilitie of ftate, be not too much different :
for I fee . . . to except againft any men in con
. . .
one onely degree is different betwixt them. And as I
affirme that one degree onely maketh no inequality,
fo I doe not allowe that one vnder the title of moft
excellent, may be challenged by one right honourable, of like feodatorye nobility, but that concerning
his degree, he is fo farre inferiour vnto him : that in a-
nother cafe he would not difdaine to receiue penci-
on and pay of him. Neither yet will I faye, that one
right honourable fhould fight with a noble man, although his eftate be moft noble : nor that one right
honourable of great ftate, may be challenged by one
noble, of fmall iurifdiction : albeit their feodatorye
nobilitie be equall.

But I will fay, that a noble man feadatory to a foueraigne Prince, albeit he be of leffe degree, may notwithftanding challenge one right honourable, that is
feodatorie to one feodatorie, and hath greater figno-
ries, for his feodatorie nobilitie doth fatisfie the other
inequalities.

And therfore I conclude in this point, that the inequalitie of perfons, is to bee confidered from their
titles, from their feodatory nobilitie, and from their
ftates, and according as they are found to haue greater or leffe partes equall, fo are they to bee iudged e-
quall or vnequall.

Heereunto I will adde one other thing, which is
this, that albeit their other qualiti s were either equal
or not much different, yet the quarrell might make

great inequality: as if a prince albeit foueraign, would fight with an Emperour, for fome thing that belongeth to the Empire, in fuch cafe he might lawfully be denied, forafmuch as the Emperour by the condition of the quarrel, is true iudge therof, and confequently alfo without comparifon of any fuperiour.

Of the inequalitie of priuate Noblemen.

Entlemen that are nobly borne, are either without any degree, or elfe beare office or dignitie, as gouernment of cities, embaffages, or commaundement in the warre: and touching thofe that haue authority, either their office is for tearme, or for life: if for tearme, then vpon any quarrell to bee decided by armes, it may ftay the execution of their office : if for life, and that his degree is fuch as maketh him fuperiour to the other, he may fight by his Champion. But if his office be not of fuch qualitie, he that hath the charge of it, is to endeuour the good fauour of his Lord, to graunt him without loofing his office, to fatisfie his honor: and if he cannot obtaine it, hee is to abandon all things, and to reforte thither whether hee is challenged, or whether his honour vrgeth him to challenge another: for as a man is not bound to any thing more ftrictly than to his honor, fo is the leffer to giue place

place to the greater.

Now in that a man is borne noble, he is equall to all Knights, that are of priuate condition : and albeit that one man were borne of a noble houfe, or right honourable, being without iurifdiction, or fuccefsion of fignorie, hee maye be challenged the fielde by any priuate Knight.

Moreouer, forafmuch as the art of warre is a noble exercife, and becaufe manye meane men haue greatly aduaunced their houfes by it, he that fhal exercife the arte of weapon, if he be without infamie, or doe exercife it without abufe, is to bee reckoned and accounted amongft noble men and Knights.

But I would not that any man fhould vpon this thinke himfelfe made honourable, for hauing beene once in the warre, and for hauing taken pay, and ferued two or three moneths without euer drawing fwoorde, or feeing enemy, or hearing found of trumpet, for this were as much as to dreame vpon the hyll Parnaffus that he is a Poet, & the morning not finde himfelfe fo. It is expedient for any man that of vnnoble would become noble, to get this nobilitie by armes, and it is meet for him that would be accounted amongft Knights, to doe the act of a Knight: and it is required of a man to make honourable proofe of his perfon more than once, and to continue long in the warres, and to be knowne for a good Souldier, and to liue as well in time of warre as of peace honeftlye, and in fuch forte that it may be perceiued he intendeth onelye to bee a Souldier, and to make that his principall butte and drift.

And

And if in the studie of letters a man doe not attaine vnto any degree of honour or nobilitie, but with paines and watchinges of many yeeres, let him then thinke likewise that hopeth to innoble himselfe by armes, to sweate often, to endure manye heates of Summer, and cold of winter, to watch many nights, and to sleepe manye times in his armour vpon the hard ground, and to spend his blood, and by many hazardes of life, to manifest his prowes to the world: and when he shall haue perfourmed all these thinges, then he may thinke himselfe truelye noble (for those are noble that deserue to be known for their deeds) and that he cannot be refused for want of nobilitye. Now amongst Souldiers, a Souldier may fight with all sortes of men, as the heads of the squadrons, seriants, and others vnder the degree of their Captain, for his authoritie representeth signorie, and they maye also challenge them, and they are to answere them, being about any enterprise, and hauing degree by a Champion, but being returned to their priuate condition, I see no cause why they should not answere in person. And one Captaine maye challenge combate of another, except they be in place so vnequall, as one may commaund the other.

And this is to be saide of all sortes of Souldiers, as well foote as horse, adding moreouer, that a man of armes hauing beene in honorable and continuall exercise of warre, and liuing in all pointes as beseemeth a man of armes, challenging a particular Captaine of foote, is not to be refused, nor may he refuse any souldier seruing on foote.

And

And I am of opinion, that a Captaine of foote might challenge a Captaine of horse, but onelye that for the most parte those places are bestowed on noble personages, and the conducting of men of armes is also bestowed on right honourable men: and therfore in this case all conditions are to be considered, and the qualitie of the enterprises that they haue, for a Captaine of foot may haue so honorable a degree, or be of so honorable familye, that there could be no cause to refuse him.

And this which I haue spoken touching captains of foote, of horse, and of men of armes, is also to bee vnderstood of footmen twixt themselues, and horsemen also, be they either men of armes, or light horse. For besides their degrees of greatnes in warre, their degrees of nobilitie which wee haue spoken of before in our treatise of noble men (if any they haue) are to be considered, and according to their greater or lesse inequalitye, they are equall or vnequall: which rule beeing generall giuen, may by men of vnderstanding easilye bee applyed vnto particular cases.

G g   With

439

With what perſons a Knight ought to enter Combate, and with what he ought not.

E haue long waded through this ſpacious diſcourſe of chiualrie, ſeeking to ſet downe who ought to be denyed Combate, which matter is ſo large and copious, as if a man would particularlye to euery mite diſcourſe thereof, it would containe a greater volume then I intend to make, in the whole ſubiect of Duello, but it ſufficeth me to haue pointed at the fountaine where water may bee fetcht: and to conclude with my opinion touching the dutie of a Knight, I haue in the beginning of this chapter touched two principall heads: that is, who they are that ought to be cleane thruſt from combate, and who are onelye to be refuſed, for in thoſe two almoſt all controuerſie of perſons that enter or not enter Duello, are as it were conteined, foraſmuch as the wicked and infamus perſons ought to be refelled by knights: and they may be refuſed who for condition are vnequall, and if a man would aske why we haue not ſaid that in theſe two heads all are contained, but almoſt all, it is for that which we haue before ſpoken, of learned men, and cleargye men, who are farre from the

liſts,

lifts, not as refelled, nor as refused, but as priuiledgd, and as fuch to the qualitie and eftimation of whofe condition it is not meete, neither to challenge nor be challenged to proofe by armes, becaufe their ftudie and exercife is far from the valour of the minde.

And to returne to our heads before propounded, I fay, that to refel the infamous and wicked, is the dutie and band of chiualrye, for a knight is bound to do fo that he doe not bring in to the exercife of armes perfons vnworthye to appeare amongft honourable perfons, whereof by their own fault they haue made themfelues vnworthye. Nor is there any credite to be giuen them in the proofe of armes, who are not receiued in ciuile teftimonie: neither are difhonourable perfons to enter into battailes, that are vndertaken for honour fake.

And if any Knight fhould make a quarrell with any perfon vncapable of Duello, the Lords (as I haue faid before) as well in right of chiualrie, as not for to fuffer the field to be difhonored, ought not to graunt the combate.

The refufall is not of band of chiualrie, but of will of Knights, becaufe that if a man will not enter combate with one of leffe condition then himfelfe, hee may lawfully doe it, appointing a meane champion to decide the quarrel. But if a man would not refpect degree, but would in perfon fight with one who for his condition or other defect were not his equall, he could not be faid to do wrong to chiualry, but rather to honour it: forafmuch as chiualrie is not the account of condition, but of valour.

And in the disputations of artes and more noble sciences, no mans linnage is respected but his worth, and therefore a man of base or high degree may bee valorous, and the honour of the listes, is not so much for ouercomming one borne of noble familie, as one that is knowne for a valiant man.

Againe, as great men account it no shame to bee called Knights with meaner men, so they ought not be ashamed to come together, to doe the oath of chiualrie: and if a man borne of a great familie, haue no respect to iniury another, I know not why by reason of his noblenes in blood, he may refuse to defend the same, and to maintaine it against him whom he iniured: and in case that combat were to follow vpon it, my iudgement is, that the iniurer or offender, howsoeuer we terme him, is to answere the other in person. And therefore as I thinke it a discommendable thing for an honorable person, to agree to make himselfe equall to a person that for his vices were odious, albeit he descended of a noble race: so I repute it a knightly course, not to bee too curious in the differences of conditions, especially when they are not so diuers as may seeme, that the frog striues to be equall with the Oxe, (according to the tale.)

Again, I will adde another case, that as I wil commend him that should not so much respect the condition as the valour of him with whom he had quarrell, so I would blame him, that being of a base estate would compare himselfe with euery great man, and would not acknowledge nor content himselfe with his owne condition.

And

And this I speak, not onely of those that are borne meerely, but of those also that being borne of noble blood, are yet of a priuate condition, and in question of honour, would be equall with right honourable personages : for if they esteeme so much of themselues for hauing blood, and being in their families of great Lords, they are to consider, that those Lords haue innobled those houses, and that they haue receiued their nobilitie from Lords, and if they haue receiued it from them, they are by so much lesse then they, by how much hee is greater that giueth another man nobilitie, than he that receiueth it.

Touching the appointing of Champions.

E haue shewen great inequalitie of noble men, wherby the lesse cannot binde the greater to answere him in person : but because no mans greatnes can make it lawfull for him vniustlye to oppresse the lesser, without leauing him sufficient meanes to reuenge himself, and no man ought to make the shadowe of his nobilitie a pretence to be able secretlye to commit defectes, without yeelding reason for them. It is very necessarye, that as in them there is respect for the degree of nobilitie, so also it should bee of honour and iustice, to prouide a meet remedy for euerye priuate person, and that the lawe of chiualry should be inuiolably kept as well of great as of small. And therefore all such as by reason of some excellent degree of nobilitie, shall be found not bound to come in person into the lists with another, are also to know, that in question of armes which they shal happen to haue with persons albeit priuate, that they shall be bound to appoint a Champion, who beeing lawfully ouercome or yeelding, he is likewise to be saide ouercome, that apointed him for his Champion.

And in this pointe I will deliuer the opinion of Doctors, that in case where combate is to be doone by a Champion, such as doe present him, ought also to be present themselues, and bee helde vnder safegarde, to the end that a mockery be not made of Duello, and that if their Champion loose the field, they doe not escape the iudgement.

The like also is to bee doone, when the quarrell is such, as the looser should be condemned in corporall punishment: but where other punishment is not requisite, then to be the vanquishers prisoner, it may sufficientlye suffice, that securitye bee giuen of the charges, and conuenient raunsome.

The lawes of giuing a Champion, are these: such ought to bee giuen as are not infamous, and are equall to them against whome they are to fight, and when one party should intend to appointe a Champion, the other may likewise appoint one: But it is meete that he that will take benefite heereof, should vse such course in his writing, that hee loose not his prerogatiue or iurisdiction as we will terme it: for if

a man

444

a man by his writing fhould fay that hee will defend the quarrell in his own perfon, and afterward would appoint a Champion, the contrary parte might with reafon refufe it.

Againe, it is to be vnderftoode, that the Champions on either fide are to fweare, that they thinke to fight in a iuft quarrell, and that they will doe their vtmoft, as if themfelues were intereffed in the quarrell: and whatfoeuer Champion fhall willinglye fuffer himfelfe to be ouercome, is to haue one of his hands cut off, and the aduerfarye hath not ouercome, but the combate may be renued: and after that a Champion hath been ouercome, he may not after that fight for any other, but for himfelfe he may.

But I will not heere omit, that albeit that nobilitie doth priuiledge the greaters to appoint Champions, fuch yet may the cafes be, that not onely a great man with an inferiour, but a maifter with his feruant, and a Prince with his fubiect is bound to fight in perfon: for feeing that promife is a band which equally bindeth the Prince and fubiect, fo no greater or leffe band hath the one than the other: and whenfoeuer one man fhall oppofe vnto another, any defect of promife and faith, he cannot vfe his Champion, but the accufer is to trye the quarrell in perfon with the accufed. And therfore when a Lord fhall accufe his fubiect or his feruant, of whatfoeuer condition hee be of violating his faith, or of women, or of treafon againft the ftate, he is to proue it in his proper perfon: and the like is alfo to bee obferued, when the fubiect or feruant fhall accufe his Lord.

But

But manye Lords haue no care nor confider not the oath and obligation of faith which they haue toward their fubiects, but rechles of their faith, doe inceffantly euery day commit newe defectes, and perhaps they think that their greatnes doth couer their defects, and do not perceiue, that by how much they are exalted aboue other men, by fo much their faults appeare the greater : for whereas they both by their example and lawes ought to inftruct others in their life, they oppofing themfelues againft lawes, do giue other men example of wicked liuing : and therefore feeing that the defect of faith is a defect fo great in Lords, it is great reafon that they fhould haue no priuiledge in quarrell of faith : and if it bee not to be graunted to Lords, much leffe is it to be graunted to perfons of other qualitie or condition.

And further it is to be vnderftoode, that befides the inequalitie of nobilitie, there are alfo fuch manner of cafes, that in refpect of perfons it is lawfull to appointe Champions, as if a man fhall not bee of eighteene yeeres, or if he be decrepite, or ficke, or in fuch forte hindered in his bodye, as hee is not fitte to fight.

Touch-

This is to be placed before the first chapter of Satisfaction.

Of the Duello or Combat.

Ow and in what manner the Duello or Combat hath bin vsed, they may knowe that haue turned ouer the Records & Annals of passed ages. And seeing it is now long since out of custome, and not permitted by the lawes, I thinke it not necessarie to bee much spoken of in this place. I will onely saie this, that in times past it was had in verie reuerent account, and Gentlemen thought it an honorable qualitie to bee able to discourse of those points and rules that were agreed vpon amongst Princes, and by them approued, concerning free and open Combat. My intention is, to giue gentlemen warning how they appoint the field with their enemies, seeing it is not permitted by the lawes to bee done publikely, as by ancient custome it was wont to be allowed. For it may so fall out, that a Gentleman hauing passed his word to meet his aduersarie in some secret place, after hee hath valiantly wounded him, and reported the victorie of him in the appointed place, his sayde aduersarie may accuse him of fellonie, and saie that hee robbed him, and so where the quarrell should haue an end, he shalbe forced to enter into newe troubles, and begin againe. It

¶ may

447

may alſo ſo chance that his aduerſarie hath ambuſhes prepared for him, & ſo he may be murdered, & being dead, his enemie may vaunt of hauing brauely conquered him by right and valour. I haue my ſelfe knowen in Countries beyond the ſeas, two Captaines, the one named Faro, the other Montarno de Garda, the Lord of Mandelot, gouernour of Leon, met together, whereof the one trecherouſlie minded, prayed the other to ſhew whether he was not priuily armed: whereupon as ſoone as Captain Montarno had opened his doublet, he preſently ranne him through, and ſeeing him fall downe dead (as hee thought) on the ground, returned into the citie with counterfeit glorie, as if he had done wonders, vntil by hap the poore Capteine was found by his friends yet liuing, to bewraie the other Captaines villanie. Like examples many haue happened, and that not ſo far hence, but many vndoubtedly are acquainted with them. I woulde in lyke manner aduertiſe Gentlemen, of an euill cuſtome which of late yeres hath inſtalled it ſelf amongſt men of all ſortes and nations: to bee delighted with broiles and hurliburlies, to ſet men together by the eares, & cauſe quarrels betwixt friends, neighbours, and kinsfolke : whereas it was wont to bee a matter of great conſequence, and of ſuch nature, as it might not be otherwiſe decided, which ſhould bring men ſo mortallye at defiaunce, as nothing but the ſword could finiſh the quarrell. Now vppon euerie occaſion Armes are taken, and one friend for a word will not only violate the ſacred reſpect which ought to be zealouſlie obſerued in friendſhippe, by turning

their

their familiaritie into ſtrangenes, their kindneſſe into malice, & their loues into hatred, but alſo accompany this ſtrange and vnnaturall alteration with a wicked reſolution of ſeeking one anothers ouerthrowe, not reſting till the enmitie be confirmed by fight, & fight ended by death.

O the reuerent eſteeme and account wherin former ages had the Combat ! And why? Forſooth becauſe no Gentleman ſought the ruine or deſtruction one of another, and neuer vndertooke tryall by the ſword but in defence of his innocencie, and to maintaine his honor vnfained and blotleſſe. Now malice and hatred ouerrunneth all, ſtrife and rancor are the bellows of quarrels, and men vpon euerie light cauſe enter into more actions of defiance, than for any iuſt occaſion offered in reſpect of iuſtice and honour.

One fault more, beſides theſe which I haue alredie mentioned, is fairely growen amongeſt vs, that if anie of our friendes ſaie to vs but one worde to this effect, Come will you go with mee, I muſt fight with ſuch a one, and I knowe not what partakers hee hath, We are preſently readie not onely to go wyth him our ſelues, but to drawe others into the minde with vs alſo, without any conſideration had of the manner of the quarrell, how iuſtly or iniuſtly it grew, and ſo often times wee bolſter wrong againſt right: whereas wee ſhould enter into examination of his cauſe, learne the quarrell, and ſearch for the occaſions and cauſes of their falling out, and beeing acquainted therewith, though wee finde him to haue reaſon for his rage, (for I know not how els to terme
that

terme that paſſion that leades men to that mortal reſolution, vpon what iuſt occaſion ſoeuer) yet ough
we not to accompany, nor to further him, no not to
ſuffer him to fight, if the matter can poſſiblye by any
other meanes be taken vp and ended: for ſo dangerous a triall in my opinion, is to be reſerued for ſuch
occaſions as neceſſarily require it: and what or how
many ſuch there be, I leaue to be perpended and conſidered by them that can beſt diſcerne matters of ſo
great waight: and ſo I will come to thoſe pointes,
which I imagine it will not be amiſſe heere to diſcourſe of.

Touching the satisfaction that ought to be made twixt Knights.

Eing wee haue already treated sufficientlie of Duello, as farre as is necessary for a Knight to vnderstande, mee thinketh it also verye conuenient to speake somewat of satisfaction, which is to bee made when a man knoweth he hath wrongfullye iniuried or charged another. And before I proceede, I cannot but greatlye condemne an olde and common opinion, which is his: that when a man hath doone or spoken anye thing good or bad, he should defend and maintaine it for good, which opinion how it is to be approued, I will laye open for euerye man of vnderstanding to dge.

Forasmuch as man is principally distinguished by his reason from brute beastes, as often as hee shall effect any thing without reason and with violence, hee worketh like a beast, and is transfourmed euen into a verye beast, as those afore time did very well vnderstand, who describing men metamorphosed into

H h   beasts,

451

beaftes, fignified no thing els but that thofe men had done acts proper to thofe beaftes, whereof they tearmed them to haue the fhape.

Now then if men be turned into beafts by doing like beaftes, we may alfo faye, that fo long they abide in that fourm, as they continue in that action or opinion, and that their abode in that is fo: and they haue no other meanes to dif-beaft themfelues (as I will terme it) than by acknowledging their fault, by repenting and making amendes thereof, and a man fhould ftrictly follow reafon, as the cheefe guide and miftres of his life: and if happily hee fhould at any time happen to offend (as it is common to man) hee fhould with all poffible fpeede recall himfelfe, feeing it is a heauenly thing to amend.

But to fpeake particularly of matters of chiualrie, we take the office and dutie of this degree to bee, to to help the oppreffed, to defend iuftice, to beat down the proud: where fome cleane contrarily doe turne their fworde, the enfigne and armes of iuftice, to oppreffe reafon, to comit iniuftice, and to confound the truth: and this wicked opinion and peruerfe cuftome is fo rooted in the common forte, as they account it a bafe thing for a man to proceede with reafon, and to confent to equitie: but albeit they be many that follow this corrupt vfe, yet the better forte of fpirites do approue that fentence which is preached. And I haue heard of *Signor Luigi Gonzaga,* who dyed Captaine of the Romifh Church, whofe valour hath beene fo well knowne, as no man ought to think that euer hee was ftayed from anye noble enterprife

through

through the basenes of his minde, that he was woont to saye, that if hee should be knowne to haue spoken or doone any bad thing, for the which hee was challenged to proue it by armes, rather then hee would fight for the false against the truth, and for the bad against the good, he would freely disclaime from it, and deny it.

And this no doubt is to bee helde a manlye and a christian like deede, for reason wils vs to doe so, and lawe and the dutie of the degree of chiualrye requires it, and all doctrine as well philosophicall as Christian, doth teach vs the same.

We are not to follow the opinion of the vulgare.

Ee see that the earth dooth naturallye bring forth venemous thinges, and thornes, and hearbes, and Plantes, either not prontable or hurtful, all which as a mother she dooth nourish, without any helpe of mans labour: but those that are good & profitable and helpful, she receiueth with noisomnes like a stepmother, so as they haue need of continual culture & yeerly renouation. And that which wee see in the earth of the seedes of things, is likewise seene in men of good and badde mindes: for the bad through our naturall corruption is conceiued, receiued, and generally embraced of vs all: whereas the good is ynwillinglye receiued, and we stoppe our eares least wee should heare of it, for there belongeth great studie to vnderstand the truth, and much paines to bring to passe that our mindes bee capable of it: and therefore by how much the paines is the greater, by so much is to be said they are fewer that haue true knowledge of the truth: in which respect, it is no meruaile if the vulgare opinion be so farre from the truth.

But because learned men haue distinguished mans condition in three sortes, the firste, such as of themselues are apt to seek out the truth, and they are tearmed the best: the second, such as finding themselues vnapt for so good a worke, do obey others that doe truly admonish them, and they are called good: and the third, such as neither themselues know, nor will hearken to others, and they are fitlye called bad. Seing that euery man cannot be in the first place, yet wee ought to beleeue such men, whose authoritie and doctrine we finde approued, and to follow their direction, and to take heede least through our obstinacie wee fall into the last degree, which is of the wicked: which as wee are to performe in all manner of our liuing, so it is expedient to doe the like in the order of things of chiualrie, abandoning the vulgare opinion, and following the steps of those, who by valour and knowledge haue laide open vnto vs, the right waye, and gouerning vs by the lawe of reason, and not after the vanities of those, who rather by
chaunce

chaunce or by violence, then by any true courſe or
iudgement of true vnderſtanding, doe rule their own
actions.

Of ſatisfactions in generall.

Nightes taking vpon them to deale
of peace, ought cheefly to prouide
that there be hope of the continuance thereof: which they are to doe
with the leaſt greeuance that may
be of both parties, not burthenyng
the one, for the eaſe of the other, for many times ſuch
things are demaunded, as are more heauye to the offender, than eaſe to the offended, and this is not a to-
ken of ſeeking peace, but reuenge : and yet it is verye
meete that when one is greeued in any thing, the o-
ther that hath doone the wrong ſhould be alike greeued: for if thou take from me, mine own reaſon com-
maunds that thou make mee full reſtauration. euen
with parte of thine owne.

But in wrongs committed, two thinges are commonly woont to be conſidered, the thing whereby a
man is wronged, and the manner how it was doone:
for from the deede commeth the iniurie, and from
the manner commeth the charge : as for example,
Henry giueth the baſtonata to *Edward* when hee had
no cauſe to take heed of him, and after he hath giuen
it: runneth away: in this action the ſtroke is the iniu-

rie,and the charge is, that *Edward* is bound to proue
that he did it shamefully. And to make them frends,
Henry will saye that hee did *Edward* this iniurie vnawares to him, and when hee had no cause to beware
of him, and after hee had stricken him, hee went his
way in such sorte, as *Edward* could not make sufficient reuenge,and that he is not a man of equal degree
to charge him,nor wrong him, more then the other
is to wrong him:and by these words manifesting the
manner how hee wronged *Edward*, hee dischargeth
him from the band of prouuing this act to bee villa-
nous: for there needs no proofe of that which is apparant,so as all the iniurie resteth on him, for which
be he great or meane,it is an ordinary matter to aske
him forgiuenes.

Moreouer the words according to conditions,the
age,and profession of the parties,may alter & change
it,that it be referred to the iudgement of the meaner.
Some men would haue, that a man should confesse
to haue done badlye or trecherouslye, for saying or
doing such a thing,and doe not perceiue that the sig-
nification of these words, is when a thing is done in
a bad and euill manner: and therefore I would not
haue any man make more account of words,then of
the meaning of them : and after that by the meaning
the offended is discharged,to seeke other wordes, is
not to vnburthen himselfe, but to burthen the other
more greeuously. But because there are two sorts of
iniuries,the one by deeds, the other by wordes, wee
will seuerally intreat of them both.

Of

Of satisfaction of iniurye by deedes.

Any I know are of opinion, that satisfaction cannot be made by words for offences by deeds, wherein I am of contrarye minde, for this is not meerelye to bee considered, from woords to deedes, but by the greeuousnes and greatnes of the shame that comes to him by the deede and the wordes, and by the shame that he accounts to himselfe, and that comes to him from others: for which of them will we repute more honourable or more shameful, he that is trecherously wronged, or he that committeth it? and the like I mean also of disaduantage, by striking one behinde, and other ill manner of outraging others.

In this case me thinketh there is no doubt, for neither is his shame the greater that did the iniurie, nor his that receiued it, (according as wee haue saide before) for if I confesse to haue committed a defect, and thou through my confession are iustified from not hauing done amisse, wherof shouldst thou not be satisfied with asking forgiuenes I cannot conceiue any so hainous an iniurie, as in my iudgement such a satisfaction may not suffice, especiallye seeing it hath euer been the vse of most gentlemanlike mindes, willingly to forgiue.

But

457

But forafmuch as there wanteth not fuch, who in cafe of greeuous iniurie, would that a man fhould fecretly be committed into their hands and difcretion, I doe not fee how it is the ready or honourable way to make agreement, for if the offended fhould by his owne hands take fatisfaction, it feemeth hee dealeth difcurteoufly, and by fuch manner of proceeding we haue feen that quarrels and enmyties haue not been ended, but redoubled: and if without other demonftration this remiffion be accepted for amendes, the matter giueth fufpect of a fecret agreement betwixt them, which is preiudiciall to the honor of him that is wronged. But if one man fhould vnaduifedly againft his will offend another, and finding his errour, fhould yeelde himfelfe and giue him his fworde, and put him felfe into his handes, vfing all humilitie and forrowfulnes, and that he that was wronged without further adoe fhould embrace him and lifte him vp, I would account a moft honourable act twixt them both : but the matter once waxt colde, and that it is dealt in by meanes, I cannot thinke that agreement may bee made by remiffion. And to confirme that which I faide, that words may be fufficient fatisfaction for iniurie by deedes : I alleadge, that if happilye one man were mightilye outraged by another, and fhould write to him that hee meant to proue it, that he had doone a vile act, and like a bad man and ill knight: and the other anfwering him, fhould confeffe as much, it is certain that no further quarrell fhould remaine, nor band of honour betwixt them.

Yea, and if being come to the liftes, in making the
articles

articles twixt the Padrini, the Padrinio of the challenged should agree to the forme of the quarrell, and
confesse that to be true, which his aduersarye alleadged, and that if the quarrel should cease, the combate
likewise should cease : which if it be so, as indeede it
is, I doe not see why those wordes, which in the car-
teis and at the fielde may satisfie me, the same words
should not likewise satisfie mee, in the presence of
honorable persons, and of the same mine aduersarye
being spoken, and he also asking me forgiuenes. And
with these reasons I do firmely conclude, that words
may satisfie iniurie by deeds.

Of the contradicting certaine vul-
gare opinions or matters
of satisfaction.

WE haue shewed before how greatly they
are deceiued, that holde opinion, that
after a man hath doone or spoken any
thing good or bad, hee is to defend and
maintaine it for good: and in the Chap-
ter before we haue spoken of the falsitie of that other
opinion, that satisfaction cannot be made by words.
to iniuries by deedes : in which opinion such as doe
stand, alleadge authoritie from generall Captaines,
who were wont to saye: hast thou stricken him? let
him doe what hee list. Which saying, how farre it is

I i   worthy

worthy to be approued, may be perceiued from that which we haue already spoken. And I doe not think that any man of good vnderſtanding, (if he ſhal truly know that he hath ſtricken another, either with his hand or cudgel) to make peace, wil ſay that he wronged him like a traitor, or ſhameſullye. But foraſmuch as wee haue ſeuerallye diſcourſed before of either of theſe opinions, now intreating of them both together, I affirme that from them may be known the falſitie of the vulgare opinion, ſo by common conſent they are receiued for good. and yet if wee will with ſincere iudgement conſider them, we ſhall finde that one of the doth repugne the other: for if I ought to maintain for good all that which I ſhal haue done, I ſhall not be able with my honour to ſay for the ſatiſfaction of him that is wróged, not only al that which hee will haue mee ſaye, but not ſo much as any one thing: and if I may ſay that which he will, it ſhall not be true that I ought to maintain for wel done, al that which I ſhal haue done. Now ſeeing that ſo manifeſt contrarietie is comprehended from ſo open contradiction, they ſhould alſo perceiue their errour, and perceiuing it, reclaime themſelues from it: eſpecially conſidering, that as theſe two opinions are contrarye twixt themſelues, ſo reſon is contrary to them both: and that ſurelye is a commendable & gentlemanlike opinion which is founded vpon law and reaſon. And according to this opinion are honorable perſons and deſirous of valour, to frame themſelues, that no one thing is to be eſteemed valorous or honourable, if it be not accompanied with reaſon.

Of

Of satisfaction to bee made vpon iniurye by deeds.

Peaking in particular of satisfactions that are to bee made, the foundation of them is to bee vpon truth, that whosoeuer hath done wrong, should confesse it, and whosoeuer hath reason in it, should maintaine it. And therefore whosoeuer being moued with iust disdain, and iust occasion, shall conuenientlye reuenge himselfe against any man, hee is not to make other satisfaction, then to say, that he is soary to haue had occasion to haue vsed such an act against him, and that if he had done it without cause, he should haue doone ill or like a badde man, or not like a Gentleman, or knight, or such like wordes, and hee may also intreat him to be freends with him: and hee that hath giuen cause thereof to the other, acknowledging his fault, should content himselfe with as much as reason requires, and not continue in his errour, if hee will not (as was saide before) remaine transfourmed into a brute beast.

And if vpon anye woordes, two should fight, and one of them should be hurte, it were not to bee doubted that without further adoe they might not

I i 2   be

461

be made freends, for that blood doth wash awaye all blot, of which soeuer of them it was: nor can any of them be reproued of defect, when both of them did manifest a bolde and knightly minde.

And if it happen that one man should any way offend another, & that he which is offended should lay hand on his weapons, and the other should fly, albeit the offended could not come to him, hee that should flye were to bee condemned for a vilde man and a coward, and the other should be honoured : forasmuch as honor is seated in the face and in the hands, and not in the shoulders and feete. But to come to be made freends, he should confesse his basenes, and ask forgiuenes of his offence.

And if one man should offend another not in any ill forte, but wrongfullye, and the other doe not reuenge himselfe being able to doe it presently, the offender according to the qualitie of the person offended, shall confesse to haue doone wrong, or to haue done against reason, or such a thing as he ought not, or not like a gentleman: and in all these fortes yet he is to aske him forgiuenes thereof.

But if happilye twixt maskers (as often it happeneth) not knowing one another, one of them bee iniured, the amends should be to say, I knewe you not, and if I had knowne you, I would not haue doone so vnto you, but if I had doone it, I should haue doone discurteously, or villanouslye, or like a bad Gentleman, asking pardon for it: the like course is to be held when one man should offend another by night in the darke.

But

But I will not omit, that sometime a peace is made twixt men, which is not an agreement of the fact: as if I say that a man stroke me and hee denyes that hee toucht me, in such case the satisfaction may be, I strok thee not: and if I haue, I haue doone an ill deede, or such like words to this effect: and by such like examples other cases may likewise be ruled. And to these and such like cases may be added those other wordes, which are commonly vsed twixt Knights, according as we haue made mention in the chapter of satisfactions in generall.

Of satisfaction to bee made vpon iniurye by word.

T hath beene saide before, that the foundation of satisfactions dooth consist in the truth, and to confirme the same, when a man hath opposed against another any defect vntruly, hee ought to confesse that the matter is not so as hee saide, and may alleadge in excuse of himselfe (if the truth be not opposite against it) that he spake it either thinking it to be so, or because it was tolde him, or els in choller: and if hee shall say that he thought so, he shall adde, he was deceiued, or that he thought amisse, and that he knoweth the truth

I i 3   to

to be otherwise: if he say it was tolde him, he shall say
that he which tolde it him, saide not the truth: and if
he say he spake it in choller, hee shall then say that he
knoweth the truth to be other, that he is soarye for it,
or discontented or greeued. And in this sort al words
spoken maye be expressed and declared with a contrary sence, as for example: I haue caide thee traitor,
when I knew thee to be an honorable and iust knight:
and as often as there is demonstration that the truth
is contrarye to that spoken, hee that is iniured, is discharged. And if a man would not make mention of
the iniurious wordes, if hee should reuoke them in
such sorte as I haue saide, or with words of honoura-
rable witnes, the charge should neuertheles be taken
away: and if one man should giue another the lye v-
pon words of wrath, hee ought also to reuoke it. But
if a man should make daintye, to saye I haue belyed
thee, he might yet in another sorte honestly prouide
for it, for he may say, I confesse the words true spoken
by thee whereupon our quarrell is growen, or els he
may expresse the very matter it selfe, and allowe it to
be true: and I will not omit, that seeking meanes to
make quietnes in controuersies, I haue sometimes so
handled a matter, as I haue made agreement by such
a way, that he which gaue the lye, hath spoken to the
other in this sorte : I would be glad to know of you
with what minde you gaue me hard words the other
day, whereupon I gaue you the lye, and I praye you
resolue me heerein: and the other hath answered, to
tell you the truth, I spake them in choller, and not v-
pon any other occasion : and the first hath replyed,
since

since you haue spoken those words in choller, I assure you that I meant not to haue giuen you the lye, vn-lesse you had spoken them with a deliberate minde, to charge me, and I saye that that my lye dooth not charge you, but rather I acknowledge you for a man of troth, and I praye you remember no discurteous words past betwixt vs, but hold me for your freend: and the other hath answered, and I do likewise iudge you a man of honor, beseeching you also to account me your freend. And this forme of satisfaction may bee applied to a thousand cases that happen daylye: and by this example other formes and rules maye be found according to the qualitie of the cases.

Moreouer, it dooth happen, that when a man is greeued at anothers ill wordes of him, hee denyeth that hee spake them, which some men make question whether it should be taken for a full satisfaction, for some would haue him say, I spake them not, but if I had done it, I had spoken falsely, or other like wordes of sence. And touching this doubt, me thinketh that if a man should speake ill of me, in denying to haue spoken it, he should greatly shame himselfe, but not-withstãding he should not giue me satisfaction, & yet he should be found to haue wronged me: & therfore it is not sufficient only to deny, but a further matter is conuenient. And if a man haue not spoken il, he may recite all things, and if he haue spoken it, he ought to saye something to satisfie the other, and the wordes which he is to say are these: I haue not spokẽ it, but if I had, I should haue spoken vntruth, or cõmitted that which I ought not, nor like a gentleman, or such like.

But

But a gentleman ſhould not be brought to deny that which hee hath ſpoken, but rather ſhould confeſſe it, and make ſatisfaction : and if hee ſhould not deny it to be true, but ſhould ſay that in ſpeaking it it, hee hath offended him, that hee ſhould not haue ſpoken it, or that he did ill, and craue pardon for it, for in all caſes where an offence is, it is requiſite to ask pardon. And a man may alſo offend in ſpeaking the truth, if his intent be to offend.

That it is no ſhame to giue ano-
ther ſatisfaction.

Oraſmuch as we are to come ordinarily to ſatisfaction by way of deniall (for ſo will we teatme reuocations of wordes, and confeſſion to haue doone iniuriouſlye) ſome perhaps may ſay, if deniall be ſo ſhamefull, as thereby (as you ſaid before) a man is infamed, and may bee refelled in other quarrels by Knightes: how wil you if I haue ſpoken any falſe thing, or done ill thing, that I by denying ſhould bring vpon me ſuch an infamie? whereto albeit we haue ſufficientlye anſwered before, where wee ſhewed, that a man ſhould rather remoue himſelfe from error, then continue in it obſtinately: yet I affirme that there is great difference of that which is done in the liſtes through force of armes, and of that which is done abroad for

loue

loue of the truth : for one is forced, and the other vo-
luntary : one for feare of death, the other for right of
reafon: the one condemneth a man for a bad Knight
that would fight againſt iuſtice, and the other ſheweth that a man will doe any thing rather then take
weapons in iniuſtice: and one ſheweth, that he which
hath once vndertaken to defend an ill quarrell, is like
to doe it another time: and the other giueth teſtimonie, that renouncing the quarrell, not to fight wrongfully, he will not be brought to take weapons but for
a iuſt and lawfull occaſion : and in ſumme, as one is
the parte of a bad Knight and diſloyall, ſo the other
is the teſtimonie of ſinceritie and true faithfulnes: for
ſeeing that no man liueth without ſinne, hee is more
to be commended amongſt men, that hauing committed any errour, and knowing it, forthwith repen-
teth him of it, and ſeeketh to make true ſatisfaction:
and a Knight that acknowledging his fault ſeeketh to
amend it, dooth not onely not deſerue blame, but is
woorthy of much commendation: as hee who like a
man gouerning himſelfe by reaſon like a Knight, taketh iuſtice for his guide, and like a Chriſtian obſer-
ueth the true law. For theſe reaſons then all Knights
ought to embrace it, and al Princes to eſteem it highlye, both the one and the other accounting no leſſe
the faith and puritie of the minde, then the pride and
bodily ſtrength. Foraſmuch as ſtrength is as profitable to mankinde, as it is gouerned by reaſon and in-
tegritie, onely of it ſelfe ſufficeth to gouerne innumerable multitudes in peace, where force that is not accompanied with ripe counſaile, is that which with
K k   the

the ruine of nations, ouerturneth all diuine and humaine lawes. And becaufe I know that the vulgare forte account fatisfaction bafenes, I will thereto anfwere no other, but that the choofing rather to fight wrongfully, then fatisfie by reafon, is iudged beaftlynes of euery man of vnderftanding.

Satisfaction done to one in Burgundie, by death for his infolencie.

Certaine quarrel rofe betwixt two Souldiers which I knew very well, one a Normand of Roan called Iames Luketo, a man very wel experienced in armes, who falling into fome words with the other (being at Geneua) gaue him a boxe on the eare, wherupon he anfwered Luketo, that becaufe hee knewe him to haue great skill in his weapon, which he had not, but beeing a fouldier would fight, and challenged him for to meete him with his peece, and going to the Generall of the armye, obtained leaue for the open fielde with his confent and the other commaunders: who were prefent at the action, and feeing that many difcharges paffed betwixt them, and yet neither of the tooke any hurt, fuffered them to charge their peeces no more, but fought to reconcile them againe, and make them freendes: whereupon it was agreed of
both

both partes, that he of Geneua, to whom the boxe on the eare was giuen by Luketo, should in presence of the Generall and other Captains of the armie, strike Lucheto on the shoulder, and say I am satisfied, wee will be freends. But the Souldier of Geneua being of a stout stomacke, when hee came to doe as it was concluded, tooke Luketo a sound blow on the eare, which Luketo taking for a great iniurie beeing in that presence, and against the order set downe, drew his sworde presently and ranne him through, and so slew him out of hand, iustly rewarding him for his insolencie : sure I thinke it was the iust iudgement of God, who vseth to shewe his iustice vpon them that are so insolent and full of contumacie and enuious malice, that not regarding neither what they passe their wordes for priuatelye among themselues, nor the intercession of noble Gentlemen and worthye personages, that seeke their safetie and welfare, care for nothing but the fulfilling of their headdynes and reuenging appetite.

My opinion concerning these reconciliations is, that it were not good in the making of them to allow any signe of reuenge, to passe betwixt the parties that are to be reconciled, so that if satisfaction in the treating of any peace betwixt two fallen out, can be made by words, me thinks it were not amisse that euen all tokens or signes of reuenge were auoyded.

Satisfaction vnto one that was tre-cherouslye hurt.

Made mention aboue(vpon occasion)of two Captaines called Montarno and Faro, the beginning of their quarrell you heard before, the end was such, Montarno being vngently and cowardlye hurt, accused Faro as hauing dealt with him not like a man, which Faro denying the deede, the matter could not be taken vp betweene them, howbeit many gentlemen trauailed in it, but they appointed to meete one the other, hauing each of them a God-father (as they call him)appointed him : wherupon the gentleman that was to go with Faro, being wise and circumspect, and a very honest man besides, saide vnto him when hee was going to encounter Montarno, looke what you doe, for you goe to a place, where God ouerthroweth the strongest, and giueth the victorye to the weakest if he fight iustly, and therefore if you haue offended Montarno, make him satisfaction : whereunto Faro answered, why what satisfaction wil Montarno haue? wherupon it was agreed that Faro should confesse that hee esteemed of Montarno as of a braue gentleman and honourable Souldier, and that whilest he did vnbutten his doublet, he meant not to offer him iniurie howsoeuer it fell out, and therefore would

would gladlye haue him to bee his freend, and so the peace was made vp betweene them. But I thinke it a folly for men to trust their enemies, hauing their wepons ready in their hands to iniurie or wrong them.

A peace made betwixt two noblemen, by the Archduke Charles, Sonne to the Emperour Maximilian.

Here were two Noblemen of account vnder Archduke Charles, Prince of Stiria, Carinthia, & some places in Croatia and of Friuli, who were both of the confines of Friuli, one of them being called the Earle Rimondo of Torre, with whome I haue serued in warres when he was Coronell of certaine companies of the Emperours in Croatia, against the Turkes, at which time the Christians had as famous a victorie, as likely hath beene heard of, by the industrie and valorous vertue of generall Pernome, and the Lord Firinbergher. But to return to our purpose, the other noble man was called Lord Mathew Ouuer, they being both in mortal enmitie, one incensed against the other, were cause of much bludshed, and the death of manye fine Gentlemen and Knights: which the Archduke Charles their Prince perceiuing to be a thing lamentable, caused both the noble men to be called to the Court, & placing them into sundrie lodgings about htmselfe (desirous of his subiects welfare) separately to eache, and first to Rimondo, disswading him from his hostile minde and hatred towardes the Lord Mathew, and finding him verie obstinate and altogether resisting all peace and agreemenr, considering hee could not be reconciled with honor, and would rather die than make a peace ignominious vnto him. Whereupon the Archduke replyed, that if hee were resolued rather to die than to yeeld to his intreatie, hee should bee resolued and looke to himselfe, for he should die in deed, and with all called for an officer criminall to execute him presently. Which soone moued the Lord Mathew to alter his resolution, and to promise the prince to bee friends with the Earle Rimondo : to whom he went also, and forced him in like manner to vowe friendship to the Lorde Mathew. The prince then hauing brought them both to consent to his purpose and demand, made them meete in his presence. where the Lord Mathew, (who had two verie excellent proper gentlewomen to his daughters) being the eldest spake first and said : Countie Rimondo, I am at peace with you, and accept you for my friend and sonne, and do giue one of my daughters in mariage vnto you, with a hundred thousand crownes : who accepted of the conditions, and so the peace was concluded to theyr great contentation, the princes great pleasure, and the ioy of all his subiects, without anie more bloudshed or mortalitie.

A dan-

A dangerous Satisfaction between two Gentlemen, one called the Bianchi, and the other Neri, whereof issued great harmes.

I Reade in the historie of Florence, of two Gentlemen in the Citie of Pistoia, who were in verie straight league of amitie together, and hauing two sonnes, it happened as the two youthes kept companie together, that once playing at cardes they fell to wordes, and from wordes to blowes in the ende, and one returned home to his father hurt. His father that was not hurt, vnderstanding the whole matter, was verie sorrie that his friends sonne was hurt by his sonne, & rebuked him bitterly, and commanded him expresly vpon his blessing to go to his friende the youthes father whome he had hurt, and to aske forgiuenesse of him for hurting his sonne. Now he seeing the youth and his sonne, and not remēbring or considering the great amitie and friendship that was betwixt himself and the youthes father, caused his men to cutte off his right hande, and so sent him backe againe home to his Father, saying that deeds could not be recompenced with wordes. Which act and vnciuill parte caused greate ruine and slaughter in Tuscane.

They

473

They therefore that purpofe to bee reconciled and make peace, or goe about to reconcile others and bring them in league, muft take heed what they doe, and neuer truft to the difcretion of him that is offended, but fee the conditions and points agreed vpon firft, and if any one doe not keepe his promife, and do contrary to his faith & word paffed, they themfelues that are the mediators and dealers in the making of the peace, as louers of honor and iuftice, to be reuenged of him, feeing fuch villanie and infolencie worthily punifhed, for fuch men are commonlye for the moft parte caufe of their owne ouerthrowe, of their parents and freends, and alfo of their countrie.

We read in hiftories of ancient times, that a King of the Perfians dying, left two fonnes, each demaunding the Empire, and yet while the matter was a debating, they conuerfed and liued together in al kindnes and brotherly louingnes, till it was in the end declared by the peeres of the Empire, which of them was chofen and elected to be the King, which the other tooke fo well, that hee would not in any cafe be brought to think either vnkindely of his brother, or euill of the electors, he hauing what he afpired vnto, and they doing what they thought beft and conuenienteft for the Countrie: Such difcretion would doe well in all men, to cut from them manye inconueniences, debates, ftrifes and quarrels.

Hauing

The nobility of Women.

Auing diſcourſed of the inequalitie in nobility, and eſpecially of priuate noblemen and gentlemen, I wil not take occaſion now to ſay any thing of the meanes and maner whereby men riſe vnto honour and dignitie, nor of the greatnes and nobilitie of kingdomes, prouinces and citties, conſidering that this matter hath been ſo largelye and laudablye handled by many, as appeares by the reading of the ancient and moderne hiſtories, which are filled with diſcourſes tending to this purpoſe: this I will onelye ſaye by the way, that thoſe places haue beene famed for moſt noble, and had in greateſt account, which haue produced braueſt men, commended vnto poſteritie for their vertue either intellectuall or actiue, morall or politicke, ciuile or militarie: and as places are made famous or enobled by reaſon of the excellét men that are there borne, ſo alſo can no place how barbarous ſoeuer it be, drowne or darken the glorie and commendation due vnto a man ennobled by valour, prudence, or other vertues whatſoeuer, as Anacharſis being noted by one to be a Scithian, anſwered as ſharpely as readily, true indeed by birth, but not by bringing vp: ſo that howbeit he was a Scithian borne, yet were his

L l   manners

manners not barbarous, nor his life Scithian like, but deserued the commendation due to ciuile and vertuous education. But I will leaue the vertues and nobilities of men, and turne my speech to women, hoping they will not be offended with me if I discouer the vertues and noble disposition of their sexe, which being such as deserue highest commendation, I vtterly disalow of their opinion, that not onely not attribute nobilitie vnto women, but also abridge them from power and abilitie, to ennoble and imparte nobilitie vnto others. We read of many excellent women both of high and low estate, in diuers histories, whose fame hath been carried through the world for rare vertue, some for valour, others for learning, others for wisedome, others for chastitie, others for other singular vertues and commendable partes: manye Queenes and noble Ladies haue gotten great renown and become glorious for armes and warlike exploites: many haue had their names dedicated to euerlasting remembrance euen by the memoriall of their owne pennes, hauing been most exquisite writers and penwomen themselues, both for prose and verse. In my opinion then are women greatly wronged by them that seeme to take from them power of transferring nobilitie to others, excluding them from so great an honor, they notwithstanding hauing great reason to be copartners with men therein: for excellency consisting in vertue of the body and the minde, and women being endewed with both beautye and vertue, and seeing that women can learne whatsoeuer men can, hauing the full vse of reason (or else nature who

doth

doth neuer do any thing in vaine)fhould haue to no purpofe giuen them the gifte of vnderftanding : I thinke they deferue fellowfhip and communing in honor with men,confidering nature hath beftowed on them afwel as on men,meanes to attain vnto lear-ning,wifedome,and al other vertues adiue and con-templatiue: which is made manifeft by the example of many that haue côfirmed the opinion of their va-lour and excellencie,by their rare vertue,and almoft incredible prowes. And to recite the worthy ades of fome,I will wholye commit and paffe by the Ama-zones,their ftory being counted fabulous, and men-tion fome, whofe valiant & vertuous ads haue been recorded in true hiftories, afwell of olde times, as of our times. The king Argus hauing by reafon of long continued wars great want of men, Thefelide a wo-man of a cittie wherin Argus was befieged by Cleo-menes king of Lacedemony,prouoked the other wo-men in the cittie to take armes,and leading them out at the gates, deliuered the Cittie from fiege, and put their enemies to fhameful flight. I wil not heer fpeak of the valour of Artemifia, of Ificrate, of Semira-mis, of Tômiris,of the women of Lacedemony, of Debora,of Iudirh,and other vertuous and magnani-mous, yea holye and facred Ladies,whofe hiftoryes are contained in the holy Scripture : but I will come vnto thofe whofe life was not fo long fince, but that we may well remember them. About the time that the Englifhmen vnder Charles the 6.had brought in fubiedion the greteft part of that kingdom,there was a yong maidé called Iane Pulzela,daughter to a fhep-hcard of the Duke of Loraine,who not yet reaching

to the fifteenth yeere of her age, was accounted to
be a Propheteſſe,and of many helde to be a witch,
but this maketh not to the purpoſe: the King beeing
in great doubt of his fortune, ſent for her to know
whether he ſhould loſe the reſt of his kingdome alſo
or no, and hauing anſwere that hee ſhould become
victorious in the end, gaue the more credite vnto it,
becauſe many of his noblemen aſſured him that ſhe
had the ſpirite of prophecie, recounting many things
vnto him which ſhe had declared in priuate mens e-
ſtates. Afterward ſhe tooke armes her ſelfe, and behaued her ſelfe in ſuch ſorte among the other Captains
and men of armes, that in a verye ſhorte time ſhe was
made Captaine generall of the whole armye, and being armed and mounted on a barbed horſe, in ſuch
ſorte as ſhe was not knowne but to be a man, made a
ſally with all her troupes both horſe and foote, and
aſſailing the enemie with an vndaunted courage, followed her enterpriſe with ſuche valour and pru-
dence, that ſhe freed the Cittie of Orleance from the
ſiege, being her ſelfe ſhot through the ſhoulder with
an arrow: thence ſhe led her companye to Troe in
Campanie, where beeing encamped, againſt the expectation of all the Captaines and Souldiers, tooke
the cittie in very ſhorte time, and cauſed Charles the
ſeauenth to be crowned in Rheymes, as the ancient
cuſtome is, hauing firſt deliuered the cittie from the
ſiege which the enemie had laide vnto it. Shortly after battering Paris, and clambring on the walles as
being famous amongſt the ſtouteſt Souldiers, notwithſtanding her legge was pierced quite through
with

with an arrowe, gaue not ouer the enterprise for all that, but persisted till she had effected it. Petrarch writeth, that he knewe a damsell at Pozzuelo called Marie, who borrowing the habit of a yong man, after the fashion men wore their apparell there, armed her selfe, and was euen the firste that fought with the enemie, and the last that retired: Vrsina wife vnto Guido the cheefe of the house of Torrello, vnderstanding how the venecians had laid siege to Guasteila a castle of her husbands, hee being abroad, armed herselfe, and led a companye of men to the place, and spoyling many Venecians, defended the Castle. Margaret daughter to Valdiner King of Suetia, and wife to Aquinus King of Norway, remained inheritrix vnto these Kingdomes in the right of her husband and of her father, and in the right of her sonne Olaus also of Dacia, but the Duke of Monopoli waging warre against her, shee encountred him with a mightie armie, defeated his forces, tooke him prisoner, and led him in her triumph after the solemn order of the Romans.

Mahomet King of the Turkes, waging warre against the Venecians, sent a great armie vnder the conduct of one of his generall Captaines, to take the isle of Metelino, and besieging Coccino very strongly, the inhabitants issued and fought verye valiantlye against the Turkes : in the same Cittie was a young maide, who seeing her father slaine by the Turkes in this fight, and the Citizens beginning to fainte and feare, got into the former companies, and skirmished so couragiouslye with the Turkes, that all the Citi-

zens

zens aſhamed to ſee themſelues ouercome in ſtout-
nes and courage by a ſimple girle, tooke hart and
vtterlye deſtroyed their enemies, and ſaued the
Cittie.

Bona Lombarda, firſt ſeruant and afterward wife
to Petro Brunoro of Parma, being in the warres that
the Venecians had againſt Franceſco Sforza Duke
of Millaine, after Pauono a caſtle in the territories of
Breſcia was taken, with her courage and gallant for-
wardnes recouered it againe.

Margaret wife to Henry King of England, and Si-
ſter to Renatus King of Naples, being informed that
her husband was ouercome in battaile and taken pri-
ſoner, preſentlye gathered certaine companies together, and leading them to a place wherby the enemie
was to paſſe, encountred him, ouercāe his camp, and
purſuing them that fled with her husband the King,
ſlewe an infinite company of men, and in the end ſaued him, and returned home with him, and got him
this moſt glorious victorie.

I remember that I being a youth, a freend of mine
ſonne to a Trumpet that was in pay vnder the Captaines of the ſignorie of Venice, was with a certaine
coſin of his ſet vpon by eleuen other yong men that
were their enemies, which his mother perceiuing,
took a Partiſan in her hauds, and defended her ſonne
and coſin, and ſorely wounding fiue of their enemies
made the reſt to flye.

Being in Rauenna, I ſawe in one of the Churches
the carued image of a Ladie, who, being wife to a
Gentleman that was cheefe of the houſe of Raſpo-
ni,

ni, had euer in her life time accompanied her huſband in all his warres, and atchiued immortall fame by her proweſſe and valour.

I was in Lombardie on a daye which was generally ſolemniſed, according to the cuſtome ouer the whole Countrie, and it happened at that time, that there was a great quarrell betweene two rich houſes, among the Farmers and countrymen of that place, the one part of which were called the Romani, and the other the Ferrariſi, both beeing vnder the Duke of Ferrara, and meeting on this vniuerſall feaſt daye at a village called Treſenta, one of the Romani ſhot a Piſtole at the cheefe of the Ferrariſi, and thinking to haue wounded him, miſſed him and hutte one of the Ferrariſi their wiues, who was of ſo valiant a diſpoſition, that howbeit ſhe was ſhot quite through, yet ſaid nothing to her freends, nor complained of it, leaſte they ſhould haue lefte their enemies and come to help her, and ſo many of them might haue in meane while been ſpoyled by the aduerſe parte, but ſnatching a weapon out of one of the countrymens handes, ſlewe him that had ſhot her, and his fellowe that fought by him, and ſo fell downe her ſelfe, not able to performe any more, liuing but foure daies after.

I haue read in the Cronicles of France, that two great men growing to be enemies, for the dukedome of Bretagne, the one pretéding an eſtate in the ſame, in right of his father, as being his by inheritance, the other claiming intereſt in it by the right of his wife, as her doury, &c. one of thé was much fauoured by the

King

King of Fraunce, and the other of the King of England: these two rising vp in arms, one of them whom the King there least fauoured, was taken and put in prison, and the Frenchmen began to spoile his countrie, and take his tenantes, and comming to a Cittie where the Lady was, wife to him that was taken, besieged it, and often assailed it though in vaine, for she like a right valiant gentlewoman, and of a manly courage, prouided that not one woman in the Cittie should bee idle, but bring her helping hand for the defence of the Cittie, and maintenance of their honour, causing some to make instruments of pitch and tarre and fire workes, others to bring stones, seething water, and other things necessary at that instant and necessitie: and very oftentimes issued very valorously and brauelye, and firing her enemies tentes, put them to great losse and confusion, slaying manye of them, but they daylye receiuing new supplies from the King, she was forced to send for some succour to the King of England, for which whilest she staied, they draue her to manye inconueniences, for the people began to mutter and to mutinie within the Cittie, finding great want and scarcitie, by reason whereof many dyed, and she was much sollicited and importuned to deliuer vp the Cittie to the enemie, and not knowing how to answere them, she desired them to staye for Gods mercie but so manye dayes, (limiting a certaine time) and if no aide came in the meane while, then shee would doe their request: those daies being expired, whilste shee was heuilie musing what answere to make her citizens, that

had

had verye earneftlye befought her againe to render, fpyed the Englifh nauie on the feas, and calling them to her window, comforted them with that fight, and caufed all things to be prepared and made in a readines, that when her Englifh freends were landed and fhouldaffault the enemy, fhe might with her companies make a fallie to meete them; and bid them welcome, to the deftruction and vtter ouerthrow of her enemies, which fhee did, and flewe fo manye of the Frenchmen, that all the countrie was amazed thereat, and fhee maintained warres againft them a long time after.

I haue read in the hiftories of the Turks, how that Selim Sultan hauing obtained the Empire after hee had poyfoned his Father and ftrangled his Brother Corcut, who was a Philofopher, with a mightye armye purfued his Brother Accomat, whom the King of Perfia Vfan Caffano much fauoured and holpe with men, prouifion, and monye: but the Bretheren meeting together, and the victorie being very doubtfull a great while, in the end Selim Sultan ouercame by the valour of his Ianizaries, for the Perfians hauing with their horfes broken quite through the whole battaile, and entring on the Ianizaries in the middeft of whom the Turke Selim Sultan was garded, they difcharged a volly of fhot vpon the Perfians, who vnufed to heare fuch a noyfe, were wonderfullye difmaied, and inftantlye forced to take their flight, by which meanes Sultan Selim obtained a wonderfull great victorie, and his brother Accomat was ftrangled by his Ianizaries, who after the fight

M m   was

was done, found among them that were taken and dead, an infinite company of Persian Gentlewomen that were come all armed as Knightes, to fight with their husbands, but Selim Sultan caused the dead to be folemnly buried, and thofe who were faued, to be fent home to their Countries very honourably.

In the yere 1571. at the time that Selim Emperour of the Turkes, and father to Amurat that now liueth, waged war againft the Venecians, the Baffa that was generall by Sea, went to the cittie Raguzi in the Ifle of Carfola, and began to batter it, which the cittizens perceiuing, and fearing the danger, fled with their goods & fuch things as they made moft account of, into the Ifle, and left none but women at home, who chofing rather to dye then fall into the Turks hands, went valiantly to the walles, and one of them putting fire to a peece of Ordirance, ftrooke away with the bullet the lantern of the Baffa, wherupon he hoifted fayle and fled, and fo the cittie was faued.

In the time of Charles the fifth, and Francis King of France, they hauing fouldiers in Italy, by reafon of the difcention and factions among the Italians, the citie of Siena was befieged, where a gentlewoman of the houfe of Picholhomini was made Coronell of 3000. other women, and atchiued wonderfull matters, to the aftonifhment of al the people. I haue been toulde by diuers, of a Portingall gentlewoman that for religions fake about 4. yeeres now paft, left of the apparell of her fexe, and went as a fouldier into Barberie, where fhe behaued her felfe fo refolutelye, that fhe was in fhort time after made a Captaine, and became

came

came very famous, fearfull to her enemies, and greatly esteemed of her freends: in the end she chanced to
go to confession, and bewraied her sex to her confes-
sor, who tolde her that it was a great sinne to delude
the worlde, in taking vpon her the person of a man,
which she could not do without offending God: besides this, he told the Bishop of it, and the whole matter was known through the Country where she was:
wherupon diuers noblemen knowing her to be a woman, desired to be maried vnto her, but shee refused
them, in regarde that she had euer loued a nephew of
the Bishops, and conuersed with him very priuately
before she was known, and therefore being discouered, would not marry any one but him, for that shee
would admit none to that neer point of acquaintáce
as he was, but him that should be her husband, being
of as good a disposition that way, as shee was in matters of valour and courage. She was seene afterward
in Lishbone apparelled like a woman, but armed like
a knight, leading a troupe of men, the conducting of
which she had obtained for her husband.

It were a worke infinite for me to rehearse all such
famous Ladies as haue been renowmed for their vertue, neither were it possible for any man truelye to
make a collection of all their gallant deeds, seing they
are in number so exceeding: but as I haue mentioned and called to remembrance some who were ex-
celling in magnanimity, courage, and greatnes of the
minde, so will I now also set downe the names of
some that passed in greatnes of vnderstanding, and
excelled in intellectuall vertues.

M m 2   Saffo

Saffo of Lesbos was inferiour to few Poets in that Arte, and superiour to many. Erinna wrote a Poeme in the Dorike tung, compared to Homers diuine worke. Corina fiue times put downe Pindarus that great Poet. Pythagoras learned many thinges of his sister Themistoclea, and his daughter Dama was so excellent in learned misteries, that shee commented and expounded the difficulte places in her Fathers workes. Areta of Cirena, after the death of her Father Aristippus, kept the schoole while she liued, and read Philosophie lector dayly, and wonderfullye encreased the auditorie. Leontia wrote against Theophrastus Aristotles scholler. Hipatia was very skilfull in Astronomie, and professed it publiquelye a long time in Alexandria. But to leaue the Grecian Gentlewomen and come to the Italian, Sempronia of Rome, was excellently well spoken both in Greeke and Latine, she was a fine Poet and wrote very sweetly. Cornelia Africanus his wife, was nothing inferiour vnto the former: nor Hortensia who was in veritie her Fathers true heire, in eloquence and Oratorie. Sulpitia a Roman Lady, in Heroical verse, deplored the pitifull time of Domitian the Emperour. In our times we haue heard of Russuida of Saxony, who was excellent in the tunges, and hath written diuers treatises and Poems, very commendably. Batista eldest daughter to Galeazo Lord of Pessaro, made many excellent proofes of her learning, and wrote many pamphlets. In the same Cittie of Pessaro was a gentlewoman called Laura Brenzara, who hath writen many verses both Latin and Italian, and was admirable

mirable for her excellencie in making of Orations
and extemporall speeches in both tungs, Latine and
Italian. At Padua where I was borne, in my time
was a Gentlewoman of good reckoning, that professed the ciuile lawe publiquelye, came dayly into the
colleges and schooles, and disputed with all the Doctors and schollers of the vniuersitie. Cassandra a gentlewoman of Venice, was commended for great skill
in languages, and spake very eloquently, she could also write very wel, as apppeered by diuers bookes she
hath set forth, among which hath been known a book
of the order of the sciences.

But I wil content my selfe, hauing produced these
examples, in proofe of the valour and vertue of women, concluding with onely one more, which as the
best, I kept to be last : heerein imitating the best ora-
tors, who euer reserue the strongest argumentes for
the last. These lines therefore shalbe adorned and
honoured with the name of this most glorious Prin-
cesse Elizabeth our gracious Queene, whose fame
hath built her towers of triumphes, euen in Countries farthest remoued from her, and forced her very
enemies in the storme of their malice and spite, to
praise her name, to admire her mercifulnes and wisedome, and to feare her power : this is such a manifest
and worthy example of womanly worthines and fe-
minine perfection, that the perfectest men must by
truths enforcement acknowledge themselues most
vnperfect, in regarde of the meanest perfection that
heauen most bountifullye hath bestowed on her sacred maiestie, who liueth yet renowmed through

M m 3   the

the whole worlde, the Sunne of Chriftendome, and the onely Starre wherby all people are directed to the place which aboundeth in peace, religion and vertue: fhe being a Princeffe trulye accomplifhed with all vertue both morall and intellectuall, with greatnes both of minde and vnderftanding, and with heauenly wifedome to gouerne royallye both in peace and warres, to the credit and glory of all her fexe. God of his mercy maintain her life in much profperity, euen a whole eternity, that as her vertue is heauenlye and immortall, fo fhee her felfe may neuer dye, but when the world and all muft perifh, be carried vp to heauen by holye Angels, there to liue in Gods eternall glory.

FINIS.

PARADOXES

OF DEFENCE,

WHEREIN IS PROVED THE TRVE
grounds of Fight to be in the ſhort auncient weapons,
and that the ſhort Sword hath aduantage of the long
Sword or long Rapier. And the weakeneſſe and imperfection of the Rapier-fights diſplayed. Together with an
Admonition to the noble, ancient, victorious, valiant,
and moſt braue nation of Engliſhmen, to beware of falſe
teachers of Defence, and how they forſake their owne
naturall fights : with a briefe commendation of
the noble ſcience or exerciſing of
Armes.

By George Siluer Gentleman.

LONDON,
Printed for Edvvard Blount.
1599.

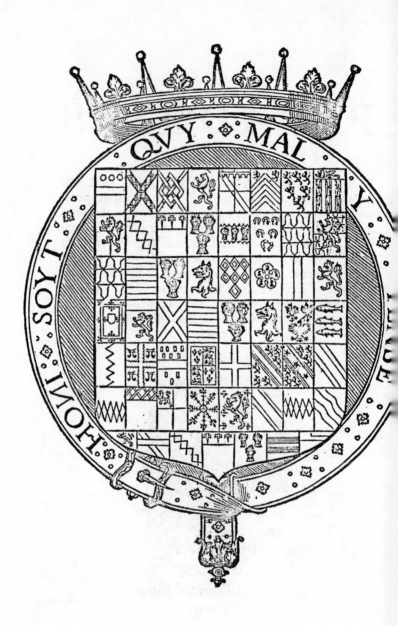

TO THE RIGHT

HONORABLE, MY SINGVLAR
GOOD LORD, ROBERT EARLE OF
Effex and Ewe, Earle Marfhall of England, Vif-
count Hereford, Lord Ferrers of Chartley, Bourchier
and Louaine, Maifter of the Queenes Maiefties horfe , &
of the Ordenance, Chancellor of the Vniuerfitie of Cam-
bridge, Knight of the moft noble order of the Gar-
ter, and one of her Highneffe moft ho-
norable Priuy Counfell.

ENCING (Right honorable)
in this new fangled age, is like
our fafhions , euerie daye a
change, refembling the Ca-
melion, who altereth himfelfe
into all colours faue white: fo
Fencing changeth into all wards faue the right.
That it is fo , experience teacheth vs : why it is
fo , I doubt not but your wifedome doth conceiue. There is nothing permanent that is not
true, what can be true that is vncertaine ? how
can that be certaine, that ftands vpon vncertain

A 3

491

grounds? The mind of man a greedie hunter after truth, finding the feeming truth but chaunging, not alwayes one, but alwayes diuerfe, for-
fakes the fuppofed, to find out the affured certaintie: and fearching euery where faue where
it fhould, meetes with all faue what it would.
VVho feekes & finds not, feekes in vaine; who
feekes in vaine, muft if he wil find feeke againe:
and feeke he may againe and againe, yet all in
vaine. VVho feekes not what he would, as he
fhould, and where he fhould, as in all other
things (Right honourable) fo in Fencing: the
mind defirous of truth, hunts after it, and hating
falfhood, flies from it, and therfore hauing mif-
fed it once, it affayes the fecond time: if then he
thriues not, he tries another way: whe that hath
failed he aduentures on the third: & if all thefe
faile him, yet he neuer faileth to chaunge his
weapon, his fight, his ward, if by any meanes he
may compaffe what he moft affects: for becaufe
men defire to find out a true defence for themfelues in their fight, therefore they feeke it diligently, nature hauing taught vs to defend our
felues, and Art teaching how: and becaufe we
miffe it in one way we chaunge to another. But
though

though we often chop and change, turne and returne, from ward to ward, from fight to fight, in this vnconſtant ſearch, yet wee neuer reſt in anie, and that becauſe we neuer find the truth: and therefore we neuer find it, becauſe we neuer ſeeke it in that weap-n where it may be found. For, to ſeeke for a true defence in an vntrue weapon, is to angle on the earth for fiſh, and to huntin the ſea for Hares: truth is ancient though it ſeeme an vpſtart : our forefathers were wiſe, though our age account them fooliſh, valiant though we repute them cowardes: they found out the true defence for their bodies in ſhort weapons by their wiſdome, they defended them ſelues and ſubdued their enemies, with thoſe weapons with their valour. And (Right honorable) if we will haue this true Defence, we muſt ſeeke it where it is, in ſhort Swords, ſhort Staues the halfe Pike, Partiſans, Gleues, or ſuch like weapons of perfeĉt lẽgths, not in long Swords, long Rapiers, nor frog pricking Poiniards : for if there be no certain grounds for Defence, why do they teach it? if there be, why haue they not found it? Not becauſe it is not : to ſay ſo, were to gaineſay the truth : but becauſe it is not cer-

English maiſters of defence, are profitable members in the common wealth, if they teach with ancient Engliſh weapons of true Defence, weight and conuenient length, within the compaſſe of the ſtatures and ſtrength of men to command, becauſe it maketh them ſafe, bold, valiant, hardie, ſtrong and healthfull, and victorious in the warres, ſeruice of their Prince, defence of their friendes and countrey. But the Rapier in reaſon not to be taught, nor ſuffred to be taught, becauſe it maketh men fearefull and vnſafe in ſingle combat, and weak, & vnſeruiceable in the warres.

A 4.

493

taine in thofe weapons which they teach. To
proue this, I haue fet forth thefe my Paradoxes,
different I confeffe from the maine current of
our outlandifh teachers, but agreeing I am well
affured to the truth, and tending as I hope to the
honor of our Englifh nation. The reafon which
moued me to aduenture fo great a taske, is the
defire I haue to bring the truth to light, which
hath long time lyen hidden in the caue of contempt, while we like degenerate fonnes, haue
forfaken our forefathers vertues with their weapons, and haue lufted like men ficke of a ftrange
ague, after the ftrange vices and deuifes of Italian, French and Spanifh Fencers, litle remembring, that thefe Apifh toyes could not free
Rome from Brennius facke, nor Fraunce from
King Henrie the fift his conqueft. To this defire
to find out truth the daughter of time, begotten
of Bellona, I was alfo moued, that by it I might
remoue the great loffe of our Englifh gallants,
which we daily fuffer by thefe imperfect fights,
wherein none vndertake the combat, be his
caufe neuer fo good, his cũning neuer fo much,
his ftrength and agilitie neuer fo great, but his
vertue was tied to fortune : happie man, happie
doale,

doale , kill or be killed is the dreadfull iſſue of this diuelliſh imperfect fight. If that man were now aliue, which beat the Maiſter for the ſcholers fault , becauſe he had no better inſtructed him , theſe Italian Fencers could not eſcape his cenſure , who teach vs Offence , not Defence, and to fight , as Diogenes ſcholers were taught to daunce, to bring their liues to an end by Art. VVas Aiax a coward becauſe he fought with a ſeuen foulded Buckler, or are we mad to go naked into the field to trie our fortunes, not our vertues? VVas Achilles a run-away, who ware that well tempered armour, or are we deſperat, who care for nothing but to fight, and learn like the Pigmeys, to fight with bodkins, or weapons of like defence? Is it valour for a man to go naked againſt his enemie? why then did the Lacedemonians puniſh him as deſperate, whom they rewarded for his vallour with a Lawrell crowne? But that which is moſt ſhamefull, they teach mē to butcher one another here at home in peace,wherewith they cannot hurt their enemies abrode in warre. For, your Honour well knowes, that when the battels are ioyned , and come to the charge,there is no roome for them *To this it will be obiected, that in the warres we vſe few Rapiers or none at all, but ſhort Swords. To that I anſwere: Thoſe are inſufficient alſo, for that they haue no hilts, whereby they are insufficient in their defence, and especially for the hãd, which being stroken although with a verie smal blow, most commonly is the losse of a mã, because the force of his hand being taken from him, he is neither able to defend his life, nor greatly to offend his enemy: and againe, since the Rapier-fight hath bene taught, for lacke of practise they haue lost the vse of the blow.*

to drawe their Bird-spits, and when they haue them, what can they doe with them? can they pierce his Corslet with the point? can they vnlace his Helmet, vnbuckle his Armour, hew a-sunder their Pikes with a *Stocata*, a *reuersa*, a *Dritta*, a *Stramason*, or other such like tẽpestuous termes? no, these toyes are fit for children, not for men, for stragling boyes of the Campe, to murder poultrie, not for men of Honour to trie the battell with their foes. Thus I haue (right Honorable) for the trial of the truth, betweene the short Sword and the long Rapier, for the sauing of the liues of our English gallants, who are sent to certaine death by their vncertaine fights, & for abandoning of that mischieuous and imperfect weapon, which serues to kill our friẽds in peace, but cannot much hurt our foes in warre, haue I at this time giuen forth these Paradoxes to the view of the world. And becaufe I knowe such straunge opinions had need of stout defence, I humbly craue your Honorable protection, as one in whom the true nobility of our victorious Aunceftors hath taken vp his residence. It will sute to the rest of your Honours most noble cõplements, to maintaine the defence of their weapons

weapons whose vertues you possesse. It agrees
with your Honourable disposition, to receiue
with fauour what is presented with loue. It sorts
with your Lordships high authority, to weigh
with reason, what is fit for marshall men. It is an
vsuall point of your Honor, which winnes your
Lordship loue in your countrey, to defend the
truth in whomsoeuer: and it addeth a supply to
that vvhich your Lordship haue of late begun
to your vnspeakeable honor and our inestima-
ble benefite, to reduce the vvearing of swordes
vvith hilts ouer the hands, to the Romane disci-
pline, no longer then they might draw them vnder their armes, or ouer their shoulders. In all
or any of these respects, I rest assured that your
Lordship vvill vouchsafe to receiue vvith fauor
and maintaine vvith honour these Paradoxes of
mine, vvhich if they be shrouded vnder so safe a
shield, I vvill not doubt but to maintaine vvith
reason amongst the vvise, and proue it by practise vpon the ignorant, that there is no certaine
defence in the Rapier, and that there is great
aduantage in the short Sword against the long
Rapier, or all maner of Rapiers in generall, of
vvhat length soeuer. And that the short Staffe

Why should we leaue the hand naked, since therby our limmes & liues are defended, our enemies discomforted, wounded, and executed? I see no reason but that the hand should be as well armed and prouided for, as anie other part of the bodie.

497

hath the vauntage againſt the long Staffe of twelue, foureteene, ſixteene or eighteene foote long, or of what length ſoeuer. And againſt two men vvith their Swordes and Daggers, or two Rapiers, Poiniards & Gantlets, or each of them a caſe of Rapiers : vvhich vvhether I can performe or not, I ſubmit for triall to your Honors martiall cenſure , being at all times readie to make it good, in vvhat maner, and againſt vvhat man ſoeuer it ſhall ſtand vvith your Lordſhips good liking to appoint. And ſo I humbly commend this booke to your Lordſhips vviſedome to peruſe, and your Honour to the Higheſt to protect in all health and happineſſe novve and euer.

Your Honors in all dutie,

George Siluer.

A N

498

AN ADMONITION

TO THE NOBLE, ANCIENT,

VICTORIOVS, VALIANT, AND

MOST BRAVE NATION OF

ENGLISHMEN.

Eorge Siluer hauing the perfect knowledge of all maner of weapōs, and being experiēced in all maner of fights, thereby perceiuing the great abuſes by the *Italian* Teachers of Offence done vnto them, the great errors, inconueniences, & falſe reſolutions they haue brought them into, haue inforced me, euen of pitie of their moſt lamentable wounds and ſlaughters, & as I verily thinke it my bounden dutie, with all loue and hūmilitie to admoniſh them to take heed, how they ſubmit themſelues into the hands of *Italian* teachers of Defence, or ſtraungers whatſoeuer; and to beware how they forſake or ſuſpect their owne naturall fight, that they may by caſting off of theſe Italianated, weake, fantaſticall, and moſt diuelliſh and imperfect fights, and by exerciſing of their owne ancient weapons, be reſtored, or atchieue vnto their natural, and moſt manly and victorious fight againe, the dint and force whereof manie

B

braue nations haue both felt and feared. Our plough
men haue mightily preuailed againſt them, as alſo a
gainſt Maiſters of Defence both in Schooles and coun
tries, that haue taken vpon thē to ſtand vpon Schoole
trickes and iugling gambolds: whereby it grew to
common ſpeech among the countrie-men, Bring me t
a Fencer, I will bring him out of his fence trickes wit
good downe right blowes, I will make him forget hi
fence trickes I will warrant him. I ſpeake not again
Maiſters of Defence indeed, they are to be honoured
nor againſt the Science, it is noble, and in mine opini
to be preferred next to Diuinitie; for as Diuinitie pre
ſerueth the ſoule from hell and the diuell, ſo doth thi
noble Science defend the bodie from wounds & ſlaugh
ter. And moreouer, the exerciſing of weapons puttet
away aches, griefes, and diſeaſes, it increaſeth ſtrength
and ſharpneth the wits, it giueth a perfect iudgement
it expelleth melancholy, cholericke and euill conceits
it keepeth a man in breath, perfect health, an
long life. It is vnto him that hath the perfection there
of, a moſt friendly and comfortable companion whe
he is alone, hauing but only his weapon about him, i
putteth him out of all feare, & in the warres and place
of moſt danger it maketh him bold, hardie, and valiant

And for as much as this noble and moſt mightie na
tion of Engliſhmen, of their good natures, are alwaye
moſt louing, verie credulous, & ready to cheriſh & pro
tect ſtrāgers: yet that through their good natures the
neuer more by ſtrangers or falſe teachers may be decei
ued, once againe I am moſt humbly to admoniſh thē, o
ſuch as ſhal find in themſelues a diſpoſition or deſire t
learne their weapons of them, that from henceforth a
ſtran

ſtrangers ſhall take vpon them to come hither to teach this noble & moſt valiant, & victorious nation to fight, that firſt, before they learne of them, they cauſe a ſufficient triall of them to be made, whether the excellencie of their skill be ſuch as they profeſſe or no, the triall to be very requiſite & reaſonable, euen ſuch as I my ſelfe would be contented withall, if I ſhould take vpon me to go in their countrie to teach their nation to fight. And this is the triall: they ſhall play with ſuch weapõs as they profeſſe to teach withall, three bouts apeece with three of the beſt Engliſh Maiſters of Defence, & three bouts apeece with three vnskilful valiant men, and three bouts apeece with three reſolute men half drunke. Then if they can defend thẽſelues againſt theſe maiſters of Defence, and hurt, and go free from the reſt, then are they to be honored, cheriſhed, and allowed for perfect good teachers, what countrey men ſoeuer they be: but if of anie of theſe they take foile, then are they imperfect in their profeſſion, their fight is falſe, & they are falſe teachers, deceiuers and murtherers, and to be puniſhed accordingly, yet no worſe puniſhment vnto them I wiſh, then ſuch as in their triall they ſhall find.

A great fauor to giue them choice of their weapons, becauſe profeſſors of armes ought to be skilfull with all maner of weapõs.

There are foure eſpeciall markes to know the Italian fight is imperfect. & that the Italian teachers and ſetters forth of books of Defence, neuer had the perfection of the true fight.

The firſt marke is, they ſeldome fight in their owne country vnarmed, commonly in this ſort, a paire of Gantlettes vpon their hands, and a good ſhirt of maile vpon their bodies. The ſecõd marke is, that neither the Italians, nor any

*2
Yet they perſwade vs that the croſſe of the Rapier without hilt or gantlet is ſufficient.*

B 2

of their beſt ſcholers do neuer fight, but they are
moſt cōmonly ſore hurt, or one or both of them ſlaine.

The third marke is, they neuer teach their ſcholers,
nor ſet downe in their bookes anie perfeċt lengthes of
their weapons, without the which no man can by nature
or Art againſt the perfeċt lēgth fight ſafe, for being too
ſhort, their times are too long, and ſpaces too wide for
their defence, and being too long, they wilbe vpon euerie croſſe that ſhall happen to be made, whether it be
done by ſkil or chance, in great danger of death; becauſe
the Rapier being too long, the croſſe cannot be vndone
in due time, but may be done by going backe with the
feete ; but that time is alwaies too long to anſwere
the time of the hand, therfor euery man ought to haue
a weapon according to his owne ſtature : the tall man
muſt haue his weapon longer then the man of meane
ſtature, or elſe he hath wrong in his defence, & the man
of meane ſtature muſt haue his weapon longer then the
man of ſmal ſtature, or else he hath wrong in his defence;
& the man of ſmal ſtature muſt beware that he feed not
himſelf with this vaine cōceipt, that he wil haue his weapon long, to reach as farre as the tall man, for therin he
ſhal haue great diſaduantage, both in making of a ſtrong
croſſe, and alſo in vncroſſing againe, and in keeping his
point from croſſing, and when a croſſe is made vpon
him, to defend himſelf, or indanger his enemie, or to redeeme his loſt times. Againe Rapiers longer, then is
conuenient to accord with the true ſtatures of men, are
alwaies too long or too heauie to keepe their bodies in
due time from the croſſe of the light ſhort ſword of perfeċt length, the which being made by the skilfull out of
any of the foure true times, vpon any of the foure chiefe
Aċti-

Actions, by reafon of the vncertaintie & great fwiftneffe in any of thefe times, they are in great danger of a blow, or of a thruft in the hand, arme, head, body, or face, & in euerie true croffe in the vncroffing, in great danger of a blow vpon the head, or a full thruft in the bodie or face: and being taken in that time & place, the firft mouer in vncroffing fpeedeth the Rapier man of imperfect legth, whether it be too long, too fhort or too heauie, and goeth free himfelfe by the direction of his gouernours.

The fourth marke is, the croffes of their Rapiers for true defence of their hands are imperfect, for the true cariage of the guardant fight, without the which all fights are imperfect.

Of fixe chiefe caufes, that many valiant men thinking themfelues by their practifes to be skilfull in their weapons, are yet manie times in their fight fore hurt, and manie times flaine by men of fmall skill, or none at all.

He firft and chiefeft caufe is, the lacke of the 3 foure Gouernours, without the which it is impoffible to fight fafe, although a man fhould practife moft painfully and moft diligently all the daies of his life.

The fecond caufe is, the lacke of knowledge in the due obferuance of the foure Actions, the which we cal bent, fpent, lying fpent, and drawing backe: thefe Actions euerie man fighteth vpon, whether they be skilfull or vnskilfull, he that obferueth them is fafe, he that obferueth the not, is in continuall danger of euerie thruft that fhalbe ftrongly made againft him.

B 3

The third caufe is, they are vnpractifed in the foure true times, neither do they know the true times frõ the falfe: therefore the true choife of their times are moft commonly taken by chance, and feldome otherwife.

The fourth caufe is, they are vnacquainted out of what fight, or in what maner they are to anfwer the variable fight: and therefore becaufe the variable fight is the moft eafieft fight of all other, moft cõmonly do anfwer the variable fight with the variable fight, which ought neuer to be but in the firft diftance, or with the fhort Sword againft the long, becaufe if both or one of them fhall happen to prefe, and that in due time of neither fidefight be changed, the diftance, by reafon of narrowneffe of fpace, is broken, the place is won and loft of both fides, then he that thrufteth firft, fpeedeth: if both happen to thruft together, they are both in dãger. Thefe things fometimes by true times, by change of fights, by chance are auoided.

The fift caufe is, their weapons are moft commonly too long to vncroffe without going backe with the feet.

The fixt caufe is, their weapons are moft commonly too heauie both to defend and offend in due time, & by thefe two laft caufes many valiãt mẽ haue loft their liues.

What is the caufe that wife men in learning or practifing their weapons, are deceiued with Italian Fencers.

No fight perfect that is not done in force & true time.

THere are foure caufes: the firft, their schoolmaifters are imperfect: the fecond is, that whatfoeuer they teach, is both true & falfe; true in their demõftrations, according with their force & time in gẽtleplay, & in their actions

actions according with true force & time in rough play or fight, falfe: for exāple, there is as much difference betwixt thefe two kind of fights, as there is betwixt the true picture of Sir *Beuis* of *Southampton*, & Sir *Beuis* himfelf, if he were liuing. The third, none cā iudge of the Craft but the Crafts-man; the vnskilfull, be he neuer fo wife, can not truly iudge of his teacher, or skill, the which he learneth, being vnskilful himfelfe. Laftly, & to confirme for truth all that fhal be amiffe, not only in this excellēt Science of Defence, but in all other excellent fecrets, moft commonly the lye beareth as good a fhew of truth, as truth it felfe.

Of the falfe refolutions and vaine opinions of Rapier-men, and of the danger of death thereby enfuing.

IT is a great queftion, & efpecially amōgft 4 the Rapier-men, who hath the vantage of the thrufter, or of the warder. Some hold ftrongly, that the warder hath the vantage: others fay, it is moft certain that the thrufter hath the vantage. Now when two do happē to fight, being both of one mind, that the thrufter hath the vantage, they make all fhift they can, who fhall giue the firft thruft: as for example, two Captaines at *Southampton* euen as they were going to take fhipping vpon the key, fel at ftrife, drew their Rapiers, and prefently, being defperate, hardie or refolute, as they call it, with all force and ouer great fpeed, ran with their rapiers one at the other, & were both flaine. Now when two of the contrary opinion fhall meet and fight, you fhall fee verie peaceable warres betweene them: for they verily thinke that he that firſt thruſteth is in great danger of his life, therefore with all ſpeede do put themſelues in ward, or Stocata, the ſureſt gard of all other, as *Vincentio* ſaith, and therevpon they ſtand ſure, ſaying the one to the other, thruſt and thou dare; and ſaith the other, thruſt and thou dare, or ſtrike or thruſt and thou dare, ſaith the other: then ſaith the other, ſtrike or thruſt and thou dare for thy life. Theſe two cunning gentlemen ſtanding long time together, vpon this worthie ward, they both depart in peace, according to the old prouerbe: It is good ſleeping in a whole skinne. Againe if two ſhall fight, the one of opinion, that he that thruſteth hath the vantage, and the other of opinion, that the warder hath the vantage, then most commonly the thruſter being valiant, with all ſpeed thruſteth home, and by reaſon of the time and ſwift motion of his hand, they are moſt commonly with the points of their rapiers, or daggers, or both, one or both of them hurt or ſlaine; becauſe their ſpaces of defence in that kind of fight, are too wide in due time to defend, and the place being wonne, the eye of the Patient by the ſwift motion of the Agents hand, is deceiued. Another reſolution they ſtand ſure vpon for their liues, to kill their enemies, in the which they are moſt commonly ſlaine themſelues: that is this: When they find the point of their enemies rapier out of the right line, they ſay, they may boldly make home a thruſt with a *Paſſata*, the which they obſerue, and do accordingly: but the other hauing a ſhorter time with his hand, as nature manie times teacheth him, ſodainly turneth his wriſt, whereby he meeteth the other in his paſſage iuſt with the point of his rapier in the face or body. And this falſe reſolution hath coſt manie a life.

That

*That the caufe that manie are fo often flaine, and manie
fore hurt in fight with long Rapiers is not by reafon of
their dangerous thrufts, nor cunningneffe of that
Italienated fight, but in the length and
vnweildineffe thereof.*

T is moft certaine, that men may with
fhort fwords both ftrike, thruft, falfe and
double, by reafon of their diftance and
nimbleneffe thereof, more dangeroufly
then they can with long Rapiers: and yet
when two fight with fhort fwordes, hauing true fight,
there is no hurt done: neither is it poffible in anie reafon,
that anie hurt fhould be done betwixt them of either
fide, and this is well knowne to all fuch as haue the perfection of true fight. By this it plainely appeareth, that
the caufe of the great flaughter, and fundrie hurts done
by long Rapiers, confifteth not in long Reach, dangerous thruftes, nor cunningneffe of the Italian fight, but
in the inconuenient length, and vnweildineffe of their
long Rapiers: whereby it commonly falleth out, that in
all their Actions appertaining to their defence, they are
vnable, in due time to performe, and continually in danger of euerie croffe, that fhall happen to be made with
their rapier blades, which being done, within the halfe
rapier; (vnleffe both be of one mind with all fpeed to depart, which feldome or neuer happneth betweene men
of valiant difpofition,) it is impoffible to vncroffe, or get
out, or to auoid the ftabbes of the Daggers. And this
hath falne out manie times amongft valiant men at
thofe weapons.

C

*Of running and standing fast in Rapier fight, the runner
hath the vantage.*

6   F two valiant men do fight being both cunning in running, & that they both vse the same at one instant, their course is doubled, the place is wonne of both sides, and one or both of them will commonly be slaine or sore hurt: and if one of them shall runne, and the other stand fast vpon the *Imbrocata* or *Stocata*, or howsoeuer, the place wilbe at one instant wonne of one side, and gained of the other, and one or both of them wilbe hurt or slaine: if both shall prese hard vpon the guard, he that first thrusteth home in true place, hurteth the other: & if both thrust together, they are both hurt: yet some vantage the runner hath, because he is an vncertaine marke, and in his motion: the other is a certaine marke, and in a dead motion: and by reason thereof manie times the vnskilfull man taketh vantage he knoweth not how, against him that lyeth watching vpon his ward or *Stocata* guard.

Of striking and thrusting both together.

7   It is strongly holden of manie, that if in fight they find their enemy to haue more skill then themselues, they presently will continually strike, & thrust iust with him, whereby they will make their fight as good as his, and thereby haue as good aduantage as the other with all his skill: but if their swordes be longer then the other, then their aduantage is great; for it is

certaine

certaine (fay they) that an inch will kill a man: but if
their fwordes be much longer then the other, then their
aduantage is fo great, that they wilbe fure by thrufting
and ftriking iuft with the other, that they will alwaies
hurt him that hath the fhort fword, and go cleare themfelues, becaufe they will reach him, when he fhall not
reach them. Thefe men fpeake like fuch as talke of Ro-
bin Hoode, that neuer fhot in his bow; for to ftrike or
thruft iuft together with a man of skill, lyeth not in the
will of the ignorant, becaufe the skilfull man alwaies
fighteth vpon the true times, by the which the vnskilfull
is ftill difappointed of both place and time, and therefore driuen of neceffitie ftill to watch the other, when &
what he will doe; that is, whether he will ftrike, thruft,
or falfe: if the vnskilfull ftrike or thruft in the time of falfing, therein he neither ftriketh nor thrufteth iuft
with the other: he may faie, he hath ftroke or thruft before him, but not iuft with him, nor to anie good purpofe; for in the time of falfing, if he ftrike or thruft, he
ftriketh or thrufteth too fhort: for in that time he hath
neither time nor place to ftrike home, and as it is faid,
the vnskilfull man, that will take vpon him to ftrike or
thruft iuft with the skilfull, muft firft behold what the
man of skil will doe, and when he will doe it, and therfore of neceffitie is driuen to fuffer the skilfull man to be
the firft mouer, and entred into his Action, whether it
be blow or thruft, the truth therof in reafon cannot be
denied. Now iudge whether it be poffible for an vnskilfull man to ftrike or thruft iuft together with a man of
skill; but the skilfull man can moft certainly ftrike and
thruft iuft together with the vnskilfull, becaufe the vnskilfull fighteth vpon falfe times, which being too long

to anfwere the true times, the skilfull fighting vpon the true times, although the vnskilfull be the firft mouer, & entred into his Action, whether it be blow or thruft; yet the fhortneffe of the true times maketh at the pleafure of the skilfull a iuft meeting together: in perfect fight two neuer ftrike or thruft together, becaufe they neuer fuffer place nor time to performe it.

Two vnskilfull men manie times by chance ftrike and thrufte together, chance vnto them, becaufe they know not what they doe, or how it commeth to paffe: but the reafons or caufes be thefe. Sometimes two falfe times meet & make a iuft time together, & fometimes a true time and a falfe time meeteth and maketh a iuft time together, and fometimes two true times meet and make a iuft time together. And all this hapneth becaufe the true time and place is vnknowne vnto them.

George Siluer his refolution vpon that hidden or doubt-
full queftion, who hath the aduantage of the
Offender or Defender.

he aduantage is ftrongly holden of many to be in the offender, yea in fomuch, that if two minding to offend in their fight, it is thought to be in him that firft ftriketh or thrufteth. Others ftrongly hold opinion that the wardr abfolutely hath ftill the aduantage, but thefe opinions as they are contrary the one to the other: fo are they contrarie to true fight, as may well be feene by thefe fhort examples. If the aduantage be in the warder, then it is not good anie time to ftrike or thruft: if the aduantage be in the ftriker or thrufter, then were it
         a friuolous

a friuolous thing to learne to ward, or at anie time to seeke to ward, since in warding lieth disaduantage. Now may it plainly by these examples appeare, that if there be anie perfection in fight, that both sides are deceiued in their opinions, because if the striker or thruster haue the aduantage, then is the warder still in danger of wounds or death. And againe, if the warder hath the aduantage, then is the striker or thruster in as great daunger to defend himselfe against the warder, because the warder from his wards, taketh aduantage of the striker or thruster vpon euerie blow or thrust, that shall be made against him. Then thus I conclude, that if there be perfection in the Science of Defence, they are all in their opinons deceiued; and that the truth may appeare for the satisfaction of all men, this is my resolution: there is no aduantage absolutely, nor disaduantage in striker, thruster, or warder: and there is a great aduantage in the striker thruster & warder: but in this maner, in the perfection of fight the aduantage consisteth in fight betweene partie and partie: that is, whosoeuer winneth or gaineth the place in true pace, space and time, hath the aduantage, whether he be striker, thruster or warder. And that is my resolution.

Of Spanish fight vvith the Rapier.

THe *Spaniard* is now thought to be a better 9 man with his Rapier then is the Italian, Frenchman, high Almaine, or anie other countrie man whatsoeuer, because they in their Rapier-fight stand vpon so manie intricate trickes,

C 3

that in all the courfe of a mans life it fhall be hard to learne them, and if they miffe in doing the leaft of them in their fight, they are in danger of death. But the *Spaniard* in his fight, both fafely to defend himfelfe, and to endanger his enemie, hath but one onely lying, and two wards to learne, wherein a man with fmall practife in a verie fhort time may become perfect.

This is the maner of Spanifh fight, they ftand as braue as they can with their bodies ftraight vpright, narrow fpaced, with their feet continually mouing, as if they were in a dance, holding forth their armes and Rapiers verie ftraight againft the face or bodies of their e-nemies: & this is the only lying to accomplifh that kind of fight. And this note, that as long as any man fhall lie in that maner with his arme, and point of his Rapier ftraight, it fhall be impoffible for his aduerfarie to hurt him, becaufe in that ftraight holding forth of his arme, which way foeuer a blow fhall be made againft him, by reafon that his Rapier hilt lyeth fo farre before him, he hath but a verie litle way to moue, to make his ward per-fect, in this maner. If a blow be made at the right fide of the head, a verie litle mouing of the hand with the knuckles vpward defendeth that fide of the head or bo-die, and the point being ftill out ftraight, greatly endan-gereth the ftriker: and fo likewife, if a blow be made at the left fide of the head, a verie fmall turning of the wrift with the knuckles downward, defendeth that fide of the head and bodie, and the point of the Rapier much indangereth the hand, arme, face or bodie of the ftriker: and if anie thruft be made, the wards, by reafon of the indirections in mouing the feet in maner of dauncing, as aforefaid, maketh a perfect ward, and ftill withall the point

point greatly endangereth the other. And thus is the
Spanifh fight perfect: fo long as you can keepe that order, and foone learned, and therefore to be accounted
the beft fight with the Rapier of all other. But note how
this Spanifh fight is perfect, and you fhall fee no
longer then you can keepe your point ftraight againft
your aduerfarie: as for example, I haue heard the like
ieft.

There was a cunning Doctor at his firft going to fea,
being doubtfull that he fhould be fea-ficke, an old woman perceiuing the fame, faid vnto him: Sir, I pray, be
of good comfort, I will teach you a tricke to auoid that
doubt; here is a fine pibble ftone, if you pleafe to accept
it, take it with you, and when you be on fhip-bord, put
it in your mouth, and as long as you fhall keepe the
fame in your mouth, vpon my credit you fhall neuer vomit: the Doctor beleeued her, and tooke it thankfully at
her hands, and when he was at fea, he began to be ficke,
whereupon he prefently put the ftone in his mouth,
& there kept it fo long as he poffibly could, but through
his extreme ficknefle the ftone with vomit was caft out
of his mouth: then prefently he remembred how the woman had mocked him, and yet her words were true.

Euen fo a *Spaniard* hauing his Rapier point put by,
may receiue a blow on the head, or a cut ouer the face,
hand, or arme, or a thruft in the body or face, and yet his
Spanifh fight perfect, fo long as he can keepe ftraight
the point of his Rapier againft the face or body of his
aduerfarie: which is as eafie in that maner of fight to be
done, as it was for the Doctor in the extremity of his
vomite to keepe the ftone in his mouth.

Yet one other pretie ieft more, fcarce worth the reading, in commendation of outlandifh fight. There was an *Italian* teacher of Defence in my time, who was fo excellent in his fight, that he would haue hit anie Englifh man with a thruft, iuft vpon any button in his doublet, and this was much fpoken of.

Alfo there was another cunning man in catching of wildgeefe, he would haue made no more ado, when he had heard them crie, as the maner of wildgeefe is, flying one after another in rowes, but prefently looking vp, would tell them, if there had bene a dofen, fixteene, twētie, or more, he would haue taken euerie one. And this tale was manie times told by men of good credit, and much maruelled at by the hearers: & the man that wold haue taken the wildgeefe, was of good credite himfelfe: marie they faid, indeed he did neuer take anie, but at anie time when he had looked vp, and feene them flie in that maner, he would with all his heart haue taken thē, but he could no more tell how to do it, then could the cunning *Italian* Fencer tell how to hit an Englifhman, with a thruft iuft vpon any one of his buttons, when he lifted.

Illufions for the maintenance of imperfect weapons & falfe
fights, to feare or difcourage the vnskilfull in their
weapons, from taking a true courfe or vfe,
for attaining to the perfect know-
ledge of true fight.

10 Irft, for the Rapier (faith the *Italian*, or falfe teacher) I hold it to be a perfect good weapō, becaufe the croffe hindreth not to hold the handle in the hand, to thruft both far & ftraight, & to vfe all maner of aduantages in the wards,

or

r fodainly to caſt the ſame at the aduerſarie, but with
he Sword you are driuen with all the ſtrength of the
ƚand to hold faſt the handle. And in the warres I would
viſh no friend of mine to weare Swords with hilts, be-
:auſe when they are ſodainly ſet vpon, for haſte they ſet
heir hands vpon their hilts in ſteed of their handles : in
vhich time it hapneth manie times before they can
ǃraw their ſwords, they are ſlaine by their enemies. And
or Sword and Buckler fight, it is imperfect, becauſe the
ʋuckler blindeth the fight, neither would I haue anie
nan lie aloft with his hand aboue his head, to ſtrike
ound blowes. Strong blowes are naught, eſpecially be-
ng ſet aboue the head, becauſe therein all the face and
ʋodie is diſcouered. Yet I confeſſe, in old times, when
ʋlowes were only vſed with ſhort Swords & Bucklers,&
ʋack Sword, theſe kind of fights were good & moſt mã-
y, but now in theſe daies fight is altered. Rapiers are lõ-
ʒer for aduãtage thē ſwords were wõt to be: whē blowes
vere vſed, men were ſo ſimple in their fight, that they
hought him to be a coward, that wold make a thruſt or
ſtrike a blow beneath the girdle. Againe, if their weapõs
vere ſhort, as in times paſt they were, yet fight is better
ʋooked into in theſe dayes, than then it was. Who is it in
heſe daies ſeeth not that the blow cõpaſſeth round like
ǁ wheele, whereby it hath a longer way to go, but the
ʰhruſt paſſeth in a ſtraight line, and therefore commeth
ǁ nearer way, and done in a ſhorter time thē is the blow,
ǃnd is more deadly then is the blow? Therefore there is
ǁo wiſe man that will ſtrike, vnleſſe hé be wearie
ꞏf his life. It is certaine, that the point for aduantage
:uerie way in fight is to be vſed, the blow is vtterly
ǃaught, and not to be vſed. He that fighteth vpon the

D

Theſe counterſeit ſhews are enough to cary the wiſeſt that know not the true fight frõ the falſe, out of the right way.

And if their weapons were ſhort, as in times paſt they were, yet they could not thruſt ſafe at body or face, becauſe in gardant fight they fall ouer, or vnder the perfect croſſe of the ſword & to ſtrike beneath the waſte, or at the legges, is great diſaduantage, becauſe the courſe of the blow to the legs is too far, & therby the head, face, & body is diſcouered: and that was the cauſe in old time, that they did not thruſt nor ſtrike at the legs, & not for lacke of skill,

as in thefe daies
we imagine. A-
gaine, if a man
in thofe daies
fhold haue fought
with a long
fword, they would
prefently haue
put him into
Gobbes Trauers.

blow efpecially with a fhort fword, wilbe fore hurt or flaine. The deuill can fay no more for the maintenance of errors.

That a blow commeth continually as neare a way as a thruft, and moft commonly nearer, ftronger, more fwifter, and is fooner done.

I I

*A confutation
of their errours.*

THe blow, by reafo that it compaffeth round like a wheele, whereby it hath a longer way to come, as the Italian Fenfer faith, & that the thruft paffing in a ftraight line, commeth a nearer way, and therefore is fooner done then a blow, is not true: thefe be the proofes.

Let two lie in their perfect ftrengths and readineffe, wherein the blades of their Rapiers by the motion of the body, may not be croffed of either fide, the one to ftrike, and the other to thruft. Then meafure the diftance or courfe wherein the hand and hilt paffeth to finifh the blow of the one, and the thruft of the other, and you fhall find them both by meafure, in diftance all one. And let anie man of iudgement being feene in the ex-ercife of weapons, not being more addicted vnto nouel-ties of fight, then vnto truth it felfe, put in meafure, and practife thefe three fights, variable, open, and guar-dant, and he fhall fee, that whenfoeuer anie man lyeth at the thruft vpon the variable fight, (where of neceffitie moft commonly he lyeth, or otherwife not poffiblie to keepe his Rapier from croffing at the blow & thruft, vp-on the open or gardant fight,) that the blowes & thruftes from thefe two fightes, come a nearer way, and a more ftronger

tronger and fwifter courfe then doth the thruft, out of
he variable fight. And thus for a generall rule, where-
foeuer the Thrufter lyeth, or out of what fight foeuer
he fighteth, with his Rapier, or Rapier and Dagger, the
blow in his courfe commeth as neare, and nearer, and
more fwift and ftronger then doth the thruft.

Perfect fight ftandeth vpon both blow and thruft, there-
fore the thruft is not onely to be vfed.

Hat there is no fight perfect without both 12
blow and thruft: neither is there anie certaine rule to be fet downe for the vfe of the
point onely, thefe be the reafons : In fight *This in truth*
here are manie motions, with the hand, bodie, and *cannot be denied.*
feet, and in euerie motion the place of the hand is altered, & becaufe by the motions of the hand, the altering
of the places of the hand, the changes of lyings, wards,
and breaking of thruftes, the hand will fometimes be in
place to ftrike, fome times to thruft, fometimes after a
blow to thruft, and fometimes after a thruft to ftrike, &
fometimes in place where you may ftrike, and cannot
thruft without loffe of time, and fome times in place
where you may thruft, and cannot ftrike without loffe of
time, and fometimes in place where you can neither
ftrike nor thruft, vnleffe you fight vpon both blow and
thruft, nor able to defend your felfe by ward or going
backe, becaufe your fpace wilbe too wide, and your diftance loft. And fometimes when you haue made a
thruft, a ward or breaking is taken in fuch fort with the
Dagger or blade of the Sword, that you cā neither thruft
againe, nor defend your felfe vnleffe you do ftrike, which

you may foundly doe, and go free, and fometimes when
you ftrike, a ward wilbetaken in fuch fort, that you cannot ftrike againe, nor defend your felfe, vnleffe you
thruft, which you may fafely doe and goe free . So to
conclude, there is no perfection in the true fight, without both blow and thruft, nor certaine rule to be fet
downe for the point onely.

That the blow is more dangerous and deadly in fight, then a
thruft , for proofe thereof to be made according with Art,
an Englishman holdeth argument againft an Italian.

Italian.

13 Hich is more dangerous or deadly in
fight of a blow or a thruft?

Englishman.

This queftion is not propounded according to art, becaufe there is no fight
perfect without both blow and thruft.

Italian.

Let it be fo, yet opinions are otherwife holden, that
the thruft is onely to be vfed, becaufe it commeth a nearer way, and is more dangerous and deadly, for thefe
reafons: firft the blow compaffeth round like a wheele,
but the thruft paffeth in a ftraight line, therfore the blow
by reafon of the compaffe, hath a longer way to go then
the thruft, & is therefore longer in doing, but the thruft
paffeth in a ftraight line, therfore hath fhorter way to go
the hath the blow, & is therfore done in a fhorter time, &
is therfore much better then the blow, & more dangerous and deadly, becaufe if a thruft do hit the face or bodie, it indangereth life, and moft commonly death en-
fueth: but if the blow hit the bodie, it is not fo dagerous.

Englishman.

Englishman.

Let your opiniõs be what they wil, but that the thruft cõmeth a nearer way, & is fooner done then the blow, is not true: & for proofe thereof reade the twelfth Paradox. And now will I fet downe probable reafons, that the *The blow more* blow is better then the thruft, and more dangerous and *dangerous then* deadly. Firft, the blow commeth as neare a way, & moft *the thruft.* cõmonly nearer then doth the thruft, & is therfore done in a fhorter time then is the thruft: therfore in refpeçt of time, wherupon ftãdeth the perfeçtion of fight, the blow is much better then the thruft. Againe, the force of the thruft paffeth ftraight, therefore any croffe being indireçtly made, the force of a child may put it by: but the force of a blow paffeth indireçtly, therefore must be direçtly warded in the counterchecke of his force: which cãnot be done but by the cõuenient ftrength of a man, & with true croffe in true time, or elfe will not fafely defẽd him: and is therfore much better, & more dãgerous thẽ the thruft, and againe, the thruft being made through the hand, arme, or leg, or in many places of the body and face, are not deadly, neither are they maimes, or loffe of limmes or life, neither is he much hindred for the time in his fight, as long as the bloud is hot: for example.

I haue knowne a Gẽtlemã hurt in Rapier fight, in nine or ten places through the bodie, armes, and legges, and yet hath continued in his fight, & afterward hath flaine the other, and come home and hath bene cured of all his *The blow cutteth* woũds without maime, & is yet liuing. But the blow be- *off the hand, the* ing ftrõgly made, taketh fomtimes cleane away the hand *arme, the leg, and* from the arme, hath manie times bene feene. Againe, *fometimes the* a full blow vpon the head or face with a fhort fharpe *head.* Sword, is moft commonly death. A full blow vpon the

necke, fhoulder, arme, or legge, indangereth life, cutteth off the veines, mufcles, and finewes, perifheth the
bones : thefe wounds made by the blow, in refpect of
perfect healing, are the loffe of limmes, or maimes incurable for euer.

And yet more for the blow:a ful blow vpon the head,
face, arme, leg, or legs, is death, or the partie fo wounded in the mercie of him that fhall fo wound him. For
what man fhall be able long in fight to ftand vp, either
to reuenge, or defend himfelfe, hauing the veines, mufcles, and finewes of his hand, arme, or leg cleane cut a-
funder? or being difmembred by fuch wound vpon the
face or head, but fhall be enforced therby, and through
He that giueth the loffe of bloud, the other a litle dallying with him, to
the firft wound yeeld himfelf, or leaue his life in his mercie?
with a ftrong
blow, commaun-   And for plainer deciding this cōtrouerfie betweene
deth the life of the blow and the thruft, confider this fhort note. The
the other.   blow commeth manie wayes, the thruft doth not fo. The
blow commeth a nearer way then a thruft moft com-
monly, and is therefore fooner done. The blow requireth the ftrength of a man to be warded; but the thruft
may be put by, by the force of a child. A blow vpon the
hand, arme, or legge is a maime incurable; but a thruft
in the hand, arme, or legge is to be recouered. The
blow hath manie parts to wound, and in euerie of
them commaundeth the life; but the thruft hath but a
few, as the bodie or face, and not in euerie part of
them neither.

Of

Of the difference betwixt the true fight & the falſe: wher-
in conſiſteth (the Principles being had with the di-
rection of the foure Gouernors) the whole
perfection of fight with all ma-
ner of weapons.

He true fights be theſe: whatſoeuer is [14]
done with the hand before the foot or
feet is true fight. The falſe fights be theſe:
whatſoeuer is done with the foot or feet
before the hand, is falſe, becauſe the hand
is ſwifter then the foot, the foot or feet being a ſlower
mouer then the hand: the hand in that maner of fight is
tied to the time of the foot or feet, and being tied thereto, hath loſt his freedome, and is made thereby as ſlow
in his motions as the foot or feet: and therfor that fight
is falſe.

Of euill orders or cuſtomes in our English Fĕce-ſchooles, &
of the old or ancient teaching of weapons, & things very
neceſſarie to be continued for the auoiding of er-
rors, and reuiuing and continuance of our
ancient vveapons, and moſt victo-
rious fight againe.

Here is in my opiniŏ in our Fence-ſchooles [15]
an euill order or cuſtome in theſe dayes v-
ſed, the which, if it might ſtand with the
good liking of our Maiſters of Defence, I
thinke it neceſſarie to be left: for as long as
it is vſed, it ſhall be hard to make a good Scholler.

That is this, at the fingle Sword, Sword and Dagger, &
Sword and Buckler, they forbid the thruft, & at the fingle Rapier, and Rapier & Dagger, they forbid the blow.
Either they are both together beft, or the thruft altogether beft, or the blow altogether beft. If the thruft be
beft, why do we not vfe it at the fingle Sword, Sword &
Dagger, & Sword and Buckler. If the blow be beft, why
do we not vfe it at the fingle Rapier, Rapier & Poinyard?
But knowing by the Art of Armes, that no fight is perfect without both blow and thruft, why do we not vfe
and teach both blow and thruft? But howfoeuer this we
dayly fee, that whē two meet in fight, whether they haue
skill or none, vnleffe fuch as haue tied thēfelues to that
boyifh, *Italian*, weake, imperfect fight, they both ftrike
and thruft, and how fhall he then do, that being much
taught in fchoole, neuer learned to ftrike, nor how to
defend a ftrong blow? & how fhall he thē do, that being
brought vp in Fēce-fchoole, that neuer learned to thruft
with the fingle Sword, Sword and Dagger, and Sword
and Buckler, nor how at thefe weapōs to breake a thruft?
Surely, I thinke a downe right fellow, that neuer came
in fchoole, vfing fuch skill as nature yeeldeth out of his
courage, ftrength, and agilitie, with good downe right
blowes and thrufts among, as fhall beft frame in his
hands, fhold put one of thefe imperfect fchollers greatly to his fhifts. Befides, there are now in thefe dayes no
gripes, clofes, wreftlings, ftriking with the hilts, daggers, or bucklers, vfed in Fence-fchooles. Our plough-
men by nature wil do all thefe things with great ftrēgth
& agility: but the Schooleman is altogether vnacquainted with thefe things. He being faft tyed to fuch fchool-
play as he hath learned, hath loft thereby the benefite
of

of nature, and the plowman is now by nature without
art a farre better man then he. Therefore in my opinion,
as long as we barre anie maner of play in fchoole, we
fhall hardly make a good fcholler: there is no maner of
teaching comparable to the old ancient teaching, that
is, firft their quarters, then their wardes, blowes, thrufts,
and breaking of thruftes, then their Clofes and Gripes,
ftriking with the hilts, Daggers, Bucklers, Wraftlings,
ftriking with the foote or knee in the Coddes, and all
thefe are fafely defended in learning perfectly of the
Gripes. And this is the ancient teaching, the perfecteft *In the warres*
& moft beft teaching; and without this teaching, there *there is no obfer-*
fhall neuer fcholler be made able , doe his vttermoft , *tas, Imbrocatas,*
nor fight fafe. Againe their fwordes in fchooles are too *times, nor an-*
long by almoft halfe a foote to vncroffe, without going *fwers.*
backe with the feete , within diftance or perfectly to
ftrike or thruft within the halfe or quarter fword. And
in feruing of the Prince, when men do meet together in
publique fight , are vtterly naught and vnferuiceable.
The beft lengthes for perfect teaching of the true fight *Long weapons*
to be vfed and continued in Fence fchooles , to accord *imperfect.*
with the true ftatures of all men, are thefe. The blade to
be a yard and an inch for meane ftatures, and for men
of tall ftatures, a yard and three or foure inches, and no
more . And I would haue the Rapier continued in
fchooles, alwaies readie for fuch as fhall thinke themfelues cunning, or fhall haue delight to play with that
imperfect weapon. Prouided alwaies, that the Schoole-
maifter or Vfher play with him with his fhort Sword,
plying him with all maner of fight according to the
true art: this being continued the truth fhall flourifh,
the lye fhalbe beaten downe , and all nations not ha-

E

uing the true ſcience, ſhall come with all gladneſſe to
the valiant and moſt braue Engliſh maiſters of Defence
to learne the true fight for their defence.

The grounds or Principles of true fight with all maner of weapons.

16

Irſt Iudgement, Lyings, Diſtance, Direction, Paſe, Space, Place, Time, Indirection, Motion, Action, generall and continuall Motion , Progreſſion , Regreſſion ,
Trauerſing, and Treading of groundes,
Blowes, Thruſtes, Faulſes, Doubles, Slipes, Wardes,
breakings of Thruſts, Cloſings, Gripes, & Wraſtlings,
Guardant fight, Open fight, Variable fight, and Cloſe
fight, and foure Gouernours.

The wardes of all maner of weapons.

17

L ſingle weapons haue foure wardes, and
all double weapons haue eight wardes.
The ſingle ſword hath two with the point
vp, and two with the point downe. The
Staffe and all maner of weapons to be v-
ſed with both handes haue the like.

The Sword and Buckler, and Sword and Dagger are
double weapons, and haue eight wardes, two with the
point vp, and two with the point downe, and two for
the legges with the point downe, the point to be caried
for both ſides of the legges, with the knuckles downeward, and two wardes with the Dagger or Buckler for
the head. The Forreſt bill is a double weapon by reaſon
                                                        of

of the head, and therefore hath eight wardes, foure with
the Staffe, foure with the head, foure of them to be vſed
as with the ſtaffe, and the other foure with the head, the
one vp, the other downe, and the other ſidewaies.

The names and numbers of times appertaining vnto fight
both true and falſe.

Here are eight times, whereof foure are 18
true, and foure are falſe: the true times
be theſe.
The time of the hand.
The time of the hand and bodie.
The time of the hand, bodie and foote.
The time of the hand, bodie and feete.
The falſe times be theſe.
The time of the foote.
The time of the foote and bodie.
The time of the foote, bodie and hand.
The time of the feete, bodie and hand.

Thus haue I thought good to ſeparate and make
knowne the true times from the falſe, with the true
wardes thereto belonging, that thereby the rather in
practiſing of weapons, a true courſe may be taken for
the auoiding of errours and euill cuſtomes, and ſpeedie
attaining of good habit or perfect being in the true vſe
and knowledge of all maner of weapons.

Of the length of weapons, and how euerie man may fit him-
ſelfe in the perfect length of his weapon, accor-
ding to his owne ſtature, with briefe rea-
ſons wherefore they ought to be ſo.
E 2

19 **T**O know the perfect length of your Sword, you fhall ftand with your fword and dagger drawn, as you fee this picture, keeping out ftraight your dagger arme, drawinge backe your fword as far as conueniently you can, not opening the elbow ioynt of your fword arme: and looke what you can draw within your dagger, that is the iuft length of your fword, to be made according to your owne ftature.

If the fword be longer, you can hardly vncroffe without going backe with your feet. If fhorter, thē you can hardly make a true croffe without putting in of your feet, the which times are too long to anfwer the time of the hand.

The like reafons for the fhort ftaffe, half Pike, Forreft bill, Partifan, or Gleue, or fuch like weapons of perfect length.

The perfect length of your two hand fword is, the blade to be the length of the blade of your fingle fword.

To know the perfect length of your fhort ftaffe, or half Pike, Forreft bil, Partifan, or Gleue, or fuch like weapons of vantage and perfect lengths, you fhall ftand vpright, holding the ftaffe vpright clofe by your body, with your left hãd, reaching with your right hand your ftaffe as high as you can, and then allow to that length a fpace to fet both your hands, when you come to fight, wherein you may conueniently ftrike, thruft, and ward, & that is the iuft length to be made according to your ftature. And this note, that thefe lengths will commonly fall out to be eight or nine foot long, and will fit, although not iuft, the ftatures of all men, without any hindrance at all vnto them in their fight, becaufe in any weapon wherin the hands may be remoued, and at libertie, to make the weapon lõger or fhorter in fight at his pleafure, a foot of the ftaffe behind the backmoft hand doth no harme. And wherfore thefe weapons ought to be of the lengths aforefaid, and no fhorter, thefe are the reafons: If they fhould be fhorter, then the long ftaffe, Morris Pike, and fuch like weapons ouer and aboue the perfect length, fhould haue great vantage againft them, becaufe he may come boldly and fafe without anie gard or ward, to the place where he may thruft home, and at euery thruft put him in danger of his life: but if thefe weapons be of their perfect lengths, then can the long ftaffe, the Morris Pike, or anie other longer weapon ly nowhere in true fpace, but fhall be ftill within compaffe of the croffe, to croffe and vncroffe, wherby he may fafely paffe home to the place, where he may ftrike or thruft him that hath the long weapon, in the head, face, or body at his pleafure.

E 3

Of the lengths of the Battel axe, Halbard, or blacke Bill,
or such like vveapons of weight, appertaining
vnto gard or battell.

20   N anie of thefe weapons there needeth
no iuſt length, but commonly they are, or
ought to be fiue or fixe foot long, & may
not well be vſed much longer, becauſe of
their weights: and being weapons for the
warres or battell, when men are ioyned cloſe together,
may thruſt, & ſtrike ſound blowes, with great force both
ſtrong and quicke: and finally for the iuſt lengths of all
other ſhorter or longer weapons to be gouerned with
both hands, there is none: neither is there anie certaine
lengthes in anie maner of weapons to be vſed with one
hand, ouer or vnder the iuſt length of the ſingle ſword.
Thus endeth the length of weapons.

Of the vantages of weapons in their kinds, places, & times,
both in priuate and publike fight.

21   Irſt I will begin with the worſt weapon,
an imperfect and inſufficient weapon,
and not worth the ſpeaking of; but now
being highly eſteemed, therefore not to
be left vnremembred; that is, the ſingle
Rapier, and Rapier and Poiniard.

The ſingle Sword hath the vantage againſt the ſingle Rapier.

The Sword and Dagger hath the vantage againſt the
Rapier and Poiniard.

                            The

The Sword & Target hath aduātage againſt the Sword
and Dagger, or Rapier and Poiniard.

The Sword and Buckler hath aduantage againſt the
Sword and Target, the Sword and Dagger, or Rapier
and Poiniard.

The two hand Sword, hath the vantage againſt the
Sword and Target, the Sword and Buckler, the Sword
and Dagger, or Rapier and Poiniard.

The Battel-axe, the Halbard, the Blacke-bill, or ſuch
like weapons of weight, appertaining vnto guard or battell, are all one in fight, and haue aduantage againſt the
two hand Sword, the Sword and Buckler, the Sword and
Target, the Sword & dagger, or the Rapier & Poiniard.

The ſhort ſtaffe or halfe Pike, Forreſt-bill, Partiſan,
or Gleue, or ſuch like weapons of perfeċt length, haue
the vantage againſt the Battel-axe, the Halbard, the
Blacke-bill, the two hand ſword, the Sword and Target,
and are too hard for two Swords and Daggers, or two
Rapiers and Poiniards with Gantlets, and for the long
ſtaffe and Morris Pike.

The long Staffe, Morris Pike, or Iauelin, or ſuch like
weapons aboue the perfeċt length, haue aduantage a-
gainſt all maner of weapons, the ſhort ſtaffe, Welch
hooke, Partiſan, or Gleue, or ſuch like weapons of vantage excepted: yet too weake for two Swords and Daggers or two Swords and Bucklers, or two Rapiers and
Poiniards with Gantlets, becauſe they are too long to
thruſt, ſtrike, and turne ſpeedily: and by reaſon of the
large diſtance, one of the Sword and Dagger-men will
get behind him.

The Welch hooke or Forreſt bill, hath aduantage a-
gainſt all maner of weapons whatſoeuer.

Yet vnderſtand, that in battels ,and where varietie of weapons be, amongſt multitudes of men and horſes ,the Sword and Target, the two hand Sword, the Battel-axe, the Blacke-bill, and Halbard, are better weapons , and more dangerous in their offence and forces , then is the Sword and Buckler, ſhort ſtaffe , long ſtaffe, or Forreſt bill. The Sword and Target leadeth vpon Shot , and in troupes defendeth thruſts and blowes giuen by battel-axe, Halbards, Blacke-bill, or two hand ſwords, far better then can the Sword and Buckler.

The Morris Pike defendeth the battell from both horſe and man , much better then can the ſhort ſtaffe, long ſtaffe, or Forreſt bill. Againe, the Battel-axe , the Halbard, the Blacke bill, the two hand ſword, and Sword & Target, amongſt armed men and troupes, when men are come together , by reaſon of their weights, ſhort-neſſe, and great forces , do much more offend the ene-mie, & are then much better weapons, then is the ſhort ſtaffe, the long Staffe, or Forreſt bill.

Of the inſufficiencie and diſaduantages of the Rapiers-fight in Battell.

22 FOr the ſingle Rapier, or Rapier & Poiniard, they are imperfect & inſufficient weapons: and eſpecially in the ſeruice of the Prince, when men ſhall ioyne together, what ſer-uice can a ſouldier do with a Rapier, a chil-diſh toy wherwith a man can do nothing but thruſt, nor that neither, by reaſon of the length, and in euerie mo-uing when blowes are a dealing , for lacke of a hilt is in daunger to haue his hand or arme cut off, or his head clouen ?

clouen . And for Wardes and Gripes, they haue none,
neither can any of thefe fine Rapier men, for lacke of vfe,
tell howe to ftrike a found blow.

Of the vantages and fufficiencie of the short Sword fight in battell.

He fhort Sword, and Sword and Dagger, 23
are perfect good weapons , and efpecially
in feruice of the Prince. What a braue weapon is a fhort fharpe light Sword, to carie,
to draw, to be nimble withall, to ftrike, to cut, to thruft
both ftrong and quicke. And what a goodly defence is a
ftrong fingle hilt , when men are cluftering and hurling
together , efpecially where varietie of weapons bé , in
their motions to defend the hand , head, face, and bodies , from blowes, that fhalbe giuen fometimes with
Swordes, fometimes with two handed Swordes, battell
Axe, Halbardes , or blacke Billes , and fometimes men
fhalbe fo neare together , that they fhall haue no fpace,
fcarce to vfe the blades of their Swordes belowe their
waftes, then their hilts (their handes being aloft) defendeth from the blowes, their handes, armes, heads, faces,
and bodies : then they lay on, hauing the vfe of blowes
and Gripes , by force of their armes with their hilts,
ftrong blowes, at the head , face , armes , bodies , and
fhoulders, and manie times in hurling together , fcope
is giuen to turne downe their points, with violent thrufts
at their faces, and bodies, by reafon of the fhortneffe
of their blades, to the mightie annoyance , difcomfort ,
and great deftruction of their enimies. One valiant man
with a Sword in his hand , will doe better feruice , then
ten *Italians*, or Italienated with the Rapiers.

F

*That all maner of double weapons, or weapons to be vſed
with both handes, haue aduantage againſt the ſingle Rapier or ſingle Sword, there is no
queſtion to be made.*

That the Sword and Buckler hath the vantage a-
gainſt the Sword and Dagger.

24   He Dagger is an imperfect ward , although borne out ſtraight , to make the
Space narrow, whereby by a litle mouing
of the hand, may be ſufficient to ſaue both
ſides of the head , or to breake the thruſt
from the face or body, yet for lacke of the circumference
his hand will lie too high or too low, or too weake, to defend both blow and thruſt: if he lye ſtraight with narrow
ſpace, which is beſt to breake the thruſt, then he lieth too
weake, and too lowe to defend his head from a ſtrong
blow : if he lye high , that is ſtrong to defend his head,
but then his ſpace wilbe too wide to breake the thruſt
from his bodie . The Dagger ſerueth well at length to
put by a thruſt , and at the halfe Sword to croſſe the
Sword blade , to driue out the Agent, and put him in
danger of his life, and ſafely in anie of theſe two actions
to defend himſelfe. But the Buckler, by reaſon of his circumference and weight, being well caried, defendeth
ſafely in all times and places, whether it be at the point,
haife Sword, the head, bodie, and face, from all maner
of blowes and thruſtes whatſoeuer, yet I haue heard manie hold opinion, that the Sword and Dagger hath aduantage of the Sword and Buckler, at the Cloſe, by reaſon of the length and point of the Dagger : and at the
point

point of the Sword , they can better fee to ward then
with a Buckler . But I neuer knew anie, that wanne the
Clofe with the Dagger vpon the Sword and Budkler,
but did wifh himfelfe out againe:for diftance being broken, iudgement faileth, for lacke of time to iudge , and
the eie is deceiued by the fwift motion of the hand, and
for lacke of true Space with the dagger hand,which cannot be otherwife , for lacke of the circumference to defend both blow and thruft , it is impoffible for lacke of
true Space in iuft time , the agent hauing gotten the
true place, to defend one thruft or blow of an hundred .
And it is moft certaine, whofoeuer clofeth with Sword
and Dagger, againft the Sword and Buckler , is in great
danger to be flaine . Likewife at the point within diftance, if he ftand to defend both blow and thruft with
his Dagger , for lacke of true fpace and diftance , if he
had the beft eye of anie man, and could fee perfectly ,
which way the thruft or blow commeth , and when it
commeth , as it is not to be denied but he may, yet his
fpace being too large, it helpeth him nothing, becaufe
one mans hand being as fwift as another mans hand ,
both being within diftance, he that ftriketh or thrufteth,
hurteth the warder: the reafon is this : the Agent being
in the firft motion although in his offence , further to go
then the warder to defend , yet the warders fpace being
too large, the blow or thruft wilbe performed home,be-
fore the warder can come to the true plaee to defend
himfelfe, and although the warder doe perfectly fee the
blow or thruft comming,fo fhall he fee his owne ward fo
farre from the true place of his defence , that although
he doe at that inftant time,plainly fee the blow or thruft
comming, it fhalbe impoffible for him to recouer the

F 2

true place of his ward, till he be wounded. But let the warder with the dagger ſay , that it is not true which I haue ſaid,for as he hath eies to behold the blow or thruſt cōming,ſo hath he as good time to defend himſelf.Herein he ſhal find himſelf deceiued to; this is the reaſon:the hand is the ſwifteſt motion, the foot is the ſloweſt, without diſtance the hand is tied to the motion of the feet, wherby the time of the hand is made as ſlow as the foot, becauſe thereby we redeeme euerie time loſt vpon his comming by the ſlow motion of the foot, & haue time therby to iudge , whē & how he can performe any actiō whatſoeuer , and ſo haue we the time of the hand to the time of the feet.Now is the hād in his owne courſe more ſwifter then the foot or eye,therfore within diſtance the eye is deceiued,& iudgement is loſt; and that is another cauſe that the warder with the dagger,although he haue *The eye is decei-* perfect eyes, is ſtil within diſtance deceiued. For proofe *ued by the ſwift* that the hand is more ſwifter then the eye,& thereby de-*motion of the hād.* ceiueth the eyes:let two ſtand within diſtance,& let one of thē ſtand ſtill to defend himſelf,& let the other floriſh & falſe with his hand, and he ſhall continually with the ſwift motions of his hand, deceiue the eyes of him that ſtandeth watching to defend himſelfe, & ſhal continually ſtrike him in diuerſe places with his hand.Againe,take this for an example, that the eyes by ſwift motions are deceiued:turne a turne-wheele ſwift,& you ſhall not be able to diſcerne with your beſt eies how many ſpokes be in the wheele,no nor whether there be any ſpokes at all, or whereof the wheele is made,and yet you ſee when the wheele ſtandeth ſtill there is a large diſtance betweene euerie ſpoke.He that will not beleeue that the ſwift motion of the hand in fight will deceiue the eye, ſhal ſtare abroad

broad with his eyes,& feele himſelf ſoundly hurt,before
he ſhall perfectly ſee how to defend himſelfe. So thoſe
that truſt to their ſight,the excellēcy of a good eye,their
great cunning, & perfect wards of the daggers,that they
can better ſee to ward then with a buckler,ſhall euer be
deceiued. And whē they be wounded,they ſay the Agēt
was a litle too quicke for them;ſometimes they ſay they
bare their dagger a litle too low : ſometimes they are
thruſt vnder the dagger,then they ſay,they bare it a litle
too high :ſometimes a thruſt being ſtrongly made , they
being ſoundly paid therewith, ſay, they were a litle too
ſlow,& ſometimes they be ſoundly paid with a thruſt,&
they thinke they were a litle too quick.So they that practiſe or thinke to be cunning in the dagger ward, are all
the dayes of their liues learning,and are neuer taught.

The Dagger is an
imperfect ward.

That the Sword and Buckler hath the vantage
against the Sword and Target.

He Sword & Target together hath but two **25**
fights;that is, the variable fight, & the cloſe
fight,for the cloſe fight, the nūber of his feet
are too many to take againſt any mā of skill
hauing the Sword & buckler,& for the variable fight although not ſo many in number,yet too many to win the
place with his foot to ſtrike or thruſt home.The ſword &
buckler-man can out of his variable,opē & gardāt fight,
come brauely off & on, falſe and double, ſtrike & thruſt
home , & make a true croſſe vpon euery occaſion at his
pleaſure:if the Sword & Target mā will flie to his gardāt
fight, the bredth of his Target will not ſuffer it , if to his
open fight,thē hath the Sword & Buckler man in effect
the ſword and Buckler to the ſingle , for in that fight by
reaſon of the bredth,the target can do litle good or none
at all.   **F 3**

Ow for the vantage of the ſhort Staffe a-
gainſt the Sword and Buckler , Sword &
26   Target, two hand ſword , ſingle Sword,
Sword and Dagger , or Rapier and Poiniard, there is no great queſtion to be
made in anie of theſe weapons: whenſoeuer anie blow
or thruſt ſhall be ſtrongly made with the ſtaffe, they are
euer in falſe place, in the cariage of the wards, for if at a-
ny of theſe ſixe weapons he carie his ward high & ſtrõg
for his head , as of neceſſitie he muſt carie it verie high,
otherwiſe it will be too weake to defend a blow being
ſtrongly made at the head , then will his ſpace be too
wide, in due time to breake the thruſt from his bodie.
Againe, if he carie his ward lower , thereby to be in e-
quall ſpace for readineſſe to breake both blow & thruſt,
then in that place his ward is too low, and too weake to
defend the blow of the ſtaffe: for the blow being ſtrongly
made at the head vpon that ward , will beate downe the
ward and his head together, and put him in great danger of his life. And here is to be noted, that if he fight
well , the ſtaffe-man neuer ſtriketh but at the head , and
thruſteth preſently vnder at the body : and if a blow be
firſt made, a thruſt followeth ; & if a thruſt be firſt made,
a blow followeth ; and in doing of any of them , the one
breedeth the other : ſo that howſoeuer anie of theſe ſixe
weapons ſhall carie his ward ſtrongly to defend the firſt,
he ſhall be too farre in ſpace to defend the ſecond, whether it be blow or thruſt.

    Yet againe for the ſhort ſtaffe: the ſhort ſtaffe hath
the vantage againſt the Battel-axe, blacke-bill, or Halbard,

bard: the fhort ftaffe hath the vantage, by reafon of the nimbleneffe and length: he will ftrike and thruft freely, and in better and fwifter time then can the Battel-axe, Blacke-bill, or Halbard: and by reafon of his iudgement, diftance and time, fight fafe. And this refolue vpon, the fhort ftaffe is the beft weapon againft all maner of weapons, the Forreft bill excepted.

Alfo the fhort ftaffe hath aduantage againft two Swords and Daggers, or two Rapiers, Poiniards and Gantlets, the reafons and caufes before are for the moft part fet downe already, the which being well confide-red, you fhall plainely fee, that whenfoeuer anie one of the Sword & Dagger men, or Rapier and Poiniard men fhall breake his diftance, or fuffer the Staffe-man to breake his, that man which did firft breake his diftace, or fuffer the diftance to be won againft him, is prefently in danger of death. And this canot in reafon be denied, be-caufe the diftance appertaining to the Staffe-man, either to keepe or breake, ftandeth vpon the mouing of one large fpace alwayes at the moft, both for his offence or fafety. The other two in the breach of their diftance to offend the Staffe-man, haue alwayes foure paces at the leaft therin they fall too great in number with their feet, and too fhort in diftance to offend the Staffe-man. Now there refteth no more to be fpoken of, but how the Staffe-man fhall behaue himfelfe to keepe that diftance, that one of the Sword & Dagger men get not behind him, while the other fhal bufie him before: to do that is very eafie, by reafon of the fmal nuber of his feet, for by a verie fmall turning of his feet, as it were in the Center point of a wheele, the other two to keepe their diftance, are driuen to runne twentie foote for one, as it

The fhort ftaffe or half Pike hath the aduantage a-gainft two fword and dagger men, or two Rapiers, Poiniards, and Gantlets.

were vpon the vttermoſt part or circle of the wheele : all this while the Staffe-man is verie well. Then it commeth thus to paſſe, whether they both labour to get behind him, or one keepe directly before him whileſt the other get behind him , yet before that be brought to paſſe, they ſhal either be both before him or iuſt againſt both ſides of him: at which time ſoeuer the Staffe-man finding either of them within diſtance, he preſently in making of his play, ſlayeth with blow or thruſt one of thē, or at the leaſt putteth him in great danger of his life. If the Staffe-man take his time , when they are both before him , that is to ſay, before they come to the half ring, iuſt againſt both ſides of the Staffe-man , then he that is neareſt within diſtance is ſlain by blow or thruſt, or put in great danger of his life. But if the Sword and Dagger men do keepe their diſtance vntill they come to the iuſt halfe ring right againſt the ſides of the Staffe-man, and then breake diſtance, that man that firſt breaketh diſtance is ſlaine with blow or thruſt, or ſore hurt, and in great danger of death: and the Staffe-man in making that play at that inſtant, muſt turne with one large pace, the which he may eaſily do , before the other can get neare enough to offend him , by reaſon that he hath to make with his feet but one large pace , but the other hath at the leaſt three paces. But if the Sword and Dagger-men will in the time that they be before him, keep their diſtance in the time of their being vpon the middle part of the outſide of the circle, right againſt both ſides of him, & will labor with all heed & diligence to be both or one of thē behind him , that troubleth the Staffe-man nothing at all, for in that very time, when he findeth them paſt the middle part of the circle, he preſently

sently turneth, by the which he shall naturally set himselfe as it were in a triangle , and both the sword and
dagger-men, shall thereby stand both before him in true
distance of three paces , from offending of him at the
least , as at the first they did. And take this for a true
ground, there is no man able to ward a sound blow
with the Sword and Dagger, nor Rapier, Poinyard, and
Gantlet, being strongly made at the head , with the
Staffe , and run in withall, the force of both handes is
such, being in his full motion and course, that although
the other do carie his ward high and strong with both
handes, yet his feete being mouing from the ground ,
the great force of the blow will strike him with his ward,
and all downe flat to ground. But if he stand fast with
his feete, he may with both weapons together, strongly
defend his head from the blow, but then you are sufficiently instructed, the thrust being presently made , after
the blow full at the bodie, it is impossible in due time to
breake it, by reason of the largenesse of his space.

*The short Staffe hath the vantage against the long staffe,
and Morris Pike, and the Forrest bill against all
maner of weapons.*

He reasons are these . The short Staffe 27
hath the vantage of the long Staffe and
Morris Pike in his strength & narrownes
of space in his foure wardes of defence.
And the Forrest bill hath the vantage of
all maner of weapons in his strength and narrownes of
space in his eight wardes of defence: and the rather because the Bill hath two wardes for one against the Staffe

G

or Morris Pike, that is to say, foure with the Staffe, and foure with the head, and is more offensiue then is the Staffe or Morris Pike: yet a questiõ may be made by the vnskilfull, concerning the fight between the long Staffe *A queſtion.* and the ſhort , in this ſort: Why ſhould not the long Staffe haue aduantage againſt ſhort Staffe, ſince that the long Staffe-man, being at libertie with his handes, may make his long Staffe both long and ſhort for his beſt aduantage , when he ſhall thinke it good , and therefore when he ſhall find himſelfe ouermatched in the length of his Staffe, by the ſtrength of the ſhort Staffe, and narrowneſſe of ſpace in his foure wardes of defence, he can preſently by drawing backe of his Staffe in his handes , make his Staffe as ſhort as the others , and ſo be readie *Anſwere.* to fight with him at his owne length. To this I anſwere, that when the long Staffe-man is driuen there to lye, the length of his Staffe that will lye behind him, will hinder him to ſtrike, thruſt , ward , or goe backe in due time. Neither can he turne the contrarie end of his Staffe to keepe out the ſhort Staffe man from the Cloſe, nor ſafely to defend himſelfe at his comming in.

Againe of the vantages of weapons.

28 Ake this for a general rule, all long Staues, Morris Pikes, Forreſt bils , Iauelins , or ſuch like long weapons, of what ſort ſoeuer , being aboue the true lengthes , the ſhorteſt haue the aduantage , becauſe they can croſſe and vncroſſe in ſhorter time then can the longer: and all maner of ſhort weapons to be vſed with both handes, as ſtaues, and ſuch like, being vnder the perfect lengthes, the

the longeſt haue the aduantage , and all maner of weapons to be vſed with one hand, that are aboue the perfect length of the ſingle Sword, the ſhorteſt haue the vantage, and all maner of weapons vnder the iuſt length of the ſhort Sword, as Fauchions, Skaines, or Hangers, Woodkniues, Daggers, and ſuch like ſhort weapons of imperfect lengthes, the longeſt haue the aduantage, becauſe the fight of theſe weapons conſiſt within the halfe or quarter Sword, wherein by the ſwift motions of their handes, their eyes are deceiued , and in thoſe weapons, commonly for their handes lieth no defence. And if two ſhall fight with ſtaues or Swordes, or what weapons ſoeuer, the one of them hauing his weapon longer then the perfect length, and the other his weapon ſhorter then the perfect length, he that hath the longeſt hath the vantage, becauſe the ſhorteſt can make no true Croſſe in true time. The ſhort Staffe or halfe Pike, Forreſt bill, Partiſan , or Gleue , or ſuch like weapons of perfect length , to be vſed with both handes , haue the aduantage againſt two Swordes and Daggers , or two Rapiers, Poiniardes, and Gantlets, and againſt all other weapons whatſoeuer, the Forreſt bill excepted.

Againe for the short Staffe or halfe Pike.

He ſhort Staffe is moſt commonly the 29 beſt weapon of all other , although other weapons may be more offenſiue, and eſpecially againſt manie weapons together, by reaſon of his nimbleneſſe and ſwift motions , and is not much inferiour to the Forreſt bill, although the Forreſt bill be more offenſiue, and hath more wardes , becauſe

G 2

the Staffe is verie vncertaine , but the Bill is a more certaine marke, by reafon of the breadth of the head, wherby as the Bill hath aduantage in his wardes in the head, fo therefore hath the Staffe the like defence, or rather more, to play vpon the head of the Bill , not onely to make a perfect good ward, but thereby, the rather to caft the Bill out of the right line, whereby the Staffe-man may thruft fafe, and endanger the Bill-man : and the rather becaufe therein he is the firft mouer, wherin there is great vantage, both in time and force. And if the Bilman be not very skilfull (all vantages and difaduantages of both fides confidered,) the fhort Staffe will proue the better weapon. Laftly note this, that long Staues, Morris Pikes, and fuch like weapons of imperfect lengthes, being to be vfed with both hands, notwithftanding their imperfect lengthes, are perfect weapons to be vfed, the one againft the other , and their fightes therein perfect, becaufe in drawing of them backe betwixt their handes, their motions are fwifter backewardes, then is the time of the Agents feet forwardes, by the which all their loft times are redeemed : therefore thefe weapons in their fightes, the one againft the other are perfect. And thefe weapons in the night are the beft weapons of all other, and haue great aduantage againft the forreft Bill , fhort Staffe, or anie maner of fhort weapons whatfoeuer : for thefe caufes, they boldly make home their fightes , and if neede be againft defperate men , that will venture themfelues to run in, they redeeme their loft times. But the other with fhorter weapons for lacke of light, can make no true defence. Thus endeth the vantages of weapons.

Note this.

Queftions

542

Queſtions and anſwers betweene the Scholler and the Mai-
ſter, of the vantages and diſaduantages betweene a
tall man, and a man of meane ſtature, hauing
both the perfeƈt knowledge in
their weapons.

Scholler.

Ho hath the aduantage in fight, of a tall 30
man, or a man of meane ſtature?

Maiſter.

The tall man hath the vantage , for
theſe cauſes : his reach being longer, and
weapon vnto his ſtature accordingly , he hath thereby a
ſhorter courſe with his feet to win the true place, wherin by the ſwift motion of his hand , he may ſtrike or
thruſt home: in the which time a man of meane ſtature
cannot reach him, & by his large pace , in his true pace
in his regreſſion further , ſetteth himſelf out of all danger, & theſe are the vantages that a tall man hath againſt
anie man of ſhorter reach then himſelfe.

Tall men haue the
vantage againſt
men of meane
ſtature.

Scholler.

What vantage hath a man of meane ſtature againſt
a tall man?

Maiſter.

He hath none : becauſe the true times in fight, and a-
ƈtions accordingly, are to be obſerued and done, as well
by a tall man, as by a man of meane ſtature.

Scholler.

Why then if this be true , that tall men haue the vantage againſt mē of meane ſtature, it ſhold ſeeme in fight

G 3

there is no perfection, other then this, when men of like ftature, reach, & length of weapon, fhall fight together, the which will feldome or neuer happen, but either in the length of their weapons, ftatures or reaches (if their fwords fhould be of iuft length) fome difference moft commonly there will be in their reaches.

Maifter.

Yes verily, the tall man hath ftill the vantage, and yet the fight is perfect, although the men that fhall happen to fight, fhall happē to be vnequall in their ftatures, reaches, or lengths of their weapons.

Scholler.

That can I hardly beleeue, vnleffe you can tell me by Art how to auoid or fafely defend my felfe, being but a man of meane ftature, againft a tall man.

Maifter.

I will tell you : there belongeth vnto this Art of defence onely to be vfed with the feet, progreffion, regreffion, trauerfing, and treading of grounds: in any of thefe you playing the part of the Patient, or Patient Agent, your feete are fwifter in their motions then are the Agents, becaufe his weight and number of his feet in his comming to win the true place to ftrike or thruft home, are greater then yours, and therefore the true time is yours to auoid him, or fafely to defend your felfe: fo the Art is ftill true, and the tall man hath ftill the vantage.

Scholler.

Yet I am not fully fatisfied herein, becaufe you tell me ftill that the tall man hath the vantage, and notwithftanding you fay the Art is true, wherein then hath the tall man the vantage, when by your Art you can defend your felfe againft him.

Maifter.

Maifter.

I will fatisfie you therein thus. The tall man hath the
vantage, he can maintaine his fight, both by nature and
Art , with more eafe then can the man of meane ftature , becaufe the man of meane ftature hath thereby a further courfe with his feete to paffe to the place,
wherein he may ftrike or thruft home , and in winning
of that place , is driuen by Art to come garded vnder his wards to defend himfelfe, becaufe in the time of
his comming , the tall man may both naturally or artifi-
cially ftrike or thruft home, in the which time, if the mā
of meane ftature fhould faile in the leaft iote of his Art,
he fhould be in great daunger of death or hurt. But the
tall man can naturally and fafely come to the true place
open, without any artificiall wards at all, and therein alfo endanger the other, or driue him ftill to trauerfe his
ground, with all the artificiall skill that he hath to defend himfelfe; and all this the tall man doth by reafon
of his length of weapon, large pace , fhort courfe, and
long reach, with great fafetie, pleafure and eafe. And for
thofe caufes the tall man hath ftill the vantage of men of
meane ftature, and yet notwitftāding the noble Science
of Defence moft perfect and good.

Foure inuincible
aduantages con-
fift in a tall man
againft a man
of meane ftature.
Long reach.
Short courfe.
Length of weapõ.
Large pace.

Of the long fingle Rapier fight betweene valiant men, ha-
uing both skill , he that is the beft wraftler, or if nei-
ther of them can wraftle , the ftrongeft man
moft commonly killeth the other, or lea-
ueth him at his mercie.

Hen two valiant men of skill at fingle Ra- 31
pier do fight , one or both of them moft cōmonly ftanding vpon their ftrength or skill
in wraftling, will prefently feeke to run into

the clofe ; but hauing both skill , not without fpeciall
care of their gard or croffe, the which they may fafely
do, by reafon of the length of their Rapiers : but hapning
both of one mind , the rather do bring themfelues together : that being done, no skil with Rapiers auaileth,they
prefently grapple faft their hilts , wrifts, armes , bodies
or neckes, as in luftring, wraftling, or ftriuing together,
they may beft find for their aduantages : wherby it moft
commonly falleth out, that he that is the beft wraftler,
or ftrongeft man (if neither of them can wraftle) ouercommeth, wrefting by ftrength , or fine skill in wraftling, the Rapier from his aduerfarie , or cafting him frō
him, either to the ground, or to fuch diftance, that he
may by reafon therof, vfe the edge or point of his rapier,
to ftrike or thruft him , leauing him dead or aliue at his
mercie. But if but one of thefe valiant men fhall feeke to
run into the clofe , and that the other fhall vfe his skill
in trauerfing of his ground , or otherwife by ftanding
vpon his gard or *Stocata* ward , to take all maner of adua-
tages at his cōming, yet all auaileth him not, becaufe the
Rapiers being long, the croffing of the blades cannot
be auoided : that being made , the oppreffor runneth
fafter forwards then can the defendant backwards , and
fo are brought together, as in the firft affault they were,
& euerie action therein accordingly performed.

Of the Rapier and Poiniard-fight betwixt valiant men, hauing both skill.

32   I F two valiant men do fight at Rapier and Poiniard hauing both skill, one or both of them
will prefently preffe hard to winne the place,
wherein in his iudgement he may thruft home. If both
be

be of one mind , the time is doubled in winning the
fame : whereby it commeth to paffe , that then he that
firft thrufteth, endangereth, killeth or hurteth the other:
and if they both thruft together , as they may do by the
equall time of their feet , then they are moft commonly both flaine , or both hurt. And this is well knowne
vnto all men of skill , that the place being once gotten,
there is neither iudgement, fpace, pace, nor time, either
by wards with their Rapier blades, or by breaking with
their Poiniards , or flying backe , that can preferue or
defend them . But if but one of them will feeke to win
by paffage, hard preffing, or otherwife the place, wherin
in his iudgement he may thruft home , it is impoffible
for the other to denie him the fame , becaufe the length
of the Rapiers winneth him the croffe ; the croffe being
taken, the place is had ; the place being had, he that firft
thrufteth, firft fpeedeth : if both thruft together, they are
both in danger : the prefently followeth (vnleffe it pleafe
God otherwife to haue it) the ftabs with their daggers,
wherein there lieth no defence.

Of the long Rapier & Poiniard-fight betweene two valiant
men, the one hauing skil, the other none : that he that
hath no skill hath the vantage.

Hen two valiant men fhal fight with lõg 33
Rapiers and Poiniards , the one hauing
skill , and the other none, he that hath no
skill moft commõly proueth himfelf the
better mã, for thefe caufes or reafons following. Firft the skilfull man as knowing the other to
haue no skill , or finding it to be fo by his fhape or

H

maner of comming towardes him , will prefently yeeld
to take the aduantage of his comming , or elfe with all
fpeed put himfelfe into his fhort ward , to be readie at
his comming to make out a ftrong *Stocata* (as the *Italians* call it:) the other knowing his imperfection in
fight , affureth himfelfe there can be no great good for
him to ftand long out at the point, prefently redoubleth
or reuiueth his fpirits with perfect refolution , to make
fhort worke, couragioufly with fome offenfiue action ,
fuch as nature fhall beft yeeld vnto him, flieth in with all
force and agilitie : the skilfull man ftandeth watching to
take fuch aduantages as his fchoolemaifter hath taught
him , in the which time , manie times it falleth out , he is
taught a new time, euen by an vnskilfull man that neuer
fought before , is fore hurt or flaine : and if it happen
they both miffe in their offenfiue actions , then by reafon thereof , and of the imperfect length of their Rapiers, they come to ftabbing with their Poiniards, wherin there lyeth no defence , becaufe diftance being broken, iudgement faileth , time is loft, and their eies (by the
fwift motions of their handes) are deceiued.

*Of the long fingle Rapier ,or Rapier and Poiniard-fight be-
tweene two vnskilfull men being valiant.*

34 Hen two vnskilfull men (being valiant)
fhall fight with long fingle Rapiers , there
is leffe danger in that kind of fight, by reafon of their diftance in conuenient length,
waight, and vnweildineffe , then is with fhort Rapiers:
whereby it commeth to paffe, that what hurt fhall happen to be done , if anie with the edge or point of their
Rapiers

Rapiers is done in a moment , and prefently will grapple and wraftle together, wherin moft commonly the ftrongeft or beft Wraftler ouercommeth, and the like fight falleth out betweene them, at the long Rapier and Poiniard , but much more deadly , becaufe in ftead of Clofe and Wraftling, they fall moft commonly to ftabbing with their Poiniardes.

Of the imperfection and infufficiencie of Rapiers in generall, of what length foeuer they be.

F two fight with long Rapiers , vpon euerie Croffe made within the halfe Rapier, if they haue Poiniardes, they moft commonly ftabbe each other, which cannot be auoided , becaufe the Rapiers being long, the Croffe cannot be vndone of either fide , without going backe with their feete , the which likewife in due time cannot be done , becaufe the hand is more fwifter then the feete,and the feete more fwifter in their courfe forwardes then backwardes, neither can the Croffe be preuented , becaufe the point of neceffitie lyeth too farre off in his offence,or elfe within compaffe of the true time of the hand and bodie, by reafon of his imperfect length: and fo by the like reafons, if two fight with long fingle Rapiers , vpon euerie Croffe made therewith, within the halfe Rapier, the Clofe cannot be auoided, wherby it commeth to paffe moft commonly , that the ftrongeft man or beft Wraftler ouercommeth . Now if two do fight with fhort Rapiers, or Rapiers of conuenient length , fuch Rapiers be inconuenient and infufficient alfo for lacke of an hilt to defend the hand and head from the blow; for no eie (in making a

35
If they ftand vpon breaking with their Daggers,he that firft winneth the place,and thrufteth home, hurteth the other for lacke of the circüference:if both thruft together, they are both fped,becaufe their Spaces of Defence are too wide to anfwere the time of the hand, and by the fwift motion thereof,the eye in that diftance is by the fame deceiued. The feete in their courfe , but not in the firft motion,alwaies note for the auoiding of great errours.

H 2

perfect ward for the head, to defend a blow, can difcerne to take the fame within three or foure inches, wherby it may as well and as often fall vpon the hand, as vpon the blade of the Rapier. Againe, the hilt as well ferueth to defend the head as the hand, and is a more fure and ftrong ward, then is the blade of the Rapier. And further, vnderftand this for truth, that in gardant and open fight, the hand without an hilt lieth open to moft blowes that fhalbe ftroken by the Agent, out of the gardant or open fight, becaufe in the true cariage of the gardant fight, the hand muft lie aboue the head, in fuch ftraightnes and narrownes of fpace, that which way foeuer the Agent fhall ftrike or thruft at the head, face, or bodie, the remouing of two or foure inches fhall faue all. And now fomewhat more for the fhortneffe or conuenient length of Rapiers.

Rapiers hauing no hilts to defend the head, the Rapier-man is driuen of neceffitie to lie at the variable fight or low ward, and being there he can neither defend in due time, head, face, nor bodie from the blowes or thruftes of him, that fhall fight out of the gardant or open fight, but is continually in great danger of the Agent, for thefe caufes following. Firft, becaufe his fpace is too wide to defend his head from blow or thruft. Secondly his Pace ftanding vpon that fight, wilbe of neceffitie too great or too narrow: if too narrow, too weak: if too large, his weight and number of his feet, are too great to endanger him, that is vpon his gardant or open fight.

Of

*Of the imperfection and insufficiencie of the fight of the
single Rapier, Rapier and Poiniard , Ra-
pier and Buckler, Rapier and
Cloke , and Rapier and
Gloue of maile.*

He Rapier fight , whether it be single or ac- 36
cõpanied with Poiniard, Buckler, cloke, or
gloue of male, is still by reason of the insufficiencie or imperfection of the Rapier, an
imperfect fight : vnperfect instruments can make no
perfect musicke, neither can vnperfect weapons make
perfect fight : let the men that handle them haue
all the knowledge that may be in all maner of weapons,
yea the full height, or perfection, and true habite by his
great labour and industry, euen as it were naturally effected in him , yet if the weapons that they shall fight
withall be imperfect or insufficient to performe whatsoeuer appertaineth vnto true fight , as concerning the
perfection of their safetie, it auaileth them nothing.
What shall we then say for the Rapier? Is the Rapier
an imperfect or insufficient weapon to perfourme
whatsoeuer appertaineth vnto the true fight? Yea:
Wherefore ? Because vnto the true fight there appertaineth foure fights, Gardant fight, Open fight, Variable fight , and Close fight : without all foure of these
fights it is impossible to fight safe: but the Rapier for
lacke of an hilt is an vnperfect weapon, and therefore
insufficient to fight safe vpon these foure fights, the
reasons are alreadie set downe in the Paradoxe before, but it is inferred to loose the benefit of two of the

H 3

beſt fights, gardant and open fight, and to flie from thē, and truſt only vnto variable fight, and cloſe fight. Now hauing proued through the imperfection or inſufficiencie of the Rapier, the imperfection of the Rapier fight, it remaineth that I ſpeake of the reſt of the weapons, or inſtruments appertaining vnto Rapier fight.

The Rapier and Poiniard fight, the Rapier & Buckler fight, the Rapier and cloke fight, & the Rapier & gloue of male fight: all theſe fights by reaſon of the imperfection of the Rapier, and Rapier fight, are all alſo imperfect fights: and for proofe of the vncertaintie and impoſſibilities of ſafetie in any of theſe fights, thus it ſtandeth. Theſe fights depend altogether vpō variable fight and cloſe fight: in anie of theſe fights it is impoſſible in true ſpace of Offence to keepe the blades of their Rapiers from croſſing, or frō breaking with the Poiniards, buckler, cloke, or breaking or catching with the gloue of male; becauſe in anie of theſe two fights, the Agent hath ſtill in true ſpace the blade of the Patients Rapier to worke vpon. Theſe things by letters cannot be made more plaine, neither is it vnknowne to the skilfull, or in fight by anie meanes to be auoided, the weapon being too farre in true ſpace to be wrought vpon, the place cannot be denied, do the patient Agent what he can for his life to the contrarie, either by blowes, thruſts, falſing, or doubling of thruſts, going backe, indirections, or turnings of the body, or what elſe ſoeuer may in the higheſt touch of wit or ſtrength, or agilitie of bodie be deuiſed or done, to keepe out the Agent: but ſtill the Agent by narrowneſſe of ſpace bringeth himſelf by ſtrōg gard to the place, where being brought, it is as impoſſible to fight ſafe, as it is for two deſperate men ſet together
ther

552

ther being both blind;becaufe in the true place (wonne
in Rapier or variable fight) their eyes by the fwift motions of their hands are deceiued , the croffes in that
fight are falfe, their diftance, iudgements and times are
loft,either to offend in fafetie, or fafely to defend themfelues : and thefe reafons, rules, or grounds of the feates
of armes are infallible and inuincible.

Now, ô you Italian teachers of Defence , where are
your *Stocatas, Imbrocatas ,Mandritas ,Puntas*, & *Puynta
reuerfas,Stramifons ,Paffatas,Carricados,Amazzas*, &*In-
cartatas*,& playing with your bodies , remouing with
your feet a litle afide,circle wife winding of your bodies,
making of three times with your feet together,marking
with one eye the motion of the aduerfary,&with the o-
ther eye the aduãtage of thrufting? What is become of
all thefe iugling gambalds , Apifh deuifes,with all the
reft of your fquint-eyed trickes , when as through your
deepe ftudies, long practifes, & apt bodies, both ftrong
& agilious, you haue attained to the height of all thefe
things?What then auaileth it you, when you fhal come
to fight for your liues with a man of skill?you fhall haue
neither time,nor place,in due time to performe any one
of them , nor gardant nor open fight fafely to keep out
a man of skill,a man of no skill, or fcholler of your owne
teaching, from the true place, the place of fafetie , the
place of vncertaintie or mifchiefe , the place of wounds
or death,but are there inforced to ftand in that mifchie-
uous, vncertaine, dangerous, and moft deadly place, as
two men hauing loft in part their chiefeft fences, moft
furioufly with their rapiers or poiniards , wounding or
flaying each other.

Thus endeth the imperfect fights of the rapier with

all maner of weapons or inſtruments thereto ap pertai-
ning, with their imperfections, through the true groūds
and rules of the Art of armes, truly diſplayed &brought
to light.

All laud be vnto the Almighty God.

*That the reaſons vſed by the Italian Fencers in commen-
ding the vſe of the Rapier and Poiniard, becauſe it
maketh peace, maketh againſt
themſelues.*

37   T hath bin commonly held, that ſince the
Italians haue taught the Rapier fight, by
reaſon of the dangerous vſe therof, it hath
bred great ciuilitie amongſt our Engliſh
nation, they will not now giue the lye, nor
with ſuch foule ſpeeches abuſe themſelues, therefore
there are fewer frayes in theſe times then were wont to
be: it cannot be denied but this is true, that we are more
circumſpect of our words, and more fearefull to fight,
then heretofore we haue bene. But whereof commeth
it ? Is it from this, that the Rapier maketh peace in our
minds; or from hence, that it is not ſo ſufficient defence
for our bodies in our fight? He that will fight when he is
armed, will not fight when he is naked : is it therefore
good to go naked to keepe peace ? he that would fight
with his Sword and Buckler, or Sword and Dagger, being weapons of true defence, will not fight with his Rapier and Poiniard, wherein no true defence or fight is
perfect: are theſe inſufficiēt weapōs therfore the better,
becauſe not being ſufficiēt to defēdvs in fight, they force
vs vnto peace ? What elſe is it, but to ſay, it is good for
                           ſubiects

*There are few
frayes, but more
valiant Gentlemē
ſlaine now then
were then.*

fubiects to be poore, that they may not go to law: or to
lacke munition, that they may not fight, nor go to the
warres: and to conclude, what more followeth through
the imperfect workes of thefe *Italian* peacemakers? They
haue made many a ftrong man in his fight weake, many
a valiant man fearefull, manie a worthie man trufting to
their imperfect fight, hath bene flaine, and manie of our
defperate boyes and young youthes, to become in that
Rapier-fight, as good men as *England* yeeldeth, and the
talleft men in this land, in that fight as verie boyes as
they and no better. This good haue the *Italian* teachers
of Offence done vs, they haue transformed our boyes into men, and our men into boyes, our ftrong men into
weakeneffe, our valiant men doubtfull, and manie worthie men refoluing themfelues vpon their falfe refolutions, haue moft wilfully in the field, with their Rapiers
ended their liues. And laftly, haue left to remaine a-
mongft vs after their deathes, thefe inconueniences behind them, falfe Fence-bookes, imperfect weapons, falfe
fightes, and euill cuftomes, whereby for lacke of vfe and
practife in perfect weapons and true fight, we are difa-
bled for the feruice of our Prince, defence of our countrey, and fafetie of our liues in priuate fight.

That the short Sword hath the aduantage againft
the long Sword or long Rapier.

Hereas for the moft part opinions are 38
generally holden, that the long Sword,
or long Rapier, hath the vantage in fight
againft the fhort Sword, which the *Itali-*
an teachers of Defence, by their falfe de-

I

monftratiōs haue brought vs to beleeue. I haue thought good that the truth may appeare which hath the vantage, to adde my helpe vnto the reafons they vfe in their owne behalfe, for that yet I could neuer heare them make a found reafon for the fame. Thefe are the reafons.

Thefe reafons are vfed by the Italians.

Firft with my long Rapier, I will put my felfe into my gard or *Stocata*, holding my hilt backe by the outfide of my right thigh, keeping in fhort the point of my Rapier, fo as he that hath the fhort Sword, fhall not be able to reach the point of my Rapier, to make his ward or Croffe with his Dagger, Buckler, Sword, or Cloke, without ftepping in of his foote, the which time is too long to anfwere the time of the hand, by reafon of my diftance. I can there ftand fafe without danger of blow or thruft, playing the Patients part: if you ftrike or thruft you do it too fhort, by reafon of my diftance: if you feek to come nearer, you muft do it with the time of your foote, in the which time I may fafely thruft home: if in that diftance you breake it not, you are flaine: if you do breake it, yet you do me no harme, by reafon of my diftance, and I may ftand faft and thruft againe, or flie backe at my pleafure: fo haue you put your felfe in danger of your life, and hauing hardly efcaped, are driuen againe to begin a new bought, as at the firft you did. Againe, if I pleafe, I can be the oppreffour, keeping the fame gard, and my point in fhort as I did before, and preffing ftrongly by putting in by litle and litle of my feete, vntill the place with my foote be gotten, wherein (in my iudgement) I may thruft home, the which I may boldly and fafely do, without refpect of anie ward at all, by reafon of my diftance, in which time of my comming he muft ftrike, thruft, ward, or go backe: if he go backe,

it

it is a great difgrace: if he ftrike or thruft, it is too fhort: if he ftand to defend, the place being alreadie gotten, where I may thruft home, the thruft being verie quicke & ftrongly made, fuch is the force and fwiftneffe there-of, that it is impoffible by nature or art, for anie man to breake one thruft of an hundred. Thefe reafons in my o-pinion may fuffice to confirme the wife, that there is no queftion to be made, but that the long Rapier hath the aduantage againft the fhort Sword.

Sir you haue pretily handled your difcourfe, concer- *A confutation of the Italians rea-*ning the vantages of the long Rapier againft the fhort *fons.* Sword, efpecially at the firft fhew, and according to common fence, but for the fubftance and truth of the true fight, you haue faid nothing, becaufe for the per-formance of anie of your allegations, you haue neither true Pace, Place, Time, nor Space: thefe are the rea-fons.Your Pace of neceffitie muft be too large, becaufe otherwife you cannot keepe fafe the point of your long Rapier, from the Croffe of the fhort Sword, vnleffe you will with a narrow Pace keepe backe your hilt fo farre, that the fpace of your offence wilbe too large or too long in diftance, and your bodie vnapt to moue and to thruft both ftrong and quicke in due time, nor aptly to keepe your diftance, to win the place with your feete, to thruft home. So now you may plainely fee, if you haue skill in the art or fcience of Defence, that to per-forme anie thing which you haue alleadged, you haue neither true Pace, Place, time nor Space. But if you will ftand vpon the largeneffe of your Pace, to keepe backe or faue the point of your long Rapier from the ward or Croffe of the fhort Sword, or vpon your *Paffatos*, in all thefe you haue great difaduantages: and

I 2

thefe are my reafons: Your number will be too great, as thus: whenfoeuer you meane out of your large pace to thruft home, you muft of neceffitie make foure times with your feet, and one with your hand, or two times with your feet, and one with your hand at the leaft: and whenfoeuer you make any of your paffages, the nūber of your feet are greater then the greateft of any of thefe times done out of the large pace: but the patient with his fhort fword, to auoyd you, or difappoint you of your thruft, hath but one time with his foot, at or before the which time, as he in his iudgemēt fhall find you in your motion, hath by the flow and great number of your motions or times, fufficient time fafely out of all danger to make himfelfe readie to take his croffe with his fhort fword.Now Sir, whether you thruft or not thruft, whether you play the part of an Agent, or Patient, it helpeth you nothing, for he that hath the fhort fword hath foure times or motions againft the long Rapier, namely, bent, fpent, lying fpent, and drawing backe, in all maner of fights thefe are to be obferued both by the Patient and Agent. Now note, he that hath the long Rapier muft of neceffitie play vpon one of thefe foure motions, or be Patient, which foeuer he fhall do, he is ftill in great danger of the croffe of the fhort fword, becaufe if he be Agent, his number is too great, he falleth into one of the foure motions, the Patient with his fhort fword, hauing but the time of the hand, or hād & foot, fafely vpon thefe actions or times taketh his croffe with the fhort Sword: that being done, he prefently vncroffeth and ftriketh or thrufteth at his pleafure him that hath the long Rapier, in the head, face, or bodie.Now here is againe to be noted, that when the croffe

is

is made, if he that hath the long Rapier ſtand faſt, he is
wounded preſently in the vncroſſing of the ſhort ſword,
if he ſtep or leape backe to ſaue himſelfe, yet the time
of the hand being ſwifter then the time of the foot, ouer-
taketh him, with blow or thruſt in the arme, hand, head,
face and bodie. Now if he that hath the long Rapier
will be patient & make no play, but lie ſtill watching to
make his thruſt or *Stocata* iuſt in the comming or mouing of the Agents feete with his ſhort ſword, then he
hath as great diſaduantage as he had when he was Patient, becauſe thē the Agent with his ſhort Sword hath
but hand and foot to make his croſſe: which is moſt ſafely to be done in that time, which we call Bent, and is as
impoſſible for the Rapier-man to preuent, as it is for an
vnskilfull to ſtrike or thruſt iuſt together with a man of
skill. Then thus I conclude, that he that fighteth with a
long Rapier, againſt him that fighteth with a ſhort
Sword, can do nothing in due time to defend himſelfe,
or hurt the other, but is ſtill in daunger of his life, or
at the mercie of him that hath the ſhort Sword, or
elſe hath no ſafe way to helpe himſelfe, but onely *Cobs*   *Cobs Trauerſe.*
Trauerſe. This *Cob* was a great quareller, and did de-
light in great brauerie to giue foule words to his bet-
ters, and would not refuſe to go into the field to fight
with any man, and when he came into the field, would
draw his Sword to fight, for he was ſure by the cunning of his Trauerſe, not to be hurt by anie man: for
at anie time finding himſelfe ouermatched would ſuddenly turne his backe and runne away with ſuch ſwift-
neſſe, that it was thought a good horſe would ſcarce
take him. And this when I was a young man, was verie much ſpoken of by many Gentlemen of the Innes of

I 3

the Court, and was called *Cobs* Trauerſe and thoſe that had ſeene anie go backe too faſt in his fight, would ſay, he did tread *Cobs* Trauerſe.

George Siluer his militarie riddle, truly ſet downe betweene the Perfection and Imperfection of fight: containing the handling of the foure fights: wherein true conſiſteth the whole ſumme and full perfection of the true fight, with all maner of wea-pons, with an inuicible concluſion.

Ardant fight ſtayeth, putteth backe, or beateth gardant fight.

Open fight ſtayeth, putteth backe, or beateth open fight.

Variable fight anſwereth variable fight in the firſt diſtance, and not otherwiſe, except it be with the perfect length againſt the imperfect.

Cloſe fight is beaten by gardant fight.

Variable cloſe & gardant fight, beateth gardant fight, open fight, variable fight, and cloſe fight.

Gardant fight in the imperfection of the Agent or Patient, winneth the halfe ſword, and preuenteth the cloſe, and whoſoeuer firſt ventureth the cloſe, looſeth it, and is in great danger of death, and not poſſible to eſcape or get out againe without great hurt.

There attendeth moſt diligently vpon theſe foure fights foure offenſiue actions, which we call certaine, vncertaine, firſt, before, iuſt, and afterwards: they are to be performed through iudgement, time, meaſure, number and waight, by which all maner of blowes, thruſts, thrufts, falfes, doubles, or flips, are preuented, or moft safely defended. And thus endeth my riddle.

Now followeth the conclufion, that whofoeuer fhall thinke or find himfelfe in his fight too weake for the A-gent, or Patient Agent, and therefore, or by reafon of his drunkenneffe, or vnreafonable defperateneffe fhall prefe within the halfe Sword, or deferately runne in of purpofe to giue hurt, or at leaft for taking of one hurt, to giue another, fhall moft affuredly be in great daun-ger of death or wounds, and the other fhall ftill be fafe and go free.

Veritas vincit.

A BRIEFE NOTE OF THREE ITA-
lian *Teachers of Offence.*

I write not this to disgrace the dead, but to shew their impudēt boldnesse and insufficiency in performance of their profession when they were liuing: that from henceforth this briefe note may be a remembrance and warning to beware of had I wist.

Here were three Italian Teachers of Offence in my time. The first was *Signior Rocko*: the second was *Ieronimo*, that was *Signior Rocko* his boy, that taught Gentlemen in the *Blacke-Fryers*, as Vsher for his maister in steed of a man. The third was *Vincentio*. This *Signior Rocko* came into *England* about some thirtie yeares past: he taught the Noblemen & Gentlemen of the Court; he caused some of them to weare leaden soales in their shoes, the better to bring them to nimblenesse of feet in their fight. He disbursed a great summe of mony for the lease of a faire house in *Warwicke* lane, which he called his Colledge, for he thought it great disgrace for him to keepe a Fence-schoole, he being then thought to be the onely famous Maister of the Art of armes in the whole world. He caused to be fairely drawne and set round about his Schoole all the Noblemens and Gentlemens armes that were his Schollers, and hanging right vnder their armes their Rapiers, daggers, gloues of male and gantlets. Also, he had benches and stooles, the roome being verie large, for Gentlemē to sit round about his Schoole to behold his teaching. He taught none commonly vnder twentie, fortie, fifty, or an hundred pounds. And because all things should be verie necessary for the Noblemē & gentlemē, he had

in

in his fchoole a large fquare table, with a greene car-
pet, done round with a verie brode rich fringe of gold,
alwaies ftanding vpon it a verie faire Standifh couered
with Crimfon Veluet, with inke, pens, pin-duft, and
fealing waxe, and quiers of verie excellent fine paper
gilded, readie for the Noblemen & Gentlemen (vpon
occafion) to write their letters, being then defirous to
follow their fight, to fend their men to difpatch their
bufineffe. And to know how the time paffed, he had in
one corner of his fchoole a Clocke, with a verie faire
large Diall, he had within that fchoole, a roome the
which was called his priuie fchoole, with manie weapons therein, where he did teach his fchollers his fecret
fight, after he had perfectly taught them their rules. He
was verie much beloued in the Court.

There was one *Auften Bagger*, a verie tall gentleman of his handes, not ftanding much vpon his skill, but
carying the valiant hart of an Fnglifhman, vpon a time
being merrie amongft his friendes, faid he would go
fight with *Signior Rocco*, prefently went to *Signior
Rocco* his houfe in the *Blackefriers*, and called to him in
this maner: *Signior Rocco*, thou that art thought to be
the onely cunning man in the world with thy weapon,
thou that takeft vpon thee to hit anie Englifhman with
a thruft vpon anie button, thou that takeft vpon thee to
come ouer the feas, to teach the valiant Noblemen and
Gentlemen of *England* to fight, thou cowardly fellow
come out of thy houfe if thou dare for thy life, I am
come to fight with thee. *Signior Rocco* looking out at a
window, perceiuing him in the ftreet to ftand readie
with his Sword and Buckler, with his two hand Sword
drawne, with all fpeed ran into the ftreet, and manfully

K

let flie at *Auſten Bagger*, who moſt brauely defended himſelfe, and preſently cloſed with him, and ſtroke vp his heeles, and cut him ouer the breech, and trode vpon him, and moſt grieuouſly hurt him vnder his feet : yet in the end *Auſten* of his good nature gaue him his life, and there left hin. This was the firſt and laſt fight that euer *Signior Rocco* made, ſauing once at Queene Hith he drew his Rapier vpon a waterman, where he was throughly beaten with Oares and Stretchers, but the oddes of their weapons were as great againſt his Rapier, as was his two hand Sword againſt *Auſten Baggers* Sword and Buckler, therefore for that fray he was to be excuſed.

Then came in *Vincentio* and *Ieronimo*, they taught Rapier-fight at the Court, at *London*, and in the countrey, by the ſpace of ſeauen or eight yeares or thereabouts.Theſe two *Italian* Fencers, eſpecially *Vincentio*, ſaid that Engliſhmen were ſtrong men, but had no cunning, and they would go backe too much in their fight, which was great diſgrace vnto them.Vpon theſe words of diſgrace againſt Engliſhmen, my brother *Toby Siluer* and my ſelfe, made challenge againſt them both, to play with them at the ſingle Rapier, Rapier and Dagger, the ſingle Dagger, the ſingle Sword, the Sword and Target, the Sword and Buckler, & two hand Sword, the Staffe, battell Axe, and Morris Pike, to be played at the Bell Saua ge vpon the Scaffold, where he that went in his fight faſter backe then he ought, of Engliſhman or Italian, ſhold be in danger to breake his necke off the Scaffold.We cauſed to that effect, fiue or ſixe ſcore Bils of challenge to be printed, and ſet vp from *Southwarke* to the Tower, and from thence through *London* vnto *Weſtminſter*,

minſter, we were at the place with all theſe weapons at
the time apointed, within a bow ſhot of their Fence
ſchoole: many gentlemen of good accompt, caried manie of the bils of chalenge vnto them, telling them that
now the *Siluers* were at the place appointed, with all
their weapons, looking for them, and a multitude of
people there to behold the fight, ſaying vnto them, now
come and go with vs (you ſhall take no wrong) or elſe
you are ſhamed for euer. Do the gentlemen what they
could, theſe gallants would not come to the place of
triall. I verily thinke their cowardly feare to anſwere this
chalenge, had vtterly ſhamed them indeed, had not the
maiſters of Defence of *London*, within two or three
daies after, bene drinking of bottell Ale hard by *Vin-
centios* ſchoole, in a Hall where the *Italians* muſt of neceſſitie paſſe through to go to their ſchoole: and as they
were comming by, the maiſters of Defence did pray
them to drinke with them, but the *Italians* being verie
cowardly, were afraide, and preſently drew their Rapiers: there was a pretie wench ſtanding by, that loued
the *Italians*, ſhe ran with ourcrie into the ſtreet, helpe,
helpe, the *Italians* are like to be ſlaine: the people with
all ſpeede came running into the houſe, and with their
Cappes and ſuch things as they could get, parted the
fraie, for the Engliſh maiſters of Defence, meant nothing leſſe then to foile their handes vpon theſe two
faint-harted fellowes. The next morning after, all the
Court was filled, that the *Italian* teachers of Fence had
beaten all the maiſters of Defence in *London*, who ſet v-
pon them in a houſe together. This wan the *Italian* Fencers their credit againe, and thereby got much, ſtill continuing their falſe teaching to the end of their liues.

K 2

This *Vincentio* proued himfelfe a ftout man not long before he died, that it might be feene in his life. time he had bene a gallant, and therefore no maruaile he tooke vpon him fo highly to teach Englifhmen to fight, and to fet forth bookes of the feates of Armes. Vpon a time at *Wels* in Somerfetfhire, as he was in great brauerie amongft manie gentlemen of good accompt, with great boldneffe he gaue out fpeeches, that he had bene thus manie yeares in *England*, and fince the time of his firft comming, there was not yet one Englifh-man, that could once touch him at the fingle Rapier, or Rapier and Dagger. A valiant gentleman being there amongft the reft, his Englifh hart did rife to heare this proude boafter, fecretly fent a meffenger to one *Bartholomew Bramble* a friend of his, a verie tall man both of his hands and perfon, who kept a fchoole of Defence in the towne, the meffenger by the way made the maifter of Defence acquainted with the mind of the gentleman that fent for him, and of all what *Vincentio* had faid, this maifter of Defence prefently came, and amongft all the gentlemen with his cap off, prayed maifter *Vincentio*, that he would be pleafed to take a quart of wine of him. *Vincentio* verie fcornefully looking vpon him, faid vnto him. Wherefore fhould you giue me a quart of wine? Marie Sir, faid he, becaufe I heare you are a famous man at your weapon. Then prefently faid the gentleman that fent for the maifter of Defence: Maifter *Vincentio*, I pray you bid him welcome, he is a man of your profeffion. My profeffion faid *Vincentio*? what is my profeffion. Then faid the gentleman, he is a maifter of the noble fcience of Defence. Why faid maifter *Vincẽtio*, God make him a good man. But the maifter of Defence wold not

not

not thus leaue him, but prayed him againe he would be pleaſed to take a quart of wine of him. Thē ſaid *Vincētio*, I haue no need of thy wine. Then ſaid the maiſter of Defence: Sir I haue a ſchoole of Defence in the towne, will it pleaſe you to go thither. Thy ſchoole, ſaid maiſter *Vincentio*? what ſhall I do at thy ſchoole? play with me (ſaid the maiſter) at the Rapier and Dagger, if it pleaſe you. Play with thee ſaid maiſter *Vincentio*? if I play with thee, I will hit thee 1. 2. 3. 4. thruſtes in the eie together. Then ſaid the maiſter of Defence, if you can do ſo, it is the better for you, and the worſe for me, but ſurely I can hardly beleeue that you can hit me: but yet once againe I hartily pray you good Sir, that you will go to my ſchoole, and play with me. Play with thee ſaid maiſter *Vincentio* (verie ſcornefully?) by God me ſcorne to play with thee. With that word ſcorne, the maiſter of Defence was verie much moued, and vp with his great Engliſh fiſt, and ſtroke maiſter *Vincentio* ſuch a boxe on the eare that he fell ouer and ouer, his legges iuſt againſt a Butterie hatch, whereon ſtood a great blacke Iacke: the maiſter of Defence fearing the worſt, againſt *Vincentio* his riſing, catcht the blacke Iacke into his hand, being more then halfe full of Beere. *Vincentio* luſtily ſtart vp, laying his hand vpon his Dagger, & with the other hand pointed with his finger, ſaying, very well: I will cauſe to lie in the Gaile for this geare, 1. 2. 3 4. yeares. And well ſaid the maiſter of Defence, ſince you will drinke no wine, will you pledge me in Beere? I drinke to all the cowardly knaues in *England*, and I thinke thee to be the verieſt coward of them all: with that he caſt all the Beere vpon him: notwithſtanding *Vincentio* hauing nothing but his guilt Rapier, and

Dagger about him, and the other for his defence the
blacke Iacke, would not at that time fight it out: but the
next day met with the maifter of Defence in the ftreete,
and faid vnto him, you remember how mifufed a me
yefterday, you were to blame, me be an excellent man,
me teach you how to thruft two foote further then anie
Englifhman, but firft come you with me: then he
brought him to a Mercers fhop, and faid to the Mercer,
let me fee of your beft filken Pointes, the Mercer did
prefently fhew him fome of feauen groates a dozen,
then he payeth fourteene groates for two dozen, and
faid to the maifter of Defence, there is one dozen for
you, and here is another for me. This was one of the va-
lianteft Fencers that came from beyond the feas, to
teach Englifhmen to fight, and this was one of the man-
lieft frayes, that I haue hard of, that euer he made in
England, wherin he fhewed himfelfe a farre better man
in his life, then in his profeffion he was, for he profeffed
armes, but in his life a better Chriftian. He fet forth in
print a booke for the vfe of the Rapier and Dagger, the
which he called his practife, I haue read it ouer, and becaufe I finde therein neither true rule for the perfect
teaching of true fight, not true ground of true fight, neither fence or reafon for due proofe thereof. I haue
thought it friuolous to recite any part therin contained:
yet that the truth hereof may appeare, let two mē being
wel experienced in the Rapier and Dagger fight, choofe
any of the beft branches in the fame booke, & make trial
with force and agility, without the which the truth betweene the true & falfe fight cannot be knowne, & they
fhall find great imperfections therein. And againe, for
proofe that there is no truth, neither in his rules, groūds

or

or Rapier-fight, let triall be made in this maner: Set two vnskilfull men together at the Rapier and Dagger, be-ing valiant, and you ſhall ſee, that once in two boutes there ſhall either one or both of them be hurt. Then ſet two skilfull men together, being valiant at the Rapier and Dagger, and they ſhall do the like. Then ſet a skilful Rapier and Dagger-man the beſt that can be had, and a valiant man hauing no skill together at Rapier & Dag-ger, and once in two bouts vpon my credit in all the ex-perience I haue in fight, the vnskilful man, do the other what he can for his life to the contrarie, ſhall hurt him, and moſt commonly if it were in continuance of fight, you ſhall ſee the vnskilfull man to haue the aduantage. And if I ſhould chuſe a valiant man for ſeruice of the Prince, or to take part with me or anie friend of mine in a good quarrell, I would chuſe the vnskilfull man, be-ing vnencombred with falſe fights, becauſe ſuch a man ſtandeth free in his valour with ſtrength and agilitie of bodie, freely taketh the benefit of nature, fighteth moſt braue, by looſing no oportunitie, either ſoundly to hurt his enemie, or defend himſelfe, but the other ſtanding for his Defence, vpon his cunning Italian wardes, *Poin-ta reuerſa,* the *Imbrocata, Stocata,* and being faſt tyed vn-to theſe falſe fightes, ſtandeth troubled in his wits, and nature therby racked through the largeneſſe or falſe ly-ings or Spaces, whereby he is in his fight as a man halfe maimed, looſing the oportunity of times & benefit of nature, & whereas before being ignorant of theſe falſe Rapier fightes, ſtanding in the free libertie of nature giuen him by god, he was able in the field with his wea-pō to anſwere the valianteſt man in the world, but now being tied vnto that falſe fickle vncertaine fight, there-

K 4

by hath loft in nature his freedome, is now become
fcarce halfe a man, and euerie boye in that fight is become as good a man as himfelfe.

Ieronimo this gallant was valiant, and would fight
indeed, and did, as you fhall heare. He being in a Coch
with a wench that he loued well, there was one *Cheefe*,
a verie tall man, in his fight naturall Englifh, for he
fought with his Sword and Dagger, and in Rapier-fight
had no skill at all. This *Cheefe* hauing a quarrell to *Ieronimo*, ouertooke him vpon the way, himfelfe being on
horfebacke, did call to *Ieronimo*, and bad him come
forth of the Coch or he would fetch him, for he was
come to fight with him. *Ieronimo* prefently went forth
of the Coch and drew his Rapier and dagger, put himfelf into his beft ward or *Stocata*, which ward was taught
by himfelfe and *Vincentio*, and by them beft allowed of,
to be the beft ward to ftand vpon in fight for life, either
to affault the enemie, or ftand and watch his comming,
which ward it fhould feeme he ventured his life vpon,
but howfoeuer with all the fine Italienated skill *Ieronimo* had, *Cheefe* with his Sword within two thruftes ran
him into the bodie and flue him. Yet the Italian teachers will fay, that an Englifhmā cannot thruft ftraight
with a Sword, becaufe the hilt will not fuffer him to put
the forefinger ouer the Croffe, nor to put the thumbe
vpon the blade, nor to hold the pummell in the hand,
whereby we are of neceffitie to hold faft the handle in
the hand: by reafon whereof we are driuen to thruft
both compaffe and fhort, whereas with the Rapier they
can thruft both ftraight and much further then we can
with the Sword, becaufe of the hilt: and thefe be the reafons they make againft the Sword.

FINIS.

BREF INSTRUCTIONS

VPŎ MY PRADOXES OF DEFENCE
for the true handling of all Mann^r of
weapons together w^t the fower grownds
& the fower gou^rnors wch gouernours
are left out in my pradoxes w^tout the
knowledge of wch no Man can fight ſaf

By *George Silver Gentleman*
[1599]

[Sloane MS. No. 376.]

571

TO THE READER.

Or as much as in my padoxes of Defence I haue admonyfhed Men to take heede of falfe teachers of Defence, yet once againe in thefe my bref inftructions I do the lyke, becaufe Diuers have wryten books treating of the noble fcience of Defence, wherin they rather teach offence then Defence, rather fhewing men therby how to be flayne than to defend them felues frõ the Dang^r of their enemys, as we may dayly fe to the great grief & ouerthrowe of many braue gentlemen & gallent of o^r ever victorious nation of great brytaine, And therfore for the great loue & Care y^t I haue for the well Doing & p^{r}f,vation of my Countrymen, feeing their Dayly ruens & vtter ou^{r}throw of Diu^{rs} gallant gent: & others wch truft only to that Impfyt fyght of y^t Rapior, yeafe although they Deyly fe their owne ou^{r}throwes & flaughter therby, yet becaus they are trayned vp therin, they thinke & do fully pfwade them felues that ther is no fight fo excelent & wher as amongft div^{rs} other their oppynyons y^t leadeth them to this errous on of y^t cheifeft is, becaufe ther be fo many flayne w^t thefe weapons & therfore they hold them fo exelent, but thefe thinges do

L

573

cheifly happen, firſt becauſe their fyght is Imprfyt for that they vſe nether the prfyt gronds of true fyght, nether yet the 4 gouʳnors wᵗout wᶜʰ no man can fight ſaf, nether do they vſe ſuch other rules wᶜʰ are required in the right vſe of prfyt defence, and alſo their weapons for yᵉ moſt prte beinge of an Imprfyt length, muſt of neceſſytie make an Imprfyt Defence becauſe they Cannot vſe them in due tyme & place, for had theſe valerous mynded men the right prfection of the true fyght wᵗ the ſhort ſword, & alſo of other weapons of prfyt length, I know yᵗ men would com ſaffer out of the field frō ſuch bloddye bankets & that ſuch would be their prfections her in, that it would ſaue many 100 mens lyues. But how ſhould men lerne prfection out of ſuch rules as are nothing els but very Imprfectiō it ſelf. And as it is not fyt for a man wᶜʰ deſyreth yᵉ clere lyght of the Day to go downe into the bottom of a deepe & Darke Dungion, belyvinge to fynd it there, ſo is it as Impoſſyble for men to fynd the prfyt knowledge of this noble ſcience wher as in all their teachings every thinge is attempted & acted vpō Imprfyt rules, for ther is but one truth in all things, wᶜʰ I wiſh very hartely were taught & practyſed here amongſt vs, &yᵗ thoſe Imprfyt & murtherous kynde of falſe fyghts might be by them abolyſhed. Leaue now to quaf & gull any Longer of that fylthy brynyſh puddle, ſeeing yō may now drink of yᵗ freſh & clere ſprynge.

O that men for their Defence would but geve their mynde to practiſe the true fyght in deed, & lerne to bere true brytiſh wards for thire defence, wᶜʰ yf they had it in prfyt practyſe, I ſpeak it of myne owne knowledge yᵗ thoſe Imprfyt Italyon Devyſes wᵗ rapyor & ponyard
would

would be clene caſt afyde & of no account of al ſuch as
blind offeſtions do not lead beyond the bonds of reaſon.
Therfore for the verye zealous & vnfayned loue yᵗ I
beare vnto yoʳ high & royal prſon my Cuntrymen pytti-
ng their cauſes yᵗ ſo many braue men ſhould be dayly
murthered, & ſpoyled for want of true knowledge of
this noble ſcience & not as ſom Imagyn to be, only yᵉ
excelence of yᵉ rapior fyght, & wher as my padoxes of
defence is to the moſt ſorte as a darke ryddle in many
things ther in ſet downe, therfore I have now this ſecond
tyme taken ſom paynes to write theſe few breef Inſtructions ther vppõ wher by they may the better attayne to
the truth of this ſcyence & laying open here all ſuch
things as was ſom thinge Intrycat for them to vndʳ ſtand
in my pʳdoxes & therfor yᵗ I haue the ful prſeſtiõ &
knowledge of the prſyt vſe of all mannʳ of weapons, it
Doth embolden me here in to wryte for the better In-
ſtruſtiõ of the Vnſkylfull.

And I haue added to theſe my breef Inſtruſtions
cʳtaine neceſarie admonytions wᶜʰ I wiſh every man not
only to know but alſo to obſʳve & follow, Chiefly al ſuch
as are deſyrous to enter into the right vſage & knowledge of their weapons, & alſo I haue thought it good
to Annexe here vnto my pʳdoxes of Defence becauſe in
theſe my bref Inſtruſtions, I haue reſerred yᵉ reader to
divʳs rules ther in ſet down.

This haue I wryten for an Infallible truth & a note of
remembrance to oʳ gallant gent: & others of oʳ brave
mynded Nation of great bryttaine, wᶜʰ bere a mynde to
defend them ſelues & to wyn honour in the feeld by
their Aſtions of armes & ſyngle Combats.

And know yᵗ I write not this for vaineglorie, but out

of An entyre loue y^t I owe vnto my natyve Cuntrymen, as on who lamentith their Loſſes, forrye y^t ſo great an errour ſhould be ſo Carefully noryſhed as a ſⁱpant in their boſoms to their vtt^r confuſyõ, as of long tyme haue byn ſeene, wher as yf they would but ſeeke the truth her in they were eaſyly abolyſhed, therfore follow the truth & fly Ignorance.

And confyd^r y^t learnyng hath no greater enemye than Ignorance, nether can the vnſkylfull euer Judge the truth of my arte to them unknowen, beware of raſh Judgment & accept my labours as thankfully as I beſtow them willingly, cenſuer me Juſtly, let no man Diſpiſe my worke herin Cauſeles, & ſo I refere my ſelf to the cenſuer of ſuch as are ſkylful herin & ſo I cõmyt yõ to the prteƈtion of the almyghty Jehovah.

yo^{rs} in al loue & fryendly Affeƈtiõ,

GEORGE SYLUER.

Admonytions

ADMONYTIONS

TO THE GENTLEMEN &
BRAVE GALLANTS OF GREAT
BRITAINE AGAINST QUARRELS &
BRAULES WRITEN BY GEORGE SILUER.
GENT.

Heras I have declaired in my prdoxes of defence of the falſe teachinge of the noble ſcyence of defence vſed here by the Italyon fencers willing men therin to take heed how they truſted ther vnto wᵗ ſuffytient reaſons & profs why.

And wher as ther was a booke wryten by Vincentio an Italiō teacher whoſe yll vſinge practiſes & vnſkylfull teaching were ſuch yᵗ it hath coſt the lyves of many of oʳ brave gentlemen & gallants, the vncʳtaintye of whoſe falſe teaching doth yet remayne to yᵉ dayly murthering & ouer throw of many, for he & the reſt of them did not teach Defence but offence, as it doth playnlye appere by thoſe yᵗ follow the ſame Imprfyt fyght according to their teaching or inſtructiōs by the orders from them prceedinge, for be the actors yᵗ follow them neuer ſo prfyt or ſkylfull therin one or both of them are eyther

L 3

577

fore hurt or flaine in their Incountrs & fyghts, & yf they alledge y^t we vfe it not rightly according to ye prfectiõ therof, & therfore cannot defend o^r felues, to wch I an-fwer yf themfelues had had any prfection therin, & that their teaching had byn a truth, themfelues would not have byn beaten & flayne in their fyghts, & vfing of their weapons, as they were.

And therfore I proue wher a man by their teaching can not be faf in his defence following their owne grounde of fyght then is their teaching offence & not de-fence, for in true fyght againft the beft no hurt can be don. And yf both haue the full prfection of true fyght, then the one will not be able to hurt the other at what prfyt weapon fo ever.

For it cannot be fayd y^t yf a man go to the feld & can-not be fure to defend him felf in fight & to com faf home, yf goid be not againft him whither he fyght w^t a man of fkyll or no fkil it may not be faid y^t fuch a man is Maft^r of the Noble fcyence of defence, or that he hath the prfection of true fyght, for yf both haue the prfection of their weapons, yf by any Device, on fhould be able to hurt the other, ther were no prfection in the fyght of weapons, & this firmely hold in yor mynd for a generall rule, to be the hayth & prfection of the true handling of al maner of weapons.

And alfo wheras y^t faid Vincentio in y^t fame booke hath written difcours of honour & honourable quarrels making many reafons to prve meanes & wayes to enter ye feeld & cõbat, both for the lye & other difgraces, al wch diabolicall devyces tendeth only to villayne & dif-truction as hurtynge, Maymynge & Murtheringe or kyllinge.

Annymating

Annymating ye mynds of yonge gentlemen & gallants
to follow thofe rules to maintaine their honors & credits,
but the end ther of for the moft prte is eyther kyllinge or
hanginge or both to their vtter vndoinge & great gref of
themfelues, & their friends, but then to late to call it a-
gaine. they confyder not the tyme & place that we lyue
in , nor do not throughly looke into the danger of the
lawe til it be to late, & for that in diuers other cuntryes
in thefe things they have a larger fcope than we have in
thefe our dayes.

Therfore it behoveth vs not upō euery abufe offered
wher by o^r bloud fhalbe Inflamed, or o^r choler kindled
p^rfently w^t the fword or w^t the ftabb, or by force of
Armes to feeke Reuenge, wch is the propre nature of
wild beafts in their rage fo to do, being voyde of the vfe
of reafon, wch thinge fhould not be in Men of difcreatiō
fo much to Degenerate, but he y^t wil not endure an Iniurye, but will feeke revenge, then he ought to do it by
Cyvill Order & prof, by good & holfom lawes, wch are
ordayned for fuch Caufes, wch is a thinge far more fyt &
requifted in a place of fo Cyvell a gou^rnment as we lyve
in, then is the other, & who fo follow^t thefe my Admony-
cions fhalbe accounted as valyent a Man as he y^t fyghteth
& farr wyfer. for I fee no reafon why a Man fhould
adventure hys lyf & eftate upō every tryfle, but fhould
rather put vp diu^rs abufes offered vnto him, becaufe it is
agreeable both to the Lawes of god & o^r Cuntrye.

Why fhould not words be Anfwered w^t words againe,
but yf a Man by his enemye be charged w^t blowes then
may he Lawfully feeke the beft meanes to defend him
felf, & In fuch a Cafe I hold it fyt to vfe his fkyll & to
fhow his force by his Deeds, yet fo, y^t his dealynge be
not

not w*t* full Rygour to the others confufyon yf poffyble it may be efchewed.

Alfo take heed how yō appoynt the field w*t* yo*r* Enemye publickly becaufe o*r* Lawes do not prmyt yt, neyther appoint to meet him in pryvat fort left yō wounding him he accufe yō of fellownye faying you have robbed him &c. Or he may laye companye clofely to Murther you & then to report he dyd yt him felf valyently in the feeld.

Alfo take heed of thyne Enemyes Stratagems, left he fynd Meanes to make yō to looke a fyde vpō fomthing, or caufe yō to fhew whether yō have on a p*r*vye Coate, & fo when yō Looke from him, he hurt or kyll you.

Take not armes vpō euery light occafyon, let not one fryend vpon a word or a tryfle violate another but let ech man zealoufly embrace fryendfhyp , & turne not famylyaritie into ftrangnes, kyndnes into mallice, nor loue into hatred, norifh not thefe ftrange & vnnaturall Alterations.

Do not wyckedly refolue one to feeke the others ou*r*throwe, do not confyrme to end thy Mallice by fyght becaufe for the moft prte y*t* endeth by Death.

Confyder when thefe things were moft vfed in former Ages they fought not fo much by envye the ruen & diftruction on of another, they never tooke tryall by fword but in defence of Innocencye to maintayne blotlefs honour.

Do not vpon Euery tryfle make an Action of revenge, or of Defyance.

Go not into the feeld w*t* thy fryend at his Intreatye to take his prte but firft know y*e* mann*r* of y*e* quarrell how Juftly or vniuftlye it grow, & do not ther in maintaine wronge

wronge againſt ryght, but examyne the cauſe of the con-
travercye , & yf ther be reaſon for his rage to lead him
to yᵗ mortall reſolution.

Yet be the cauſe neuer ſo Juſt, go not wᵗ him neyther
further nor ſuffer him to fight yf poſſyble it may by any
meanes be otherwyſe ended & wyll him not to enter into
ſo dangerous an action , but leue it till necceſytie requireth it.

And this I hold to be the beſt Courſe for it is fool-
iſhnes & endleſſe troble to caſt a ſtone at euerye Dogge
yᵗ barks at you. this noble ſcyence is not to cauſe on
man to abuſe another iniuriouſlye but to vſe it in their
neceſſyties to defend them in their Juſt Cauſes & to
maintaine their honour & Credits.

Therfore flye al raſhnes, pryde, & doynge of Iniurie
all foule faults & errours herin, pᵗſume not on this, &
therbye to think it lawfull to offer Iniurye to Anye,
think not yoᵗſelf Invincible , but conſyder yᵗ often a
verye wretch hath kylled a taule man, but he yᵗ hath
humanytie, the more skylful he is in this noble ſcience,
the more humble, modeſt, & Vᵗtuous he ſhould ſhew
him ſelf both in ſpeech & Action, no lyer, no vaunter
nor quarreller, for theſe are the cauſes of Wounds, Diſhonour & Death.

Yf you talke wᵗ great men of honourable qualitie wᵗ
ſuch chiefly haue regarde to frame yoᵗ ſpeeches & Anſwer
ſo reverent, yᵗ a fooliſh word, or froward Anſwer geve
no occaſyon of offence for often they breed Deadly hatred, Cruell murthers & extreem ruens &c.

Ever ſhun al occaſyons of quarrels, but marſhall men
cheiflye generals & great comanders ſhould be exelent
skylfull in the noble ſcience of defence, therby to be

M

able to anſwer quarrels, Combats & Chalenges in Defence of their prince & Cuntry.

Vale.

*Bref Inſtructions vpō my pradoxes of Defence for the
true handlyng of all Mannʳ of weapons together
wᵗ the fower grownds & the fower goúnors
wᶜʰ gouernours are left out in my
pradoxes wᶜout the knowledge of
wᶜʰ no Man can fight ſaf.*

Cap. I.

The fower grownds or	1.	*Judgment*
principls of yᵗ true	2.	*Diſtance*
fyght at all manner of	3.	*Tyme*
Weapons are theſe 4, viz.	4.	*Place.*

He reaſon wherof theſe 4 grownds or pʳnci-
ples be the fyrſt & cheefeſt, are the follow-
inge, becauſe through Judgment, yō kepe
yoʳ dyſtance, through Diſtance yō take yoʳ
Tyme, through Tyme yō ſafly wyne or
gayne the Place of yoʳ aduʳſarie, the Place beinge woon
or gayned yō haue tyme ſafly eyther to ſtryke, thruſt,
ward, cloze, grype, ſlyp or go back, in the wᶜʰ tyme
yoʳ enemye is diſapoynted to hurt yō, or to defend himfelf, by reaſon that he hath loſt his true Place, the reaſon yᵗ he hath loſt his True place is by the length of
Tyme

Tyme through the numbᵍ of his feet, to wᶜʰ he is of neceffytie Dryven to yᵗ wilbe Agent.

The 4 gouᵗnors are thofe yᵗ follow.

1. The fyrft gouʳnor is Judgment wᶜʰ is to know when yoʳ Adverfarie can reach you, & when not, & when yō can do the lyke to him, & to know by the goodnes or badnes of his lyinge, what he can do, & when & how he can pʳforme itᵢ

2. The fecond gouʳnor is Meafure. Meafure is the better to know how to make yoʳ fpace true to defend yoʳ felf, or to offend yoʳ enemyeᵢ

3. The third & fourth gouʳners is a twyfold mynd when yō prefs in on yoʳ enemye, for as yō have a mynd to go
4. forwarde, fo yō muft haue at yᵗ inftant a mynd to fly backwarde vpō any ac̆tion yᵗ fhalbe offered or don by yoʳ aduʳfarieᵢ

Certaine general rules wᶜʰ muft be obfyved in yᵗ prfyt vfe of al kynde of weapons.
Cap. 2.

1. Yrft when you com into the feeld to encounter wᵗ yoʳ Enemy, obfyve wel the fcope, Even-nes & vneunnes of yoʳ grounde, put yoʳfelf in redynes wᵗ yoʳ weapon, before yoʳ enemye Com wᵗin diftance, fet the fvnn in his face travers yf poffible yō can ftill remembrynge yoʳ gouʳnors.

2. Let al yoʳ lyinge be fuch as fhal beft like yoʳfelf, euer confyderinge out what fyght yoʳ Enemye chargeth yō, but be fure to kepe yoʳ diftance, fo yᵗ nether hed, Armes,

M 2

583

hands, body, nor legges be wᵗin hys reach, but yᵗ he

"*Put in his foot,*" *i.e. advance.* muſt fyrſt of neceſſytie put in his foote or feet, at wᶜʰ tyme yō haue the Choyſe of iij Actions by the wᶜʰ yō may endangʳ him & go free yoʳſelf.

"*His cominge in.*" *It muſt be remembered that in Silver's time the lunge was unknown, at leaſt to Engliſh fencers, & the only movements of the feet were "paſſes" and "traverſes," which with "ſlips" conſtituted a great part of the defence as well as of the attack. "Paſſes" were ſteps either forwards or backwards and the "traverſes" were ſteps in a lateral direction. "Slips" were little ſhort ſteps either lateral or backwards. Theſe movements were alſo much uſed in feints of attack.*

1. The fyrſt is to ſtrike or thruſt at him, at yᵗ inſtant when he haue gayned yō the place by his cominge in
2. The ſecond is to ward, & Aftʳ to ſtrike or thruſt from yᵗ, remembringe yoʳ gouʳnors
3. The thyrd is to ſlippe alyttle backe & to ſtrike or thruſt after hym.

but euer remember yᵗ in the fyrſt motion of your Adverſarye towarde yō, yᵗ yō ſlyde a lyttle back ſo ſhall yō be pʳpred in due tyme to prforme anye of the iij Actions Aforeſaid, by diſappointynge him of his true place, whereby yō ſhall ſaſlye defend yoʳſelfe & endanger him.

remember alſo yᵗ yf through fear or polyſye, he ſtrike or thruſt ſhort, & ther wᵗ go back, or not go back, follow him vpon yoʳ twofold gouʳnors, ſo ſhall yoʳ warde & ſlype be prformed in lyke mannʳ as before, & yoʳſelf ſtil be ſaf.

Kepe yoʳ dyſtance & ſuffer not yoʳ aduʳſarie to wyn or gayne the place of you, for yf he ſhall ſo do, he may endanger to hurt or kyll you.

"*To wyn or gayne the place;*" *i.e. to come within ſtriking diſtance.* Know yᵗ the place is, when on may ſtryke or thruſt home wᵗout puttinge in of his foot.

Yt may be obiected againſt thys laſt ground, yᵗ men do often ſtrike & thruſt at the half ſword & yet the ſame is prfytly defended, where to I anſwer yᵗ that defence is prfytly made by reaſon yᵗ the warder hath his true ſpace before the ſtryker or thruſter is in his force or entred into his action.

Therfore

Therfore alwaies do p'vent both blow & thrust, the *"Space" is the*
blow by true fpace, & the thruft by narrow fpace y^t is *diftance which the fword blade*
true croffinge it before the fame cominto their full force, *has to traverfe in*
other wyfe the hand of the Agent beinge as fwyft as y^e *changinge from*
hand of the patient, the hand of ye Agent beinge the *one pofition to another: thus*
fyrft mou^r, muft of neceffytie ftrike or thruft y^t prte of *from "medium"*
ye patient wch fhalbe ftryken or thruft at becaufe the *to "quarte" or "tierce" would*
tyme of y^t hand to the tyme of ye hand, beinge of lyke *be a "narrow*
fwyftnes the fyrft mou^r hath ye aduantage. *fpace," while*

from "tierce" to
4. When yor enemy fhal prefs vpon you, he wilbe Open *"feptime" or*
in one place or other, both at fyngal & dubble weapon, *from "feconde".*
or at the leaft he wilbe to weake in his ward vpon fuch *to "quarte"*
p^rffinge, then ftrike or thruft at fuch open or weakeft *would be a very*
prte y^t yo fhal fynd neereft. *"wyde fpace."*

5. When yo attempt to wyn the place, do it vpon gard,
remembringe yor gou^rnors, but when he p^rffeth vpo yo
& gayneth yo The place, then ftrike or thruft at him *A time hit or*
in his comynge in, *thruft.*

Or yf he fhal ftryke or thruft at yo, then Ward it,
& ftryke or thruft at him from yor warde, & fly backe *Parry and Ripofte.*
Inftantly accordinge to yor gou^rnors, fo fhall yo efcape *Silver is very*
faflie, for that the fyrft Motion of the feete backwarde *careful to em-*
is more fwyft, then the firft motion of the feet forwarde, *phafife the neceffity of "fly-*
wher by yor regreffyon wilbe more fwyfter, then his *ing backe," i.e.*
courfe in prgreffyon to Anoye you, the reafon is, that *getting away,*
in the fyrft motyon of his prgreffyon his Numb^r & *immediately after an attack,*
Waight is greater then yo^rs are, in yor firft motyon of *whether it be*
yor regreffyon, neu^rthelefs al men knowe that the co- *fuccefsful or otherwife.*
tynual courfe of the feet forwarde is more fwyft then
the Contynuall Courfe of ye feet backwards.

6. yf yor enemye lye in varyable fyght, & ftryke or *Time hits &*
thruft at yo then be fure to kepe yor Diftance & ftrike *thrufts.*

M 3

or thruſt at ſuch open prte of him as are neereſt vnto you, viz, at the hand, Arme, hed, or legg of him, & go back w^t all,

yf ij men fight at varyable fyght, & yf w^{t}in diſtance, 7. they muſt both be hurt, for in ſuch fight they Cannot make a true Croſſe, nor haue tyme trulye to Judge, by reaſon y^t the ſwyft motyon of the hand, beinge a ſwyfter moue^r, then the eye Deceyveth the eye, at what weapon ſoeuer yō ſhal fyght w^t all, as in my pradoxes of defence in the   chapter therof doth appere.

The "grype" *is the ſeizing of the ſword-hilt with the left hand,— for this purpoſe a* "guanto da preſa," *or gripping gauntlet with the palm protected with fine mail, was ſometimes uſed. To* "indirect" *is to either manœuvre or force him from the true line of direction.*

Looke to the grype of yor Enemye, & vpō his ſlype 8. take ſuch warde as ſhal beſt fyt your hand, from wch warde ſtrike or thruſt, ſtil remembrynge yor gouernors,

yf yō can Indirect yor enemye at any kynde of weapon, 9. then yō haue the aduantage, becauſe he muſt moue his feet to direct him ſelf Againe, & yō in the meane tyme may ſtrike or thruſt at him, & fly out faſt, before he can offer anything at you, his tyme wilbe ſo longe.

A Demi-volte.

When you ſhall Ward blow or thruſt, made at yor 10. right or left prte, w^t any kynd of weapon, rememb^r to Draw yor hynde foot a lyttle c^{r}culerlye, from that prte to wch the ſame ſhalbe made, wher by yō ſhall make yor defence the more prſyt, & ſhal ſtand the more Apt to ſtrike or thruſt from yt.

A

A declaration of al the 4 generall fyghts to be
vfed w' the fword at dubble or fyngle,
longe or fhort, & w' Certaine
p'ticuler rules to them
Annexed.

Cap. 3.

1. Pen fyght is to Carrye yor hand & hylt a loft *The "Guardia* aboue yor hed, eyther w^t poynt vpright, or *alta" of Maroz-* point backwards wch is beft, yet vfe that w^{ch} *zo & "Terza* yō fhall fynd moft apteft, to ftrike, thruft, or *Viggiani.* ward.

2. Gardant fyght in gen^rall is of ij forts, ye fyrft is true *A "hanging"* gardant fyght, wch is eyther prfyt or Imprfyt. *guard.*

   The prfyt is to carry yor hand & hylt aboue yor hed *"True gardant"* *is a High Prime.* w^t yor poynt doune to wards yor left knee, w^t yor fword blade fomewhat neer yor bodye, not bearing out your poynt, but rather declynynge in a lyttle towards yor faid knee, y^t yor enemye crofe not yor poynt & fo hurt *Command.* you, ftand bolt vpright in this fyght, & yf he offer to preffe in then bere yor hed & body a lyttle backwarde.

   The Imprfyt is when yō bere yor hand & fword hylt *To ftand with the* prfyt hayth aboue yor hed, as aforefayd but leanynge *body leaning* *forward is an* or ftoopinge forwarde w^t yor body & therby yor fpace *"imperfea"* wilbe to Wyde on both fyds to defend the blow ftryken *pofition.* at the left fyde of yor hed or to wyde to defend a thruft from the ryght fyde of the body,

   Alfo it is Imprfyt, yf yō bere yor hand & hylt as aforefayd, berynge yor poynt to farr out from yor knee, fo y^t yor enemy May Crofs, or ftrike Afyde yor poynt, & therby endanger you,

   The

*"Baſtard gar-
dant" is a kind of
high ſeconde, but
more central.*

The ſecond is baſtard gardant fyght wch is to Carrye yor hand & hylt below yor hed, breſt hye or lower w^t yor poynt downwarde towarde yor left foote, this baſtard gardant ward is not to be vſed in fyght, ecept it be to Croſſe yor enemyes Ward at his comynge in to take the grype of him or ſuch other advantage, as in diu^{rs} placs of y^e ſword fyght is ſet forth.

*"Forehand
ward" is a
medium guard.*

Cloſe fyght is when yō Croſs at ye half ſword eyther 3. aboue at forehand ward y^t is w^t poynt hye, & hande & hylt lowe, or at true or baſtard gardant ward w^t both yor poynts doun.

Cloſe is all mann^r of fyghts wherin yō have made a 4. true Croſe at the half ſword w^t yor ſpace very narrow & not Croſt, is alſo cloſe fyght.

*The Italian
terms were im-
perfectly under-
ſtood in England
at the end of the
XVIth century,
& Silver has
evidently miſcon-
ſtrued them.*
*"Quinta
guardia" of
Capo Ferro.*

Variable fyght is al other mann^r of lyinge not here before ſpoken of, wher of theſe 4 that follow are the cheefeſt of them.

Stocata: wch is to lye w^t yor right legge forwarde, w^t (1.) yor ſword or rapior hylt back on the out ſyde of yor right thygh w^t yor poynt forewarde to ward yor enemye, w^t yor dagg^r in yor other hand extendinge yor hand to wards the poynt of yor rapior, holdinge yor dagg^r w^t ye poynt vpright w^t narrow ſpace betweene yor rapior blade , & the nayles of yor dagg^r hand , kepynge yor rapior poynt back behind yor dagg^r hand yf poſſyble,

*"Prima
guardia" of
Capo Ferro,
"Guardia alta"
of Alfieri, &
"Guardia di
becha poſſa" of
Marozzo.*

Or he may lye wyde below vnd^r his dagg^r w^t his rapior poynt doun towards his enemyes foote, or w^t his poynt fourth w^t out his dagg^r.

*"Quarta
guardia" of
Alfieri.*

Imbrocata: is to lye w^t yor hylt hyer then yor hed, beringe yor knuckles vpwarde, & yor point depending towarde yor Enemys face or breſt.

Mountanta: is to Carrye yor rapior pummell in the palm

palm of yoᵘ hand reſting it on yoᵘ lyttle fynger wᵗ yoᵘ
hand belowe & ſo movntynge it vp a loft, & ſo to com
in wᵗ a thruſt vpō yoᵘ Enemyes face or breſt, as out of
yᵉ Imbrocata.

4.   Paſſata; is eyther to paſs wᵗ yᵉ Stocata, or to carrye
yoᵘ ſword or rapior hylt by yoᵘ right flanke, wᵗ yoᵘ
poynt directly againſt yoᵘ Enemyes belly, wᵗ yoᵘ left
roote forwarde, extendinge fourth yoᵘ daggᵘ hand wᵗ
the poynt of yoᵘ dagger forwarde as yō do yoᵘ ſword,
wᵗ narrow ſpace between yoᵘ ſword & daggᵘ blade, &
ſo to make yoᵘ paſſage vpon him,

   Alſo any other kynd of varyable fyght or lyeinge
whatſoeuer a man can deviſe not here expreſſed, is
cōtayned vnder this fight.

*The "ſhort
ſyngle ſword
fight" was a
fight with a one-
hand ſword,
and without the
aſſiſtance of a de-
fenſive weapon in
the left hand.
The "ſword
dubble" is any
kind of ſingle-
hand ſword
aſſiſted by a
defenſive weapon
in the other.*

Of the ſhort ſyngle ſword fyght againſt
the lyke weapon.
Cap. 4.

1.   F yoᵘ enemye lye a loft, eyther in open or true
   gardant fight, & then ſtrike at the left ſyde of
   yoᵘ hed or body yoᵘ beſt ward to defend yoᵘ ſelf,
is to bere it wᵗ true gardant ward, & yf he ſtrike
& com in to the cloze, or to take the grype of you yō
may then ſaſly take the grype of him as it appereth in
the chapter of the grype,

A high prime.

2.   but yf he do ſtrike & not com in, then inſtantly vpō
yoᵘ ward, vncroſe & ſtrike him either on the right or
left ſyde of yᵉ hed, & fly out inſtantly.

*A direct
"ripoſte."
"Fly out" ſug-
geſts a lateral
movement of the
feet, but might
alſo mean a back-
ward one.*

3.   Yf yō bere this wᵗ forhand ward, be ſure to ward his
blowe, or kepe yoᵘ diſtance, otherwyſe he ſhall decue

          N   you

you wᵗ euery falſe, ſtil endangeringe yoʳ hed, face, hand, Armes, bodye, & bendynge knee, wᵗ blow or thruſt. Therfore kepe well yoʳ dyſtance, becauſe yō can very hardly deſerne (being wᵗ in dyſtance), by wᶜʰ ſyde of yoʳ ſword he will ſtryke, nor at wᶜʰ of thoſe prts afore-ſayd, becauſe the ſwyft motion of yᵉ hand deceyveth the eye,

A ſimilar guard is favoured by ſome modern Auſtrian ſabre players.

yf he lye aloft & ſtrike as aforeſaid at yoʳ head, yō may 4. endanger him yf yō thruſt at his hand, hilt, or Arme, turninge yoʳ knuckles dounwarde, but fly back wᵗ all in the inſtant yᵗ yō thruſt,

A time thruſt in "quarte" at the ſword hand.

A "quarte" parry, followed by "ripoſte" or "grip."

yf he lye a loft as aforeſaid, & ſtrike a loft at the left 5. ſyde of yoʳ hed, yf yō wil ward his blow wᵗ forehand ward, then be ſure to kepe yoʳ diſtance, except he com ſo cʳtaine that yō be ſure to ward his blow, at wᶜʰ tyme yf he com in wᵗ all, yō may endanger him from yᵗ ward, eyther by blow, thruſt or grype,

yf he lye a loft & yō lye a lowe wᵗ yoʳ ſword in the 6. varyable fyght, then yf yō offer to ward his blow made at yoʳ hed, wᵗ true gardant ward yoʳ tyme wilbe to longe Due in tyme to make a ſure ward, for that it is bettʳ to bere it wᵗ forehand ward, but be ſure to kepe yoʳ diſtance, to make him com in wᵗ his feet, wher by his tyme wilbe to longe to do yᵗ he intendeth.

A time hit with "oppoſition."

yf ij Men fight both vpō open fyght he yᵗ firſt break- 7. eth his diſtance, yf he attempt to ſtryke at the others hed, ſhalbe ſurely ſtryken on the hed himſelf, yf the patient Agent ſtrike ther at in his Comynge in, & ſlyp a lyttle back wᵗ all, for yᵗ ſlydinge back maketh an indirection, wherby yoʳ blow Croſſeth his hed, & maketh a true ward for yoʳ owne, this will yt be, becauſe of his length of tyme in his cōmynge in,

Alſo

8. Alſo yf ij fyght vpon open fyght, it is better for the
    patient to ſtrike home ſtrongly at the Agents hed, when
    the ſaid Agent ſhal preſs vpon him to wyn the place then
    to thruſt, becauſe the blow of the patient is not only hurt-
    ful to the Agent, but it alſo maketh a true Croſe to defend
    his owne hed,

9. yf he charge yō a loft, out of the open or true gardant
    fyght, yf yō anſwer him wᵗ yᵉ Imprfyt gardant fyght, wᵗ
    yoʳ body leanynge forwarde, yoʳ ſpace wilbe to wyde on
    both ſyde to make a true ward in due tyme, & yoʳ arme
    And body wilbe to neere vnto him, ſo that wᵗ the bend-
    ing in of his body wᵗ the tyme of hand & foote, he may
    take the grype of you,
        but yf yō ſtand vpright in true gardant fyght, then he
    cannot reach to take the grype of you, nor otherwiſe to
    offend yō yf you kepe yoʳ diſtance, wᵗout puttinge in of
    his foote or feete wherin his number wilbe to great, &
    ſo his tyme wilbe to longe, & yō in that tyme may by
    puttinge in of yoʳ body take the grype of him, yf he preſs
    to com in wᵗ vſing only yoʳ hand, or hand & foote, & ther
    vpon yō may ſtryke or thruſt wᵗ yoʳ ſword & fly out wᵗall
    accordinge to yoʳ governors, ſe more of this, in the chap-
    ter of the grype.

    " Number wilbe to great," i.e. will have to make too many ſteps or paſſes.

0. yf he wil ſtil prſſe forcibly a loft vpō you, Charginge
    yō out of the open fyght or true gardant fyght, Intendinge
    to hurt yō in the face or hed, or to take the grype of yō
    Againſt ſuch a on, you muſt vſe both gardant & open
    fyght, wherby vpon euery blow or thruſt that he ſhall
    make at you, you may from yoʳ wards, ſtrike or thruſt
    him on the face hed or bodye as it appeareth more at
    large in the 5ᵗʰ Chapter of theſe my Inſtructions.

1. yf yō fyght wᵗ on yᵗ ſtandeth only vpon his gardant fyght *A variety of*

guards to be uſed in order to prevent fatigue. or yf he ſeeke to com in to yō by the ſame fyght, then do yō ſtrike & thruſt Contynually at al mann^r of open place that ſhall com neereſt vnto you, ſtill remembringe yor gou^rnors, ſo ſhall he Contynually be in dang^r, & often wounded, & weryed in that kynd of fyght, & you ſhalbe ſaf, the reaſon is, he is a c^rtaine marke to you, & yō are an vnc^rtaine marke to hym.

And further becauſe he tyeth him ſelf vnto on kynd of fyght only, he ſhalbe wearyed for want of Change of lyinge, & yō by reaſon of many changes ſhal not only ſtyll fyght at eaſe, & much more braue, but you haue lykewyſe iiij fyghts to his one, to wytt, gardant, open, cloſe, & variable fyght, to his gardant only, therfore y^t fight only is not to be ſtode vpon or vſed.

But yf al this will not ſ^tue, & although he hath receyved 12. Many Wounds, wyl contynually run on to com in, & forcibly breake yor dyſtance, then may you ſaffly take the grype of him, & hurt him at yor pleaſure w^t yor ſword, as appeareth in the chapter of the grype, & he can nether hurt nor take ye grype of yō, becauſe the numb^r of his feet are to many, to bringe his hand in place in due tyme, for ſuch a on ever geueth yō the place, therfore beſure to take yor tyme herin.

In "Sword and Buckler" or "Sword and Dagger" fight-ing, ſtrike with the defenſive weapon inſtead of gripping, and trip up his heels.

Lonergan, 1771.

"ſyckfyt" (ſic ſit). In the lyke ſort may yō do at ſword & dagg^r, or ſword & buckler, at ſuch tyme as I ſay, y^t yō Maye take the grype at the ſyngle ſword fyght, yō may then inſteed of the grype, ſoundly ſtryke him w^t yor buckler on the hed or ſtabb him w^t yor dagg^r & inſtantly eyther ſtryke vp his heeles or fly out, & as he lyketh y^t coolinge card to his hot braine, ſyck fyt, ſo let him com for another.

yf ij fyght & that both lye vpō the true gardant fyght 13. & that one of them will neede ſeek to wyn the half ſword
by

by preſſinge in, yᵗ may yō ſaflye do, for vpō yᵗ fyght the
half ſworde may ſafflye be woon, but he yᵗ firſt cōmeth in,
Muſt fyrſt go out, & yᵗ prſently, otherwiſe his gard wilbe
to wyde aboue to defend his hed, or yf fyt for yᵗ defence,
then wil it be to wyde vndᵉʳneath to defend yᵗ thruſt frō
his body wᶜʰ things the patient Agent may do, & fly out
ſaf, & yᵗ Agent cannot avoyd it, becauſe the moving of
his feet maketh his ward vnequall to defend both prts in
due tyme, but the one or the other wilbe diſceived & in
danger, for he being Agent vpon his firſt entrance his tyme
(by reaſon of yᵗ numbʳ of his feet), wilbe to longe, ſo yᵗ yᵉ
patient Agent may firſt enter into his action, & the Agent
muſt be of force an after doer, & therfore cannote avoyde
this offence aforeſaid.

The "patient Agent" is the man who ſtands upon the defenſive, the "Agent" being the one who attacks.

4.   yf he com in to encounter the Cloze & grype vpō yᵉ
baſtard gardant ward, then yō Maye Croſſe his blade wᵗ
yoʳˢ vpō the lyke gardant ward alſo, & as he cometh in
wᵗ his feet & haue gayned yō the place, yō may prſently
vncroſſe & ſtryke him a ſound blowe on yᵉ hed, & fly
out inſtantly, wher in he cannot offend yō by reaſon of
his loſt tyme, nor defend him ſelf vpon yoʳ vncroſſing,
becauſe his ſpace is to wyde wherby his tyme wilbe to
longe in due tyme to prvent yoʳ blowe, this may yō do
ſafly.

5.   yf he cō in vpon the baſtard gardant ward, bearing
his hylt lower than his hed, or but breſt hye or lower,
then ſtrik him ſoundly on the hed wᶜʰ thinge yō may
eaſylye do, becauſe his ſpace is to wyde in due tyme to
ward the ſame.

6.   yf yoʳ Enemy charge you vpō his Stocata fyght, yō
May ly variable wᵗ large Diſtance & vncᵉʳtaine wᵗ yoʳ
ſword & bodye at yoʳ pleaſure, yet ſo yᵗ yō may ſtryke,

N 3   thruſt

thruſt or Ward, & go forth & back as occaſion is, to take yᵉ advantage of this cōmynge in, whether he doth it out of the Stocata, or paſſata, wᶜʰ advantage yō ſhalbe ſure to haue, yf yō obſrue this rule & be not to raſh in yoʳ actions, by reaſon yᵗ yᵉ numbʳ of his feet wilbe great, & alſo becauſe when thoſe ij fyghts are met together, it is hard to Make a true Croſſe, therfore wᵗout Large dyſdance be kept of them, Commonly they are both hurt or ſlayne, becauſe in narrow diſtance their hands haue free Courſe & are not tyed to the tyme of yᵉ foote, by wᶜʰ ſwyft motion of the hand the eye is deceyved, as yō may read more at large in the   cap: of my prdoxes of defence.

" The number of his feet will be great "—i.e. he will have to make too many steps or "paſſes."

You may alſo vſe this fyght, againſt the longe ſword, or longe rapior, ſyngle & dubble,

vpon this ground ſom ſhallow wytted fellow may ſay, yf the patient muſt keep large diſtance then he muſt be dryven to goback ſtyll, to wᶜʰ I anſwer yᵗ in the contynnuall motion & travers of his ground he is to travers circuler wyſe, forwards, backwards, vpō the right hand, & vpō the left hand, the wᶜʰ travers is ſtill a certaintye to be vſed wᵗin him ſelf, & not to be pʳvented by yᵉ Agent, becauſe the Agent cōmeth one vpō an vncʳtaine marke, for when he thinketh to be ſure of his purpoſe, the patient is ſomtymes on the on ſyde, & ſom tymes on yᵉ other ſyde, ſomtymes to far back, & ſomtymes to neere, ſo yᵗ ſtil the Agent muſt vſe the numbʳ of his feet wᶜʰ wilbe to longe to anſwer yᵉ hand of yᵉ patient Agent, & it cannot be denyed but the patient Agent by reaſon of his large diſtance, ſtil ſeeth what yᵉ Agent doth in his cōmyng, but the Agent cannot ſe what the other doth, til the patient Agent be into his Action, therfore

This is exactly the traverſe recommended by Roworth.

to

to late for him eyther to hurt the patient, or in due
tyme to defend him felf, becaufe he entreth his aɗtiõ
vpõ yᵉ knowledge of the patient, but he knowᵗ not
what yᵉ patient Agent will do til it be to late.

7.   yf the Agent fay yᵗ then he wil ftand faft vpon fom
fure gard & fomtymes moving & travᵣfing his ground,
& kepe large diftance as yᵉ patient do, to wᶜʰ I anfwer,
yᵗ when ij men fhal meete yᵗ haue both the prfeɗion
of their weapons, againft the beft no hurt canbe don,
other wife yf by any devife on fhould be able to hurt
the other, then werther no prfeɗion in yᵉ vfe of weapons,
this prfeɗion of fyght being obfrved, pᵣventeth both
clofe fyght, & al mannᵣ of clozes, grype & wreftling &
al mannᵣ of fuch other devics what fo euer.

8.   Alfo yf he charge yõ vpõ his Stocata, or any other
lying aftᵣ yᵗ fafhion, wᵗ his poynt low & large paced,
then lye yõ a loft wᵗ yoᵣ hand & hylt aboue yoᵣ hed,
eyther true gardant, or vpõ the open fight, then he cannot reach yõ yf yõ kepe yoᵣ diftance wᵗout putting in
of his foot or feet, but yõ may reach him wᵗ the tyme
of yoᵣ hand, or wᵗ the tyme of your hand & body, or
of hand, body & foot, becaufe he hath al redy put in
his body wᵗin yoᵣ reach & haue gayned yõ the place,
& yõ are at lybertye & wᵗout his reach, til he put in
his foot or feete, wᶜʰ tyme is to longe to anfwer the tyme
of yoᵣ hand, & his fpace to wyde in that place to make
a ward in due tyme to defend his hed, Armes & hande,
one of wᶜʰ wilbe alwaies wᵗ in yoᵣ reach.

note ftil in this yᵗ yoᵣ weapons be both fhort of yᵉ
Equal & convenient length of yᵉ fhort fword.

9.   yf out of his varyable fyght he ftrike at yᵉ right or
left fyde of the hed or body, then yoᵣ beft ward is to
bere

bere it wᵗ fore hand ward, otherwiſe yoʳ ſpace wilbe to
wyde & to far to make yoʳ ward in due tyme.

Yf he lye variable aftʳ the mannʳ of the paſſata then 20.
yf yō lye a loft as is aboue ſaid, yō haue the Advantage,
becauſe he yᵗ lyeth varyable cannot reach home, at hed
hand or arme, wᵗout putting in of his foote or feet, &
therfore it cannot be denyed, but yᵗ he yᵗ playeth aloft,
hath ſtil the tyme of the hand to the tyme of yᵉ foot,
wᶜʰ fight beinge truly handled is aduantage invincible.

Yf he lye variable vpō the Imbrocata, then make a 21
narrow ſpace wᵗ yoʳ poynt vpwarde, & ſodainly yf yō
can Croſe his poynt wᵗ yoʳ blade put aſyde his poynt
ſtrongly wᵗ yoʳ ſword & ſtrik or thruſt at him , & fly
out inſtantly, euer remembring yoʳ gouernors yᵗ he deceve yō not in taking of his poynt.

*From this it
appears that in
Silver's time the
knees were very
little bent.*

*A time hit or
thruſt at the arm
or upper parts.*

yf he ſtrike or thruſt at yoʳ lege or lower prte out of 22.
any fyght, he ſhal not be able to reach the ſame vnleſs
yō ſtand large paced wᵗ bendinge knee, or vnleſs he com
in wᵗ his foote or feete, the wᶜʰ yf he ſhal ſo do, then
yō may ſtrik or thruſt at his arme or vpper prte for
then he putteth them into the place gayning yō the
place wherby you may ſtrike home vpō him & he
cannot reach yō.

but yf he ſtand large paced wᵗ bendinge knee then
wyn the place & ſtrike home freely at his knee, & fly
back ther wᵗ.

yf he com to the cloſe fight wᵗ yō & yᵗ yō are both 23
croſt aloft at yᵉ half ſword wᵗ both yoʳ points vpwards,
then yf he com in wᵗ all in his Croſſing bere ſtrongly
yoʳ hand & hylt ouʳ his wriſt, cloſe by his hylt putting
it ouer at yᵉ backſyde of his hand & hylt prſſinge doune
his hand & hylt ſtrongly & ſodainly, in yoʳ entring in,
& ſo

& ſo thruſt yor hylt in his face, or ſtrike him vpō y^e *Recommended* head w^t y^r ſword, & ſtrike vp his heeles, & fly out, *alſo by Lonergan, 1771.*

24. yf yō are both ſo croſt at ye baſtard gardant ward, & yf he then preſs in, then take the grype of him as is ſhewed in ye chapter of ye grype,

Or w^t yor left hand or arme, ſtrike his ſword blade *Beating the* ſtrongly & ſodainly towarde yor left ſyde by wch meanes *ſword away with the gauntleted* yō are uncroſt, & he is diſcou^red, then may yō thruſt *left hand.* him in the body w^t yor ſword & fly out inſtantly, wch thinge he cannot avoyd, nether can he offend yō

Or being ſo croſt, yō may ſodainly vncroſe & ſtrike *An alternative.* him vpō the hed & fly out inſtantly wch thinge yō may ſafly do & go out free.

25. yf yō be both croſt at ye half ſword w^t hys poynt vp & yor poynt doune in the true gardant ward, then yf he preſs to com in, then eyther take ye grype of him, *Again the* as in the chapter of the grype, or w^t yor left hand or *alternatives of* arme, ſtrike out his ſword blade towards yor left ſyde as *"gripping" and beating the* aforeſaid, & ſo yō may thruſt him in the body w^t yor *ſword off.* ſword & fly out inſtantly.

26. Do yō neuer attempt to cloze or com to ye grype at theſe weapons vnleſs it be vpō the ſlow motiō or diſorder of yor enemye,

but yf he will cloze w^t you, then yō may take the *When he en-* grype of him ſafly at his cōmynge in, for he y^t firſt by *cloſes, "grip" him.* ſtronge preſſing in adventureth the cloze looſeth it, & is in great danger, by reaſon y^t the numb^r of his feet are to great, wherby his tyme wilbe to longe, in due tyme to anſwer the hand of ye patient Agent, as in the chapter of the grype doth plainly appere,

27. Alwaies remembring yf yō fyght vpō the variable fight y^t yō ward vpō forehand ward, otherwiſe yor ſpace

O wilbe

wilbe to wyde in due tyme to make a true gardant ward, to defend yor ſelf.

yf yō fyght vpō open fyght, or true gardant fyght, 28. neuer ward vpō forehand ward for then yor ſpace wilbe to wyde alſo, in due tyme to make a fureward,

yf he lye aloft w^t his poynt towarde you, aft^r the 29. mann^r of the Imbrocata, then make yor ſpace narrow w^t yor point upwarde & put by his poynt, & ſtrike or thruſt as aforeſaid but be fure herin to kepe yor diſtance, y^t he deceue you not in taking of his poynt.

| *" Parrying" and "Ripoſting."* | *Of diu'rs aduantages y' you may take by ſtrykinge frō yo' warde at y' ſword fyght.* |

Cap. 5.

A parry in "high tierce" with its ripoſtes.

IF yor enemy ſtrike at the right ſyde of yor hed, 1. yō lyinge true gardant, then put yor hilt a little doune, Mounting yor poynt, ſo that yor blade May Croſſe a thwart yor face, ſo ſhal yō make A true ward for the right ſyde of yor hed, from the wch ward yō may inſtantly ſtrike him on the ryght or left ſyde of the hed, or to turne doune yor poynt, & thruſt him in the bodye, or you may ſtrike him on the left ſyde of the body, or on the out ſyde of his left thygh.

Or yō may ſtrike him on the out ſyde of the right thygh, on of thoſe he cannot avoyd yf he fly not back inſtantly vpō his blowe, becauſe he know^t not wch of theſe the patient Agent wil do.

A parry of "prime" with its ripoſtes.

Yf yō lye vpō yor true gardant ward, & he ſtrike 2. at the left ſyde of yor hed, yō haue the choyſe from yor ward to ſtrike him ſrom yt, on the right or left ſyde of the

the hed, or to turne doune yor poynt, & thruſt him in
the bodye, or yō May ſtryke him on the out ſyde of
the right or left thygh, for the reaſon aboue ſayde in
the laſt rule, except he fly out inſtantly vpō his blowe.

3. Yf he charge yō vpon the open or true gardant fyght,
yf yō wil anſwer him w^t the lyke, then kepe yor diſtance,
& let yor gatheringe be all waies in y^t fyght to warde
his right ſyde ſo ſhal yō w^t yor ſword choake vp any
blowe that he can make at yō, from the wch ward yō
May ſtryke him on the right or left ſyde of ye hed, or
thruſt him in the bodye.

but yf he thruſt at your face or body, then yō may
out of yor gardant fight break it doun warde w^t yor *A thruſt parried*
ſword bering yor poynt ſtrongly towarde yor right ſyde, *with the*
from the wch breaking of his thruſt yō may likwiſe ſtrike *"ſeconde," and*
him frō the right or left ſyde of ye hed, or thruſt him *its ripoſtes.*
in the bodye.

4. Yf yō meet w^t on y^t cannot ſtrike frō his warde, vpō
ſuch a on yō may both dubble & faulſe & ſo deceue
him, but yf he be skylful yō muſt not do ſo, becauſe he
wilbe ſtil ſo vnc^{r}taine in his traverſe that he will ſtyll
p^{r}vent you of tyme & place, ſo y^t when yō think to *To "dubble" =*
dubble & falſe, yō ſhal gayne him the place & ther vpō *to "remiſe."*
he wilbe before yō in his action, & in yor comynge he *To "faulſe" =*
will ſtil endanger yō, *to "feint."*

5. yf yō fyght vpō the variable fyght, & that yō receue *A parry of*
a blow w^t forehand ward, made at the right ſyde of yor *"tierce" with*
hed or body, yō haue y^e choiſe of viij offenciue Actions *its ripoſtes.*
frō y^t ward, the firſt to ſtryke him on the right ſyde,
eyther on the hed ſhould^r, or thygh, or to thruſt him
in the body, or to ſtryke him on the left ſyde either on
the hed ſhold^r or thygh, or to thruſt him in the body,

O 2 the

the lyke may yō do yf he ſtrike euʳ at yoʳ left ſyde, as is aboue ſaid, yf yō bere it wᵗ fore hand ward.

In this forehand ward kepe yoʳ diſtance, & take heed 6. yᵗ he deceyue yō not wᵗ the dounright blowe at yoʳ hed out of his open fyght, for being wᵗ in diſtance yᵉ ſwift motion of yᵉ hand May deceue yoʳ eye, becauſe yō know not by wᶜʰ ſyde of yoʳ ſword his blow wil com

Alſo ſe yᵗ he deceue yō not vpō any falſe offerynge to 7. ſtryke at the on ſyde, & when therby yō haue turned yoʳ poynt aſyde, then to ſtrike on the other ſyde, but yf yō kepe diſtance yō are free from yᵗ, therfore ſtyll in all yoʳ actions remembʳ y gouʳnors

yf he wil do nothinge but thruſt, Anſwer him as it 8. is ſet doune in the 16ᵗʰ ground of yᵉ ſhort ſword fyght & alſo in divⁿˢ places of the 8ᵗʰ chaptʳ.

How to engage
with a man who
uſes point.

Alſo conſyder yf he lye at the thruſt vpon yᵉ ſtocata, 9. or paſſata, & yō haue no waye to avoyde him, except yō can Croſſe his ſword blade wᵗ yoʳˢ, & ſo Indirect his poynt, therfore kepe narrow ſpace vpō his poynt, & kepe well yoʳ diſtance in vſing yoʳ travers.

but yf he put forth his poynt ſo yᵗ yō may Croſs it wᵗ fore hand ward, for yf yō wacth for his thruſt then lye vpō forehand ward wᵗ poynt alittle vp. yf he lye wᵗ his poynt Mounted, & yf yō ſyngle yoʳ thruſt vpō the out ſyde of yoʳ ſword to warde yoʳ right ſyde, or back of yoʳ ſword hand, ſtrike or bere his poynt out towarde yoʳ right ſyde, & ther vpon putting forward yoʳ body & left foote Circuler wyſe to warde his right ſyde yō May ſtrike him vpō his ſword Arme, hed, face or bodye.

Or yf yō take it on the Inſyde of yoʳ ſword blade to warde yoʳ left ſyde then wᵗ yoʳ ſword put by his poynt ſtrongly & ſodainly towarde yoʳ left ſyde, drawing
yoʳ

yor left foote Circuler wyſe back behind the heele of
yor right foote, & ſtrike him on the inſyde of his ſword
hand or Arme or on the hed, face, or body, & fly out
accordinge to yor gou^rnors

This May yō vſe againſt y^e ſword & dagg^r longe or
ſhort, or rapior & ponyard, or ſword & buckler.

10. Alſo rememb^r yf he haue a longe ſword, & yō a ſhort
ſword, euer to Make yor ſpace ſo narrow, y^t yō may
alwaies break his thruſt before y^t be in force yf poſſible
yō may, & alſo to kepe large diſtance whether he charge
yō out of the Stocata, paſſata, or Imbrocata &c,

of this yō may ſe more at large in the 8th chapter.

*The mann^r of Certaine gryps & Clozes to be
vſed at y^e ſyngle ſhort ſword fyght &c.*

Cap. 6.

1. F he ſtrike aloft at the left ſyde of yor hed, and
run in w^t all to take the Cloze or grype of
you, then ward it gardant, & enter in w^t yor
left ſyde puting in yor left hand, on the inſyde
of his ſword Arme, neere his hylte, bering yor hand ou^r
his Arme, & Wrape in his hand & ſworde vnd^r yor Arme,
as he cometh in, Wreſting his hand & ſword cloſe to
your bodye turninge back yor right ſyde from him, ſo
ſhal he not be able to reach yor ſword, but yō ſhall ſtyll
haue it at lybertye to ſtryke or thruſt him & endanger
the breakinge of his Arme, or the takinge away of his
ſword by y^t grype.

2. Yf yō are both Croſt in Cloſe fyght vpon the baſtard
gardant ward alowe, yō May put yor left hand on the
out ſyde of his ſword at the back of his hand, neere or

O 3   at

at the hylte of his ſword Arme & take him on the inſyde
of y^t arme w^t yor hand, aboue his elbowe is beſt, & draw
him in towarde yō ſtrongly, wreſtinge his knuckles dounwarde & his elbowe vpwarde ſo may yō endang^r to break
his arme, or caſt him doune, or to wreſt his ſword out
of his hand, & go free yor ſelf.

in like ſort vpō this kynd of cloze, yō may clape yor 3.
left hand vpō the wriſt of his ſword arme, holding it
ſtrongly & ther w^t thruſt him hard from yō, & p^{r}ſently
yō may thruſt him in the body w^t yor ſword for in y^t
Inſtant he can nether ward, ſtrike, nor thruſt,

yf he ſtrike home at the left ſyde of yor hed, & ther 4.
w^t all com in to take the cloze or grype of your hilt
or ſword arme w^t his left hand, firſt ward his blow
gardant, & be ſure to put in yor left hand und^r yor ſword
& take hold on the out ſyde of his left hand, Arme or
ſleve, putting yor hand vnder the wriſt of his Arme w^t
the toppe of yor fing^{rs} vpwarde, & yor thumb & knuckles
dounwarde, then pluck him ſtrongly towarde yor left
ſyde, ſo ſhal yō indirect his feet turning hys left ſhould^r
towarde yō, vpō wch inſtant yō Maye ſtrike or thruſt
him w^t yor ſword & fly out ſaf, for his feet being indirected, although he hath his ſword at lyberty, yet
ſhal he not be able to Make any offencyve fight againſt
yō becauſe his tyme wilbe to longe to direct his feet
againe to vſe his ſword in due tyme.

Alſo yf he attempt the cloze or grype w^t you vpon 5.
his baſtard gardant ward, then croſſe his ſword w^t the
lyke ward, & as he cometh in w^t his feet you haue the
tyme of yor hand & bodye, wherby w^t yor left hand or
Arme yō May put by his ſword blade, wch thinge you
muſt ſodainly & ſtrongly do, caſting it towarde yor left
                                                                    ſyde

ſyde, ſo may yō vncroſſe & thruſt him in yᵉ body wᵗ yoʳ
ſword & fly out inſtantlye, for yf yō ſtay ther he wil
direct his ſword againe & endanger yō, this may ſafly
be don, or yō May vncroſſe & turne yoʳ poynt vp, & ſtrike
him on the hed, & fly out inſtantly.

6.   Yf he preſſe in to the half ſword vpō a forehand ward,
then ſtrike a ſound blow at the left ſyde of his hed
turnyng ſtrongely yoʳ hand & hylt preſſing doun his
ſword hand & arme ſtrongly, & ſtrike yoʳ hilt full in
his face, beringe yoʳ hilt ſtrongly vpō him, for yoʳ hand
beinge vppʳmoſt yō haue the aduantage in yᵗ grype, for
ſo May yō breake his face wᵗ yoʳ hylt, & ſtrike vp his
heels wᵗ yoʳ left foote, and throwe him a great fall, al
this May ſafly be don by reaſon yᵗ he is weake in his
cōmynge in by yᵗ moving of his feet, & yō repell him
in yᵉ fulnes of yoʳ ſtrength, as appeareth in the Chapter
of yᵉ ſhort ſingle ſword fyght, in the 23ʳᵈ grownde of
the ſame,

7.   remember that yō neuʳ attempt the Cloze nor grype
but looke to his ſlyppe, Conſyder what is ſaid in the 8ᵗʰ
genʳall rule in the Second Chapter, & alſo in the 26ᵗʰ
ground of the ſyngle ſword fyght in the 4ᵗʰ Chapter.

Of the ſhort ſword & dagger fyght
Againſt the lyke Weapon.

Cap. 7.

1. BSRVE at theſe weapons the formʳ rules, defend wᵗ yoʳ ſword & not wᵗ yoʳ daggʳ, yet yō
may croſs his ſword wᵗ yoʳ daggʳ, yf yō may
conveniently reach the ſame therwᵗ, wᵗ out
puttinge in of yoʳ foote, only by bendinge in of yoʳ body,
other

other wyfe yor tyme wilbe to longe, & his tyme wilbe fufficient to difplace his owne, fo y^t yō fhal not hyt it w^t yor dagg^r, & fo he may make a thruft vpon yō, this tyme y^t I here Meane, of puttinge by of his fword is, When he lyeth out fpent w^t his fword poynt towarde you, & not elfe, wch thinge yf yō can do w^tout puttinge in of yo^t foote, then yō may vfe yor dagg^r, & ftrike ftrongly & fodainlye his fword poynt ther w^t vp, or doune, to indirect the fame, that don, inftantly ther w^t ftrike or thruft at him w^t yor fword,

Alfo yō may put by his fword blade w^t yor dagg^r When 2. yor fwords are Croft, eyther aboue at forehand ward, or belowe at the baftard gardant ward & ther w^t inftantly ftrike or thruft w^t yor fword & fly out accordinge to yor gou^rnors, of this yō may fee more at large in ye Chapter of the fyngle fword fyght in the 24th ground of the fame.

Alfo yf he be fo foolehardye to com to the cloze, 3. then yō may gard w^t yor fword & ftabb w^t yor dagg^r, & fly out faf, wch thinge yō may do becaufe his tyme is to longe by the numb^r of his feet, & yō haue but the fwyft tyme of yor hand to ufe, & he cannot ftabb til he haue fetted in his feete, & fo his tyme is to late to endang^r yō, or to defend himfelf.

Know y^t yf yō defend yo^rfelf w^t yor dagger in other 4. fort than is aforefaid, yō fhalbe endang^r to be hurt, becaufe the fpace of yor dagg^r wilbe ftill to wyde to defend both blow & thruft for lacke of Circomference as ye buckler hath.

Alfo note when yō defend blow & thruft w^t yor fword 5. yō haue a neerer courfe to offend yor enemye w^t yor fword then when yō ward w^t yor dagg^r, for then yō may for the moft prte from yor warde ftrike or thruft him.

Yō

6. Yō muſt neyther Cloze nor com to the grype at
theſe weapons, vnleſs it be by the ſlow motyon or diſ-
ordour of yor adv^rſarie, yet yf he attempt ye Cloze, or
to com to the grype w^t yō, then yō may ſafly Cloze &
hurt him w^t yor dagg^r or buckler & go free yor ſelf,
but fly out according to yor gou^rnors & ther by yō ſhal
put him from his attempted Cloze, but ſe yō ſtay not
at any tyme w^tin diſtance, but in due tyme fly back
or hazard to be hurt, becauſe y^e ſwyft motion of the
hand being w^tin diſtance will deceue the eye, wher
by yō ſhall not be able to Judge in due tyme to make
a true ward, of this yō may ſe more in the chapter of
the back ſword fyght in the 12th ground of the ſame.

7. yf he extend forth his dagg^r hand yō may make yor
fyght at the ſame, remembring to kepe diſtance & to
fly back according to yor gou^rnors.

Every fight & ward w^t theſe weapons, made out of
any kynd of fyght, muſt be made & don according as
is taught in the back ſword fyght, but only y^t the
dagg^r muſt be vſed as is abouſaid, in ſteed of the grype.

8. yf he lye bent vpō his Stocata w^t his ſworde or
rapior poynt behind his dagg^r ſo y^t yō cannot reach the
ſame w^tout putting in of yor foote, then make al yor
fight at his dagg^r hand, euer remembring yor gou^rnors,
& then yf he draw in his dagg^r hand, ſo that yō may
Croſe his ſworde blade w^t yo^{rs}, then make narrow
ſpace vpō him w^t yor poynt & ſodainly & ſtrongely
ſtryke or bere his poynt towarde his right ſyde, in-
dyrecting the ſame, & inſtantly ſtrike or thruſt him
on the hed, face, Arme, or body, & fly back ther w^t
out of diſtance ſtil remembring yor gou^rnors.

9. yf he lye ſpent vpō his variable fyght then kepe yor
P diſtance

diftance & make yo͞r fpace narrow vpō him, til yō may
Croffe his fword or rapior point wᵗ yo͞r fword poynt,
wher vpon, yō having won or gayned the place, ftrike
or thruft inftantly.

yf he lye bent or fpent vpō the Imbrocata bere vp 1
yo͞r point, & make yo͞r fpace narrow & do the lyke.

Of the fhort fword & dagger fyght againft the longe fword & dagger or longe rapior & poinard.
Cap. 8.

I F yō haue the fhort fword & daggʳ, defend 1
wᵗ yo͞r fword & not wᵗ yo͞r daggʳ, except yō
haue a gautlet or hylt vpō yo͞r dagger hand,
then yō may ward vpō forehand ward, vpon
the dubble wᵗ the poynt of yo͞r fword towarde his face.

Lye not aloft wᵗ yo͞r fhort fword yf he lye alowe 2
variable on the Stocata or paffata &c, for then your
fpace wilbe to wyde to make a true Crofe in due tyme,
or to farr in his courfe to make yo͞r fpace narrow, the
wᶜʰ fpace take heede yō make very narrow, yea, fo yᵗ
yf it touch his blade, it is better.

I fay make yo͞r fpace narrow vntil yō can crofe his 3
fword blade ftrongly & fodainly, fo fhal you put by his
point out of the right lyne, & inftantly ftrike or thruft,
& flyp back according to yo͞r gouʳnors.

but take heede unlefs yō can furely & fafly crofe go
not in, but although yō can fo crofe, & ther vpon yō
enter in, ftay not by yt but fly out according to yo͞r
gouʳnors,

yf wᵗ his longe fword or rapior he charge you aloft 4
out of his open or true gardant fyght ftrykyng at the
right

right ſyde of yo̅ʳ hed, yf yo̅ haue a gautlet or cloſe hylt vpon yoʳ daggʳ hand then ward it dubble wᵗ forehand ward, bering yoʳ ſword hylt to warde yoʳ right ſhouldʳ, wᵗ yoʳ knuckles upwarde & yoʳ ſword poynt to warde the right ſyde of his breſt or ſholder, croſſing yoʳ dagger on yoʳ ſword blade, reſting yt ther on vpon yᵉ hyer ſyde of yoʳ ſword beringe yoʳ hylts cloſe together wᵗ yoʳ dagger hilt a little behind yoʳ ſword hilt bering both yoʳ hands right out together ſpent or verye neere ſpent when yo̅ ward his blowe, Meetinge him ſo vpon yoʳ ward that his blow may light at yoʳ half ſword or wᵗin, ſo that his blade may ſlyde from yoʳ ſword & reſt on yoʳ daggʳ, at wᶜʰ inſtant tyme thruſt forth yoʳ poynt at his breſt & fly out inſtantly, ſo ſhal yo̅ co̅tynually endanger him & go ſaf yoʳ ſelf.

Yf he ſtrike a loft at the left ſyde of yoʳ hed, ward as aforeſaid, bering yoʳ ſword hilt towarde yoʳ left ſhouldʳ wᵗ yoʳ knuckles doun warde, & yoʳ ſword poynt towarde the left ſyde of his breſt or ſholdʳ, bowing yoʳ body & hed a little forewarde towarde him, & remembʳ to bere yoʳ warde on both ſyds yᵗ he ſtrike y̅ not vpon the hed, then vpo̅ his blow meet his ſword as is aforeſaid wᵗ yoʳ dagger croſt ouʳ yoʳ ſword blade as before, & when his ſword by reaſon of his blowe vpon yoʳ ſword ſhal ſlyde doune & reſt vpon yoʳ dagger, then ſodainly caſt his ſword blade out to warde yoʳ left ſyde wᵗ yoʳ dagger, to indirect his point, & ther wᵗ thruſt at his breſt fro̅ yoʳ ward & fly out inſtantly, the like may you do yf his ſword glance out fro̅ yoʳⁿ, vpo̅ his blowe.

al this may ſafly be don wᵗ yᵉ ſhort ſword & cloſe hylted dagger or gautlet

Stay

Stay not w^t in diſtance of the longe ſword or rapior 6. w^t yor ſhort ſword, nor ſuffer him to wyn the place of you, but eyther Croſe his ſword, or make yor ſpace verye narrow to croſe it before his blow or thruſt be in force, yet keping yor diſtance wher by he ſhall ſtrike or thruſt at nothing, & ſo he ſhalbe ſubiect to the tyme of yor hand againſt the tyme of his feet.

Kepe diſtance & lye as yō thinke beſt for yor eaſe & 7. ſafty, yet ſo y^t yō may ſtrike, thruſt, or ward, & when yō find his poynt Certaine, then make yor ſpace narrow & croſe his ſword, ſo ſhal yō be the firſt mou^r, & enter firſt into yor action, & he beinge an aft^r doer, is not able to avoyd yor Croſe, nor narrow ſpace, nor any ſuch offence as ſhalbe put in execution againſt hym.

havinge Croſt his longe ſword or rapior w^t yor ſhort 8. ſword blade, & put his poynt out of the ſtrait lyne by force then ſtrike or thruſt at him w^t yor ſword & fly out inſtantly accordinge to y^r gou^rnors.

Stand not vpō gardant fyght only, for ſo he will 9. greatlye endanger yō out of his other fyghts becauſe yō haue made yor ſelf a c^rtaine marke to him, for in contynuynge in y^t fyght only yō ſhal not only weary yor ſelf, but do alſo exclude yo^rſelf frō the benyfyt of the Open, variable, & cloſe fyghts, & ſo ſhal he haue four fyghts to yor one, as yō may ſe in the Chapter of the ſhort ſyngle ſword fyght in the 15th ground therof.

Yf he lye in Open or true gardant fyght, then yō 10 may vpon yor open & gardant fight ſafly bringe yor ſelf to the half ſword, & then you may thruſt him in the body , vnder his gard or ſword when he bereth it gardant, becauſe he is weak in his garde, but fly out inſtantly, & he cannot bringe in his point to hurt yō

except

except he go back w^t his foote or feet, wch tyme is to
longe to anfwer the fwyft tyme of the hand.

yf he put doune his fword lower to defend y^t thruft
then will his hed be open, fo y^t yō may ftrike him on
the hed ou^r ouer his fword & fly out ther w^t, w^ch
thinge he cannot defend, becaufe his fpace is to wyde
to put vp his blade in due tyme to make a true ward
for the fame.

1.   Underftand y^t the whole fom of the long rapior
fyght is eyther upon the Stocata, Paffata, Imbrocata,
or Mountanta, al thefe, and al the reft of their devycs
you may fafly prevent by kepinge yor diftance, becaufe
therby you fhal ftil dreue him to vfe the tyme of his
feet, wherby yō fhal ftil p^rvent him of ye true place,
& therfore he cannot in due tyme make any of thefe
fyghts offencive vpon you by reafon y^t the number of
his feet will ftill be to great, fo y^t he fhal ftil vfe the
flow tyme of his feet to the fwyft tyme of yor hand,
& therfore yō may fafly defend yor felf & offend him,

Now you plainly fe how to p^rvent al thefe, but for
the bett^r example note this, wher as I fay by kepeinge
of diftance fom may obieft y^t then the rapior man will
com in by degrees w^t fuch warde as fhall beft lyke him,
& dryve back the fword man contynually, to whome
I anfwer, y^t can he not do, by reafon y^t ye fword mans
travers is made c^rculer wyfe, fo y^t the rapior man in
his cōmyng hath no place to carrye the poynt of his
rapior, in due tyme to make home his fyght, but y^t
ftil his rapior wil lye w^t in the compafs of the tyme
of the fword mans hand, to make a true croffe vpon
him, the wch crofe beinge made w^t force he may fafly
vncrofe, & hurt the rapior man in the Arme, hed,

P 3   face

face or body, w^t blow or thruſt, & fly out ſaf before
he ſhal haue tyme to direct his poynt againe to make
his thruſt vpō y^e ſword man.

Yf ye rapior man lye vpon the ſtocata, firſt make yor
ſpace narrow w^t yor ſhort ſword, & take heed y^t he
ſtrike not doune yor ſworde poynt w^t his dagger & ſo
Jump in & hurt you w^t the thruſt of his longe rapior,
wch thing he may do becauſe he haue cōmaunded
your ſword, & ſo yō are left open & diſcov^red & left
onlye vnto the vnc^rtaine ward of yor dagg^r, wch ward
is to ſyngle for a man to venter his lyf on, wch yf yō
myſſe to prforme Neuer ſo lyttle yō are hurt or ſlaine.

To p^rvent this danger yō muſt remember your
gou^rnors, & p^rſently vpon his leaſt motion be ſure of
yor diſtance, & yor narrow ſpace, then do as follow^t.

Yf he lye vpō his ſtocata, w^t his rapior point w^t in
or behind his dagg^r hand out ſtrait, then lye yō variable in Meaſure w^t yor right foote before & yor ſword
poynt out directly forth w^t yor ſpace very narrow as
neere his rapior poynt as yō may, betwixt his rapior
poynt & his dagger hand, from wch yō may ſodainly
w^t a wriſt blow, lyft vp yor poynt & ſtrike him on the
out ſyde or in ſyde of his dagg^r hand, & fly out w^t all,
then make yor ſpace narrow as before, then yf he thruſt
home at yō, yō are redy p^rpred for hys thruſt, or yō
may thruſt at his dagger hand, do wch yō ſhal thinke
beſt, but yor blow muſt be but only by moving of yor
wriſt, for yf yō lyft vp yor hand and Arme to fetch a
large blowe then yor tyme wilbe to longe, & yor ſpace
to wyde in due tyme to make a true ward to defend
yor ſelf from his thruſt, ſo ſhall yō hurt him although
he haue a gantlet therone, for yor thruſt wil run vp
                                                    between

between his fing^rs, & yor blow wil cut of the fyng^rs of
his gantlet, for he cannot defend himſelf from on blow
or thruſt of 20, by reaſon that yō haue the place to
reach home at his hand, & for y^t cauſe he cannot
p^rvent it, nether can he rech home to you w^tout putting
in of his foot or feet, becauſe his diſtance is to large,
but upon eu^r blow or thruſt y^t yō make. at his hand
ſlypp back a little, ſo ſhal yō ſtill vpō eu^r blow or
thruſt y^t yō make at him, be out of his reach,

but yf vpon yor blow or thruſt he wil enter in w^t
his foote or feet to make home his ſtocata or thruſt
vpō you, then by reaſon of yor ſlydynge back, you
ſhalbe prepared in due tyme to make a prſyt ward to
defend yo^rſelf w^t yor ſworde.

Therfore euer reſpect his rapior poynte & remember
to make & kepe narrow ſpace vpon it w^t yor ſword
poynt, that yō may be ſure to break his thruſt before
it be in ful force.

Yf he thruſt at yor hyer prts w^t his poynt a lyttle
mounted, then make narrow yor ſpace w^t yor poynt
vpon his, yf yō Croſe his blade on the inſyde between
his rapior & his dagg^r, yf he preſs in then frō yor croſe
beat or bere backe his poynt ſtrongly towarde his right
ſyde, and havinge indirected his poynt, ſtrike him on
the inſyde of the rapior or dagg^r hand or Arme, or on
the hed, face, or body, & fly out inſtantly,

Or you may vpon his p^rſſinge in w^t his thruſt Slypp
yor poynt doune as he cōmeth in, & put vp yor hylt
& ward it gardant, & ther w^t from that ward caſt out
his poynt, & ſodainly ſtrike him in one of the placs
aforeſaid, & fly out inſtantlye remembringe yor gou^rnors.

Yf he lye faſt & do not com in, then ſtrike & thruſt
at

at his dagg^r hand, w^t yor wrist blow and slypp back
ther w^t euery tyme

but yf he lye fast & beat doune yor poynt w^t his
dagger, & then thrust at you from his Stocata then
turne vp yor hilt w^t yor knuckles vpwarde & yor nayles
dounwarde, takinge his blade vpō the backsyde of
yo^rs towarde yor left syde & bere it gardant towarde y^t
syde, & so may yō offend him as before is said vpō y^t
ward.

The lyke may yō do vpon him yf he lye out w^t his
poynt, when yō haue crost ye same w^t yo^rs, & strike it
to eyther syde, & so indirect his poynt, and then strike
or thrust & fly out.

The lyke must yō do, yf he lye with his point
directly towarde yor bellye

but yf yō crose his poynt so mounted or dyrect as
abouesaid, vpō ye out syde of yor sword w^t his poynt
a little hyer than yor hylt, so y^t you may crose his
blade, then yf he thrust ouer yor blade syngle uncros-
ing the same, then may you break it w^t yor forehand
ward out towarde yor right syde, & yf he com in ther
w^t, then strike him on the out syde of his rapior hand
or Arme, or on the hed or face, & fly out ther w^t

but yf he thrust in ouer yor sword as abouesaid &
press in his blade strongly dubble w^t the helpe of his
dagger, then put doune yor poynt & turne vp yor hylt
gardant, so shal yō safly defend it beringe it gardant
out towarde yor left syde & from yt strike him in between his rapior and dagger in on of the foresaid
places, & fly out,

but yf from this crose he slypp his poynt doune to
thrust vnd^r yor sword, then strike doune his poynt towarde

warde his left foote & ther w^t ſtrike him on the out
ſyde of his rapior hand or arme, hed, face, or body, &
fly out inſtantly, according to yor gou^rnors.

Alſo yō may vpon this of his poynt doune, then
turne yor poynt ſhort ouer his blade in yor ſtepp-
ynge back, & put yor poynt doune in the inſyde of
his blade turnynge vp yor hilt gardant as aforeſaid, &
then yf he thruſt at yō, bere it gardant towarde yor
left ſyde, & then haue you the ſame offenciue blowes
& thruſts againſt him as is aboueſaid vpō y^e ſame
ward.

2. Yf he lye aft^r the Stocata w^t his poynt doune towarde yor foote, then croſe his blade on ye out ſyde,
& yf he turne his poynt ou^r yor blade to make his
thruſt vpon you, then turne vp yor hilt & bere it gardant as aboueſaid, bering it out towarde yor left ſyde,
& frō y^t ward offend him as is aboueſaid

3. Alſo in this fyght take heed y^t he thruſt yō not in
the ſword hand or arme, therfore euer reſpect to draw
it back in due tyme, remembring therin yor twofold
gou^rnor, in yor comyng in, to make yor croſe or narrow
ſpace.

4. Yf at ſword & dagger or buckler he ſtrike in at the
out ſyde of yor right legge ward it w^t the back of yor
ſword, carrying yor poynt doune holding yor knuckles
dounwarde & yor Nayles upwarde, bering yor ſword
out ſtrongly towarde yor right ſyde, vpon wch ward yō
may ſtrike him on the out ſyde of the left legge, or
thruſt him in ye thigh or belly

5. The lyke may yō do yf he ſtrik at yor other ſyde, yf
yō ward his blowe w^t the edge of yor ſword yor hand
& knuckles as aforeſaid, caſting out his ſword blade

Q   towarde

towarde yoʳ left ſyde, this may be vſed at ſhort or
longe ſword fyght.

    you muſt neuer vſe any fyght againſt the longe 2⸿
rapior & daggʳ wᵗ yoʳ ſhort ſword but variable fyght,
becauſe yoʳ ſpace wilbe to wyde, & yoʳ time to longe,
to defend or offend in due tyme.

    Alſo yō muſt vſe large diſtance euer, becauſe out of 2⸿
yᵗ fyght yō can hardly make a true croſe becauſe being
wᵗ in diſtance yᵉ eye is deceiued to do it in due tyme

    remembʳ in putting forth yoʳ ſword point to make 2⸿
yoʳ ſpace narrow, when he lyeth vpō his ſtocata, or
any thruſt, yō muſt hold yᵉ handle thereof as it were
a longſt yoʳ hand, reſting the pomell thereof in the
hollow prte of the mydl of the heele of yoʳ hand towarde the wriſt, & the former prte of the handle muſt
be holden betwixt the fore fynger & thumbe, wᵗout
the Myddle Joynt of the fore fynger towarde the topp
ther of, holding yᵗ fynger ſomethinge ſtrait out gryping round yoʳ handle wᵗ yoʳ other iij fingers, & laying
yoʳ thumbe ſtrait out vpō the handle, ſo yᵗ yoʳ thumbe
lye al alonge vpon yᵉ ſame, ſo ſhal yō lay yoʳ point
out ſtrait towarde his, the better to be able to prforme
this aǎtiō prfytly, for yf yō grype yoʳ handle cloſe
ouʳthwart in yoʳ hand, then can yō not lay yoʳ poynt
ſtrait vpon his to make yoʳ ſpace narrow, but yᵗ yoʳ
poynt wil ſtil lye to wyde to doe the ſame in due tyme,
& this is the beſt way to hold yoʳ ſword in al kinde of
variable fyght

    but vpō yoʳ gardant or open fyght then hold it wᵗ 2⸿
ful gryping it in yoʳ hand, & not laying yoʳ thumb
alonge yᵉ handle, as ſom vſe, then ſhal you neuer be
able ſtrongly to ward a ſtronge blowe.

This

;o.   This haue I written out of myne entyre loue yᵗ I
bere to my country men, wiſshing them yet once
againe to follow the truth, & to fly the vaine Imprſyt
rapior fight, the bettʳ to ſaue themſelues from wounds
& ſlawghter, for who ſo attayneth to the pʳfectiō of
this true fyght wᶜʰ I haue here ſet forth in theſe my
bref Inſtructions, & alſo in my pradoxes of defence,
ſhal not only defend them ſelues, but ſhal ther by
bring thoſe that fyght vpō that Imprſyt fyght of yᵉ
rapior vndʳ their mercye, or elſe put them in Cobbs
travers, where of yō may read in the 38 Chapter of
my pradoxes aforeſaid.

Of yᵉ ſword & Buckler fyght,
Cap. 9.

WORD & Buckler fight, & ſword & daggʳ
fyght are al one, ſaving yᵗ yō may ſafly defend both blowe & thruſt, ſyngle wᵗ yoʳ
buckler only, & in likeſort yō may ſafly
ward both blowes & thruſts dubble, yᵗ is wᵗ ſword &
buckler together wᶜʰ is great aduantage againſt yᵉ
ſword & daggʳ, &c, & is the ſureſt fight of al ſhort
weapons.

Of the two hand ſword fight againſt yᵉ like weapon.
Cap. 10.

HESE weapons are to be vſed in fight as the
ſhort ſtaf, yf both play vpō dubble & ſyngle
hand, at the ij hand ſword, the long ſword
hath the advantage yf the waight ther of
be not to heavye for his ſtrength yᵗ hath it, but yf
Q 2   both

both play only vpon dubble hand, then his blade wᶜʰ
is of cōvenyent length agreeing wᵗ his ſtature yᵗ hath
it, wᶜʰ is according with the length of the meaſure of
his ſyngle ſwordblade, hath the advantage of yᵉ ſword
yᵗ is to long for yᵉ ſtature of the contrarye prtye, becauſe he can croſe & vncroſe, ſtrike & thruſt, cloze
& grype in ſhorter tyme than the other can.

Of the ſhort ſtaf fyght, being of cōvenient length, againſt
yᵉ like weapon.

Cap. 11.

HE ſhort ſtaf hath iiij wards, yᵗ is ij wᵗ yᵉ
point vp, & ij wᵗ the poynt doune,

At theſe weapons euer lye ſo that yō may 1.
be able to thruſt ſyngle & dubble, & to ward,
ſtrike, or thruſt in due tyme, ſo ſhal yoʳ enemye, yf
he fyght only vpō dubble hand be driuen of neceſſitie,
ſeeking to wyn the place, to gayne yō the place wher
by yō may ſafly hurt him, & go free yoʳ ſelf by reaſon
of yoʳ diſtance, & when yō ſhal ſeeke to wyn the place
vpon him he ſhal not be able to gaine the place vpon
you, nor to kepe the place frō you wher by he ſhal
eyther be hurt, or in great danger of hurt, by reaſon
of yoʳ large reach, true place & diſtance, yoʳ fight being truly handled keeping it ſelf from Cloze & grype.

And in like ſort ſhal it be betweene two, wᶜʰ ſhal 2.
play vpon the beſt, yᵗ is, yf they play both dubble &
ſyngle handed.

yf yō fynd yoʳ ſelf to ſtrong for yoʳ aduʳſarie in any 3.
mannʳ of ward, whether the ſame be aboue or belowe,
put by his ſtaf wᵗ force, & then ſtrike or thruſt from it,
                                                                but

4. but yf yō fynd him to ſtrong for yō vpō hys blowes from a loft, ſo yᵗ yō can hardly bere them vpon yoʳ ward, then when he ſtryketh in a loft at yoʳ hed, & by hys maine ſtrength would beat doune yoʳ ſtaf, & ſo geue yō a hurt before yō ſhalbe able to com againe into yoʳ ward,

Againſt ſuch a on giue the ſlypp in this ſort, ſo-dainly dray back the hyer prte of yoʳ body a lyttle & yoʳ for moſt foote wᵗ all, & ſlyp in the poynt of yoʳ ſtaf vndʳ his ſtaf, & thruſt ſingle at him, & fly out wᵗ all, ſo ſhal you be ſure to hyt him & go out free,

5. yf he lye a loft wᵗ his ſtaf, then lye yō wᵗ your hindʳ hand alowe, wᵗ yoʳ poynt vptowards his ſtaf making yoʳ ſpace narrow becauſe yō may croſe hys ſtaf to ward his blow before it com in ful force, & then ſtrongly & ſodainlye indirect his poynt, & ſo thruſt at him ſyngle, the wᶜʰ yō may do before he can remoue his feet, by reaſon of the ſwyftnes of yoʳ hand & fly out ther wᵗ, do this for both ſyds of yᵉ hed yf cauſe require yt, ſo ſhal yō ſaue both yoʳ hed, body, and al prts, for yoʳ vppʳ prts are garded, & yoʳ lower prts to farr out of his reach.

6. yf he lye a lowe wᵗ his poynt doune, then lye yō wᵗ yoʳ poynt doune alſo, wᵗ yoʳ formoſt hand lowe & yoʳ hindʳ moſt hand hye, ſo yᵗ yō may croſe his ſtaf, & do in al things as is before ſaid in the other

7. yf he lye vpō the thruſt then lye yō wᵗ yoʳ ſpace narrow lying vp or doune wᵗ yoʳ poynt in ſuch ſort as you may croſe his ſtaf, & therby yō ſhal be able to put or beat by his thruſt before it be in ful force, & then ſtrike or thruſt, euer remembring yoʳ gouernors.

yf vpon this any wil obiect yᵗ yf this betrue, then it

617

is in vaine to ſtrike, or thruſt, becauſe he yᵗ doth it
is ſtil in danger, this doubt is anſwered in the ſhort
ſingle ſword fight, in the 12ᵗʰ ground thereof

Yf yoʳ aduʳſarie ſtrike a loft at any ſyde of yoʳ hed 8
or body, ward it wᵗ yoʳ point vp & making yoʳ ſpace
ſo narrow yᵗ yō may croſe his ſtaf before it com in ful
force bearing or beating doune his blow ſtrongly, back
againe towards yᵗ ſyde yᵗ he ſtryketh in at you, & out
of yᵗ ward, then Inſtantly, eyther ſtrike frō yᵗ ward,
turning back yoʳ ſtaf, & ſtrike him on yᵗ ſyde of the
hed yᵗ is next yoʳ ſtaf,

Or lyft vp yoʳ ſtaf againe, & ſo ſtrike him on the
hed or body, or thruſt at his body dubble or ſyngle,
as yō may find yoʳ beſt aduantage ever in holding yoʳ
ſtaf, let ther be ſuch convenient ſpace between yoʳ
hands, wher in you ſhal fynd yoʳ ſelf apteſt to ward,
ſtrike or thruſt to yoʳ beſt lyking

Yf yō play wᵗ yoʳ ſtaf wᵗ yoʳ left hand before & yoʳ 9
right hand back behind, as many men do fynd them
ſelues moſt apteſt when yᵗ hand is before, & yf yoʳ
aduerſarie vpō his blowe com in to take the cloze of
you, when yō fynd his ſtaf croſt wᵗ yoʳˢ neere his
hand then ſodainlye ſlyp vp yoʳ right hand cloſe to
the hindʳ ſyde of yoʳ formoſt hand, & pʳſently looſing
yoʳ for muſt hand & put it vndʳ your owne ſtaf, &
then croſe or put by his ſtaf ther wᵗ & wᵗ yoʳ hand
take hold of his ſtaf in ſuch ſort yᵗ yoʳ lyttle ſyngʳ be
towards the poynt of his ſtaf, & yoʳ thumb & fore
ſingʳ towards his hands, & pʳſently wᵗ yoʳ right hand
mount yᵉ point of yoʳ owne ſtaf caſting the point
thereof back ouer yoʳ right ſholdʳ, wᵗ yoʳ knuckles
doun wards, & yoʳ nayles vpwards, & ſo ſtabb him in
the

the body or face wᵗ the hindʳ end of yʳ ſtaf, but be
ſure to ſtabb him at his cōmyng in, whether yō catch
his ſtaf or not, for ſomtymes his ſtaf will lye ſo farr
out yᵗ vpon his cōmyng in yō cannot reach it, then
catch yᵗ arme in his comynge in wᶜʰ he ſhal firſt put
forth wᵗ in yoʳ reach, but be ſure to ſtabb, for his ſtaf
can do yō no hurt, and having ſo don, yf yō fynd yoʳ
ſelf to ſtrong for him, ſtrike vp his heeles, yf to weake
fly out.

10.　The like muſt yō do yf yō play wᵗ yoʳ right hand
before, & yoʳ left hand back behind, but yᵗ yō neede
not to ſlyde forth yoʳ left hand, becauſe yoʳ right hand
is in the right place of yoʳ ſtaf alredye to vſe in yᵗ
aƈtion, but then yō muſt diſplace yoʳ left hand to take
hold of his ſtaf, or the grype as is a foreſaid, & to vſe
the ſtabb as is aboue ſaid,

11.　yf both lye a loft as aforeſaid, & play wᵗ yᵉ left hand
before, yf he ſtrike at the Ryght ſyde of yoʳ hed or
body then muſt yō croſe his ſtaf before his blow be in
ful force, by making yoʳ ſpace narrow, & then ſtrike
it ſtrongly back againe towards his left ſyde, & from
yᵗ ward yō may turne back yoʳ ſtaf & ſtrike him backwards ther wᵗ on the left ſyde of the hed, or lyft vp
yoʳ ſtaf & ſtrike him on the right or left ſyde of the
hed, body, or arme, or thruſt him in the body, the
lyke blowes or thruſts may you make at him whether
he ſtrike or thruſt, having put by his ſtaf, remembring
yoʳ gouʳnors.

　　The like ordʳ muſt yō vſe in playing with the right
hand before,

12.　but yf he thruſt at yō cōtynually then euer have a
ſpeciall care to cōſyder, whether he lye a loft or be-
　　　　　　　　　　　　　　　　　　　　　　lowe,

lowe, & do continually thruſt at yō ther from, then
looke that yō euer lye ſo yᵗ yō make yoʳ ſpace ſo narrow
vpon him, yᵗ yō be ſure to croſe his ſtaf wᵗ yoʳˢ, & put
it before it be in full force, and frō yᵗ ward, thruſt at
him ſyngle or dubble as yō fynd it beſt, & yf he remembʳ not to fly back at yᵗ inſtant when he thruſteth
it wilbe to late for him to avoyd any thruſt yᵗ yō ſhal
make at him,

Of the ſhort ſtaf fyght againſt the longe ſtaf.
Cap. 12.

F yō haue a ſtaf of the cōvenient length 1.
againſt a ſtaf of longer length than is cōvenient then make yoʳ ſpace narrow, & ſeeke
not to offend vntil yō haue ſtrongly & ſwyftly
put by his point the wᶜʰ yō ſhal wᵗ eaſe accompliſh,
by reaſon of yoʳ narrow ſpace & yoʳ force, then ſtrike
or thruſt as yō ſhal thinke beſt.

This ſhort ſtaf fight againſt yᵉ longe ſtaf is don in 2.
the ſame ſort that ſhort ſtaf fight to ſhort ſtaf is don,
but yᵗ the man wᵗ the ſhort ſtaf muſt alwaies remembʳ
to kepe a narrow ſpace vpon yᵉ long ſtaf, wher ſo
euer the longe ſtaf ſhal lye, Hye or lowe, cōtinually
make yoʳ ſpace narrow vpō him, ſo ſhal yō be ſure yf
he ſtrike or thruſt at yō, to take the ſame before it be
into his full force & by reaſon yᵗ yoʳ force is more wᵗ
yoʳ ſhort ſtaf than his can be at the poynt of his longe
ſtaf, yō ſhal caſt his ſtaf ſo farr out of yᵉ ſtreit lyne wᵗ
yoʳ ſhort ſtaf, yᵗ yō may ſafly enter in wᵗ yoʳ feet, &
ſtrike or thruſt home at him.

Yet this pʳſent ſhift he hath at yᵗ inſtant, he may 3.
ſlypp

620

flypp back his ſtaf in his hands, wch tyme is ſwyfter
then yor feet in cōmynge forwarde, wher by he wil
haue his ſtaf as ſhort as yo^rs, yet by reaſon y^t at ye firſt
yō caſt his ſtaf ſo farr out of the right lyne, that yō
had tyme to enter in w^t yor feet, yō ſhal then be ſo
neere him, y^t yō may make narrow ſpace vpō him
againe, ſo y^t he ſhal haue no tyme to ſlyp forwarde
his ſtaf agayne in his former place, nor to go back w^t
his feet, & ſo to recou^r the hind^r end of his ſtaf againe,
becauſe yf he ſlyp forth his ſtaf to ſtrike or thruſt at
you, that may yō ſafly defend becauſe of your narrow
ſpace vpō him, & ther w^t al yō may ſtrike or thruſt
him frō yor warde, eyther at ſyngle or dubble,

4. but yf he wil go back w^t his feet thinking by y^t
meanes to recou^r the whole length of hys ſtaf againe,
y^t can he not do in cōvenyent tyme because the tyme
of yor hand is ſwyft^r than ye tyme of his feet, by reaſon
wherof yō may ſtrike or thruſt him in his goyng back.

5. Againe it is to be remembred in y^t tyme y^t yō keepe
him at y^t bay, vpō the drawing in of his ſtaf, the hind^r
end therof lying ſo farr back behind him wilbe ſo
trobbleſom vnto him, that he can make no prſyt fight
againſt yō & cōmonly in his drawing in of his ſtaf it
wilbe to ſhort to make true fight against you, nether
to offend yō nor defend him ſelf.

6. yf he attempt the Cloze w^t yō then ſtabb him w^t
the hind^r end of yor ſtaf as is ſaid in ye fyght of ye ij
ſhort ſtaves of cōvenyent length, in the 9th ground
therof

Note. Rememb^r y^t at Morris pyke, forreſt byll,
longe ſtaf & two hand ſword, y^t yō lye in ſuch ſort
vpō yor wards y^t yō may both ward, ſtrike, & thruſt,

R   both

621

both dubble & ſyngle, & then returne to yoͬ former wards ſlyps & lyinge againe & then are yō as yō wer before

The like fight is to be vſed wͭ yͤ Javelen, prtyſon, halbard, black byll, battle Axe, gleve, half pyke &c.

*Off the fight of the forreſt byll againſt
the like weapon & againſt the ſtaf.*

Cap: 13.

HE forreſt byl haue the fyght of the ſtaf but yͭ it hath iiij wards more wͭ the hed of the byll, yͭ is one to bere it vpwards, another to beat it dounwards ſo yͭ the carrage of yoͬ byll hed be wͭ the edge neyther vp nor doune but ſyde wyſe.   1.

The other ij wards are on to cast his byl hed towards the ryght ſyde, thother towards yͤ left ſyde.

And vpon eiͬ on of theſe wards or catches run vp to his hands wͭ the hed of yoͬ byll & then by reaſon yͭ yō haue put his ſtaf out of yͤ right lyne, yō may catch at his hed neck arme or leggs &c wͭ yͤ edge of yoͬ byll, & hook or pluck him ſtrongly to you & fly out wͭall.

Yf yō caſt his ſtaf ſo farr out yͭ yoͬ byll ſlyde not vp to his hands, then yō may ſafly run in ſlyding yoͬ hands wͭin one yard of yͤ hed of yoͬ byll, & ſo wͭ yoͬ byl in one hand take him by yͤ legg wͭ the blade of yoͬ byll & pluck him to yō & wͭ yoͬ other hand defend yoͬ ſelf from his gryps yf he offer to grype wͭ you.   2.

Yf you fight byll to byll do the like in al reſpects as wͭ yͤ ſtaf in yoͬ fyght, for yoͬ byll fight & ſtaf ſyght   3.

is

is al one, but only for the defence & offence wᵗ the hed of yᵉ byll, & wher yᵉ ſtaf man vpō the cloze yf he vſe yᵉ ſtabb wᵗ the butt end of his ſtaf, the byll man at yᵗ tyme is to vſe yᵉ catch at his legg wᵗ yᵉ edge of his byll, as in yᵉ ſecond ground aboue is ſaid.

4. Remembʳ euer in al yoʳ fyght wᵗ this weapon to make yoʳ ſpace narrow whether it be againſt the ſtaf or byll ſo yᵗ what ſo euer he ſhal do againſt you, yō ſhal ſtill make yoʳ ward before he be in his ful force to offend you.

5. Alſo yf yō can reach wᵗin the hed of his byll wᵗ the hed of yoʳ byll then ſodainly wᵗ the hed of yoʳ byll ſnach his byll hed ſtrongly towards you, & therwᵗall indirect his byl hed & forcibly run vp yoʳ byl hed to his hands, ſo haue yō the lyke advantage as aboueſaid, wheras I ſpake of runyng vp towards his hands.

6. Yf he lye alowe wᵗ his byl hed then yf yō can put yoʳ byll hed in ouʳ the hed of his bylle & ſtronglye put doune his byl ſtaf wᵗ yoʳ byl hed, bearinge it flat, then yō may prſently run vp yoʳ byll hed ſingle handed to his hands & fly out therwᵗ, ſo ſhal yō hurt him in yᵉ hand & go free yoʳſelf.

7. The like may yō do wᵗ yoʳ byll againſt the ſhort ſtaf yf yō can preſs it doune in yᵉ lyke ſort, but yf he haue a longe ſtaf then run vp dubble handed wᵗ both hands vpon yoʳ byll, wᶜʰ thynge yō may ſafly do becauſe yō are in yoʳ ſtrength & haue taken him in the weak prte of his ſtaf.

8. Yf he lye hye wᵗ his byll hed then put vp yoʳ byll hed undʳ his & caſt his byll out to yᵗ ſyde yᵗ yō ſhal fynd fytteſt, ſo haue yō the aduantage to thruſt or hook at him & fly out.

R 2   Or

Or yf yō caſt his byl farr out of the right lyne then run in & take him by the legg wᵗ yᵉ edge of yorᵉ byll, as is ſaid in the 2ⁿᵈ ground of this chapter.

Yf yō ward his blow wᵗ yorᵉ byll ſtaf wᵗin yorᵉ byll 9. hed, then anſwer him as wᵗ yᵉ ſhort ſtaf.

Note yᵗ as the byl mans aduantage is to tak the ſtaf wᵗ yᵉ hed of yᵉ byll ſo the ſtaf man by reason yᵗ yᵉ hed of yᵉ byll is a faire mark hath yᵉ aduantage of him in yᵉ caſting aſyde of the hed of the byll wᵗ his ſtaf or beating yᵗ aſyde, the wᶜʰ yf yᵉ byll man looke not very well into it the ſtaf man ther vpon wil take al mannʳ of aduantages of yᵉ ſtaf fyght againſt him.

" *The Chapter on the Morris pike is unique, as no other work ſpeaks of parries with that weapon.*"— *W. London.*

Of the fyght of yᵗ morris pyke againſt the lyke weapon.

Cap: 14.

F yō fight wᵗ yorᵉ enemy having both morris 1. pyks wᵗ both poynts of yorᵉ pyks forwards, alowe upon yᵉ ground, holding the butt end of the pyke in one hand ſyngle wᵗ knuckles vpwards & the thumb undrneth, wᵗ the thumbe & forefingʳ towards yorᵉ face & the lyttle fynger towards the poynt of yᵉ pyke, bering the butt end of the pyke frō the one ſyde to yᵉ other right before the face, then lye yō wᵗ yorᵉ arme ſpent & yorᵉ body open wᵗ yorᵉ hand to yᵉ right ſyde wᵗ yorᵉ knuckles Dounwards & yorᵉ nailes vpwards.

Or yō may lye in yᵗ ſort, wᵗ yorᵉ hand over to the left ſyde wᵗ yorᵉ knuckles vpwards & yorᵉ nayles Dounwards, wherby al yorᵉ body wilbe Open. yf then he ſhal ſodainlye rayſe vp the point of his pyke wᵗ his other hand

hand & com to thruſt at yō, then in the Mountinge of his poynt or his cōynge in ſodainlye toſſe vp the poynt of yor pyke w^t yor hand ſyngle & ſo thruſt him in the leggs w^t yor pyke & fly out therw^t.

Or els you May ſtand vpō yor ward & Not toſſe vp yor pykes poynt but breake his thruſt by croſſynge the poynt of his pyke w^t the Mydds of yor pyke by caſting vp yor hand, w^t the butt end of yor pyke aboue yor hed, & ſo bering ouer hys point w^t yor ſtaf, to the other ſyde as for example,

2.   Yf yō lye w^t yor hand ſpent towards the left ſyde of yor bodye, then ſodainlye bere his poynt ouer ſtrongly towards yor right ſyde.

Yf yō lye w^t yor hand ſpent towards yor right ſyde then bere his poynt towards yor left ſyde, & ther vpon gather vp yor pyke w^t yor other hand & thruſt at him & fly out.

Yf he cōtynew his fyght w^t his point aboue, & yō lye w^t yor pyke breſt hye & hyer w^t your hand & point ſo, y^t yō may Make yor thruſt at his face or body w^t yor poynt Direɛtly towards his face, holding yor pyke w^t both your hands on yor ſtaf yor hinder hand w^t yor knuckles vpwards & yor formuſt hand w^t yor knuckles dounwards & ther ſhaking yor pyke & faulſing at his face w^t yor poynt as Neere his face as you may, then ſodainlye Make out yor thruſt ſyngle handed at his face & fly backe w^t all, wch thruſt he can hardly breake one of 20 by reaſon y^t yō haue made yor ſpace ſo narrow vpon his gard, ſo y^t yō beinge firſt in yor aɛtion he wil ſtil be to late in his defence to defend himſelf.

4.   but note while yō lye faulſinge to Deceve him looke well to yor leggs y^t he in the Meane tyme toſſe not vp the

poynt

poynt of his pyke ſyngle handed & hurt yō therw^t in y^e ſhynes.

Yf he lye ſo w^t his poynt vp a loft as you do then 5. Make yor ſpace Narrow Mountinge yor point a lyttle & croſe his pyke w^t yo^{rs} & ſtronglye and ſodainly caſt his poynt out of the right lyne and thruſt whome from the ſame ſyngle or dubble as you fynd yor beſt aduantage, & fly out therw^t.

Or yō may run in when yō haue caſt out his poynt ſlydinge both yor hands on yor ſtaf til yō com· w^{t}in iij quarters of a yard of the hed of yor pyke & ſtabb him therw^t w^t one hand & w^t yor other hand kepe him of from ye grype.

Now yf he be a man of ſkyll, notw^{t}ſtandinge ye 6. Making of y^t faulte in ſuffering you to do ſo yet this help he hath, as yō are cōmynge in he will ſodainlye draw in his pyke poynt & fly back w^{t}all, then haue yō no helpe but to fly out inſtantly to the myddle of yor pyke & from thence backe to ye end & then are yō as at the firſt begynnynge of yor fyght yō were.

Yf you fynd y^t he lye farr out of ye right lyne w^t 7. his poynt or y^t yō can ſo farr Indirect y^e ſame then caſt yor pyke out of yor hands, croſe over vpon the myds of his pyke, by wch meanes yō ſhal entangle his pyke, then while he doth ſtryve to get his pyke at lybertye, run you in ſodainlye drawing yor Dagg^r & ſtrike or ſtabb at him.

Then yf he haue the prfection of this fyght as well 8. as you, he wilbe as reddy w^t his dagg^r as yō are w^t yo^{rs}, then muſt yō fyght it out at the ſyngle dagg^r fyght as is ſhewed in the 15th Cap: then he y^t hath not the prfection of y^t fyght gow^t to wracke.

And

9. And here note y^t in al the courfe of my teachinge of thefe my breef Inftructions yf both the prtyes haue the ful prfection of ye true fyght then the on will not be able to hurt thother at what prfyt weapon fo euer.

0. But yf a Man y^t haue the prfection of fight fhal fight w^t on y^t haue it not then muft y^t vnfkylful man go to wrack & thother goe free.

Of the fingle Dagger fyght againft the lyke weapon.
Cap: 15.

1. IRST know y^t to this weapon ther belongeth no Wards nor gryps but againft fuch a one as is foolehardy & will fuffer himfelf to haue a ful ftabb in the face or bodye to hazard the geving of Another, then againft him yō may vfe yor left hand in throwinge him afyde or ftrike vp his heeles aft^r yō haue ftab^d him.

2. In this dagg^r fyght, yō muft vfe cōtynual motion fo fhal he not be able to put yō to ye cloze or grype, becaufe yor contynuall motion difappointeth him of his true place, & the more ferce he is in runynge in, the foon^r he gayneth you the place, wherby he is wounded, & yō not any thing the rather endangered.

3. The mann^r of handling yor cōtynuall motion is this, kepe out of diftance & ftrik or thruft at his hand, Arme, face or body, y^t fhal prefs vpon yō, & yf he defend blow or thruft w^t his dagg^r make yō blow or thruft at his hand.

4. Yf he com in w^t his left legg forewards or w^t the right, do you ftrike at y^t prte as foone as it fhalbe w^tin yor reach, remembring y^t yō vfe contynual motion
in

in yoʳ prgreſſion & regreſſyon according to yoʳ twyfold gouʳnors.

Although the daggʳ fyght be thought a verye dan- 5. gerous fyght by reaſon of yᵉ ſhortnes & ſynglenes therof, yet the fight therof being handled as is afore-ſaid, is as ſaf & as defencive as is the fight of any other weapon, this endeth my breef Inſtrućtions.

Finis.

Sundry

Sundry kinds of play or fight. Thornborow.

1 Unc^rtaine variable
2 fyngle
3 gardant.

iij *different kinds of fight.*

1 y^t forceth or p^rffeth on
2 he y^t goeth back w^t fom blow or thruft
3 he y^t ftandeth to his wards or paffato

} w^t an Imp^rfit ward & out of ye way.

1. Againft him y^t p^rffeth y^e, naked play is beft becs he ufeth his foote, ye open lofty play ye hand.

2. ye 2nd is beft followed w^t ye variable & vnc^rtaine handling els fhould yō be a ma^rke to yor enemy & too flow in motion.

3. ye 3rd muft be incountred w^t ye gardant play wherin you fhal try him at ye B fword or how he can efcape ye prting blow or thruft.

When yō gather kepe yor place & fpace equal & only be a patient & rememb^r y^t ye gardant play bringeth yō fafly in & keps yor enemy out.

Know this ord^r of play els ye beft may be deceaved, to be ufed againft al thefe differencs & bring ye good-

S   nes

nes therof in ſuſpitiõ, for al theſe plaies are good in
their kynd, tyme & occaſiõ offered by divᵣſitie of play,
but not on of them to be continually uſed & played
vpon as a pᵣfectiõ againſt euery aſſault.

1. In yᵉ naked play yõ muſt ſet yoᵣſelf vpright wᵗ
yoᵣ feet in a ſmale ſpace, obſᵣving yᵉ place of yoᵣ hand
wher yõ may ſtrike or thruſt moſt quickly & redely
& ſo take yᵉ tyme of him yᵗ pᵣſſeth on (vſing yᵉ tyme
of his feet) wᵗ yoᵣ blowe or thruſt wher he is moſt
open.

1. In yᵉ variable play, yõ dryve him to his ſhyfts
changing yoᵣſelf into ſundry kynds of blowes thruſts &
lyings, wᶜʰ yõ muſt not ſtay upon,

2. ſeeking to + him ſtil in his playes as yõ may,
wherby yõ ſhal force him to fly, or els to ſtand to yᵉ
proof of his B ſword play.

3. the gardant play is to be vſed againſt yᵉ blowe,
thruſt & paſſata yᵗ cometh wᵗin dangᵣ of hurt, for
treading yᵉ right way & keping yoᵣ place & hand in
ſpace & ſtrength you cannot looſe yᵉ tyme to defend
frõ either of thoſe offers.

theſe Judged of in reaſon & known by ſom practiſe
wil make yõ deale ſafly againſt al ſorts, ſkilful or vn-
ſkilful, ſo yᵗ feare or Angᵣ hinder not yoᵣ Knowledge.

Of Tymes.

1. The tyme of yᵉ $\begin{cases} \text{hand} \\ \text{foote} \\ \text{hand \& foot} \\ \text{foot \& hand. naught} \end{cases}$

Of

Of place space. strength & tyme.

1. yᵉ tyme of yᵉ hand is when yō strike frō a wʳᵈ or stand in place to strike.

2. the tyme of yᵉ foot is when yō step forward to strike or when yō gather towarde yoʳ own right syde.

3. yᵉ tyme of yᵉ hand & foot is when yō tread yoʳ ground in courfe to strike rather than pʳffing forwards, or when yō slide back or go back, yoʳ hand & foot being then of equal agillitie.

4. yᵉ tyme of yᵉ foot & hand is when yō handle yoʳ gardant play vfing then a flowe motiō in both.

ther is but i good way to gather vpō yoʳ enemy, gardant. Al other are dangerous & fubieĉt to yᵉ blowe on yᵉ hed or thruft on yᵉ body.

for no way can ward both but as aforfᵈ.

yoʳ hand & feet in good play muft go together, whether it be in quick or flow motion.

In gathering forwards or towʳᵈs yoʳ right syde yoʳ hand falleth frō yoʳ place, space, & ftrength & fo falleth out yᵉ lofs of tyme.

when yō gather & fuffer yᵗ gouʳne yoʳ fight, defend only. when yō do, be fingle, or not fixed towards on any lying, but alfo yᵉ quicknes of yoʳ hand in its pʳpʳ place carried,

In breaking yᵉ thruft when yō lye aloft fingle or gardant & fpace yoʳ arme fomwhat bowing in warding yᵉ blowe, haue refpeĉt to yoʳ place of hand & ftrength, yoʳ arme ftrait. this courfe in yoʳ tyme is beft pʳformed, the on of thefe wᵗ yoʳ hand aloft yoʳ point downe thother yoʳ hand in place yoʳ more high yoʳ fpace lefs curious.

S 2   Dubble

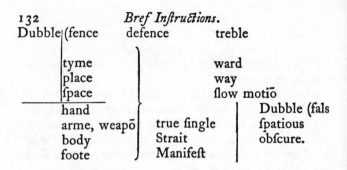

Dubble|(fence   defence   treble

tyme   ward
place   way
ſpace   flow motiō

hand   Dubble (fals
arme, weapō| true ſingle   ſpatious
body   Strait   obſcure.
foote   Manifeſt

II
93ʳᵉ
    tyme is cheefly to be obſʳved in both actions vpō
wᶜʰ (place / ſpace) waiteth.

    Upon theſe 3 yᵉ 4 following, vpon theſe 4 yᵉ firſt
3, upon theſe yᵉ later 3.

    to hurt or defend, a tyme in both is to be obſʳved
to yᵉ furtherance of wᶜʰ place is to be gotten, wᵗout wᶜʰ
tyme wilbe to long to pʳform yᵗ wᶜʰ is intended, yᵉ ſpace
is to be noted betwene ij oppoſits & in reſpect of
touching, or in regard of ſaving as alſo for pʳſving of
tyme, by yᵉ ſmale way it hath either to yᵉ body, or
puting by yᵉ weapon.

    the next 4 muſt be vſed together to pʳforme thother
iij rules, for yᵉ hand being nymble & quick of itſelf
may els be hindered in yᵉ want of any of theſe, the
weapon muſt be framed & inclyned to sʳve yᵉ agilitie
of yᵉ hand eyther in hurting or defending.

4
□
    the body vpright or leanyng to yᵉ weapon, yᵗ it
hindʳ not yᵉ diſpoſitiō of thother ij the foot anſwerable
to them plying yᵉ hand & ward al in ſtrait ſpace, yᵉ wʳᵈ
wᵗ hand high wᵗ yᵉ point downe, the arme ſtrait out as
redy for both actions.

                                      the

the way vnd^r ye wrd w^tdrawing ye body from harmes,
the motiō flowe y^t ye actiō of ye hand be not hindered.

the reſt are ye diſpoſitions of ye placed diſplaced
handlings

Slowfoot : ſwift hand : quick foot : ſlow hand.

tread : ſtride : follow : falaway :

When yō ſeek to offend w^t blow or thruſt, yor place of
hand is loſt, ye way to redeeme it is to ſlyde back vnd^r
yor lofty ward as aforeſd alwaies y^t yor adu^rſarie lye
aloft redy to ſtrike or thruſt or vſe his hand only,

yf yō would offend him y^t lyeth lowe vpō ye thruſt
then when yō diſplace yor weapon frō aloft yō may
aft^r yor blow at hed or arme or neereſt place, ſtand &
thruſt before yō go backe becauſe he is out of place &
ſpace & cannot +, & therby looſeth his tyme to annoy
yō & yō may thruſt & retyre for a new aſſault.

this not ſo ſownd,

In ſtriking or thruſting neu^r hind^r yor hand w^t puting
forth yor foote but kepe ye place therof til yō haue offended w^t ye one only ye bending of yor body very
little foreward may ſufficte, els yō looſe a dubble tyme,
on in ſetting forth yor foot thother in reco^uring yor
loſt place of yor fōt both to y^e loſs of tyme & yor
purpoſte.

Strike : thruſt : ward : breake :

the dubble offence is in ſtriking & thruſting.

the iij fold
defence in
$$\begin{cases} \text{warding y}^e \text{ blow} \\ \text{breaking or puting bye y}^e \text{ thruſt} \\ \text{ſlyding back vnd}^r \text{ yo}^r \text{ hanging ward.} \end{cases}$$

wyn y^e place : ſtanᵈd faſt, ſtrike home
offend, defend, & go ſaf.

S 3   al

al vnd^r play is beaten w^t moſt agil, ſingle & y^e lofty the lofty w^t y^e gardant,   His   when w^t his foot he ſeeke y^e low lying is out of place to ofend defend or not ſo for lack of tyme ſpace & croſſing, yf he lye out w^t his long^r weapō it is put bye frō aloft, who hath place tyme & reach of body & arme al w^t y^e +.

93 re y^e reading y^e enterlyyinge of other things therto adioyn-ing.

the lofty naked play is beaten w^t y^e ward becs of $\left\{ \begin{array}{l} \text{Croſs} \\ \text{ſpace} \\ \text{tyme} \end{array} \right\}$

to Defend, y^e lofty naked ſingle looſe play ſ^{r}veth to win y^e Tyme of y^e lowe & dubble play.

the bent gardant requireth yor arme ſtrait high & out y^e point down towards (93 re II wel) y^e body & foote y^t way inclyned.

CHISWICK PRESS:—CHARLES WHITTINGHAM AND CO.
TOOKS COURT, CHANCERY LANE, LONDON.